Social Movements in Politics

Perspectives in Comparative Politics

Series Editors: Professor Kay Lawson, San Francisco State University and Sorbonne, Paris. Professor Stephen Padgett, University of Liverpool, UK

Covering important themes in comparative politics this series is designed to bridge the gap between introductory textbooks and research literature in journals and monographs. Each book in the series surveys the theoretical literature associated with a particular topic area and then tests the theories against three country case studies.

Titles in series (in preparation)

Miriam Feldblum *Immigration*
Paul A. Godt *Health Care*
Ludger Helms *Executives in Western Democracies*
Charles Olsen *Social Inequality*
Joseph Rudolph and Robert Thompson *Ethnicity*
Michael Sturm *Budget Deficits*

Social Movements in Politics:
A Comparative Study

Cyrus Ernesto Zirakzadeh

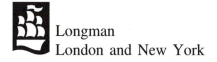
Longman
London and New York

Addison Wesley Longman Limited
Edinburgh Gate
Harlow, Essex CM20 2JE, England
and Associated Companies throughout the world.

Published in the United States of America by
Longman Publishing, New York

© Addison Wesley Longman Limited 1997

First published 1997

ISBN 0 582 20947-1 CSD
ISBN 0 582 20946-3 PPR

British Library Cataloguing-in-Publication Data

A catalogue record for this book is
available from the British Library

Library of Congress Cataloging-in-Publication Data
Zirakzadeh, Cyrus Ernesto, 1951–
    Social movements in politics : a comparative study / Cyrus Ernesto
Zirakzadeh.
        p. cm. — (Perspectives in comparative politics)
    Includes bibliographical references and index.
    ISBN 0–582–20946–3 (ppr). — ISBN 0–582–20947–1 (csd)
    1. Social movements—Political aspects—Case studies.
2. Political participation—Case studies. 3. Sendero Luminoso
(Guerrilla group) 4. NSZZ "Solidarność" (Labor organization)
5. Grünen (Political party) I. Title. II. Series.
HN17.5.Z57 1997
306.2—dc21   96–53294
                                                                              CIP

Set by 35 in 10/12pt Times Roman
Produced by Longman Singapore Publishers (Pte) Ltd
Printed in Singapore.

For Vanessa and Daniel

Contents

Series editors' preface   ix
Preface   xi
Acronyms   xiii

Part I   How we think about social movements   **1**

1   Recent traditions in social-movement theorizing   3

**Part II   Germany's Greens and the politics
of party-movements**   **23**

2   A world to be remade: sociopolitical circumstances
    of Green politics   25

3   Political antecedents   43

4   Clashing shades of Green   63

**Part III   Poland's Solidarity and movements
against dictatorial regimes**   **95**

5   A world to be remade: sociopolitical circumstances
    of Solidarity   97

6   Political antecedents   111

7   Discord within Solidarity   129

**Part IV   Peru's Shining Path and agrarian-based
movements**   **167**

8 A world to be remade: sociopolitical circumstances
of Shining Path   169

9 Political antecedents   185

10 Diverse directions along the Shining Path   199

Part V   Conclusions   **225**

11 From history to theory   227

References   241
Author index   257
Subject index   259

Series editors' preface

Social Movements in Politics by Cyrus Ernesto Zirakzadeh is the first volume in a new series of books, published by Addison Wesley Longman of England, entitled *Perspectives in Comparative Politics*. The purpose of this new series is to fill a serious gap in the literature available for the study of comparative politics by providing books that are at the same time genuinely comparative, scholarly, timely, and written for a student and general readership.

The format for all these books is straightforward. Each has an introductory chapter, giving a historical and theoretical overview of the relationship between the subject at hand and the world of politics and government. This introduction is then followed by three case studies, in each of which the author explains the nation's constitutional-political system, gives the history of political and state involvement, and then develops the specific topics of importance as they apply to the case: the nature of the political organizations active in this domain and the tactics they employ; the external factors constraining policy; the policies presently in place; the degree of satisfaction with such policies; and probable future directions. A final chapter compares the three cases, making clear the points in common, but also giving ample recognition to the contextual differences that govern what has been accomplished, and what yet may be.

The books in this series are intended for use as advanced undergraduate, upper division or graduate level texts, as well as for a broader audience interested in the topic. They are not directed toward other specialists on the subject, but it is our hope that each will be seen as a serious and substantial work by those who know the topic best.

Such an approach requires authors (or teams of authors) deeply interested in a particular problem of politics and/or government, and well informed about the manifestation of that problem in three different nations. A great deal of effort goes into finding these authors, and we are pleased that we now have six other books under contract with authors recruited from both Europe and North America. We are particularly pleased to be launching this exciting new series with *Social Movements in Politics* by Cyrus Ernesto Zirakzadeh.

Professor Kay Lawson,
San Francisco State University and
the Sorbonne, Paris.
Professor Stephen Padgett,
University of Liverpool, UK.

Preface

This book is an exploration and application of contemporary social-movement theory. It is intended to familiarize advanced students in the social sciences with different ways that European and North American scholars since the Second World War have thought about social movements. A further aim is to promote reflection on similarities and differences between three social movements that captured worldwide attention during the 1980s and early 1990s: Germany's Greens, Poland's Solidarity, and Peru's Shining Path.

The first chapter elaborates three major theoretical traditions that for almost half a century have informed studies of social movements: (1) modernization theories, which stress the human costs of social change; (2) theories about organizational resources and political opportunities, and (3) identity-formation theories. Chapter 1 examines the assumptions and logic of each theoretical tradition and their implications for empirical research.

The next nine chapters discuss the social and political circumstances of and the ideological debates within the Greens, Solidarity, and Shining Path. Using themes and questions from the three major theoretical traditions as springboards for reflection, the book offers a multidimensional picture of each movement, which highlights (1) the recent social changes and national political situation that activists in each movement confronted; (2) the pre-existing traditions of popular protest from which each movement drew symbols, leaders, and other resources, and (3) the competing social goals and political strategies and tactics that major factions in each movement espoused.

The book's final chapter compares the three cases and contrasts the historical record with the representations of social movements made by each of the major theoretical traditions. The chapter closes with a call for a fourth theoretical approach to social movements that emphasizes their internal politics.

The three extended case studies form the heart or core of the book. Complex descriptions of social movements, informed by multiple theoretical traditions, are valuable for several reasons. First and perhaps most importantly, they can enhance one's resistance to simplistic generalizations and black-and-white judgements about popular protest. In addition, by mulling over others' efforts to control their destinies, we sometimes alter how we think about ourselves. As we learn in depth about other people's struggles, we sometimes become inspired by their attempts and achievements and develop greater awareness of and self-confidence in our own political potential. Last but not least, we can sometimes educe from historical details general lessons that help us understand the difficulties and advantages of current forms of nonelite politics.

Because historical studies of social movements can affect the way one views oneself and one's political situation, a passive, distant approach may not be the best way to read this book. A reader probably will benefit more if, while reading, she or he asks: How do *I* think about social movements? Do I like them, fear them, or am I indifferent to their existence? Do these accounts of Solidarity, the Greens, and Shining Path seem plausible to me, and why (or why not)? And finally, are there any social movements occurring near me at this time? If so, how are they being represented in the conventional press and by government officials, and what alternative interpretations does this book suggest?

I have been studying social movements and social-movement theorizing for about 20 years. I am indebted to many people and their writings for my ideas. In the following pages I cite numerous works that have influenced me. In addition, I have benefited from ongoing discussions about popular politics with William Caspary, Michael McCann, and George Shulman. Their books and articles will not be cited here (Mike specializes in US public law; George writes on the history of European and US political thought; and Bill studies the political thought of John Dewey), but our endless conversations have profoundly affected my style of reasoning. I also thank the 'Frontiers of Social Movement Theorizing' group within the American Sociological Association for holding international conferences where people who love to talk about social movements can exchange opinions, stories, and theories. Betty Seaver has been a wonderful reader and friend, patiently helping me clarify my thoughts and writing. Kay Lawson and Stephen Padgett, my series editors, were very generous with their time, helping me look afresh at some early arguments and conclusions. Andrei Markovits kindly shared his knowledge about contemporary German politics and, as a good friend often will do, asked questions that helped me clarify some of my positions. Needless to say, he and other readers of earlier drafts of my manuscript are not responsible for any errors of fact or interpretation in this book – I am the responsible party.

The University of Connecticut provided a good setting for writing this particular book. The library's excellent alternative press collection helped me piece together local 'Left' histories for Germany, Poland and Peru. Sociology and political-science graduate students taking my 'Comparative Political Movements' seminar challenged my conclusions and inspired me with their enthusiasm. My colleagues in the social sciences, especially Bob Asher, Garry Clifford, Myra Ferree, Betty Hanson, and Henry Krisch, cheerfully shared scholarly references, empirical findings, and personal views about social movements in politics.

Finally, I thank Barbara, Vanessa, and Daniel Zirakzadeh for once again encouraging me and putting up with those moments when I become so involved with my writing that I forget our rituals, such as dinner. I could not have completed this book without their daily support and constant humour. I love them dearly.

Acronyms

Germany

AL	Alternative Slate (of Berlin)
APO	Extraparliamentary Movement
A3W	Action for a Third Way
AUD	Action Group for an Independent Germany
BBU	Federal Association of Citizens' Initiatives for Environmental Protection
BUF	Federal Conference of Independent Peace Groups
CDU/CSU	Christian Democratic Party/Christian Social Union
FDP	Free Democratic Party
FRG	Federal Republic of Germany
GAZ	Green Action Future
GDR	German Democratic Republic
GLU	Green List for Environmental Protection
JUSO	Working Group of Young Socialists
KB	Communist League
KPD	Communist Party of Germany
NPD	National Democratic Party
SPD	Social Democratic Party
SDS	Socialist German Students' League
SPV-Greens	Alternative Political Alliance – Greens
USP	Environmental Protection Party
WGA	Voters League, Nuclear Power, No Thanks!

Poland

KO	Citizens' Committees
KOR	Workers' Defence Committee
KPN	Confederation for an Independent Poland
KSS-KOR	Committee for Social Self-Defence – KOR

KKW	National Executive Commission
OPZZ	National Federation of Trade Unions
PPN	Polish League for Independence
PPR	Polish Workers' Party
PZPR	Polish United Workers' Party
RMP	Young Poland Movement
ROPCiO	Movement for the Defence of Human and Civil Rights
SdRP	Social Democracy of the Polish Republic
SKS	Students' Solidarity Committee
TKK	Temporary Coordinating Commission
UD	Democratic Union

Peru

APRA	American Revolutionary Popular Alliance
CGTP	General Confederation of Peruvian Workers
CTP	Confederation of Peruvian Workers
ELN	National Liberation Army
IU	United Left
MIR	Movement of the Revolutionary Left
MRTA	Túpac Amaru Revolutionary Movement
PCP	Communist Party of Peru
PCP-BR	Communist Party of Peru – Red Flag
PCP-SL	Communist Party of Peru – Shining Path
PCP-U	Communist Party of Peru – Unity
SINAMOS	National System of Support for Social Mobilization

Miscellaneous

EEC	European Economic Community
NATO	North Atlantic Treaty Organization
UFW	United Farm Workers
US	United States
USSR	Union of Soviet Socialist Republics

Part I

How we think about social movements

Chapter 1

Recent traditions in social-movement theorizing

All mass movements generate in their adherents a readiness to die and a proclivity for united action; all of them, irrespective of the doctrine they preach and the program they project, breed fanaticism, enthusiasm, fervent hope, hatred and intolerance; all of them are capable of releasing a powerful flow of activity in certain departments of life; all of them demand blind faith and singlehearted allegiance.

Eric Hoffer, *The True Believer*

The term *social movement* connotes different things to different people. For example, many people look upon the ideologically nonviolent and democratic civil rights movement in the United States as a quintessential social movement (Chong 1991). Others would place the German Nazi Party of the 1930s in that category (Arendt 1951; Fromm 1941; Hoffer 1951). Some apply the term to almost any formally organized group of citizens that periodically petitions the state for aid, such as Mothers Against Drunk Drivers (Judkins 1983; McCarthy and Wolfson 1988; Schwartz and Shuva 1992). Still others think of social movements as largely unorganized, illegal, and episodic actions, such as ghetto riots, wildcat strikes, or spontaneous boycotts of unpopular taxes (Piven 1976).

This is a study of three social movements of the 1980s that confronted very different social and political regimes and each of whose members had distinctive goals, strategies, and problems in mind. The movements are West Germany's Greens, Poland's Solidarity, and Peru's Shining Path. Each will be looked at from three perspectives: (1) in terms of the national political and social context that conditioned the movement's goals and strategies; (2) in terms of previous efforts by groups to change social and political conditions, and (3) in terms of the activists' own beliefs and strategic and tactical decisions.

But first, let me clarify the construction I put on *social movement* in order to prevent possible misunderstanding by readers. Further, I would like to describe briefly some major postwar traditions of thinking about movements, for each tradition has greatly influenced my own reading of recent political events.

What is meant by *social movement*?

Like *social class* and *political representation*, *social movement* is a term that various authors use in different ways. I employ *social movement* whenever discussing political phenomena that have at least three partially overlapping yet distinguishable characteristics.

First, a social movement is a group of people who consciously attempt to build a radically new social order. Here, I agree with J. Craig Jenkins (1981: 82), who writes that social movements are 'a series of collective actions conducted to bring about change in social structures', and the movements are guided by 'a vision, however dimly articulated, of the alternative order desired and of the basic measures necessary to put it into effect'. Participants in social movements not only challenge decisions made by authorities and make demands on authorities but try to make lasting, large-scale, and significant changes in the texture of the society. Or, to borrow a phrase from movement analyst John Wilson (1973: 3), participants see themselves as engaged 'in the building of new social worlds'.

By reading social movements as in part collective attempts to build 'new social worlds', I am, of course, oversimplifying. Obviously, not *every* person in *every* group that I ordinarily call a 'social movement' wishes to transform the society in toto. Movements are never simply 'radical' in the sense that all participants want completely to replace the status quo with a new social order. Social movements range widely in terms of proportion of participants who desire radical change. And as Dennis Chong (1991) points out, in every social movement, some proportion of the activists primarily seek immediate gratification and private benefits, such as an increase in local prestige, and are neither steadfastly nor deeply committed to long-term social change.

Furthermore, in most movements participants want to change the world in significant ways but also consciously want to preserve specific institutions. Peasant rebels in the Chiapas region of Mexico, say, may want to protect precapitalist property arrangements from international market pressures and state economic policies (Harvey 1994). Because participants in social movements, in fact, vary greatly in the amount of transformation desired, one could conceivably categorize social movements by degree and substance of transformative impulses. A social movement differs from an interest group or political party in that at least a plurality of its participants intentionally seek a far-reaching restructuring of the society. When an influential portion of the membership of an organized group steadfastly advocates innovative and fundamental social changes, I call that group a social movement.[1]

Second, when I use the term *social movement*, I have in mind political activity by people from a broad range of social backgrounds that, following current scholarly convention, I call 'nonelite'. These are people, generally speaking, who in their daily lives lack substantive political clout, social prestige, or personal wealth, and whose interests are not routinely articulated or represented in the political system. In the words of Cornel West (1993: 29), they have often been 'culturally degraded, politically oppressed, and economically exploited'. Doug McAdam (1982: 36) describes them as deprived of 'any real influence over the major decisions that affect their lives'. William Gamson (1975: 140) says they lack 'routine access to decisions that affect them'.

My position, then, coincides with that of many social-movement scholars who reserve the term *social movement* for a form of political activity by the nonpowerful, the nonwealthy, and the nonfamous (Jenkins 1981; Tarrow 1989b; Tilly 1978). According to most social-movement scholars today, participants accurately see themselves as opposing the interests of individuals and groups who either control unusual amounts of wealth or enjoy a monopoly of influence within the political system. This does not imply that participants perceive themselves, their opponents, and their actions in classical Marxian categories, such as 'proletariat', 'monopoly capitalism', and 'class struggle'. Indeed, most social-movement scholars agree that participants do *not* see their antagonists abstractly – for example, as 'the capitalist mode of production', 'private property', or 'the bourgeoisie' in its entirety. As Frances Fox Piven observes (1976: 311–12), social movements take place in particular settings, such as sweatshops and overcrowded slums. Consequently, participants, although desirous of transforming a social situation in dramatic ways, often direct their actions toward visible targets, such as local plant managers or landlords. But many social-movement scholars believe that movement activists do typically perceive themselves as outside centres of power and as involved in economically inegalitarian relations, and that these perceptions are accurate.

The third distinguishing characteristic of a social movement is the use of politically confrontational and socially disruptive tactics – such as the occupation of buildings and street blockades – to influence government officials, to deter social opponents, and/or to attract supporters. Although movement activities are often intentionally disruptive and confrontational, movement participants do not regularly engage in criminal behaviour. Even movements that political leaders and cultural authorities deem beyond the pale frequently utilize nondisruptive and civil tactics, such as lobbying and lawsuits, that are constitutionally sanctioned. Social movements balance disruption and confrontation with cooperation, legality, and consensus building. In other words, *social movement* signifies a *style* of politics different from the style of interest groups or political parties. Participants in a social movement sometimes intentionally disrupt social routines and, from the viewpoint of their targets and of many government officials, often technically violate the law – especially those parts of the legal code dealing with public order and public safety. But, again, social movements (despite opponents' charges) are never simply outlaw organizations. They are better seen as groups that walk on both sides of the legal fence.[2]

Are movements historically significant?

Many North American and western European social theorists agree that the term *social movement* refers to nonelite attempts to transform societies radically through complex mixtures of socially disruptive and nondisruptive tactics. But they disagree on whether social movements, despite participants' aspirations, significantly alter the course of social and political history or help nonelites.

University of Chicago sociologist Robert Park, for example, often interpreted social movements in an evolutionary manner. Early in this century, he argued that

> every institution may in turn be described as a movement that was once active and eruptive, like a volcano, but has since settled down to something like routine activity. It has, to change the metaphor, defined its aims, found its place and function in the social complex.
>
> (Park 1972: 22)

Park likened social movements to acorns that in appropriate soil have the potential to become mighty trees that shade and protect.

Park at times qualified his generalization about the historical significance of social movements and about their popular benefits. He occasionally categorized the movements in terms of scope of change sought, and suggested that the historical impact of a given movement is inversely related to the utopian ambitions of its leaders. Some leaders, Park argued, are grandly revolutionary and seek to sweep away almost every aspect of the society. Others are more moderate and seek limited change in selected institutions. European and North American labour movements of the nineteenth and twentieth centuries, for example, were comparatively 'minor' and 'slowburning' movements, especially when juxtaposed to, say, the French Revolution. Because of their modest aims, these movements succeeded in bringing about courts of arbitration and long-lasting labour laws. The French revolutionaries' ambitious radicalism, in contrast, spurred a counterrevolution that in the opinion of Park and some later scholars, such as Crane Brinton (1938), defeated almost all of their short-term accomplishments.

During the 1940s, 1950s, and early 1960s, North American and western European scholars echoed many of Park's conclusions and arguments. They too held that social movements have significantly affected the course of history. Unlike Park, however, they believed that social movements were inimical to civility, democracy, and liberty. (Even Park, who generally held a historically evolutionary theory of movements, sometimes deplored rash and impatient behaviour by movement activists. In particular, he warned of a subset of social movements that he called 'crowd movements', which usually disrupted without creating (Park 1972: 47–8, 96).) William Kornhauser (1959), for one, emphasized in his widely read book how certain types of movements unravel the social fabric and destroy desirable social arrangements. Other influential writers who routinely stressed the possible negative effects of social movements included Hannah Arendt (1951), Eric Fromm (1941), Eric Hoffer (1951), and Seymour Martin Lipset (1955, 1960).[3]

Movements, modernity, and social turbulence

During the decades that immediately followed the Second World War, negative interpretations predominated among western European and North American social-movement theorists. They typically depicted social movements derogatorily and dwelt on their childish, immoral, and antidemocratic features. These negative judgements were rooted in part in painful memories of National Socialism in Germany, Fascism in Italy, and McCarthyism in the United States.[4]

Intellectuals often explained the rise of social movements in terms of the pace and extent of contemporary social change. Social scientists, in particular, were profoundly impressed by the rapidity of change in social norms and practices worldwide. Societies everywhere were becoming much more urban, literate, bureaucratized, mechanized, and organizationally large scale. Global social homogenization seemed to be converging toward the heavily industrialized lifestyles of northern England, the US iron and steel belt, and southern California. Conversely, local communities, small workplaces, precapitalist forms of exchange, and voluntary associations appeared to be anachronisms that were facing extinction.

Scholars in that period tended to read contemporary social movements as direct consequences of the rush to modernization and commonly used a social-psychological line of reasoning: most movement activists were recent urban immigrants, people from small towns and from petit-bourgeois rural families (Fromm 1941; Lipset 1955). It was believed that what the newcomers sought in social movements was a psychological balm to heal the social dislocation and personal loneliness inherent in modern life. Indeed, as daily life in Europe and North America became noticeably more industrialized, bureaucratic, urban, and large scale, people felt increasingly socially unimportant and normatively out of place. Market dislocations, labour organizations, and big business posed additional economic threats to small merchants, artisans, and workers with small-town backgrounds. Uprooted and lonely, economically vulnerable, and disconcerted by their declining social status, the urban immigrants turned to movements in large part as a therapeutic resort. Movements provided an environment in which they could safely express anxieties, anger, and frustrations.

Scholars in the 1940s, 1950s, and early 1960s often argued that the new movement participants were systematically exposed to simplistic, conspiratorial ideologies that identified hidden conspiracies behind the problems posed by modern life. According to early postwar theorists, movement participants were led by ideologues who routinely pointed to selected populations in cities – such as 'Jews', 'bankers', 'Communists' – as conspirators against petit-bourgeois values and small-town social structures. Except for the scapegoatism, the ideologies were substanceless and betrayed a naivety about both the causes of modernity and the social benefits that modernity offered. Leaders of social movements uniformly failed to propose specific policies and institutional reforms that might improve the urban immigrants' daily lives. Instead, they offered up crudely melodramatic ideologies in which traditional ways of life were depicted as unproblematic and in which an urban minority was cast into the role of the proverbial snake in the Garden of Eden.

A good deal of the postwar literature on movements attempted to explain the attraction of movements whose political programmes did not promise tangible, practical benefits. Usually, the explanations involved theories about the disappearance of traditional interpersonal social linkages and the unprecedented social psychologies of the new urban dwellers. Several scholars argued that movement activists' seemingly selfless commitment was an inadvertent consequence of the increasing paucity of community activities, neighbourhood ties, and small-scale organizations (Kornhauser 1959). The translocal dimensions of modern culture (for example, mass media), of education (for example, metropolitan school systems), and of work (for example, corporations with large factories at multiple sites), meant that local institutions and groupings, which once helped the individual deal with life's exigencies, had lost their personal significance. Local union chapters, neighbourhood churches, and extended families no longer protected against illness, illiteracy, and hunger. Metropolitan and national organizations and agencies now ministered in some degree or other to people's immediate needs.

As overarching institutions superseded local associations as providers of needed goods and emotional support, interest in those associations waned and they slowly disappeared. Urban residents no longer worked regularly with their neighbours in pursuit of common interests. At best, they had a passing interest in others' circumstances, were unfamiliar with one another's fates, and were indifferent to much of the human travail about them. For a goodly number, urban life was increasingly private and somewhat lonely.

According to many of the postwar social-movement theorists, most city dwellers, because they were no longer involved in multiple local organizations that address proximate concerns, lacked familiarity with broader social interests and the practical political experience needed to question simplistic ideologies. Firsthand involvement in local affairs in premodern times had prevented people's attention and loyalties from being captured by a single abstract and intangible ideology. It was presumed by the theorists that people active in social movements thought 'ideologically', in terms of only one correct way of perceiving the world, and would not reassess and diversify beliefs in light of contrary evidence and experience. Instead of using common sense and accepting the paradox that there may exist many, and perhaps even logically incompatible, truths about how the world works, participants in a social movement would not deviate from the fixed 'Truth' as stated either in manifestos or by movement leaders. Nor would they accept the possibility that their assumptions about the world were incomplete or partially mistaken and would inevitably require revision. Further, having lost a sense of community and control over their lives, people in urban, industrialized, and commercialized environs were desperately seeking a new source of meaning, a way to regain dignity. The modern city, lacking intermediary bodies conducive to the enhancement of positive personal qualities, psychologically predisposed its people to join social movements with Manichean, intolerant doctrines. As Hannah Arendt (1951: 323–4) put it, a member's uncritical faith in a movement's hate-filled ideology

> can be expected only from the completely isolated human being who, without any other social ties . . . derives his sense of having a place in the world only from his belonging to a movement.

Or in the words of Eric Hoffer (1951: 44),

A rising mass movement attracts and holds a following not by its doctrine and promises but by the refuge it offers from the anxieties, barrenness and meaninglessness of an individual existence.

Movements' special rituals, such as secret salutations and special award ceremonies, reinforced feelings of comradeship and, conversely, lessened feelings of social awkwardness. In addition, violent actions against scapegoats, including physical attacks on 'the rich' and 'the powerful', gave members opportunities to vent frustration with the new social order, even though the attacks yielded no tangible benefits to movement activists.

Many scholars believed that the absence of tangible goals and the prevalence of scapegoat ideologies made social movements dangerous to liberal democratic constitutional systems. It was thought that participants in social movements were so loyal to simplistic ideologies and so disconnected from concrete goals and problems that they forgot the instrumental and moral value of pragmatism, dialogue, and compromise. To them, all that mattered was remaining true to the movement's doctrine. As a result, they shamelessly violated both written law and unwritten codes of decency; hate-filled ideology was their moral compass.

Ideological correctness, however, was merely one of the troubling political features of the social movements of the times. Scholars were made uneasy by the movements' internally undemocratic and authoritarian policy-making processes. According to theorists, movement participants, deprived of firsthand experience in solving local social problems and unburdened by competing institutional loyalties, trusted without qualification their leaders' decisions. Moblike credulity replaced common sense and independence of thought. Consequently, some social scientists in the postwar period believed that to understand a social movement, it is sufficient to study the decisions of its leaders. There was, after all, no independent reasoning and deliberation below the top echelon. Even the local chapters and organizations, such as youth groups, were little more than transmission belts for what the leaders of a movement deemed necessary for their followers to be told.

Like ideological loyalty, hierarchical relations within social movements were interpreted by scholars to be consequential to the profound psychological needs of participants and, more indirectly, to modernization. Uprooted and insecure, participants were thought not to be open to judicious reasoning and to intelligent discussion of their circumstances and political options (Ardent 1951: 315–16, 352). They wanted someone to blame; they wanted assurance that their older ways of life were valuable; and they wanted promises that the new social orders would not prevail. Hence, they were easily manipulated by the peddlers of nostalgia and scapegoat rhetoric.

Many scholars during the 1940s, 1950s, and early 1960s feared that contemporary social movements were not abnormalities but indications of historical trends. They believed that as the world became more and more 'modern' (that is, more bureaucratic, industrialized, urbanized, secularized, commercially competitive, and migratory), market dislocations would continue, anomie would abound, and anti-modern and violent social movements would become widespread. Fascism in Italy,

Nazism in Germany, Stalinism in the Soviet Union, and McCarthyism in the United States thus not only were despicable but augured an era of impatient, enraged politics.

Wanting to demonstrate scientifically that movements such as Stalinism were not simply the result of a uniquely charismatic leader or of a singular confluence of conditions, some scholars combed the historical record for other cases of social movements amid rapid modernization. One of their motivations was to strengthen the thesis that the movements of the mid-twentieth century were not historical anomalies but troubling manifestations of a broader, general sociological law of human behaviour: with rapid modernization come angry, tyrannical, and highly ideological social movements. Thus, Christian millenarianism during the Middle Ages was creatively reinterpreted as an expression of middle-class disorientation amid rapid urbanization, as was the Populist movement during the 1880s in the United States and the street violence in Paris during the French Revolution.[5]

Second wave of movement theorizing

Around the middle of the 1960s, an alternative view of social movements gained ascendancy. The assumptions, questions, and theories that scholars articulated differed strikingly from those found in earlier writings. Indeed, one historian of sociology declared that the radical change in patterns of thinking about social movements 'is perhaps as close as social science comes to an authentic "paradigm shift", in Thomas Kuhn's sense' (Rule 1988: 182).

The new forms of interpretation arose partly because a younger generation of movement specialists either had directly participated in recent movements for social justice and peace or had heard sympathetic reports of such events as the Montgomery Bus Boycott (McAdam 1988). In their minds and experience, participants in social movements were not excessively intolerant or violent; nor did movement activists appear indifferent to tangible changes in society. On the contrary, the activists seemed remarkably pragmatic in their politics, civil in their interpersonal behaviour, and thoughtful and articulate about their ethical principles and long-term social goals. As James Rule (1988: 183) put it,

> By the 1960s, a new generation of social scientists was responding, mostly
> sympathetically, to protest movements of blacks and university students. A theoretical
> view of movements and social contention as irrational, retrograde, destructive forces
> would no longer do.

The new scholars who wrote about social movements were mistrustful of 'liberal-democratic' polities, of 'free-market' economies, and of the spread of capitalism around the world (Gamson 1968; Perlman 1975). Many contended that the so-called liberal democratic states frequently violated citizens' rights to privacy and obstructed citizens' rights of dissent, association, and free speech. Many also maintained that 'free-market' economies were, in fact, sophisticated systems of private power, day-to-day oppression, and endless exploitation, with big business enjoying benefits paid for by other classes. Some scholars added that international trade and loans created poverty and inequality abroad, regardless of arguments to the contrary advanced by the makers of foreign policy. After 1970, the once nearly ubiquitous theme of social modernization disappeared from the majority of scholarly writings on social movements, and the general theme of structural inequality (political and economic) became commonplace.

According to most of the new social-movement analysts, in every known society a relatively small and identifiable group systematically influences decisions made in the political system and monopolizes the resources needed to create wealth (McAdam 1982). Occasionally, members of that elite may disagree among themselves about specific policies, but generally they harmoniously advance their common interest in reproducing current patterns of inequality in status, wealth, and power.

The younger analysts further differed from their predecessors in terms of psychological model favoured. According to the former, participants in social movements shrewdly calculate the probable costs and rewards of alternative courses of action, and then act accordingly. The participants are not, contrary to the assertions of earlier analysts, blind dogmatists overwhelmed by rootlessness and general vulnerability. The decision to participate is made, usually, only after the person (1) has found the stated aims of the movement relevant to his or her immediate situation, and (2) has calculated the cost:benefit ratio associated with participation. In this scenario, participation is neither a desperate nor a knee-jerk reaction to anxieties produced by modernity; it is a practical and considered activity, a form of 'bargaining by riot' (Thompson 1971: 115–23) that is 'deliberate and purposeful' (Piven 1976: 309) and 'a continuation of politics by other means' (Garner and Zald 1985: 138).

One somewhat surprising implication of this logic is that the poorest, most socially disorganized, and most politically powerless strata in every society tend to avoid participation in movements despite daily indignities and deprivations. The costs are too great for those who already have little economic security and political protection (Migdal 1974; Piven 1976: 316–18; Scott 1985). To borrow from E. E. Schattschneider (1960: 8) (a theorist of party politics who was often cited with approval by the new social-movement scholars), 'People are not likely to start a fight if they are certain that they are going to be severely penalized for their efforts.'

To explain why often acquiescent nonelites would sometimes form and join movements, the new generation of social-movement theorists looked closely at national and local political contexts, and developed ideas about how certain types of political circumstances facilitate movement organization. One can discern within the second wave of scholarship three distinguishable traditions of theorizing, which for our purposes can be called 'resource-mobilization theorizing', 'indigenous-community theorizing', and 'political-process theorizing'. As we shall see, although each tradition of theorizing highlighted very different political processes, they were similar in that they rejected the sociological and psychological logic of the preceding generation of theorists. Writers in all three traditions assumed (1) the existence of significant political and economic inequalities in all known societies; (2) the prudential nature of movement participation, and (3) the natural propensity of desperately poor people to avoid participation in movements.

Some post-1960 scholars, who labelled themselves 'resource-mobilization theorists', contended that in every society most people are unhappy with the status quo, are ignored and mistreated by their government, and suffer economic injustices. Despite widespread grievances, moral outrage, and personal discontent, people seldom form or join movements, partly because they often lack experience in politics and confidence about political matters and partly because they often lack adequate material and organizational resources with which to do battle against vested interests. According to resource-mobilization theorists, a movement for and by an aggrieved population usually appears only after alliances are forged between an aggrieved constituency and a group or person who has the appropriate political experience, vision, and/or resources to help that constituency. A researcher therefore should study the process by which a movement initially attracts outside resources, which often requires that one or more persons assume the role of an 'issue entrepreneur' and creatively bring in resources from third parties (McCarthy and Zald 1977).

The remarkable history of the US farmworker movement during the 1960s illustrates how one 'issue entrepreneur', Cesar Chavez, attracted resources from established labour organizations, sympathetic consumers, and selected government officials. Previously, most American union activists had looked upon California's farmworkers as almost impossible to unionize because of their extreme poverty (which made them chary of risking even a day's wages); because of the seasonal nature of their employment; because of the here-today-gone-tomorrow nature of their lives (which militated against development of feelings of group solidarity); and because many were Mexican citizens (a status that generated fears of deportation). In addition, farm owners had at their disposal compliant police forces and numerous vigilante groups. Lacking numerous key resources – such as time, money, legal expertise, judicially defensible rights, and even sound equipment for strikes – farmworkers for decades had been unable to mount a challenge to the owners' prerogatives, and workers understandably had become reluctant to join any movement organization that asserted it worked for their interests. According to several resource-mobilization analysts, Chavez's brilliance as an organizer was to foresee the need to enlist financial, legal, and media support from such nonunion groups as the National Council of Churches, local university communities, and the liberal wing of the Democratic Party. Through his patient courting of such contacts, Chavez was able to launch an effective national boycott of California's grapes and, ultimately, to win concessions from owners, despite their considerable local sources of power. According to one chronicler of the United Farm Worker movement,

> students and clergy marched through grocery stores, harassing store managers, conducting 'shop-ins', and closing off entrances; liberal politicians, including two presidential candidates (Senators Kennedy and McGovern), joined prominent celebrities in endorsing the boycott; liberal clerics sermonized their congregations on the boycott; universities and Catholic schools cut off standing orders to grocers that continued to handle 'scab' grapes; and millions of consumers shunned grapes and the grocery stores that continued to handle them. By the summer of 1970 the grape growers faced a closed marketplace.
>
> (Jenkins 1983: 65)

In the wake of the boycott's surprising success, thousands of migrant workers, once notoriously difficult to recruit, themselves contacted the United Farm Workers' offices, spontaneously launched their own marches and set up strike committees, and began to direct their own grievance committees on farms with UFW contracts. Thus, by rallying appropriate outsiders, Chavez helped establish a social movement among a highly discontented population.

A second theoretical tradition that developed after 1960 still lacks a convenient and widely used label, but it might best be called the 'indigenous-community approach'.[6] Resource-mobilization theorists, as we have seen, emphasize leaders' abilities to construct effective alliances. Indigenous-community thinkers, in contrast, explore how local-level social institutions, such as neighbourhood clubs, union locals, and community churches, can provide organizational building blocks, communication networks, and leadership skills for later social movements (Adam 1987; Evans and Boyte 1986; Morris 1984; Tarrow 1994).

Unlike many of the early postwar scholars, who believed that modern life was increasingly lonely, the indigenous-community theorists maintained that the rhythms of modern life – in particular, the day-to-day social interactions in heavy-industry cities – have produced a wealth of local associations that facilitate the formation of indigenous social movements. For example, according to Charles, Louise, and Richard Tilly (1975), European factory towns are hardly socially disorganized. On the contrary, large factories and their nearby working-class residential districts contain numerous public spaces where every day people regularly meet, discuss common grievances, and plan collective actions. Similarly, Aldon Morris (1984) believes that the great urban migration of southern African Americans to cities in the North resulted in the spontaneous expansion of churches, schools, clubs, and other associational forms that allowed previously isolated rural people to congregate, to discuss common grievances, and, ultimately, to plan collective actions. Both Wayne Cornelius (1971) and Janice Perlman (1975) note that residents of rapidly growing Latin American cities do not suffer profoundly from loneliness and social disorganization. Even new arrivals in metropolises quickly form associations to help satisfy physical needs (medical care, water, police protection) and emotional and mental needs (recreational groups, sports clubs, choirs, libraries). Having observed hundreds of such associations, Cornelius and Perlman contend that theories of the profound social disorganization and loneliness of urban life grossly misrepresent city life in Latin America.

Indigenous-community theorists see most urban dwellers as leading busy social lives. They belong to multiple formal associations, regularly attend local meetings, and communicate through numerous informal friendship networks. Because of such ties, individuals find partners and allies for future group struggles relatively easily. Further, the neighbourhood associations' tried and tested strategies and routines for raising funds and collecting materials and for building morale are highly instructive. Over time a leader cohort naturally emerges. Those leaders, in constant communication with friends and neighbours, inventively address local concerns and promote local values, and, if the times seem right, organize disruptive collective actions. They are attuned to the potentialities of their communities and draw on local institutions and networking for resources – such as money, copying machines, and feelings of solidarity – to help the movement succeed. Social movements thus arise naturally out of people's daily, local, and largely apolitical patterns of social interaction.

A subset of the indigenous-community theorists further explored how fledgling movements learn from local organizations' political experience. Supposedly, the victory of one group often inspires nearby discontented groups and also models useful strategies and tactics. In addition, a movement usually leaves in its wake a corps of practiced leaders, evocative symbols, and communication networks that a successor movement can utilize. Movements, in other words, do not spring full-blown from Zeus's forehead, but often arise in ongoing and identifiable traditions of popular protest and local creative politicking (Tarrow 1989a, b; Tilly 1978, 1986; Zirakzadeh 1989).

After the mid-1960s, a third popular approach to the study of social movements gradually evolved alongside the resource-mobilization and indigenous-community approaches. By the mid-1980s it had become widely known as the 'political-process approach'.[7] Political-process theorists, such as Anne Costain (1992), Doug McAdam (1982), Joel Migdal (1974), John Duncan Powell (1971), and Christian Smith (1991), held that constitutions, national-level policies and policy-making processes, and intragovernmental struggles over power profoundly influence both people's decisions to participate in a movement and the strategies and tactics that a movement adopts. For example, a fledgling movement has a better chance of attracting new participants and their resources if its constitution includes references to civil liberties and if the formally declared civil liberties of early movement activists have been shown to be, in fact, protected. If the civil rights of movement spokespersons are protected after they hold assemblies, print and distribute literature, and demonstrate in public, then the movement has a better chance of recruiting new members. If, on the other hand, movement spokespersons appear to be hounded by agents of the state, and their civil liberties appear to have been negated, the movement's chances of attracting new participants plummet.

Another relevant political circumstance affecting a movement's capacity to attract new participants is the degree of unity and the number and nature of divisions within the governing elite. Some social problems and political arrangements, such as an economic depression or intense electoral competition, may generate splits among government officials and may lead factions to seek allies among groups of the nonwealthy. Then an alliance between a fledgling movement and a governing faction might be struck that temporarily protects the participants from state harassment – a circumstance that can persuade more people to join the movement. The temporary alliance between the northern wing of the US Democratic Party and the civil rights movement during the early 1960s, for example, brought a number of people into the movement because it seemed to have guardians in high places.

Finally, the actions of international groups – foreign governments, international humanitarian organizations, international alliances of political parties, and multinational corporations – bear upon people's calculations in regard to joining a movement. International groups may offer a movement resources, such as money, legal expertise, or equipment. As a movement acquires more resources relative to its political and economic opponents, more people may become participants because the movement's chances of being effective seem more realistic.

According to almost all of the newer generation of social-movement theorists, a leader of a fledgling movement cannot create and control the movement simply by peddling 'exciting ideas' about change or by vilifying a minority population. Before an aspiring leader can hope to be influential, a broader constellation of political circumstances and associational ties has to be in place. Only then can she or he speak plausibly about the practicality of participation, persuade hesitant onlookers to join, and then nudge the newcomers toward particular courses of action.

Like the earlier generation of movement theorists, most of the post-1960 generation believed that a new era of movement activism had commenced. The worldwide spread of liberal democratic constitutions and rights, growing divisions among elites about how to respond to intense global economic competition, and ongoing urbanization and industrialization combined to make movements increasingly likely phenomena. Whereas the earlier generation of movement theorists viewed the prospect of more movements with dread, the newer generation tended to view the prospect as an opportunity to redistribute political and economic power democratically and fairly. Contemporary movements were seen as signs of increasing political health – not disease.

Fashioning identities

After the mid-1960s, few scholars saw social movements as simply uncalculated expressions of rage against modernity and as only threats to democracy. Growing numbers saw them as pragmatic political responses by 'have-nots' to inequities, oppression, and exploitation.

However, this was not the last word. In Europe, culturally sensitive approaches to the study of social movements appeared during the mid and late 1960s and had attracted significant numbers of adherents by the end of the 1970s. A similar theoretical evolution occurred in both North and South America during the late 1970s and 1980s. For convenience, I shall call writers associated with this third major wave of social-movement theorizing 'identity-formation' theorists.[8]

Identity-formation theorizing was developed and refined by scholars in diverse social-science disciplines, including history (Evans 1979; Goodwyn 1978; Hill 1972; Kelley 1994; Thompson 1963), sociology (Breines 1982; Laclau 1985; Melucci 1985, 1988; Touraine 1981, 1985), anthropology (Escobar and Alvarez 1992; Kubik 1994), and political science (Ackelsberg 1991; Apter 1987; Apter and Sawa 1984; Gaventa 1980). They periodically cited one another's work, generally developed their insights independently of one another, and shared the belief that 'culture' – broadly understood as how we interpret social arrangements, how we see our places within those arrangements, and how we see our immediate opportunities, powers, and limitations – profoundly informs and shapes our political actions. Accordingly, patterns of social and personal cognition and patterns of political action should not be treated as unrelated phenomena, for political activity is an expression and embodiment of cognition.[9] For example, our style of perceiving social arrangements determines whether we see a given phenomenon – say, a sudden rise in local unemployment – as a problem deserving of public discussion and government action or as a temporarily inconveniencing but ultimately healthy 'market correction' that should not occasion meddling. Similarly, whether we write a letter to a local newspaper criticizing a specific government policy depends in part on our beliefs about the efficacy of such an action and about our own abilities to question the wisdom of public-policy makers and also to persuade others through our prose.

Although the subtle features of the identity-formation argument vary from scholar to scholar, the basic position is as follows. We never view events directly but through intellectual prisms (or lenses) composed of our presumptions about our society and ourselves. The prisms give our observations meaning (e.g. whether we see crowds of people thrusting clenched fists into the air as principled protesters or a violent mob), shape our emotions (e.g. whether we are frightened or inspired by demonstrators), and determine whether in our political responses to social circumstances we are tolerant or outraged, passive or active, cooperative or confrontational. Although we may almost always believe ourselves to be completely open-minded, unbiased, and uncommitted to any cultural myth when thinking about public affairs, we can never escape our cultural presumptions. Indeed, we need our interpretive lens to organize our observations, to make judgements, to see alternatives, to predict consequences of imagined alternative courses of actions, and to determine what political actions (if any) are effective and appropriate. Cultural assumptions thus profoundly (and inevitably) influence both our understanding of our powers and our exercise of them.

The identity-formation theorists further maintained that although people constantly receive ideas from the social environment – for example, from friends and family, from schools and churches, from the mass media – the mind is hardly soft, formless clay upon which social forces impress ideas. Human beings have the capacity to amend, sift, enhance, and reject the ideas that are presented to them. We are both consumers of currently available ideas and producers of fresh ideas about our situations and ourselves. True, we are partly taught by many people and institutions to view the world in particular ways, but to an important degree we also endlessly define and redefine our social identities.

One can discern two theoretical subapproaches within the rapidly growing post-1960 literature on social movements and identity formation. Each emphasized the ability of nonelites to redefine their identities and related this cultural process to movement politics, but each also treated the relationship between identity formation and movement politics in a slightly different way.

First, some intellectuals viewed social movements primarily as reflections of autonomous developments in what is sometimes called popular culture (Apter and Sawa 1984; Evans and Boyte 1986; Hill 1972; Kelley 1994). That is, within society rich cultural currents are being constantly developed by ordinary folks in everyday, prepolitical public spaces, such as churches, cafes, recreational clubs, and street corners, where people talk, exchange opinions, and develop new images about what their sufferings mean and about how to address them. When recruited into social-movement organizations, new members bring along their own previously developed ideas, which often differ from those of the organizational leaders and bring on intramovement conflict and concession. For example, African Americans who joined the Communist Party in the 1930s accepted many Leninist ideas but also held on to notions of black nationalism that party leaders strongly opposed. The upshot was a complex process of factional conflict, ideological compromise, and cultural cross-pollination within the party (Kelley 1994: 123–58).

According to the autonomous popular-culture approach, to understand a social movement's activities, goals, and popular support, one must be sensitive to: (1) the specific, local popular-culture context (for example, local magazines, clubs, discussion groups, churches, and so on); (2) cultural diversity; and (3) the inevitable consequent ideological conflict and debate within a movement. Scholars of this persuasion strongly opposed broad generalizations about movements, and decried attempts to portray any movement as homogeneous in connection with member beliefs. Such attempts, in their opinion, were certain to eventuate in serious mis-understandings of movement activities and social bases of support.

The other subset of identity-formation theorists, whose position I call the 'autonomous movement-culture approach', held that social movements themselves are 'climates', 'environments', or 'atmospheres' in which new subversive ideas are invented and nurtured. Like hothouses, movements are safe, nourishing settings; there nonelites can think out loud about ideas that elites deem silly, dangerous, or immoral. In addition, daily practices of movement activists – such as the use of nonhierarchical titles: *comrade, brother, sister* – and daily rituals in which one feels surrounded by allies, give people a sense of security and equality, and the courage to think the unthinkable (Goodwyn 1978; Kubik 1994).

Many autonomous movement-culture theorists also noted that social movements – because they tend to be understaffed and decentralized in organizational structure – usually rely heavily on part-time volunteers to run local-level projects and offices. This organizational peculiarity is culturally significant (the theorists argued) because it allows people who normally do not hold positions of authority in their workaday lives to become experienced in running meetings and addressing crowds. Gradually, the grassroots volunteers acquire confidence in their own capabilities to act and think independent of elites, and begin to think the unthinkable (Apter and Sawa 1984: 230–1;[10] Breines 1982; Fantasia 1988; Goodwyn 1978: 305–6).

Last, many autonomous movement-culture theorists focused not on disruptive activities that social movements promote but on movements' far less dramatic educational projects, including street-corner harangues, poetry readings, and local concerts. According to the theorists, most movements have what Alberto Melucci (1985: 798–800) called extensive communication 'networks' that include bookstores, radio programmes, workshops, and magazines. Through these media, movements often successfully and unobtrusively radiate unconventional ideas throughout society and encourage nonelites to entertain uncommon and (from the elites' perspectives) sacrilegious ideas. Thus social movements not only reflect popular culture but also produce and shape it (Apter and Sawa 1984; Goodwyn 1978; Kubik 1994).

Like most second-wave social-movement theorists, most identity-formation theorists (both the autonomous popular-culture theorists and the autonomous movement-culture theorists) contended that highly unequal distributions of power, status, and wealth exist in all known societies, including so-called liberal democratic political orders (Apter and Sawa 1984; Goodwyn 1978; Kelley 1994). According to identity-formation theorists, elites often try to legitimize inequalities of power and wealth before nonelites by disseminating ideas about the advantages of the status quo and the dangers of alternatives. The educational/indoctrinational processes occur in myriad ways, including the manipulation of curricula in schools and the government's and big business's direct and indirect influence over the news media. According to all identity-formation theorists, despite elites' efforts to mould the thinking of nonelites, the latter repeatedly question the elites' definitions of reality in both daily expressions of popular culture (e.g. street-corner conversations) and within organized social movements. Social movements thus should be understood as manifestations of an *ongoing cultural struggle* between the haves and the have-nots over how to understand and whether to tolerate current inequalities and inequities.

Furthermore, like the first postwar generation of social-movement theorists, some identity-formation theorists viewed modern social trends uneasily because of the increasingly large roles that the nation-state, mass media, and big business play in shaping popular culture. According to these identity-formation theorists, people in modern societies increasingly look upon themselves as either helpless victims or passive consumers of others' ideas. Modern means of communication, such as television and metropolitan newspapers, have reduced nonelites' opportunities to discuss public issues directly with others and to pose questions about elites' representations of reality (Edelman 1988; Gitlin 1980). Finally, the twentieth-century evolution of scientific and legal languages has further intimidated people from second-guessing elites' wisdom, because the idioms and rules for argumentation are foreign to everyday speech. In these and other ways, modernity seems to have promoted a culture of timidity. According to US historian Lawrence Goodwyn (1978: 315), because of distinctively modern cultural conditions,

> Americans seem to have lost the capacity to think seriously about the structure of their own society. Words like 'inevitability', 'efficiency', and 'modernization' are passively accepted as the operative explanations for the increasingly hierarchical nature of contemporary life.

Other identity-formation scholars, however, believed that modern social trends provide numerous new places where nonelites can freely mingle and exchange opinions (Melucci 1985, 1988). Cities, for example, because of their size, density, and anonymity, give nonelites many opportunities to meet, question, and plan. Secularization, literacy, and modern forms of communications (radio, magazines, and the like) also facilitate the formation of movement networks. Thus, according to some authors, recent trends in social history – including the spread of electronic modes of communication – foretell a likely growth in social-movement activity, as momentarily successful tactics and novel programmes of social change are more easily communicated across cities, regions, and even national borders.

From theories to observations

In the following chapters, I will draw on the above traditions (and subtraditions) of social-movement analysis. I will use their insights and logics to understand three widely known social movements of the 1980s: the West German Greens, Poland's Solidarity, and Peru's Shining Path.

Although some commentators have considered the above three theoretical approaches incompatible (Evans and Boyte 1986; McAdam 1982), I treat them as complementary, although I certainly see differences in emphases and concerns. The first approach (of the 1940s, 1950s, and early 1960s) focuses largely on rapid, large-scale social change; emphasizes distinctively modern threats to economic security and social status; and views human beings as socially isolated and as emotionally reactive to deeply felt fears and pains. The second approach, in contrast, focuses largely on political processes and opportunities, emphasizes ongoing political struggles between organized groups, and views human beings as involved in myriad social groups and as prudent calculators and choice makers. The most recent, the cultural, approach focuses on beliefs about one's self and one's social and political situation, emphasizes small-scale educational projects, and sees humans as susceptible to intellectual conversions and as constantly able to reinterpret their situations.

Each of these approaches seems partly true and worth keeping in mind when reconstructing the histories of social movements. The first reminds us that humans are reactive animals who respond to changes in their environment; the second, that humans are far-seeing animals who contemplate consequences, benefits, and disadvantages associated with different available courses of action; and the third, that humans are interpretive animals who constantly reimagine their situations and identities.

None of the approaches seems by itself to give a 'full' or 'complete' account of the social movements in politics, however. Each, indeed, may be misleading; for it may, by itself, give an overly deterministic, rationalistic, or voluntaristic picture of movement politics. Humans, after all, are not simply blindly terrified by harmful change; nor are they merely prudent calculators; nor are they only creative dreamers. But the assumptions about human nature and the general logic of each theoretical approach ring *partly* true, and therefore each approach seems potentially useful in thinking about social movements in politics.

The three theoretical traditions provide me with themes and questions to use in narrating the histories of the Greens, Solidarity, and Shining Path. First, drawing upon the insights of the first generation of postwar social movement theorists, I will look closely at large-scale social changes in Germany, Poland, and Peru and will consider the specific discontents that modernization – in particular, rapid urbanization, rapid industrialization, and the evolution of big enterprises, capitalist business cycles, and the vagaries of the international economic order – generated. In thinking about the context of social movements, I also will look briefly at the political histories of Germany, Poland, and Peru and will consider the limits and opportunities each political system posed for peaceful, nondisruptive reform.

Then I will adopt a more mid-range view of each country and look at the legacies left by the earlier organized efforts toward social change. I will consider how the Greens, Solidarity, and Shining Path were shaped by earlier grassroots actions that provided the new movements with experienced leaders, organizational resources, rallying calls and meaningful symbols, and lessons about practical politics.

Finally, I will recount each movement's activities (political and cultural) and some of the intramovement debates that preceded and followed them. I will draw upon earlier information about premovement popular culture and the broader social and political context to help understand the diversity of goals, priorities, and strategies within each movement. But I will also view movements as autonomously generating new ideas about their societies and about immediate possibilities for social change.

The following chapters, because they are informed by three very different theoretical traditions, will, when combined, provide multidimensional histories of the Greens, Solidarity, and Shining Path. Such multidimensional accounts of specific movements are valuable because they help us reflect on how everyday people who do not hold public office periodically try to change their world and become agents in their own histories. From knowledge about the particulars we can begin to generalize and form new hypotheses about how social movements in other times and places originated, developed, and interacted with other social and political forces.

Furthermore, when examining others' efforts to control their destinies, we sometimes change how we think about ourselves. After learning about other peoples' struggles, we sometimes acquire self-confidence in our own political potential; we sometimes gain practical wisdom about the difficulties and advantages of different forms of nonelite rebellions and nonrebellious politics; and we sometimes indirectly gain fresh perspectives on our own social, political, and cultural histories. The careful study of particular social movements, in other words, is somewhat akin to looking into a mirror for the first time: we are surprised by what we discover about ourselves, our circumstances, and our alternatives. The brighter and sharper the mirror and the larger its surface, the more we can see of ourselves.

The multidimensional pictures also may help us be better scholars and more thoughtful citizens because we may become more circumspect whenever generalizing about other social movements, their goals, their causes, and their long-term implications. Detailed pictures of social movements remind us that they are highly complex phenomena that are affected by multiple social and political conditions, that combine diverse groups and heterogeneous beliefs, and that involve many political traditions. Once we discover both that movements have multiple personalities and that they tend to be internally riddled with struggles over goals, priorities, and tactics, we will be less likely to be satisfied with simplistic, single-sentence statements about the origins, goals, and likely behaviour of movements around us, as can be seen on tonight's televised news or in the morning's newspapers. Multidimensional examination of these three movements may lead some of us to expect (and perhaps demand) more subtle analyses of other movements, by other analysts.

Last, detailed and complex pictures of social movements can teach us the difficulty of evaluating a specific movement, given that each movement is probably the outcome of various conditions and probably contains heterogeneous, changing, and seemingly contradictory elements, beliefs, and plans of action. As with other political phenomena (such as elections, court decisions, and major pieces of legislation), social movements can be maturely judged only if an investigator is willing to adopt a balanced, multidimensional, and evolutionary approach. The attainment of 'complete balance' in political judgements is perhaps an unachievable goal. But even if complete balance is elusive, by attempting to see diverse social and ideological forces working upon and within a movement, we can help reduce the always-present temptation to praise or damn a social movement without qualification.

I would like to close these preparatory remarks with a brief caveat concerning methodological challenges facing students of social movements, and with mention of the research opportunities facing future social-movement scholars.

The so-called historical record with respect to social movements (even the most famous movements) is *very* incomplete and, in many ways, frustratingly unreliable. Social movements are usually short-lived, and movement activists seldom keep extensive archives or writings. Former activists, moreover, are difficult to track down, are usually preoccupied with more recent political events, and seldom are disinterested respondents during interviews. At the same time, one can never fully trust the accuracy of government and journalistic accounts of movements. Indeed, one must always take government and journalistic reports with a grain of salt, for the authors of the reports are generally politically motivated by a desire to demonize (and occasionally to romanticize) particular movements (Edelman 1988; Gitlin 1980).

There is, in short, always more to learn about any given movement and about its socioeconomic origins, its political predecessors, its cultural inventions, and its historical evolution. The following readings of the Greens, Solidarity, and Shining Path are syntheses based on *currently* available information from scholarly and journalistic reports. Readers should not treat my interpretation of the three movements as historically 'definitive', for the interpretations reflect theoretical frameworks that I find useful (a different set of theoretical frameworks would result in different story lines), and the accuracy of the descriptions will require updating as more information becomes available.

But although one of my goals is to educate readers about three social movements, I do not wish solely to convey information. I also wish to inspire potential future social-movement scholars, partly because there is so much that we do not know. I hope that the following narratives will introduce readers to some surprising and previously unknown facts that will spark curiosity about these three movements *and* about other movements closer to the readers' homes. My goal is to whet readers' appetite for studying social movements, and also to help readers see movements around them as complex, puzzling, and interesting phenomena. If the reader periodically puts down the book and asks, 'If this is true about the Greens, I wonder if it is also true about the movement that occurred last week in . . .', I will be very happy.

Notes

1. Other scholars who define social movements in terms of a group's deliberate attempt to transform society include Goldberg (1991), Killian (1964), and Morris (1984). A few

scholars dispute this way of defining social movements. Piven (1976: 300–1), for example, contends that the concept of social movement should not emphasize participants' plans for radical social change. She concedes that her usage departs from scholarly norms and is somewhat idiosyncratic.

2. Social-movement theorists are not of one mind as to whether to view transient mobs, local street gangs, and unorganized riots as social movements. Piven (1976) is convinced the term *social movement* should refer in part to these phenomena; Jenkins (1981: 82–3) excludes them. I am of mixed opinion but tend to agree with Jenkins.

3. Many of these authors were primarily fearful of right-wing movements and Soviet communism. They were much more ambivalent (if not sympathetic) toward radically democratic and democratically socialist movements. See, for example, Lipset (1950) on Saskatchewan's Cooperative Commonwealth Federation, and Arendt (1965) on local experiments in participatory democracy during selected revolutions.

   Because this chapter is a survey of social-movement theorizing over several decades, I must oversimplify specific authors' often complex positions in order to highlight commonalities. In reality, scholars seldom work from a single theoretical script and frequently combine diverse viewpoints and approaches. For present purposes (introducing readers who are generally unfamiliar with social-movement scholarship to major points of view within existing social-movement literature), the identification of specific authors with archetypical positions seems heuristically justifiable and pedagogically wise.

4. For additional discussions of social-movement theorizing immediately after the Second World War, see Eyerman and Jamison (1991), Halebsky (1976), Jenkins (1981), McAdam (1982), Morris and Herring (1981), Rogin (1967), Rule (1988), and Scott (1990).

5. Perhaps the most famous reinterpretation of Christian millenarianism in terms of a crisis of modernity is Cohn's (1961). For critiques of interpretations of the French Revolution and the US Populist movement in terms of 'the mob' and 'anomie', see Rogin (1967), and Rudé (1959).

6. This label was inspired by Morris's (1984) description of his own approach to the study of the civil rights movement.

7. The label 'political-process approach' became widely used after the publication of McAdam's seminal book (1982). For a study of Latin American politics that foreshadows some of McAdam's reasoning, see Powell (1971). For a creative application of McAdam's political-process approach to a social movement with international dimensions, see Smith (1991).

8. In choosing this label, I am slightly modifying Cohen's (1985) insightful distinction between 'identity-oriented' and 'resource-mobilization' social-movement theories.

9. Eyerman and Jamison (1991) coined the evocative phrase 'cognitive praxis' to convey the role activists' innovative language and thinking play in shaping movement activity.

10. Apter and Sawa's study of protest politics in Japan combines elements of both the autonomous popular-culture approach and the autonomous movement-culture approach. Hence, I cite their book as an illustration of both currents of identity-formation theorizing.

Part II

Germany's Greens and the politics of party-movements

Participants in a social movement, by definition, attempt to restructure their society. They want to remove features that to them seem harmful and immoral, and to establish social institutions and values not yet widely found or accepted, save in their imaginations. Critics sometimes find such commitment to reordering the world dangerous and fanciful, and accuse movement activists of being unrealistic or cantankerous. Yet research shows that activists are seldom simply utopians or cranks (Clark 1984; Halebsky 1976; McAdam 1988). Activists are certainly like many political actors, dreamers in part and malcontents to some extent. But they are also optimists, reformers who articulate a vision of a better world *and* who believe that they have found the means to move toward its realization.

What sorts of tactics and strategies do movement activists utilize? According to political-process theorists, movement activists select tactics and strategies partly in light of constitutional arrangements and of ongoing intraelite struggles for power. Movement activists know that political contexts provide opportunities and constraints on the types of activities that might affect the political behaviour of elites and nonelites. Constitutionally recognized rights of assembly and speech, for example, open doors to certain types of political activity, and make certain tactics and strategies sensible and appealing.

As we shall see throughout this book, activists within a single movement utilize diverse tactics and strategies, sometimes including armed assaults upon the state's security personnel and wanton destruction of private property. But they do not always (or even typically) engage in violence or illegal actions. They generally first explore legal opportunities to pressure their government into abetting the desired societal transformations.

Since the mid-nineteenth century, many social-movement leaders in North America and western Europe have argued that because of their countries' liberal-democratic constitutions, elections could function as the Archimedean fulcrum needed to move their societies. In theory, election campaigns offer an invaluable opportunity to educate citizens about issues and to inculcate new values and ways of thinking. Further, victories at the polls enable members of a movement to enter the governance process and 'work from within', so to speak, legislating major social change notwithstanding elites' opposition.

The United States Populist Party of the 1880s (Goodwyn 1978), the German Social Democratic Party of the late nineteenth century and early twentieth (Schorske 1972), and the Saskatchewan Cooperative Commonwealth Federation of the mid-twentieth century (Lipset 1950) all illustrate the recurrent belief among European and North American movement activists that one can remake society through a shrewd use of electoral processes and institutions. The Green Party alliance in the Federal Republic of Germany provides yet another, more recent example of what might be called the party-movement tradition of Western radicalism.

To understand better the German Greens' decision to pursue an electoral strategy, let us investigate their political situation – in particular, West Germany's constitutional arrangements, its party system, and patterns of elite consensus and conflict. In addition, let us review some recent major changes within West German society. Social-movement theorists writing immediately after the Second World War typically argued that rapid social change – in particular, urbanization, industrialization, and the expansion of big business – generates widespread fear, uncertainty, and anxiety. These feelings, in turn, enable social-movement activists to attract sizeable followings. If we tentatively accept the reasoning of the earliest postwar wave of social-movement theorists, then an examination of recent social change in Germany may provide us with clues as to how the Greens, a fledgling movement in the 1980s, attracted support.

Chapter 2

A world to be remade: sociopolitical circumstances of Green politics

The Green party-movement appeared in the FRG during a recession in the world capitalist economy, and after Western powers, led by the United States, had rearmed the FRG with nuclear weaponry that placed the country in a precarious position were the Cold War to heat up. It was also a time when the West German party system was stagnant; major parties were imitating one another rather than offering telling criticisms of the current order and imaginative proposals for substantive change. These confluent national circumstances, alongside growing fears among young West German adults about how the country's rapid industrialization and its postwar consumer culture threatened the environment, affected the Greens' dreams and provided an opportunity to mobilize others.

Towards a new constitutional order

At the close of the Second World War, the Soviet Union, Britain, France, and the United States stationed armies in their treaty-stipulated zones of the defeated enemy, Germany.[1] The Soviet Union occupied what later became organized as the German Democratic Republic (or the GDR, or colloquially, East Germany), while the other three powers controlled zones in what later became the Federal Republic of Germany (the FRG, or colloquially, West Germany).

At first, the occupiers' overriding goal was to dismantle Germany's military apparatus and Nazi Party, and thereby prevent future military aggression by the German state. The rapid escalation of the Cold War, however, soon altered the policy priorities of Britain and the United States. Soviet troops, after all, were occupying Romania and Hungary; machinery and livestock were being transported from the Soviet zone and Poland into the Soviet Union; and the Soviet Union had begun to provide material aid to West Germany's Communist Party.

Britain and the United States, wary of their wartime ally's expansionary moves, decided to remake their zones in their own image. With the somewhat grudging cooperation of France (whose leaders tended to fear a united Germany more than they feared the Soviet Union), the three governments created a new entity: the Federal Republic of Germany.

Many government leaders in Britain, the United States, and France believed that Germany's previous democratic regime (the Weimar Republic, 1919–33) had been dangerously flawed and that specific problems with its constitution had contributed to the rise of the Nazis. The occupying countries therefore were in accord that 'their' Germany needed to have a constitutional order that broadly resembled other North Atlantic states and that it was imperative that the mistakes of the interbellum period not be repeated.

What specific constitutional errors did the occupiers seek to avoid? First, many British, US, and French leaders contended that the Weimar constitution had failed to establish an effective system of institutional checks and balances between the major branches of government; in theory, branch rivalry would have prevented any single party from attaining too much power. The Weimar constitution gave Germany's president and chancellor, who were not directly accountable to parliament, broadly defined emergency powers, which enabled them to rule by decree whenever they deemed that the political order was in danger. During the early 1930s President Paul von Hindenburg and his chancellors used the emergency-power provisions to impose unpopular policies, such as reductions in wages and social services. Adolf Hitler, von Hindenburg's last chancellor, pressured the parliament into expanding the constitution's already generous emergency-power provisions, and then used those powers to outlaw rival parties, to purge the civil service of democratic sympathizers, and to restructure the labour movement. By the time of von Hindenburg's death in 1934, the executive branch was virtually unfettered.

In the opinion of many policy makers for the occupying nations, Hitler's ability to bully parliament into expanding the constitution's emergency-power provisions was partly a result of a second widely perceived problem with the Weimar constitution: an unqualified proportional-representation system of voting. Some countries, such as the United States and Great Britain, have a winner-take-all form of election: only the leading vote getter in an electoral district sits in the legislative body; regardless of number of votes received, no other candidate is seated. In theory, proportional representation allows parties that win lesser percentages of the vote to have a legislative presence because seats are allocated according to the proportion that each party receives. For example, a party winning 3 per cent of the ballots cast in a federal election is entitled to 3 per cent of the seats in the federal legislature. Defenders of the system contend that a benefit is that all voices in the society are heard; no mobilized minority is ignored. But in the 1940s, many politicians in the Western occupying countries believed that unqualified proportional representation entailed dangers that were revealed by the Nazis' seizure of power (Rogers 1995: 119–38).

Allegedly, in a proportional system of representation, numerous small parties, each with inflexible attitudes and a core of intensely loyal constituents, can obstruct discussion, compromise, and coalition building. In the case of the Weimar republic during the 1920s and early 1930s, at times 12 to 24 parties were present in the *Reichstag* (Germany's parliament), and no party controlled an absolute majority of the seats. Many Western politicians and diplomats believed that this situation was inimical to effective governance, especially when combined with Germany's hyper-inflation and its capitalists' and petit bourgeoisie's intense fears of Marxist parties. Parties in the Reichstag endlessly blocked and undercut one another's legislative initiatives. They gave higher priority to unflinching loyalty to their programmes and to enhancing their prospective electoral fortunes through dramatic acts of principled noncooperation than to governing the country responsibly in a time of enormous economic difficulty. Because of the surfeit of intransigent parties, prime ministers constantly underwent and lost votes of confidence. Cabinet after cabinet quickly fell while urgent issues – such as widespread unemployment and an inflation rate that topped 26 billion per cent in 1924 (Dalton 1993: 18) – went unaddressed.

Frustrated with the lack of leadership in the parliament, voters increasingly cast their ballots for parties that openly opposed the political status quo. By the early 1930s, parties that advocated the dismantling of parliament held a majority of the seats within that institution. The Nazis, in particular, attracted voters by (1) denouncing the irresponsibility of other democratically elected leaders, and (2) blaming international conspiracies and domestic minorities, such as Gypsies, homo-sexuals, and Jews, for the country's current social ills. In the opinions of key policy makers for the Western occupying nations, proportional representation thus propelled a dangerous antidemocratic party to power. (It should be noted that many scholars today see a very weak and indirect causal relationship between the Weimar Repub-lic's system of proportional representation and the Nazis' political success. For different views on this causal hypothesis, see Bracher (1969), Hermens (1951, 1984), Lakeman (1984), Powell (1982: 74–174), and Smith (1984: 78–81, 94–7).)

In many occupiers' opinions, Hitler's increasingly powerful party also benefited from a third constitutional weakness: a highly politicized judiciary. Throughout the late nineteenth century and early twentieth, conservative political parties and business elites had used court decisions to undermine laws passed by Germany's liberal parliaments and had protected the privileges of old wealth. Whenever the government suspended civil liberties and punished liberal and socialist opponents, members of the judiciary, never sympathetic to the ideologies such people acted upon, unhesitatingly ignored constitutional limits upon the state's authority by reading the Weimar constitution in excessively narrow ways. During Hitler's chancellor-ship, judges once again routinely disregarded legal precedent and constitutional provisions that ran counter to Hitler's personal decrees and allowed the government to ban non-Nazi parties and to seize Jewish property.

The leaders of the British, US, and French governments bore these constitutional weaknesses in mind when 'requesting' (read: insisting) that a group of representat-ives from each occupied West German regional state (or *Land*) write a new con-stitution for the non-Soviet zones of occupation. Many German political leaders were ambivalent about this charge. Most hoped that one day soon the two Germanys would be reunited, and feared that a constitution would institutionalize political differences between them and make future unification much more problematic. The representatives, as a compromise, offered to draft not a constitution per se but a 'Basic Law' that would function as a *provisional* constitutional framework until the zones became one nation. The occupying countries tolerated what they saw as primarily a modification involving mere semantics.

The Parliamentary Council (the assembly that was to design the Basic Law) attempted to placate the occupiers by designing a federal political order that apportioned government authority among ten states (or *Länder*) and the semiautonomous city-state of Berlin. According to the Basic Law, the Land cabinets and parliaments popularly elected by the citizens of each state were to be given primary legislative authority in education, transportation, social services, and environmental protection. The civil service of each Land government, besides administering its own laws, was to implement the vast majority of domestic laws made by the federal government. This administrative arrangement in effect gave the Land governments considerable discretionary power. Land governments also were to appoint representatives to a federal council (the *Bundesrat*) that had the right to review and veto all proposed federal legislation affecting the 'material interest' of the Länder. Thus political events and struggles within each Land would have direct implication for federal laws.

Today, most observers agree that when compared to almost all other European and North American nation-states, the degree of legislative and administrative decentralization within West Germany was extraordinary (Allen 1992: 251–2; Katzenstein 1987: 15–17, 19–22), as was the power of the Länder to affect federal legislation. During the late 1940s, some members of the Parliamentary Council expressed discomfort at the creation of such an extremely decentralized and potentially anarchic political order. The occupying powers, however, believed that the dispersion of authority among several smaller (and sometimes competing) Land governments would help protect civil liberties from a strong central state and also help secure international safety by reducing the likelihood that a single powerful party could command political loyalty throughout Germany and then possibly pursue an aggressive foreign policy.

The Parliamentary Council also established new election procedures at the municipal, state, and federal levels. Among them was the so-called 5 per cent rule: to gain representation in a legislative body, a party must receive at least 5 per cent of the ballots cast. It was a requirement designed partly to impede the access into government of small hate-oriented parties that represented the views of handfuls of voters. The Nazis, after all, had been in the Weimar parliament and thereby wreaked havoc even though they won only 2.6 per cent and 3 per cent of the vote in the December 1924 and 1928 elections respectively (Conradt 1986: 8; Dalton 1993: 21). The 5 per cent rule was also intended to conduce broad platforms that would attract many voters and offend few.

Finally, the writers of the Basic Law, following the occupiers' directives, put in place a constitutional court with unusually broad authority to decide explicitly political questions, such as the limits of the federal government's authority vis-à-vis the Länder and citizens' rights. Like the Supreme Court of the United States, the Federal Constitutional Court had authority to declare null and void laws that violated the provisions of the Basic Law. Besides powers of judicial review, it had authority to identify and outlaw political parties whose words and actions demonstrated antidemocratic intentions.

Economic expansion and stagnation

Britain, the United States, and France also influenced the shape and pace of West Germany's economic recovery. At first, recovery seemed a distant dream. Battles and enormous air strikes toward the end of the Second World War had devastated the transportation system and destroyed much of the housing stock. Hundreds of thousands of Germans were going hungry, lacked shelter, and could not find work. They were clearly suffering, yet political leaders of Britain, the United States, and France were ambivalent about helping to rebuild the economy because of the Germans' purported propensity for war. Indeed, initially many of the occupiers' officials hoped to cripple Germany's industrial base permanently. During the mid-1940s, US Secretary of the Treasury Henry Morgenthau, for example, advocated the transformation of Germany into an agricultural society (Black et al. 1992: 60–1).

At first, the reconstruction of heavy industry was prohibited, and large concentrations of private capital were discouraged. In addition, all occupying nations – France and the Soviet Union in particular – dismantled industrial plants and capital equipment and then seized heavy machinery as reparations.

The United States and Britain, however, soon realized that the consequences of the deindustrialization were continuing high unemployment and serious shortages of food, energy, and durable goods. The enforced impoverishment of West Germans was, in turn, producing heavy burdens for British and US taxpayers, whose money was being spent on supporting desperately hungry and unemployed people in the occupied zones. British and US policy makers concluded that industrial development had to be quickly encouraged and that the process would probably require the formation of large businesses that could pool capital and plan and invest on an appropriate scale.

French leaders, contrariwise, insisted that German economic redevelopment must be slow, must be initiated by smaller firms, and must be carefully monitored. Britain and the United States avoided publicly criticizing the French stance because the French Communist Party was posing a serious electoral threat, yet they increasingly held that rapid reindustrialization of Germany was necessary both to prevent further expansion of the Soviet Union in central Europe and to mitigate the domestic fiscal burden imposed by a paternalistic occupation policy.

During the late 1940s conflicts of interest and opinion among the three Western allies came to a head. Britain, having wearied of helping the United States do global battle against communism, announced that it could not continue to provide current levels of aid to West Germany, Greece, Turkey, and other nations; West Germany would have to carry its own economic weight; this meant, according to British policy makers, the formation there of large organizations that could coordinate investment and plan for infrastructure development. The United States generally agreed with the British position, but the Anglo-American advocacy of economic redevelopment immediately provoked public outcries and demonstrations in France.

The 1947 Marshall Plan provided a tentative resolution to the mismatch in perceived national interests. The United States would offer interested European governments large grants to be spent on American capital goods, raw materials, and foodstuffs. The arrangement enabled American producers to sell abroad and all European nations – Germany *and* its former enemies – to import necessities.

Big business quickly made its appearance in West Germany, specializing in industrial and manufactured goods for North America and western Europe. The early 1950s Korean War added to international demand for German industrial goods. Shortly afterward, seven western European countries, including West Germany, France, the Netherlands, and Italy, agreed to establish a common market, which greatly reduced tariffs and legal barriers to the movement of labour and capital among the signatories. The arrangement was beneficial for West Germany because of that country's lack of raw materials, its comparative disadvantage in food production, and the new sales opportunities for industrial goods. By the early 1960s West Germany was Europe's predominant economic power in terms of industrial production and the world's leading exporter of manufactured goods. The West German gross national product grew 51 per cent between 1961 and 1970, and unemployment averaged a mere 1 per cent (Katzenstein 1987: 104–5). During the 1950s and 1960s, average household income grew nearly sevenfold (Dalton 1993: 82). Luxury items of the early 1950s, such as automobiles, became widely affordable. Political leaders pointed with pride to an 'economic miracle'.

The speed and relative longevity of the economic boom had several social consequences. Because jobs multiplied primarily in cities, residential patterns shifted dramatically: during the 1950s (the beginning of the boom years), approximately a third of the population lived in the countryside; by 1990, only a fifteenth (Dalton 1993: 83). As telling, the proportion of the workforce in agriculture dropped from 25 per cent in 1950 to 5 per cent in 1981 (Conradt 1986: 22).

The urbanization of West Germany coincided with and contributed to the expansion of mass media. By the early 1960s, about two-thirds of adults watched evening televised news, and three-fifths read daily newspapers (Conradt 1986: 40). Most radio and television broadcasts were (and are) regulated and managed by nonprofit public corporations, but the print media were (and are) privately owned and heavily concentrated in the hands of a few companies and families. Between the mid-1950s and the mid-1980s, mergers and consolidations in the newspaper industry reduced the number of independent editorial staffs from 225 to fewer than 120 (Dalton 1993: 170). Perhaps the most controversial of the owned publishing houses was (and is) the so-called Springer chain, headed by the highly conservative magnate, Axel Springer. Approximately 60 per cent of the regular newspaper-reading population turned to magazines and newspapers (including West Germany's one major nationwide tabloid, the *Bild-Zeitung*) produced by the Springer chain (Conradt 1986: 40). Springer, himself, although initially apolitical, during the late 1950s and early 1960s became highly critical of leftist politics, decried restrictions on free trade and possible reunification with East Germany, and through editorial involvement with his numerous publications, regularly portrayed protesters extremely negatively and as dupes of international communism (Conradt 1986: 41; Dalton 1993: 170, 178).

Despite the migration to cities, urban jobs soon exceeded available workers. Business leaders during the early 1960s began to argue that more workers (especially low-wage) were needed if the economy were not to sputter and contract. A constant labour shortage was contributing to excessively high wage levels that both reduced profit margins and fuelled inflation. Such tendencies, business people argued, would sooner or later dissuade firms from investing further in either physical capital or product development. Such an eventuality could jeopardize the country's international competitiveness and, in turn, lead to painful economic contractions, lay-offs, and closings.

The West German government tried to allay the fears of the business community by opening the borders to foreign labourers, especially from Turkey and southern Europe. The number of immigrant workers increased from 100,000 in 1957 to 2.5 million in 1973. In larger cities, such as Hamburg and Frankfurt, foreigners by the late 1970s made up as much as 20 per cent of all workers (and perhaps as much as 40 per cent of all manual workers) (Conradt 1986: 69; Katzenstein 1987: 214).

Most West German officials and citizens tended to view the immigrants as 'guest workers' who would lead quiet, frugal lifestyles, accumulate money, and then return with their nest eggs to their native countries. They would perform the menial, arduous, low-paying jobs that the better-paid and better-educated West Germans could afford to avoid. Meanwhile, smaller payrolls would entail less cost, increased profits, and expanded production and product lines. Everyone would benefit: West Germany would retain its competitive position in the world economy; skilled and white-collar workers would still bring home substantial paycheques; and the *gastarbeiters* would enjoy better life prospects than awaited them elsewhere.

Many foreign workers did not live out the unwritten 'guest worker' scenario. A goodly number stayed on for more than a decade, taking advantage of the amenities of West German cities and social services, raising families, and becoming a permanent feature of the German social landscape. In 1981, 4.7 million foreigners were residing in West Germany, and more than a third of the children born in some cities were to families of foreign workers (Conradt 1986: 70; Katzenstein 1987: 216–18, 230).

During the 1960s, big business also voiced concern about possible forthcoming shortages of skilled and white-collar workers in the increasingly automated economy. Many business leaders believed that unless the workforce became more technically knowledgeable, prosperity would come to an end.

The government moved to overcome the projected labour shortfall by dramatically expanding the postsecondary educational system, by increasing subsidies for students, and by opening universities to applicants from a broader range of social backgrounds. The number of universities increased from 112 in 1950 to 735 in 1980 (Katzenstein 1987: 319), and the number of students in Germany's postsecondary schools increased 500 per cent between 1950 and 1975 (Dalton 1993: 83). Partly because of the new higher-education policies and partly because of the increased automation of production processes, West Germany had an unusually well-educated workforce by the close of the 1970s, when almost half of all wage earners held white-collar jobs (Conradt 1986: 24). A new working class had been born – one that did no factory manual labour and that expected a materially comfortable lifestyle in exchange for years of study.

During the 1960s West Germany's average annual growth rate slowed slightly, to 5 per cent, and the rate of inflation began to creep upward. Citing inflationary pressures, businesses signed conservative three-year wage contracts that ultimately cut the purchasing power of workers (Allen 1992: 266). Wildcat and general strikes, including strikes by immigrant workers, occurred in significant numbers for the first time since the postwar occupation. Still, the economy remained basically healthy: in a typical year only 223,000 workers could not find jobs, and the decade's average unemployment rate for the 1960s was less than 1 per cent (Conradt 1986: 26).

Then came the 1970s, and the economic order, which the government had once proudly hailed 'a miracle', fell to earth. The international oil crisis of 1973 and 1974 caused oil prices to quadruple, making exports much costlier. At the same time, new manufacturing competitors appeared in East Asia that challenged the recently hegemonic position of West German exports in the world economy. West Germany's annual GNP growth rate dropped from 5 per cent in 1973 to 0 per cent in 1974, and to −2 per cent in 1975 (Pulzer 1995: 189). It rose briefly in the late 1970s, but in the first three years of the 1980s annual average growth was just 0.8 per cent (Conradt 1986: 26). Heavy industry was especially hard hit: employment in the Saar steel industry fell from 22,000 in 1978 to 12,500 in 1985 (Dyson 1989: 162). Between 1970 and 1976, West Germany suffered a net loss of 1.3 million jobs (Kolinsky 1984: 173). Official unemployment for the nation rose from under 1 per cent in 1970 to almost 5 per cent in 1975 to more than 9 per cent in the early 1980s (Pulzer 1995: 189; E. O. Smith 1989: 53–5, 73). By 1983, 2.5 million people (approximately 10 per cent of the official workforce) were 'pounding the pavement' (Conradt 1986: 27).

Remilitarization

In 1979, NATO leaders agreed to station US Cruise and Pershing II missiles on West German soil in response to the earlier placement of 300 SS-20 missiles in the Soviet Union. The West German government concurred with NATO's policy, prompting numerous demonstrations that would evolve into a set of broader antinuclear and antiestablishment campaigns.

Plans for the placement of foreign weapons on West German soil were hardly novel, however. Since the closing days of occupation, the United States, hoping to create a powerful Cold War ally, had worked to remilitarize West Germany.

Not surprisingly, the semisecret US efforts to rearm a former enemy during the late 1940s and early 1950s fuelled controversy both inside and outside West Germany. French and British leaders in particular feared dire consequences in light of their experience with German aggression during two world wars. One French parliamentarian strongly opposed to what was happening declared, 'I don't know if they [German armed forces] would frighten the Russians, but, by God, they'd frighten me' (Dalton 1993: 392).

Most West Germans also opposed remilitarization, the presence of foreign troops, and the stores of unknown quantities of weaponry. Peace demonstrations proliferated in the early 1950s (to be described in more detail in Chapter 3), and groups called for referenda as a method of challenging the ongoing, somewhat secretive rearming. The government chastised the pacifist, religious, and communist groups that advocated submitting the question to referenda. Their proposals were, in effect, 'attacking the constitutional order', 'threatening peace', and 'working in the service of communism' (Hülsberg 1988: 33). The Federal Constitutional Court ruled that the proposed referenda were unconstitutional, which temporarily set back the initiators.

Despite numerous rallies and marches in West Germany and other countries, the US government indefatigably pursued the rearmament of Germany during the late 1940s and 1950s, the Korean War redoubling its resolve. Many US foreign-policy experts saw the invasion of South Korea as a tactic of the international communist movement: if US troops were redeployed in East Asia, a successful Soviet invasion of western Europe could be accomplished. The reasoning led them to recommend the prompt rearming of West Germany, despite European fears of a dangerous outcome.

The hopes of the United States provided a window of opportunity to West German leaders who were against the occupation. Using military bases and allies in central Europe as bargaining chips, they succeeded in negotiating, in addition to economic support, an end to the state of war with Great Britain, the United States, and France. By 1955 the military occupation was terminated, and West Germany's sovereignty was recognized.

The Western powers, however, still had the right to station troops and weapons within the country. West Germany was a nominally sovereign state with constraints on its foreign policy. The three former occupiers further specified that West Germany could introduce a military draft and create a sizeable standing army, conditional upon the understanding that in time of war, all West German forces would be under the supreme commander of the North Atlantic Treaty Organization (NATO). For better or worse, Germany's fate thenceforth would be closely tied to that of NATO (and the United States in particular) and would reflect US and NATO allies' positions. Locating nuclear missiles controlled by NATO in West Germany was simply a continuation of the country's postwar semisovereign status in international affairs. As a result, the proposed stationing of the Cruise and Pershing II missiles generated opposition not only among pacifists and other leftists who did not feel threatened by the Soviet bloc, but also among nationalists who were offended by the obvious lack of control that their country had over its military policies.

Changing structure of production

We have talked about the general expansion and contraction of the West German economy, about some of the international conditions that directly and indirectly impinged on West German economic and political history, and about West Germany's distinctive labour-market conditions – in particular, an immigrant-labour sector and a white-collar sector trained in the new universities. We have said little so far about the organization of production in West Germany, which has hardly been a 'classic' laissez-faire system. On the contrary, local, state, and federal levels of government have affected business through extensive regulation and in some cases direct investment.[2]

State involvement in the development of private business has had a long history, and partly reflects the efforts of political leaders to catch up to earlier-industrializing nations, such as Britain.

The modern German nation-state, in terms of market development, industrialization, and state building, appeared late in world history. Before the mid-nineteenth century, there had been no unified German political and economic order but a collection of largely nonindustrialized German-speaking kingdoms, principalities, duchies, and city-states, each with its own laws, currency, and customs regulations. Prussia successfully established a German federation with most of the smaller states in 1871, and leaders of the new state quickly sought to industrialize the expanded country by directly aiding large firms and banking houses and by encouraging the formation of bank–business cartels. This process of state-led and big business-led industrialization differed considerably from that of earlier industrialized countries, such as the United States and Britain, where small and medium-sized firms predominated and where banks and the state played a marginal role in coordinating production and codesigning industrial policy.

The new industries of the late nineteenth century recruited peasant workers. Enduring the unaccustomed hardships of factory life and lacking political rights, many workers formed and joined militant trade unions and radical political parties, such as the Social Democratic Party (the SPD), which denounced German capitalism and advocated its wholesale overthrow. The German government tried to undermine the appeal of working-class radicals by providing extensive social-welfare services, but the labour movement persisted in denouncing the absence of democracy both in government and workplace.

Shortly after the First World War, groups of militant workers sought to replicate the Bolshevik Revolution on German soil. Workers' and soldiers' soviets appeared in major cities, and a soviet socialist republic briefly existed in Bavaria. Many owners of large businesses thought that unless concessions were made, a successful communist revolution was imminent and, hence, agreed to a democratic constitution for Germany that incorporated provisions for universal suffrage and popular referenda. They also acceded to the establishment of autonomous shopfloor 'works councils', through which workers could discuss working conditions and communicate with owners.

To prevent disruptions in production, the government mandated a system of worker consultation. In all medium-sized and large firms, councils comprising representatives of management and labour were to decide day-to-day issues of production and wages. Owners won, in exchange for this loss of unilateral control, social peace: strikes were outlawed.

During the Third Reich (1933–45), the Nazis systematically repressed independent trade unions, banned the works councils, and outlawed the Socialist and Communist Parties. Ironically, despite the Nazis' efforts to destroy proletarian organizations, the Social Democratic Party, Communist Party, and numerous union organizations emerged from the Second World War with their prestige relatively intact, if not enhanced, because of their consistent opposition to the Nazis. In contrast, big business was stigmatized for a time because of its frequent collaboration with the Nazis. Many idealistic young adults joined the leftist parties, and many citizens supported left candidates in early postwar elections.

Temporarily enjoying a position of moral supremacy, the German labour movement was able in the latter 1940s to persuade the newly established federal and Land governments to legislate worker codetermination. Yielding to popular pressure, the federal government and several of the Länder passed laws requiring large and medium-sized firms to have supervisory boards of representatives of management and elected representatives of workers. The boards were authorized to decide policies concerning investment and the application of technology. In addition, works councils were established in all businesses with five or more full-time employees. Also, the Land governments legislated programmes of extensive social services and support, including job retraining, medical care, and housing subsidies.

Big business, nevertheless, retained a privileged place in the minds of most government policy makers. After all, Germany's stunningly rapid industrialization in the late nineteenth century had been accomplished largely through the coordinated efforts of government, big business, cartels, and trusts. Many political leaders believed that economic history proved that the big-business community had the skills and wisdom to redevelop the economy. So, almost immediately, government officials (with US blessing) conveniently ignored or watered down the laws of codetermination. Labour courts failed to enforce many stipulations of the proworker labour laws. In 1952 the federal government passed the Works Constitution Act, which excluded unions from shopfloor councils and reduced the number of labour representatives on companies' supervisory boards. Four years later, the Federal Constitutional Court outlawed the Communist Party on the grounds that it threatened West German democracy.

Besides attempting to pre-empt anticipated labour shortages, the postwar West German government tried to facilitate continuous economic growth by encouraging cooperation and facilitating mergers within big business. Ironically, during and immediately following the occupation years, many Länder and the federal parliament had passed anticartel laws to please US policy makers, who believed that large companies that had cooperated with the Nazis should not be nationalized but divided. The anticartel laws, however, soon were conveniently overlooked. Mergers and collusion became widespread, and banks coordinated corporations' policies with the federal and Land governments' blessings. The ceaseless competition and anarchy that many critics associate with capitalism was replaced by a much more coordinated and organized form of private production.

As mentioned above, the local, regional, and federal governments have extensive holdings in otherwise 'private' companies. Together, they control more than 25 per cent of the shares in more than 500 otherwise 'private' companies, including minority holdings in steel, utilities, and banking (Dalton 1993: 361; Katzenstein 1987: 103). The federal government, in addition, built the transportation infrastructure and owns and operates the freight and passenger railways and almost all of the television and radio stations. Meanwhile, local governments own and operate local utilities and public-transportation firms.

Officials of the federal and Land governments have since the 1950s met regularly with leaders of large business and labour associations to discuss aspects of possible new legislation regarding taxes, land use, budget expenditures, factory safety, and consumer protection. Alongside the official consultations, there are frequent meetings held in private quarters with no minutes distributed to the general public. Business and union leaders, of course, come well prepared to the official and private discussions, relying on extensive research departments that collect and analyse relevant data.

Neither government elites nor business and union leaders believe that the extensive consultative process is inappropriate in a democracy. After all, they argue, such cooperation contributes to an overall healthy economic climate, and a healthy business climate benefits not only a few plutocrats and unionized workers but the entire society. Some West Germans are critical of the consultative process, however. They argue that the interests of smaller and less organized groups – such as consumers, the chronically unemployed, guest workers, and retirees – are not fully considered in economic decisions made behind closed doors.

The early founders of West Germany's economy often described it as a 'social market economy'. What they meant was, first, that most decisions about investment, hiring, firing, prices, and wages were for the most part in the hands of private individuals and corporations. This, in fact, has generally been the postwar practice. Although the government has passed protective laws regarding workers' treatment – for example, defining excessive noise levels – the vast majority of day-to-day decisions about employment conditions are left to contractual agreements between firm owners and employees.

In addition, the phrase 'social market economy' implied that West Germans were not to be wholly vulnerable if, by any chance, changing market conditions did not lead to job opportunities or a dignified standard of living. The government would provide a web of social services – such as a mandatory social security programme, subsidized housing, universal health insurance, unemployment insurance, educational grants, and job retraining – to protect citizens from the sometimes unfortunate vicissitudes of a free-market and free-trade economy. Federal and Land social services, although not exceptional by standards of northern Europe's social-democratic regimes, have been considerably more ambitious than what is found in the United States. And the range of services increased dramatically between 1950 and 1970. Partly as a consequence of these expenditures, public-sector spending grew from less than 30 per cent of the gross national product in the early 1950s to more than 50 per cent in the early 1980s (Dalton 1993: 360). The increases prevailed over the objections of business groups that assailed the entailed costs as fuelling inflation and as generally deleterious to the economy.

Growing popular dissatisfaction

Between the mid-1950s and the mid-1980s, most owners of large businesses, top civil servants, and the leaders of West Germany's three major parties were firmly of the belief that boundless economic growth was possible and desirable, and that the modified market economy could automatically yield improved standards of living. The 'German Model' of prosperity, to borrow a phrase coined in the 1976 SPD election campaign, was rapidly becoming the envy of the world. Most West Germans probably shared the elites' opinion during the 1950s and 1960s, but popular scepticism about both the potential and desirability of the model increased after the mid-1970s, when annual growth rates grew erratic and unemployment climbed steadily.

To some extent, rising popular dissatisfaction with the economic status quo preceded the late 1970s because of ongoing and striking inequalities in the distribution of wealth. Public opinion surveys even before the recessions of the mid- and late 1970s revealed that a majority believed that the political order was 'on the side of the rich' (Conradt 1986: 29). This popular view partly reflected actual experience. Economic historian Eric Owen Smith (1983: 188) contends that capital ownership in the 1970s was 'highly concentrated' with 'only 20 per cent of the households' in West Germany owning more than 85 per cent of all productive property (business assets and shares). He also notes that 'income inequality was generally more marked in 1950 than in 1928 or 1913' (1983: 29). Meanwhile, leaders of organized labour had convinced workers to trim wage demands during the mid-1960s so that the inflationary pressures anticipated by business and government would not damage the economy. The pressures never materialized, however, and employers enjoyed greater profits. Outraged, hundreds of thousands of industrial workers carried out wildcat strikes each year between 1969 and 1972 in an effort to right the imbalance (Hancock 1989: 116–17; Semmler 1982: 47).

After the early 1970s, questions of internal inequality were complicated by two new trends. First, there was growing disparity between the wealth of foreign 'guest workers' and that of German citizens. A new underclass seemed to be emerging. For example, foreign workers suffered significantly higher unemployment rates in the late 1970s than did other German workers, and the gap seemed to be growing. By 1983, the official unemployment rate for foreign workers was 14.9 per cent, compared to 9.5 per cent for the total workforce (migrant and native) (Katzenstein 1987: 229–32). In addition, regional disparities became increasingly obvious between the booming and technological oriented economies of the southern Länder, and the declining, rust-belt economies of the North (Dyson 1989: 161–3; Markovits and Allen 1989: 302).

In January 1970 unions for the first time brought their own economic projection data to meetings with business and government leaders. Government officials, in turn, began to invite in their own experts, and consultations between government, business, and labour became less frequent and cordial. During the middle and late 1970s, friction between labour and business increased as each group articulated its views on how to respond to the oil crisis and foreign competition. Government officials and business people urged workers to reduce labour costs; workers perceived business as not making equal sacrifices and that mismanagement, failure to consult workers about production issues, and excessive executive perks were the primary causes of inefficiency.

By the late 1970s, large-scale labour strikes had become more common than at any time in West Germany's postwar history (although its strike incidence still remained low compared to other western European countries). Industrial workers demanded both significant wage increases to keep up with inflation and shorter workweeks as a way to combat spiralling unemployment. The period of overt industrial strife symbolically culminated in a two-month strike by West German printers and metalworkers, the largest strike in the history of the Federal Republic.[3]

To revive the economy, successive federal and Land governments since the late 1970s have tried to freeze the size of the public sector, and to cut back tax levels and thus enable businesses to control a larger proportion of their revenues and consumers to have more discretionary funds. The reforms were largely rhetorical: few of the proposed reductions in public services occurred. Still, the new budget controls meant that teachers, social workers, and other public-sector employees could no longer expect significant improvement in income, career, or lifestyle. In addition, hundreds of thousands of postsecondary students preparing for white-collar careers saw their hopes dashed as doors closed. The share of university graduates finding public-sector jobs tumbled from 60 per cent in the early 1970s to 25 per cent by the end of the decade, and unemployment rates among university graduates began to converge with the high unemployment rates among workers in general (Katzenstein 1987: 321–2). Now aspiring scientists, engineers, clerical workers, and public-sector employees who had thought they could find jobs with the state or big business and thus be protected from the turbulence of free-market winds, knew better. To quote Wilhelm Bürklin (1987: 113–14), 'the expectations of the young educated classes increasingly collided with conditions in the labour market'.

White- and blue-collar disillusionment with the direction of the economy was reinforced by the visible damage done to the environment by rapid and extensive industrialization. The dense concentrations of industry on waterways meant unsightly waste, death of wildlife, and unusable water. Factory smoke led to deforestation. As cars multiplied, so did urban smog. Growing use of electricity posed a difficult choice: the construction of controversial nuclear energy plants in a very densely populated country *or* the continued use of dirty coal-consuming plants.

Nuclear power became an especially ticklish problem for West German policy makers. The government launched an ambitious programme during the 1970s, in the hope of decreasing dependency on foreign oil producers, cutting energy costs, and reviving the now sluggish economy. According to government spokespersons, nuclear power would not only reduce dependency on Middle East powers but make the country's products cheaper to make *and* offer a cleaner alternative to coal-derived energy. In many West Germans' minds, however, the 1979 Three Mile Island accident in the United States corroborated the antinuclear activists' position that nuclear power was inescapably dangerous for all and highly profitable for a few energy companies.

In the meantime, the publication of best-selling books by highly reputable scientists, such as the Club of Rome's report, *Global 2000*, accelerated many citizens' naturally growing awareness of an environmental dark side to the high level of production (Markovits and Gorski 1993: 80, 132). Roughly 30 years of economic growth at a pace unprecedented in European economic history had very high and very visible costs that had been foolishly played down. Perhaps the damage to nature was beyond repair. Or perhaps it could be repaired only through drastically changed forms of production and levels of consumption.

Party convergence

While West Germany's economic and environmental difficulties unfolded, its party system atrophied. The economic programmes of the major parties, which during the occupation had been ideologically distinct, had been converging for several decades; by the 1970s none of the major parties was proposing a distinctive solution to the souring of the country's once widely lauded economic model (Dyson 1989; Frankland and Schoonmaker 1992: 25–9).[4]

The period of rapid economic growth (roughly 1950–70) had coincided with the development of what many call the 'two-and-a-half party system'.[5] In 1949, 15 parties received enough votes to be represented in the federal parliament – a highwater mark. All but three – the Christian Democrats (CDU/CSU), the Free Democratic Party (FDP), and the Social Democratic Party (SPD) – would disappear by the close of the 1950s.

After 1953 the Social Democratic Party and the Christian Democrats regularly controlled about 80 per cent of the seats in the federal parliament. However, apart from 1957 to 1961, neither was able to win a majority of the seats. For either the SPD or the CDU/CSU to secure a majority of the votes during the selection of the chancellor and for passage of key legislation, they had to form coalitions, once with each other but usually with the Free Democratic Party, which normally received between 8 and 12 per cent of the ballots cast in federal elections. In exchange for its support, the FDP received concessions, usually a combination of ministerial appointments and support for some of its own legislative agenda.

The Christian Democrats headed ruling coalitions from 1949 through 1957, and then ruled alone at the federal level for four years. The CDU/CSU coined the phrase 'social market economy', which, as we have seen, referred to an effort to synthesize (1) the Christian value of social solidarity and scepticism toward the unregulated market, and (2) the protection of individual initiative and competence from state regulation.

The CDU/CSU's primary coalition partner until 1957 was the FDP. Leaders of both favoured free-market and free-trade policies and close cooperation between Germany and the United States. The FDP, however, was generally hostile to statesponsored social services and more conscientious about protecting civil liberties from the state than was the other member of the coalition.

As we have noted, the economy grew spectacularly during the 1950s. Export industries, such as automobiles, chemicals, and electronic equipment, expanded rapidly. Led by the export sector, GNP skyrocketed, surpassing the growth rates of almost every other western industrialized country. In 1955, for example, the annual growth rate was an almost unbelievable 15 per cent.

The CDU/CSU reaped the electoral rewards of a booming economy – especially in the 1957 elections, when it garnered 50.3 per cent of the vote. This was the first time (and only time) in West German history that a party received an absolute majority of the ballots cast in a parliamentary election. From there it was a downhill slide because of ageing leadership, the growing popularity in the 1960s of a small right-wing nationalist party (the National Democratic Party, the NPD), a recession in the mid-1960s, and the government's heavy-handed treatment of journalists critical of it. The CDU/CSU's decision in the late 1960s to raise taxes to cover a growing public debt prompted the FDP to resign from the coalition government. Then, to some observers' surprise, the CDU/CSU formed a new coalition government, but with the SPD, the second-largest party in the federal parliament and hitherto the CDU/CSU's primary electoral rival.

Having been excluded from the federal government during the late 1940s, 1950s, and early 1960s, the SPD had undergone profound ideological changes since the days of occupation. Founded in the 1860s, it had originally adopted a working-class, socialist ideology. Its most famous leaders and chief theoreticians argued that it was possible for a working-class party to win a majority of seats in parliament and then to use the democratic process gradually to pass legislation that would transform Germany into a socialist order. Many observers during the late 1940s expected the SPD to become the ruling party of West Germany after occupation, partly because of the acute, generalized material deprivation immediately after the war and partly because of the SPD's moral prestige for steadfastly resisting the Nazis. The immediate success of Germany's export-oriented industrialization surprised the leaders of the SPD, who were then further discouraged by the party's repeated failure to escape the '30 per cent ghetto' in the 1953 and 1957 federal elections. Unable to garner more than a third of the ballots cast, SPD leaders decided in 1959 to imitate some of the CDU's more popular economic positions and to de-emphasize the party's traditional Marxist rhetoric (including past proposals for extensive nationalizations of industry and systematic state planning of the economy). They did an ideological about-face: endorsed free trade, pledged to preserve West Germany's modified market economy, and declared support for greater economic and military cooperation with the West. Stated differently, the party moved theoretically from Marx to Keynes: it abandoned its traditional stance as an electoral party primarily for the urban working class to seek positions that would attract middle-class votes. The SPD, of course, did not completely adopt the positions of its opponents. It continued to distance itself from the CDU/CSU primarily in the areas of secular education (where the SPD proposed extensive expansion of opportunities, especially in higher education), foreign policy (where the SPD proposed greater international economic cooperation between rich and poor countries), and economic policy (where the SPD promised to help small and middle-sized firms and to check the allegedly abusive actions of big business). The SPD, nonetheless, was attempting to win the hearts and minds of many social groups – from small business owners to pensioners to housewives to students – instead of confining itself to the interests of industrial workers alone.

The three years of the CDU/CSU–SPD coalition government greatly benefited the Social Democrats; many voters began to see them as reliable and effective.

Many voters, for example, credited SPD economic ministers for leading West Germany out of the short but sobering recession of 1966–67. Many also liked the SPD's strident support of a nuclear nonproliferation treaty and its efforts to improve East–West relations. In the 1969 federal elections, the SPD finally broke out of its '30 per cent ghetto'; it received 43 per cent of the vote and formed a coalition government with the FDP as the junior partner. The series of such coalitions lasted until 1982.

During the 1970s, the CDU/CSU criticized the SPD–FDP governments for being soft on terrorists and wildcat strikers, for being unable to pull the country out of the economic crisis caused in part by rising international oil prices, and for being naively trusting toward the Soviet bloc. The governments were also criticized from the left (in particular, by a dissident group of socialist democrats who belonged to the SPD's youth organization, the Working Group of Young Socialists, JUSO) for supporting US policies in Vietnam, for not supporting union demands for increases in real wages, and for cutting social welfare programmes while increasing defence expenditures.

As the economic crisis deepened in the late 1970s and early 1980s, the SPD and FDP failed to discover solutions to the sluggish economy and rising unemployment. The coalition governments, leaning on past successes, incrementally changed public policies to contain social expenditures, to seek greater economic aid from the United States in exchange for West German cooperation with US foreign policy aims, to promote nuclear power, and to encourage the development of industrial exports through selected tax incentives and grants. In addition, the SPD–FDP governments tried, with the support of organized business, to develop infrastructure, such as new airport facilities and motorways, partly to reduce transportation costs for private businesses.

The CDU/CSU, no longer a ruling party, made essentially the same policy recommendations, although it favoured more stringent limits on wage increases. In the opinion of many dissatisfied voters – especially unemployed young adults – the two largest parties offered no real choice. Political scientists Gene Frankland and Donald Schoonmaker (1992: 26) report that socially discontented Germans saw the two parties – in terms of economic prescriptions and visions, environmental insensitivity, and pro-US foreign policy – as 'Tweedledum and Tweedledee'. As high unemployment continued, voters became increasingly discouraged and restless. In 1980 and 1983, disproportionate numbers of Germany's voting unemployed and young adults would cast ballots for a new electoral coalition, the Greens, which launched its first two campaigns for the federal parliament.

Conclusion

The Greens appeared in West Germany during a period of rapid social change. Some changes were of the type that the theorists of the 1940s, 1950s, and 1960s had emphasized: rapid urbanization, growing market fluctuations and employment insecurity, and the consolidation of big business. But the early social-movement theorists had not anticipated several other changes, such as the radical expansion of higher education, the influx of immigrant workers, growing reliance on nuclear power, and the pollution of rivers and forests. The changing social circumstances that immediately predated and accompanied the rise of the Greens thus only partly corroborate the argument about rapid modernization made by the first wave of social-movement theorists. Uprootedness, anomie, and loneliness existed; but there were other social issues as well, such as new dangers to health, exploitation of immigrants and other blue-collar workers, and rising unemployment among former university students.

In addition, the constitutional and political circumstances facing the Greens partly favoured the formation of a new party. West Germany's federal political system and its modified system of proportional representation – with a relatively low threshold of 5 per cent of the vote – offered multiple opportunities for a social movement to launch an electoral campaign and perhaps win a seat. The three major parties of the time – the CDU/CSU, FDP, and SPD – held strikingly similar visions of the processes and desirability of economic growth, the desirability of nuclear power, and the appropriateness of a pro-US foreign policy. A major left-wing party, advocating radical transformation of society, did not exist. The major parties, instead, celebrated the impressive increase in Germany's economic productivity between 1950 and 1970, and were deaf to growing cries of discontent. Although the 5 per cent requirement for elections was somewhat daunting (since the end of the 1950s, no challenger to the three major parties had managed to win at least 5 per cent of the vote in national elections) and although the private news media was largely hostile to leftist politics, perhaps space was available for a new party that would openly question the status quo.

Thus, the grievances generated by a broad range of recent social changes, combined with the political openings provided by postwar constitutional arrangements and by the major parties' similar economic and social policies, helped make the late 1970s and early 1980s opportune for a new social movement.

Notes

1. For histories of Germany's occupation, see Black et al. (1992: 54–95) and Rogers (1995). See Hancock (1989) and Pulzer (1995) for highly readable introductions to the political history of postwar West Germany.
2. More information about West Germany's economic history may be found in Allen (1992), Dyson (1989), Katzenstein (1987, 1989), Semmler (1982), and Smith (1983).
3. For more information on postwar labour policies and politics in West Germany, see Hancock (1989), Katzenstein (1987: 125–67), Markovits (1982), and Markovits and Allen (1989).
4. For discussions of West German parties' consensus on economic policy, incrementalism in West German economic policy making, and the SPD's struggles to develop a new economic programme, see Dyson (1989), Esser, Fach, and Dyson (1983), Hancock (1993), Katzenstein (1987, 1989), and Padgett (1987).
5. For a comprehensive discussion of West Germany's parties and party system, see Padgett and Burkett (1986).

Chapter 3

Political antecedents

Some social-movement theorists – especially those who adopt either a resource-mobilization approach, an indigenous-community approach, or an autonomous popular-culture approach – have interpreted social movements as the offspring of earlier forms of nonelite politics, which provide the prerequisite leaders, resources, and ideas for a new movement.

Several journalists and scholars who study German politics, such as Kim Holmes (1983), Werner Hülsberg (1988), Andrei Markovits and Philip Gorski (1993), and Elim Papadakis (1984), have seen such cross-pollination processes at work in the case of the West German Greens. As Markovits and Gorski (1993: 81) put it, the Green party-movement

> does not lend itself easily to metaphors of diffusion and intensification . . . did not 'spread' from a central location . . . or a central organization. . . . Rather it possessed the character of a 'crazy quilt', gradually sewn together out of a multitude of smaller leftovers and scraps of 'new materials'. . . .

According to such authors, before the Green party-movement officially formed in 1980, other groups of nonelites had tried to change German society and politics. Rearmament, the Social Democrats' acceptance of a social market economy, and the West German government's support of US foreign policies, including military involvement in Vietnam – all had provoked petition drives, street blockades and battles, or other forms of protest not sanctioned by political or economic elites. In addition, the deterioration of both the once-robust economy and the once-beautiful landscape led to numerous disruptive actions by angry labourers and citizens associations. Meanwhile, in the booming cities, squatter communities, student neighbourhoods, and feminist cultural networks generated an alternative set of social experiments and cultures that consciously rejected the values and institutions of the 'German model' of economic development.

These diverse challenges to the postwar status quo provided the Green party-movement with much of its programme, most of its ambivalence toward established parties, and a great deal of its organizational resources. In addition, many leaders of the Greens had participated in earlier collective actions, and brought to the new party their earlier perspectives on and prejudices about what West German politics could and should become.

This chapter takes seriously the biological metaphor of a social movement 'born' from earlier nonelite politics and looks at the diverse social and political groups whose ideals, agendas, methods, personnel, and organizational networks the Greens inherited.[1] It begins with West Germany's early postwar peace movement.

Evolution of politics for peace

As we noted in Chapter 2, during the 1950s groups of concerned citizens protested both the rearmament of West Germany and the stationing of NATO's weapons on West German soil. Some groups, in addition, made more radical demands and called for immediate reunification with East Germany. Protestant churches and, to a much lesser extent, Catholic clergy played key roles in funding and organizing protests against rearmament. Activists from and factions within the trade-union federation, the Social Democratic Party, and the Communist Party (which would be declared unconstitutional by the Federal Constitutional Court in 1956 and ordered to disband) also participated. By the close of the 1950s, rallies and demonstrations of upwards of 100,000 people took place. Some radical trade-union leaders even called for a general strike against nuclear weapons, although most ultimately shied away from the issue because of other priorities and concerns, such as protecting jobs from breakneck automation (Cooper 1988: 84–5; Hülsberg 1988: 35; Markovits and Gorski 1993: 43).

Leaders of the SPD more often than not opposed the proposed political strikes and the public marches against rearmament. They thought that such strikes and marches were politically counterproductive; the actions had the unintended effect of legitimizing conservative politicians' ongoing efforts to check civil liberties and democratic processes. Demonstrations also frightened middle-class voters, who in Springer's newspapers and magazines read skewed accounts that routinely confused the words *pacifist* and *communist*. Also, organized protests against rearmament and the stationing of nuclear weapons enabled conservatives to redirect popular concerns from economic inequalities and hardships to questions about lawlessness and social disorder.

In 1957 the Social Democrats, facing a forthcoming federal election, turned to the issue of rearmament. The SPD viewed rearmament as an unpopular policy, especially in light of recent revelations of the government's semisecret negotiations with the United States concerning the stationing of nuclear warheads. But because a contrary stance might bring about the perception that it was a half-hidden ally of the Soviet Union, the party qualified its criticisms of the government's pro-US economic policy and rearmament programme and avoided declaring support for street demonstrators. The effort was unavailing. During the campaign, the Christian Democrats and their allies in the print media effectively painted all critics of rearmament – both the lively demonstrators and the much more sedate SPD parliamentarians – as communist sympathizers.

After its trouncing at the polls, the SPD temporarily had nothing to lose by being visibly active in extraparliamentary protests against nuclear weapons and thereby regaining a following among the propeace constituency. The SPD for a time was a cosponsor of the Battle Against Nuclear Death campaign, which included large rallies and demonstrations, petition drives, and attempts to hold referendums on military-policy questions. Many of the younger party members were ardently against nuclear weapons and were delighted by the party's new interest in peace politics. They were accordingly shocked when the SPD suddenly withdrew from the campaign in 1959, and again when the leadership openly recognized the effectiveness and desirability of a market economy at the 1959 Bad Godesberg conference.

Shortly thereafter, a large number of participants in the Battle Against Nuclear Death campaign dissolved their ties with the SPD and joined other, nonparty antiwar organizations. A majority of the campaign's executive committee, for example, joined the Easter March of the Opponents of Atomic Weapons group, which was headed by a dynamic Protestant priest in Hamburg.

The Easter March organization planned sombre, peaceful marches each year that expressed disapproval of war and of nuclear weapons. Partly because of the influx of former SPD members, its goals and activities quickly metamorphosed. Planners of the marches began to articulate neo-Marxist critiques about how militarism is spawned by capitalist-organized economies. The organization also changed its name to the more secular-sounding Campaign for Disarmament and then to Campaign for Democracy and Disarmament. It also began to seek support from diverse tiny communist associations and clubs (especially Trotskyist and Maoist) and from the left wings of the SPD and the trade-union federation. In addition, the tone of the marches and rallies changed: no longer quiet and sombre but loud and festive, and hence increasingly popular among young adults. In 1960 only 1,000 people had participated in the Easter marches and rallies; in 1964, 130,000 (Burns and van der Will 1988: 91–5; Markovits and Gorski 1993: 47–9).

Most veterans of the short-lived Battle Against Nuclear Death campaign remained in the SPD, however, and trusted that they would be able to rekindle the party's radical and proletarian traditions. Many belonged to the Socialist German Students' League (or SDS), the SPD's youth organization. The SDS was established in 1954 to recruit and train new party members from campus milieus. During the late 1950s SDS leaders roundly criticized the older leaders of the SPD for retreating from the party's original principles and anticapitalist programme. The SPD's leaders, in turn, found many of the activities of the SDS politically embarrassing, such as its participation in a Congress against Nuclear Weapons conference, at which known members of Germany quasi-illegal communist splinter parties were present. Between 1959 and 1961, the SPD systematically severed its relationship with the SDS, and the SDS increasingly turned to leftist university professors for organizational support and ideological direction. Herbert Marcuse, in particular, intrigued SDSers with his controversial theory that workers in advanced industrialized societies had been rendered apolitical and nonrevolutionary by their high incomes and mass culture (Burns and van der Will 1988: 19–21; Markovits and Gorski 1993: 50–1). Other sources of inspiration were the guerrilla campaigns of Che Guevara and Franz

Fanon's anti-imperialist indictment *Wretched of the Earth* (Hülsberg 1988: 39). In 1964 the SDS began to organize protests against selected foreign guests of the German government, such as the brutal Congolese president, Moise Tshombe, and the shah of Iran.

According to a growing number of SDS theoreticians, such as Rudi Dutschke, only students and other 'decommodified' groups (economically marginalized groups, such as prisoners, the chronically unemployed, and Third World peasants) both acutely suffered from market economies and lacked the material comforts and cultural pacifiers, such as television, that made large-scale production, regimented working life, and daily toil at home bearable. The marginalized populations alone could see the need for a complete overthrow of capitalism and for starting a radically new social, economic, and cultural order. Other classes, such as industrial workers and white-collar professionals, were rendered conservative by their high levels of consumption, stable incomes, electronic gadgets, and television and other forms of mass entertainment. Radical socialists, therefore, should say farewell to the traditional industrial working class as a social force capable of transforming capitalism. Instead, they should seek alliances with and should advance the political education of the 'decommodified' groups, such as students, who were not yet fully integrated into an affluent capitalist labour market.

Extraparliamentary protests

During the late 1960s, the somewhat smallish SDS (only slightly more than 2,000 members at the height of its popularity) and the larger Campaign for Democracy and Disarmament joined forces and organized a series of protests that scholars have come to call the Extraparliamentary Movement, or APO. What immediately triggered the wave of protests was the government's tacit support of US military intervention in Vietnam and the government's increasing repression of protesters.

The Vietnam War dismayed West Germans, young and old. Many feared that they would be dragged into an escalating military conflict between the United States and the communist world, and that if a war broke out between the superpowers, West Germany would become a central battlefield.

By 1966 demonstrations against the Vietnam War had fanned out from academic communities in Berlin (a long-time hothouse for antiwar politics, partly because Berliners were exempt from conscription and therefore the city attracted a large number of pacifist youths) to university towns and large cities across West Germany. Traffic intersections were blocked; buildings were occupied; teach-ins were held. These activities coincided with a growing level of labour unrest, especially among immigrant workers, as West Germany struggled with its first serious postwar recession.

Unused to popular contestation, the Christian Democratic government increasingly pushed for passage of emergency-power laws to deal with the problem. The government had been proposing constitutional amendments that would give it emergency powers during times of international and domestic disorder since 1958. It wanted the right to suspend constitutionally guaranteed civil liberties, such as the right to assembly, whenever domestic tranquillity was seriously threatened. Leaders of the FDP and SPD, remembering the abuse of emergency powers during the Weimar Republic, had initially opposed the suggested changes. However, after 1966 the SPD became part of the CDU/CSU's governing coalition and its new circumstance affected its political calculations. Now sharing in governance, it did not want to look 'soft' on lawlessness and in consequence began to express support for the CDU/CSU's emergency-power legislation. Trade union leaders, peace organizations, and the SDS, attempting to dissuade the SPD, organized numerous mass demonstrations during the autumn and winter of 1967–68. The federal parliament approved the constitutional amendments in May 1968.

Many SDSers, even before the passage of the emergency-power laws, had been taken aback by the SPD's apparent indifference to violations of civil rights. In the summer of 1967, for example, police in West Berlin shot a young bystander during a demonstration against the shah of Iran. Upon his death, more than 100,000 youths protested against the police behaviour. The Christian Democratic chancellor refused to express regret or to acknowledge administrative wrongdoing. The SPD, perhaps fearful of the electoral consequences of siding with what the Springer newspapers were calling 'rampaging youths', avoided an official response.

Angered by the government's intransigence and the SPD's silence, some younger SDSers argued that a state-sanctioned murder had occurred and that illegal and even violent resistance was justified. The conservative press fanned middle-class fears of long-haired radicals by selectively reporting SDS's more bombastic rhetoric. In April 1968, Dutschke, the charismatic SDS leader, was shot three times on West Berlin's main boulevard. Thousands of youths and workers went into the streets and marched side by side, protesting the near-fatal assault. Some blocked the offices of the Springer conglomerate and engaged in vandalism. Soon demonstrators and police clashed. Bloody street battles spread throughout West Germany, and at least two demonstrators were killed.

Shortly after the Dutschke shooting, 60,000 people, including a large number of unionists, marched in Bonn against the impending passage of the emergency-power legislation. Trade unionists, anti-Vietnam War activists, students, and professors insisted that passage would endanger much-needed public expression of collective dissent. After the laws were passed with the SPD's parliamentary support, many activists concluded that the party had proven itself irredeemably corrupt and even speculated that earlier it had secretly agreed to support the laws in exchange for inclusion in the governing coalition.

Extraparliamentary politics in decline

The story of the extraparliamentary Left after the spring and summer of 1968 is one of rapid fragmentation and novel experimentation. Passage of the emergency-power laws convinced a sizeable number of the street protesters that West Germany's politics was hopelessly antidemocratic, militaristic, and socially unjust. Some retreated bitterly into personalistic and even mystical adventures. Hashish, vegetarianism, and self-cleansing seemed to be more productive ways to live one's life. In the words of one disillusioned sixty-eighter: 'What does Vietnam have to do with me? I've got orgasm problems!' (Markovits and Gorski 1993: 82.)

Other former extraparliamentary activists, who came to be informally known as 'spontis', lived in tiny utopian communities within cities, where they thought spontaneous humanistic impulses – not the dogmas of radicals or the repressive norms of conventional society – would guide human relations. Pleasure and unpredictability were celebrated as a new summum bonum – a way of life far superior to nongratifying, mind-numbing careers in enormous public and private bureaucracies and factories. Slogans of the often playful-sounding spontis included 'A bit more pleasure principle can't hurt!' and 'Experiment without knowing where you'll land!' (Markovits and Gorski 1993: 85–6.) Participants in the sponti subculture instinctively explored alternative ways of deciding public issues that, in their opinion, went significantly beyond traditional bourgeois and Marxist conceptions. For example, they often lived in communal apartment complexes, with all members equally sharing chores, furnishings, and purchases. Group policies were decided through face-to-face discussion and unrestricted debate. Self-declared spokespersons often described their small-group self-government as 'grassroots democracy', 'spontaneist', and 'undogmatic', and viewed it as superior to the two-and-a-half party system by which the country was currently being governed. However, except for the experiments in small-scale and face-to-face direct democracy, there were few identifiable goals or strategies for change in what might be called 'sponti politics'. Typical group activities were street dancing or the sudden presentation of flowers to police, and they would be undertaken with no particular aim in mind other than to express the rejection of conformity, of the consumer culture, and of social and political authorities. The sponti movement attracted many young individuals, despite its lack of specific goals. By 1975, groups loosely associated with the sponti subculture had large followings on campuses, where they attempted to counter communist and socialist-inspired student organizations.

A less colourful but nonetheless creative and socially critical student subculture emerged alongside the spontis during the mid-1970s. Biobakeries, cooperative businesses, collective day-care centres, and leftist periodicals mushroomed in quarters of cities where people between the ages of 15 and 25 were concentrated. Alternative movie houses, coffeehouses, bars, and bookstores also appeared. These activities and places provided a loose communications network and conveyed understandings and interpretations of public events that differed considerably from the images commonly found in the Springer-dominated news media (Hülsberg 1988: 73–5; Markovits and Gorski 1993: 83–5).

Illegal squatter settlements also appeared during the middle and late 1970s, as growing numbers of unemployed youths lived in previously vacant buildings. By the early 1980s more than 500 such settlements existed in 50 urban areas (Conradt 1986: 227). In Berlin, young squatters had been seizing empty buildings since the late 1970s, and by the early 1980s occupied almost 160 apartment houses that had been scheduled for demolition. Battles in Berlin between police and thousands of squatters and their allies led to a drawn-out struggle of more than four years (Burns and van der Will 1988: 175–8; Eckert and Willems 1986: 130–3, 141–2; Papadakis 1984: 123–30).

Alongside these various experiments in alternative lifestyles and residential habits, appeared another distinctively post-APO political phenomenon: terrorist organizations (Burns and van der Will 1988: 55–8, 109–11, 117–18; Markovits and Gorski 1993: 65–75). Throughout the 1970s, terrorist groups bombed department stores and bridges, and killed and kidnapped civilian government leaders, industrialists, and bankers. Like many spontis, the terrorists often had previous histories of involvement in the SDS and, ironically, in the pacifist-inspired antinuclear-arms groups of the 1960s. Disillusioned by the parliamentary parties' foreign and domestic policies, the terrorists saw violence as the last means available for achieving change. The groups' spokespersons contended that only shocking violence could ignite a widespread rebellion, either by inspiring others to stand up to the government or by provoking the government into senseless acts of brutality that would reveal its true nature. Injustice and oppression clearly existed; the masses just needed to be shown how to fight.

The crest of the terrorist wave passed during the last half of the 1970s, although politically motivated murders and sabotage of nuclear power plants and of military bases continued well into the 1980s. Contrary to the revolutionary theories advanced by terrorist groups, kidnapping and murders neither revolutionized nor mobilized broad sectors of the people against the West German state. The violence did, however, prompt the Social Democratic government, already sensitive to charges from the conservative news media of being soft on radicals, into supporting a series of tough security bills that were passed between 1974 and 1978. After 1977 the police had the legal right to ask for identification from people in public places, even if not pursuant to a specific crime. The police also acquired the right to detain for up to 12 hours suspicious persons who could not provide proper identification. The government could hold suspected terrorists incommunicado for up to 30 days. Security forces could screen lawyers defending suspected terrorists, as well as monitor defence lawyers' telephone calls (Markovits and Gorski 1993: 75–8).

The security laws of the mid and late 1970s, like the emergency-power legislation of the late 1960s, were not easily approved. The incommunicado detention, for example, passed the federal parliament by only one vote. Many parliamentarians, political activists, and Free Democrats, in particular, denounced the SPD's new legislation on the grounds that it violated citizens' constitutional rights. It must be said here that several SPD parliamentarians refused to go along.

Radicalizing the SPD

Although a plurality of the 1968 street demonstrators severed their ties with the SPD, many demonstrators remained in the party and attempted to resuscitate its radical spirit. Their faith in the SPD had been sparked in part by the exciting 1969 elections. For the first time in two decades the SPD won more than a third of the ballots cast – 40 per cent – in a federal election, which enabled the SPD to form a coalition with the FDP and without the CDU/CSU. The openly procapitalist, pro-NATO, and pronuclear weapons Christian Democrats would not be in power at the federal level for the first time in postwar history. The SPD's charismatic leader, Willy Brandt, spoke glowingly of a 'social renewal' to be generated by novel democratic experiments at the workplace and in neighbourhoods and asked young adults for their help. Many of the sixty-eighters took him at his word and joined the SPD's young socialists club, commonly known as JUSO.

The Jusos never became the quiet junior partner that many SPD leaders had expected them to be. Instead, they actively sought to return SPD leaders to the party's anticapitalist and propeace principles.

The popularity of the Jusos was remarkable. Between 1968 and 1974, their number more than doubled, from 150,000 to 350,000 (Hülsberg 1988: 46). In several cities, such as Munich, Frankfurt, and Berlin, Jusos were very active and close to being the centre of gravity of Socialist politics (Conradt 1986: 96).

The Jusos articulated a number of strategic theories that the Greens later would echo. They first of all advocated the 'democratization of all areas of life' – a phrase that, for the Jusos, referred to a dual political strategy of cooperating with the SPD politicians while simultaneously organizing local communities so that they could autonomously fight for their own goals. Because of their concern for developing local groups' autonomous political capacities and power, the Jusos participated in many neighbourhood-level campaigns for strictly parochial aims, such as freezing local rents, preventing the widening of a local highway, and building community playgrounds. The Jusos believed that by patiently working in what government officials considered the low-yield vineyards of community politics, they would soon be able to establish an independent electoral base for themselves from which they could challenge the conservative leaders of the SPD. Further, many believed that by addressing immediate concerns of citizens, they could awaken German voters to broader questions of social justice and bring about a long-term partisan realignment that would benefit the SPD in general and the Jusos in particular.

Many Jusos reasoned as well that the SPD could continue to attract votes in urban neighbourhoods only if it renounced its currently conservative positions on matters of law and order and on rapid capitalist development. According to JUSO theorists, the SPD should immediately reclaim its once-progressive positions on matters of social justice.

JUSO leaders wanted to devise an effective political strategy and keenly recognized that some SPD politicians would be loath to give up what thus far had seemed to be a successful and proven middle-of-the-road path to power and prestige. To undermine the power of conservative SPD cliques and make them more responsive to grassroots concerns, the Jusos proposed novel intraparty decision-making procedures, such as informal 'primaries' (akin to caucuses in the United States) to select electoral candidates rather than having the party's inside cliques handpick them. The Jusos also proposed that party officials take instructions from local constituencies, who, the Jusos believed, would oppose the continuance in power of unresponsive leaders. Another recommendation that later would be found in the Greens' system of organization: strict limits on the number of offices a single party official could hold.

Many Jusos, in addition, wanted the economy to be restructured along the lines of radically participatory (and therefore radically decentralized) principles. According to an ideological current within JUSO known as the Stamokaps, workers should comanage enterprises, although some key industries (including the banking and credit system) should be nationalized.

The Jusos were divided about whether to ally themselves with other revolutionary groups, such as Trotskyists and other Marxist parties. Many splinter groups had arisen within West Germany, and they often participated in local-level campaigns to protect neighbourhood interests. These so-called K-groups seemed useful allies, in the opinion of a significant number of Jusos. On the other hand, Germany's major communist party had reappeared in 1968–69 under a slightly new name – German Communist Party, instead of the Communist Party of Germany – and was attempting to create a broad electoral alliance among all parties and social groups to the left of the CDU/CSU. To build bridges with the SPD, the German Communist Party avoided making the sorts of stinging attacks on the SPD that the Jusos routinely levelled. Ironically, the rhetoric of the German Communist Party was far less radical and militant-sounding than the rhetoric of the Jusos, which was forthrightly critical of West Germany's social market economy, characterizing it as a 'mature capitalist' order ruled by and for a minority of wealthy industrialists (Hancock 1989: 84).

The Jusos were internally divided over the validity and usefulness of Marcuse's and the SDS's recent theories about the contribution of marginals and intellectuals to the development of a social revolution. Some Jusos believed that class background was not a defining feature of a person's politics. In principle, all West Germans – including small business owners – could be converted to socialist positions if their immediate concerns were visibly and effectively addressed by community activists. Other Jusos held an orthodox Marxist position that only wage labourers are open to novel, socialist ideas; West Germans from petit-bourgeois backgrounds could not be relied on to support a restructuring of the economy and a radical redistribution of income and wealth.

The Jusos relentlessly denounced SPD leaders for retreating from the party's earlier commitment to international peace, social justice, and socialism. At one point, the Stamokaps faction within JUSO suggested that the SPD–FDP coalition acted as an 'agent of monopoly capitalism' (Markovits and Gorski 1993: 97). Jusos urged SPD leaders to advocate immediate withdrawal from NATO, greater power to factory workers' councils, a 35-hour workweek, and nationalization of selected industries. They also advocated periodic and open cooperation between the SPD and the newly legalized German Communist Party and various K-groups.

Despite their unending criticisms of the conservative spirit of the post-Bad Godesberg SPD, the Jusos remained loyal to the party, largely because of Brandt's ongoing efforts to normalize relations with the communist bloc. On the whole,

Brandt was viewed as a potential ally, and older SPD leaders, such as Helmut Schmidt, as obstacles to change. The solution, the reasoning went, was to strengthen intraparty democratic procedures – for example, making party officials accountable to the rank and file through primaries and threats of recall.

The Brandt government was rocked in 1974 by a spy scandal, and power within the party shifted to the more conservative wing, headed by Schmidt. As Chancellor, Schmidt retreated from many of Brandt's social and international reforms and supported the construction of nuclear power plants and closer ties with NATO, including the stationing of nuclear missiles. Also, he quickly saw to the passage of resolutions forbidding Jusos to participate in rallies and local-level activities in which the German Communist Party or any of its ancillary groups were present.

Whereas Brandt had frequently tried to appease the Jusos, even if only on a symbolic level, Schmidt had little patience with the party's youthful and socially radical naysayers. He insisted that the rest of the world envied West Germany's economic achievements and that the proper task of the party was not to seek a foolish transition to an imagined socialist and participatory democratic utopia but to consolidate the country's accomplishments. His words to the federal parliament in 1968:

> In the case of a generation which has tried so hard in the past twenty years to create what we have now, it is inevitable that here and there were mistakes. . . . No one need feel morally guilty if, after such a difficult life, he wants to lie back on the sofa, take off his shoes and watch television, if he wants to enjoy himself a little and be glad because once again everything is back to normal.
>
> (Hülsberg 1988: 27)

Many Jusos who had cheered for Chancellor Brandt felt completely alienated from the SPD by Chancellor Schmidt. Some left the party to join nonpartisan pro-test groups, and some subsequently joined an alternative party movement formed in the 1980s, the Greens. According to political scientists Gene Frankland and Donald Schoonmaker (1992: 74), 'As many Greens later noted, Schmidt was one of their best recruiters.'

While the Jusos attempted to transform the SPD from within, a subset of former APO activists were attempting to change Germany through the teaching of young-sters. A number of late-1960s student protesters entered the teaching profession in the early 1970s to try to inculcate in their young charges new values and ways of perceiving the world. In Bremen, for example, a radical teacher sought to instruct children about class structure by having them visit different city neighbourhoods and ask residents about their lives. Similarly, four teachers in a Hessian community were said to have taught their pupils popular-front slogans (Conradt 1986: 65).

Brandt (and later Schmidt) and other SPD leaders were highly sensitive to charges that the party was a Trojan horse for communist forces. Christian Democrats, after all, indefatigably argued that the SPD was allowing communists to infiltrate the German civil service, especially the teaching professions, and that the domestic triumph of communists tragically complemented the SPD's naive negotiations with Soviet bloc nations. According to leaders of the CDU/CSU and to journals published by the Springer conglomerate, the SPD's foreign policies and domestic laxness were undermining military security and fuelling disrespect for established order, as illustrated by the emergence of terrorist organizations, squatter communities, and other groups that flaunted both the law and capitalist values.

In 1972, partly to reduce the carping directed at his ongoing efforts to improve West Germany's relationships with Soviet bloc countries, Brandt issued a decree that prohibited the hiring of any civil service applicant with known 'anticonstitutional' partisan sympathies or with a history of participation in anticonstitutional organizations or activities. The decree also stated that public employees were eligible for dismissal if they belonged to organizations engaged in anticonstitutional activities or if they were observed attending activities that suggested their lack of support for a 'free democratic order'.

People representing a broad range of political perspectives – among them, trade unionists, civil libertarians, and communists – deplored the decree as overly broad and therefore a threat to democratic freedoms. What, after all, constituted 'anticonstitutional activity' – throwing bombs or merely attending a demonstration? Moreover, the decree contradicted Article 3 of the Basic Law, which prohibited the state from discriminating against citizens on the basis of their political views.

Despite widespread and bitter opposition, the government implemented the decree, which the Constitutional Court later declared constitutional. The government carried out loyalty checks on more than 3 million West Germans and disciplinary actions against 2,000 public officials, and rejected on political grounds of more than 2,200 applicants for public-service jobs (Markovits and Gorski 1993: 99; Pulzer 1995: 125–6).

Many Jusos were outraged by what, from their perspective, was obvious legal harassment of politically committed civil-service employees and an attempt by the government to regiment people's politics. According to their figures, the law ended the careers of tens of thousands of aspiring civil servants. No longer were one's after-hours political activities a personal matter beyond the jurisdiction of the state. Agreeing with the critics, US-based social scientists Andrei Markovits and Philip Gorski (1993: 91) contend that the so-called decree against radicals 'was arguably one of the most ignominious acts committed by the German social democrats since 1945'.

As we have seen, the decree was only one factor in the increasingly strained relations between the Jusos and the SPD. Schmidt's open disdain of them and his policies of streamlining social welfare, encouraging business, cooperating with NATO, and building reactors were other contributing factors. Frustrated, many Jusos withdrew from the Socialist sphere of politics at the close of the 1970s and later joined the Greens, providing it with invaluable energy, skills, strategies, and experience. The former Jusos, however, also filled the party movement with explosive myths about what could and could not politically work in West Germany. Questions of coalition-building between the Greens and the SPD, in particular, would generate hot debates within the party movement; for the previously failed project to radicalize the SPD from within left many former Jusos with 'lasting bitterness, mistrust and disgust' (Markovits and Gorski 1993: 99).

Citizen-action groups

While many young, politically radical adults were experimenting with diverse political and nonpolitical methods of changing society, more established middle-class adults were becoming increasingly active in local pressure organizations, soon to be known as citizen-action groups.

As early as the mid-1960s, middle-class West Germans had tried to organize at the grassroots level in order to influence local public officials. These groups typically engaged in voter mobilization behind particular candidates. The major political parties, especially the SPD and CDU/CSU, encouraged the formation of citizen-initiative groups at that time because, in theory, the groups would demonstrate and plead for social policies that the parties were advancing. To the parties' surprise, the citizen groups often acted independently of the wishes of the major parties and pushed issues that the parties found either unimportant or incompatible with their overriding goal of sustaining rapid industrial growth.

Around 1972 the number of politically active, middle-class, local groups multiplied, became less tied to election campaigns, and began to lobby peaceably for schools and other government services. By 1979 approximately 1.5 million West Germans – a disproportionate number of whom were university-educated – belonged to roughly 50,000 of the groups (Mewes 1983: 53–4). Some of the local activists either had once been Jusos or were active in the urban sponti subculture. A larger number were not normally politically active, were economically content and socially conservative (not anticapitalist), earned above-average incomes, and were either middle- and upper-level civil servants, or holders of middle-level managerial positions in service-sector enterprises. Stated differently, the citizen-action groups were the political activity of choice among Germany's university-trained middle classes (Hancock 1989: 117; Markovits and Gorski 1993: 100).

During the early 1970s, citizen-action groups almost exclusively engaged in institutional forms of politics, working the courts and lobbying local governments and Land legislatures. The political beliefs and interests of the activists were strikingly heterogenous. Writes Russell Dalton (1993: 194), 'Citizen-action groups cover the entire political spectrum and address almost all possible issues.' Typically, a group would pressure local governments into addressing overlooked local problems, such as construction of a progressive kindergarten, cleaning up a polluted lake, reducing noise pollution, or protecting tenants' rights. Once a designated problem had been solved, a group usually disbanded (Dalton 1993: 193). It would be overly simple, however, to view the groups as ephemeral, for many a local problem took years of work. Moreover, some activists would migrate from one local action group to another, producing relatively permanent local core groups of activists.

Most citizen-action groups involved no more than 30 regularly active members and generally reached decisions democratically through open discussions and formal votes (Dalton 1993: 193). Further, they seldom resorted to confrontational tactics or rhetoric but instead attempted to open communication with government officials and municipal councils. Groups would sometimes engage in colourful demonstrations, such as bicycle marches or bus boycotts, that were in a sense a watered-down version of some of the more daring actions of the extraparliamentary protesters of 1968.

During the mid-1970s, a growing number of citizen-group activists formed translocal federations around broader common concerns – for example, protection of the environment. Some federations were citywide and regionwide, such as the Berlin Squatters Movement, which tried to transform a rundown section of the city. The first enduring nationwide federation was formed in response to the federal government's decision to end the country's dependency on foreign oil through an ambitious nuclear-energy programme. Construction sites for reactors were occupied by teams from dozens of citizen groups, who also jointly organized rallies that sometimes attracted participants in the tens of thousands.

Local governments usually sought both to make peace with the citizen-action groups and to include them in local policy-making loops. Some city governments, for instance, established city advisory councils, wherein citizen-action groups could review and suggest policies. Federal officials, however, were annoyed by what they deemed meddling in complex policy questions and subversion of democratic politics. The SPD–FDP governments of the 1970s, for example, viewed citizens' resistance to the building of roads and reactors as obstructing economic development and causing increased unemployment. The Christian Democrats, too, regarded many of the opposition groups as a 'plague on the land' that threatened the authority of elected officials (Roth 1991: 78–9).

As the 1970s progressed, the citizen-action groups became more popular, probably involving a larger number of people than belonged to the political parties (Dalton 1993: 193; Katzenstein 1987: 357; Mushaben 1985: 31). Political analyst Horst Mewes (1983: 54) notes that 'In itself this degree of citizen participation in local protest actions was unprecedented in the political history of postwar Germany.' The vast majority of the groups remained concerned with geographically narrow goals, such as opposing local rezoning laws or the construction of an expressway through a neighbourhood. But a growing number of their activists began to articulate a generalized prejudice against all bureaucracy, and viewed neither capitalism nor particular parties but the arrogance of state-level bureaucrats and planners as the primary source of local problems. For these activists, local-level referenda and greater citizen involvement in local politics seemed the only remedy for bureaucrats' dismissiveness of citizen dissatisfaction and concerns.

Members of smaller radical parties, such as the German Communist Party and Maoist parties, increasingly attended citizen-action groups' meetings and protests during the 1970s, and tried to expand their agendas and radicalize their goals. The Jusos, who since the early 1970s had advocated community activism in such works as *Local Politics – for Whom?*, also attended citizen-action groups' meetings, despite the SPD elders' opposition. The vast majority of groups nonetheless remained nonpartisan in spirit and continued to be strikingly modest and nonradical in their goals.

During the late 1970s individuals and small groups intent on violence sometimes would throw stones during a large citizen-action group rally and thus provided police with a reason to use batons and tear gas. Police would spy on groups with reputations for unruly behaviour. Toward the close of the 1970s, the occupation of nuclear-reactor construction sites sometimes led to violence and hundreds of injuries. Most citizen-action groups, however, refrained from violent forms of protest and insisted that demonstrations be orderly. The organizing slogan for one occupation aptly describes the tension between violence and disobedience: 'Flowers for the police, wire cutters for the fence' (Hülsberg 1988: 62).

In the late 1970s some citizen-action groups began to advocate 'marching' through the electoral system. Newly formed coalitions of the groups, frustrated by government officials' failure to halt road construction and reverse other unpopular decisions, began to campaign for their own lists of nonparty-affiliated candidates. These 'rainbow' or 'alternative' candidates were, in theory, to replace career politicians from established parties, who seemed disregardful of constituencies. To the surprise of many observers, in scattered rural and urban communities alternative-list candidates won enough votes to enter the political system at the local level.

Encouraged by their successes, some groups proposed forming a nationwide coalition to compete in the European Economic Community's elections and, later, West Germany's federal elections. The goal of running candidates was, once again, not to implement a particular ideology or platform but to demonstrate widespread popular concern about the specific harms that rapid industrialization was causing, and to use electoral muscle as a method of compelling the SPD, FDP, and CDU/CSU to confront quality-of-life issues that they thus far had seemed so reluctant to do. These cross-local electoral coalitions, as we will see in Chapter 4, would, through painful negotiations, coalesce into the Green party-movement of the 1980s.

New social movements

Of the many political groups that flourished during the 1970s and provided the social bases for the Greens, perhaps none would have as much of a love–hate relationship with the party-movement as the so-called new social movements. The new social movements were loosely coordinated groups with national-level policy agendas and with relatively coherent proposals for transforming the values of West German society. Three groups that were especially important for the development of the Greens' politics were the new women's movement, the new ecology movement, and the new peace movement.

As in other parts of western Europe and North America, a distinctive, nationwide women's movement materialized in West Germany following the anti-Vietnam War mobilizations of the late 1960s. As in the case of the United States, the new women's movement in West Germany emerged in part because of women activists' anger at being excluded from leadership roles within antiwar organizations. Tired of being treated contemptuously as servants and sex objects in the offices and meetings of the SDS, women activists responded by criticizing the hypocrisy in male activists' calls for universal equality and peace. A female member of SDS, for example, hurled a tomato at a male SDS speaker after he and his fellow male speakers had berated a feminist speaker during a 1968 SDS conference. In the words of a slogan used at one women's congress in 1969, women activists should 'liberate the socialist eminences from their bourgeois dicks!' (Markovits and Gorski 1993: 87).

The new women's movement in West Germany was new not in the sense that there had never been women's groups addressing women's concerns but in the sense that forerunner groups had sought to achieve goals through conventional parties and government bureaux that were led first and foremost by men. Before the Second World War, the vast majority of politically active German women who were concerned with the problems of women at work and in the home tended to place their faith in parties – especially the SPD. They hoped that in the long run, rule by the SPD would yield policies supportive of women's aims. In contrast, the new women's movement was a current of women's politics that sought to liberate women by creating 'autonomous spaces' (that is, spaces from which men were excluded) where women could comfortably discuss issues related to sexuality, child rearing, and home life – issues that men's groups dismissed as secondary to the 'more important' issues of wage earning.

Within ten years, numerous women's magazines, publishing houses, and bookstores had been established. Local associations of women disrupted beauty pageants and walled up entrances to pornography shops. Homes for battered women, women's psychotherapy centres, women's restaurants, and even women's driving schools were in place. Most of these activities were organized exclusively on the local level, for fear that large-scale actions and organization might facilitate the counterspread of distinctively male notions of hierarchy and centralized authority. The new women's movement thus was deliberately uncoordinated at the national level and a highly parochial phenomenon (Kolinsky 1989: 195–6).

Of the many concepts that members of the new women's movement explored, perhaps none was more derided by Germany's mainstream press than the idea that women could understand and love one another in ways that surpassed men's understanding of and love for women. Music festivals for women – with tens of thousands of women drinking and dancing to rock'n'roll – and women's communes became the substance of lurid stories of lesbianism in the sensationalist press. Despite the news media's frequent ridicule, the flood of books and journals by the new feminists and the sheer extent of media coverage enticed thousands of normally apolitical women to experiment with women's consciousness-raising groups each year. There they found a supportive audience of women with whom to discuss all manner of personal concerns. After an evening of speaking their minds, some visitors left the groups never to return, and of those who came back, few remained active for more than a year.

On the other hand, local women's groups did leave an important, enduring institution: feminist shelters for battered women. These places of respite from male domination were run in a strictly democratic manner, with few hierarchical distinctions between residents and volunteers. The feminist shelters provided an opportunity for women to regain self-respect, to discover and develop skills in running meetings and interacting with others, and to acquire a sense of power (Ferree 1987: 185–7).

The primary goal of the new women's movement never was to capture positions of power in existing economic and political institutions but to nurture distinctively female values and patterns of thinking. To be sure, the new feminists also had certain political goals – such as the passage of more reasonable abortion laws and tougher laws against rape and domestic violence. But the West German movement first and foremost wished to encourage a deeper awareness and appreciation of women's different nature – in particular, women's purported greater propensity toward pacifism, mutual respect, and cooperation.

In contrast to the persistently organizationally decentralized new women's movement, the new ecology movement was increasingly centralized, year by year. In 1972, 16 citizen-action groups established the Federal Association of Citizens' Initiatives for Environmental Protection (BBU). Within a decade membership had grown to more than 1,000 affiliated groups and more than 300,000 individuals (Burns and van der Will 1988: 185; Mewes 1983: 55).

At first, the BBU simply sought government protection of the environment. Little thought was given to changing modern values or changing economic and political institutions. Reduction of particular, local instances of land, water, and air pollution was basically the extent of the BBU agenda.

During the mid-1970s the BBU programme became much more politicized. Frustrated by the federal government's repeated refusals to reconsider its ambitious plans to construct reactors, growing numbers of BBU activists began to look at pollution as having political–institutional origins. Environmentally oriented citizen-action groups in 1973 challenged government plans to construct a nuclear reactor in the upper Rhine region. During the public debate on the matter, it was discovered that four members of the nuclear-power examining committee for the Land of Baden-Württemberg were also members of the board of directors of the power company that was planning the nuclear power plant. The conflict of interest corroborated growing suspicions within many citizen-action groups that graft, corruption, and misinformation were the defining features of energy politics in West Germany. To combat the party politicians' and business interests' backroom style of policy making, environmentally oriented citizen-action groups started to call for local referenda and government investigations. In 1975 groups began to occupy reactor sites, build 'alternative' settlements, and thereby halt construction.

In the late 1970s a more radical ecological sensibility began to replace the environmental-protection thinking of the citizen-action groups that belonged to the BBU. Its leaders began to advocate what they called an 'ecological economy', which would be in harmony with the 'natural balances' of the earth and that would never exhaust the organic reproductive processes of land, sea, and air. An ecological economy would entail slower growth rates than those the West German governments had pursued during the postwar years, and would also entail more spartan habits of consumption and new moral and ethical thinking in everyday life, sometimes called 'ecological humanism'.

The BBU also began to use themes of worldwide crisis and global destruction when discussing environmental problems. Dark notions about 'irrevocable damage to nature' and threats to 'the earth's survivability' began to appear frequently in

BBU speeches and writings. Chancellor Schmidt's support during the late 1970s for the stationing of a new generation of NATO-owned nuclear weapons in West Germany reinforced the BBU's increasingly apocalyptic world view.

The solution, the ecologists argued, was to reorganize social life according to the principles of 'simplification, decentralization, and deconcentration'. In contrast to advocates of economies of scale, who insisted that large-scale production is efficient and encourages specialization and therefore innovation, leaders of the BBU argued that 'small is beautiful', that large businesses, cities, and enormous governmental systems are economically inefficient as well as spiritually destructive. In smaller settings, human beings see one another more fully and are more tolerant, more responsible, more humble, and more self-restrained. There is a reverence towards others and towards the natural environment that industrial society and patterns of living pervert. The ecologists' goal, therefore, was not simply prevention of pollution, elimination of nuclear power plants, and the establishment of natural refuges. It was more socially radical and ambitious, including political decentralization and local autonomy; a simpler, smaller-scale, and face-to-face lifestyle; and labour-intensive modes of production (Dobson 1990).

Most ecological theorists within the BBU admitted that the creation of a new social order would not be easy; it would require the sacrifice of many material comforts that most people wrongly view as necessities. The theorists concluded that the BBU would have to teach West Germans (and sooner or later all humans) a new way of understanding the world. In particular, the BBU would have to teach people to reject the dominant Western ideology, secular humanism, which puts human beings as masters of the world and deems the natural environment merely the 'raw material' with which humans satisfy their myopic desires. People would have to learn to embrace an ecological metaphysics in which 'nature' is viewed as a fragile, coherent, interdependent system, and in which humans are viewed as merely one of nature's parts and as morally responsible for protecting the larger natural system.

Within the ecological movement, several identifiable ideological subcurrents appeared during the late 1970s and early 1980s (Dobson 1990: 171–204; Hülsberg 1988: 65–6; Markovits and Gorski 1993: 105–6, 125–41). Some self-described ecofeminists believed that women were more likely to learn nature's moral lessons, because their unique childbearing capacity gives them a healthier, more wholesome relationship to nature. Men, at least for the moment, were too alienated from nature, because of their biological differences and because of their competitive and hierarchical social activities, to play a decisive role in remaking society. To achieve significant ecological reforms, West German culture first had to be feminized, which in part meant that men's social and political power had to be curtailed.

Some nonfeminist participants in the ecology movement retained ties to K-groups and the Jusos and saw the postwar consumerism mentality as an outgrowth of the day-to-day workings of industrial capitalism. According to the so-called ecological-socialists, bureaucracies in places of production and commercialized lifestyles (induced by advertisements) have jointly created human beings who feel alienated, angry, and manipulated. Men and women tragically cope with these socially induced feelings by channelling natural, spontaneous desires for harmony with nature into harmful, artificial desires for the possession of more and more manufactured goods. To end antiecological thinking, struggles against patriarchy are not enough. Attention also has to be given to transforming current class structures, greatly reducing the concentration of private economic power, and transforming the mass media.

Another subset within Germany's ecological movement was inspired by a particular reading of the Bible. Protestant ecological activists believed that teachings about the Creation and about humans' roles as guardians of God's Creation mean that ecological organizations should be concerned not only about environmental destruction but also all other threats to the world's existence, including the arms race and the growing environmental destruction and widespread economic suffering in less industrialized countries. The so-called eco-Christians maintained that any serious programme for reform must address events outside the borders of Germany and must include reflections on international relations. To prevent a widespread ecological disaster, what is needed is a widespread moral conversion from materialism to Christian-inspired spiritualism.

Only a few ecological theorists looked to the industrial working class as a leader in bringing about a postindustrial ecological revolution. Most believed that the proletariat was too spiritually based and too wedded to technological gadgetry and consumerism to overthrow industry. They made the assumption that to compensate for the monotony and servility imposed by modern industrial production, workers spent more and more leisure time acquiring freshly minted technological gadgets; electronic toys and disposable plastic goods had become the opiate of the masses. A postindustrial revolution would have to come primarily from other social groups.

The third new social movement that had profound impact on the Greens' goals, resources, and strategies was the new peace movement, whose history partly overlapped with that of the new ecology movement. The BBU approached some of West Germany's peace organizations during the late 1970s, and began to cosponsor public demonstrations with the new peace organizations by 1980.

The so-called eco-pax alliance was partly the outcome of a new surge in peace politics, prompted by Chancellor Schmidt's support for the stationing of US Pershing II and Cruise missiles on West German soil. After the 1968 demonstrations against Vietnam and the passage of the emergency-power legislation, the West German peace movement had temporarily gone into dormancy, with few organizations able to mobilize large numbers of demonstrators. Schmidt, whom critics dubbed 'the missile chancellor', supported the deployment of NATO's nuclear weaponry despite military authorities' warning that West Germany's chances of surviving a war between the superpowers was now zero because destruction of the missiles would be one of the Soviet Union's first priorities.

A backlash ensued. A number of conservative military leaders, upset with Schmidt's decision to make Germany an expendable pawn in the Cold War, angrily resigned their commissions and, prompted by concerns about national security, joined diverse peace organizations. Meanwhile, several new Christian organizations formed during Schmidt's rule and declared themselves unadulterated pacifists who were 'ready to live without the protection of military arms' (Markovits and Gorski 1993: 109; see also Burns and van der Will 1988: 209–11, 216–17). Several key figures in the SPD, citing the party's traditional commitment to peace, also broke ranks with Schmidt. Finally, a number of small militant organizations, including groups of young anarchists, squatters, spontis, and 'violent pacifists' appeared. Some of the youth groups began to ally with one another and formed the Federal Conference of Independent Peace Groups (BUF) in 1982. Unlike participants in the 1950s peace organizations, many of the youths were unabashed supporters of social disruption, intentionally engaged in offensive behaviour, and seemed undeterred by the possibility of street violence (Mushaben 1984: 178–9).

The new peace movement, like the new women's movement, was highly decentralized; and only a small number of its activists desired nationwide coordination. In the words of Alice Cooper and Klaus Eichner (1991: 160–1), 'The ideal of grassroots democracy and an abhorrence of hierarchy pervaded most of the movement.' Most analysts believe that despite the absence of an overarching decision-making body with extensive authority over local groups, the new peace movement succeeded in involving large numbers of people in demonstrations, on a scale unprecedented in postwar West Germany (Cooper and Eichner 1991: 152; Markovits and Gorski 1993: 110). For example, more than 2 million people signed a petition calling for a European referendum on disarmament (Mushaben 1985: 32).

The unprecedented popular support for the new peace movement was due in part to the way in which its spokespersons defined the problem of nuclear weapons. The Americans' traditional and increasingly hawkish rhetoric and policies toward the Soviet Union – positions encouraged by the new US president, Ronald Reagan – and Chancellor Schmidt's decision to station NATO's intermediate-range missiles on West German soil had already induced considerable suspicion among West Germans that their homes were being sacrificed for the good of outsiders. Leaders of the new ecological movement (especially leaders of the BBU) extended the growing debate over the national costs of the government's military policies into one over the survivability of the world. This broader understanding of the implications of stationing NATO weapons facilitated the participation of environmental-protection groups (especially citizen-action groups) in the mobilizations against missiles.

Among the people who played key roles in the development and diffusion of ecological arguments about the costs of stationing NATO's missiles were BBU leader Jo Leinen and peace activists Petra Kelly and Roland Vogt. They and others organized an array of 'eco-pax' conferences and demonstrations. According to the eco-pax thinkers, nuclear weapons and reactors are profoundly similar in origins and in consequences. Both atomic bombs and atomic reactors invite the destruction of humanity and the extermination of all life on the planet by means of a 'nuclear winter'. Moreover, both nuclear weapons and nuclear power are caused by the same cultural sickness: Europeans' and North Americans' drive to master the world and to use nature as raw material. So long as nature is not revered and protected but sacrilegiously abused as mere material to be controlled, Europeans and North Americans will go on building reactors, bombs, and other mechanisms that can easily destroy the entire planet. The only true solution to the arms race (and to the concomitant drive for greater and cheaper nuclear energy) is ecological reasoning – or so the eco-pax theorists reasoned.

Conclusion

Before the Greens appeared on the national scene in the late 1970s and early 1980s, multiple radical political theories, nonelite traditions of protest, and alternative cultural milieus had already evolved in West Germany. Some of these oppositional groups collaborated with one another; many did not. Different groups – say, the Campaign for Democracy and Disarmament, the SDS, the spontis, the Stamokaps, the citizen-action groups, the BBU, Berlin's urban squatters, the Christian pacifists, and the new women's movement – were troubled by different problems, upheld different values, and adopted different tactics and strategies.

The richness of nonelite oppositional politics provided key resources for the Green party-movement, such as communications networks, organized constituencies, social goals, and tested leaders. Moreover, some Green leaders hoped that by unifying these multiple disgruntled groups, they would forge a sufficiently large electoral coalition to remake the world.

But Germany's rich oppositional environment, while suggesting a political strategy, also posed a problem: to lead a broad electoral coalition, Green leaders had to find a way to link the energies, strategic ideas, and personnel of social groups with strikingly different objectives and grievances. The Greens had to discover an ideological common ground.

Let us now borrow the analytic perspective developed by cultural interpreters of social movements and examine more closely the diverse and changing beliefs of Green activists. What were their interpretations of their current political circumstances? What were their social goals? And what were their strategies for attracting and unifying pre-existing groups and mobilizing potential constituencies?

Note

1. For other overviews of the nonelite politics that preceded the Greens, see Burns and van der Will (1988), Hülsberg (1988: 29–76), Markovits and Gorski (1993: 29–112), and Papadakis (1984).

Chapter 4

Clashing shades of Green

Some theoretical approaches and subapproaches to social movements – such as the resource-mobilization approach, the political-process approach, and the indigenous-community approach – explore the social and political circumstances that facilitate or hamper the emergence of social movements. The identity-formation approach, in contrast, focuses directly on activists' perceptions, beliefs, goals, and strategies and asks 'what conventional and innovative ideas do activists in a particular movement hold and bring to a movement?' and 'what cacophony of ideological factions and wings does a particular movement contain?' The social and political circumstances that occasion a movement shift to the background. Now, analysis centres upon how movement activists think about their social movement.

This chapter explores the political beliefs of West German Greens between 1980 and the mid-1990s. It discusses their programmes and programmatic disagreements, and considers briefly how the novel ideas of the Greens affected German politics.

The political thinking of the West German Greens has fascinated many observers because it combines several seemingly incongruent elements.[1] Especially during its formative years (1979–81), the party-movement attracted activists with diverse beliefs, priorities, and styles of reasoning: advocates of guest workers' rights, cultural conservatives unhappy with the CDU/CSU, middle-class citizen groups upset over visible damage to the local environment, radical feminists, radical ecologists, pacifists, opponents of nuclear war, urban squatters, former spontis, unemployed youths, lesbian- and gay-rights advocates, and former Jusos angry at the SPD for its embrace of the so-called German Model of economic growth, its support of legislation that circumscribed civil liberties, and its pro-American, Cold War foreign policy.

Spokespersons for the Greens, during election campaigns and in their federal programmes, argued that their seemingly diverse goals and concerns were complementary and linked to each other. But beliefs often clashed, and after the Greens began winning seats in West Germany's federal and state parliaments, the members' disparate beliefs repeatedly threatened to pull the movement apart.

Electoral experiments before the Greens

What we today call the Green party-movement evolved during the last half of the 1970s, when small groups of disgruntled West Germans, often belonging to citizen-action groups, began to form 'alternative' electoral organizations in towns and cities. Almost all of the new slates developed spontaneously, without coordination from a central authority and without long-term goals other than the correction of specific local problems. Some slates formed regionwide alliances that competed for seats in Land parliaments. In 1979 one set of the new slates formed a self-named 'Green' coalition for the upcoming European Community elections.

A coincidence of political events during the late 1970s prompted diverse young activists in West Germany, already involved in protest organizations, to consider the creation of new electoral slates. One important set of events involved the unsuccessful occupation of nuclear-reactor construction sites, especially in the communities of Whyl, Brokdorf, and Grohnde. Since 1975 environmentally concerned students and radicals had taken over construction sites and created small settlements of houses and education centres. Gradually, the power companies and the government in their expulsion attempts resorted to force, especially in Brokdorf and Grohnde. Demonstrations likewise became more violent. Among the tens of thousands of protesters massed at a construction site at Grohnde in Lower Saxony in 1977 were some who had come determined to resist removal. A battle broke out; thousands were caught up in the contagion; hundreds were injured. The bloody outcome was extensively covered by the popular press. That reportage, plus news of the surprising victories of French ecologists in their local elections, convinced many antinuclear activists that civil disobedience had become an ineffective and probably counterproductive way to try to change the government's energy policies. An electoral route seemed much more promising (Fogt 1989: 93; Hülsberg 1988: 80; Markovits and Gorski 1993: 103–4; Padgett and Burkett 1986: 173–5).

That same year the West German government, to prevent further terrorism, suspended the civil rights of suspected terrorists. The SPD's endorsement of the controversial move greatly exacerbated the ongoing conflict between the party's leadership and its more radical members, especially leaders of JUSO. Soon key activists on the SPD left, such as Jochen Steffen, resigned in disgust. Many joined organizations and projects headed by radical ecologists such as Petra Kelly, who argued,

> We can no longer rely on the established parties, and we can no longer depend entirely on the extra-parliamentary road. The system is bankrupt, but a new force has to be created both inside and outside parliament.
>
> (Hülsberg 1988: 78)

At first, results of local elections were discouraging because of the small level of support. Nonetheless, the absence in certain regions of the 5 per cent requirement in local elections allowed the new environmental parties to win a few seats. This sparked hope.

In the Land of Lower Saxony, several environmental coalitions captured seats in the October 1977 local elections. The Environmental Protection List, a new electoral group in Hildesheim, won only 1.6 per cent of the ballots cast; but it was enough to capture one council seat. Another group, Nuclear Power, No Thanks, won 2.3 per cent of the vote and a council seat in the Hameln town elections. In Erlangen, an alliance of ecologists, spontis, and former Social Democrats won 2 per cent.

There also were scattered successes outside Lower Saxony. For example, in March 1978, newly formed parties opposed to the construction of nearby nuclear plants won 6 per cent of the vote and two council seats and 6.6 per cent and three seats in two small towns within the Land of Schleswig-Holstein (Hülsberg 1985: 8; Scharf 1994: 65).

After the 1977 local elections in Lower Saxony, more than a dozen local electoral lists explored the formation of a regionwide coalition. Their purpose: to win enough votes in Land elections to draw the government's attention to the heavy pollution of the North Sea and the opening of a nuclear-waste dump.

Some founders of the regionwide alliance were socially and politically conservative. For example, members of the fledgling Environmental Protection Party (USP) of Lower Saxony, which was headed by former Christian Democrat, Carl Beddermann, intended neither to create a permanent party nor to challenge the overall authority of the established parties. They simply wanted to scare major parties into addressing environmental concerns. In the words of Markovits and Gorski (1993: 193):

> The USP's founders and first members were anything but young radicals. Indeed, they were hostile towards the *Chaoten*, the longhaired radicals with whom they had little, if anything, in common, and whose participation they perceived as detrimental to their cause. The USP advocated a solution to ecological problems from within the system.

In December 1977 the USP, hoping to improve its regionwide electoral fortunes, joined forces with the Green List for Environmental Protection (GLU) in Lower Saxony, an organization committed to a more radically ecological ideology. GLU leaders advocated not only immediate protection of the natural environment but also a 'total socio-ecological alternative' (Hülsberg 1988: 82) that included an unregulated economy and an end to the progrowth, materialist culture.

Seeking enough resources and votes to clear the 5 per cent hurdle, the GLU–USP coalition allowed members of other citizen-action groups to join. Some members of the small Communist League (KB) infiltrated the coalition. As a consequence of the expansion to the left, the coalition's 1978 electoral programme included demands for greater women's rights and a shorter workweek.

The coalition performed respectably in the Land elections of 1978: 3.9 per cent of the ballots cast. Still, Beddermann and other leaders of the USP were alarmed by the nonenvironmental issues that the coalition was increasingly addressing, and resigned immediately after the election.

Meanwhile, in Germany's three northern city-states – Berlin, Hamburg, and Bremen – electoral experiments were being undertaken not so much by environmentally oriented citizens' groups, but by socially and culturally radical groups that were growing in the cities' youthful countercultures. In each city-state, communist groups, the SPD, and local social movements formed alternative lists for local elections. But the ideological profile of these new electoral slates varied from place to place.

In Berlin small communist parties – local organizations of feminists, gay activists, lesbian activists, building squatters – and members of the city's sponti subculture formed the Alternative Slate (AL) on the eve of the 1979 local elections. The AL emphasized social issues, including social and political rights for women and homosexuals, protection of low-income housing stock, health care, and length of the workweek. Some AL candidates addressed local environmental concerns, such as air pollution, but those concerns were not a key part of the AL programme. Partly because of the AL's social agenda, many local journalists portrayed it as a communist front. Even Otto Schily, a Berlin-based social activist who joined the AL and later would play a leading role in Green-party politics, expressed ambivalence about the involvement in the AL of known communist organizers and at one point disparagingly described the AL as the 'KPD [Communist Party of Germany] under a new name' (Fogt 1989: 98).

Despite published reports that the AL might be a communist Trojan horse, the group did relatively well in local elections. In the 1979 Land elections, it received 47,000 votes, or 3.7 per cent of the ballots cast. The AL also won more than 5 per cent of the vote in each of four borough elections in Berlin and therefore was able to send ten representatives to those boroughs' councils (Hülsberg 1988: 89).

In Hamburg, the role of communist organizations in the newly forming electoral coalitions was again a source of controversy. Members of the local Communist League had joined numerous citizen-action groups and various women's, immigrants', prisoners', ecosocialist and youth groups during the mid- and late 1970s. The KB then helped in the formation of a broad 'rainbow' coalition for local elections. The Rainbow Slate's electoral programme resembled that of Berlin's Alternative List in that Rainbow candidates addressed the concerns of women, homosexuals, foreigners, students, the unemployed, and other politically marginalized populations. Only 10 per cent of the Rainbow Slate's 14-page programme addressed environmental questions per se, whereas 50 per cent discussed social issues (Frankland and Schoonmaker 1992: 127).

The formation of the Rainbow Slate convinced other social groups to form their own alternative slates. For example, a list of environmentally concerned but socially conservative candidates soon appeared under the label 'Green Slate' and contended that the Rainbow Slate was controlled by 'communists, queers and criminals'. The Rainbow Slate retorted that the Green Slate contained a significant number of 'Neo-Nazis' (Hülsberg 1988: 85; Mewes 1983: 57). Meanwhile, a more centrist group, Independent Germans' Action, proposed a vague 'third way' of organizing society that would be neither communist nor capitalist but would terminate environmental destruction in the West, the arms race, and economic and natural exploitation of the Third World. Bitter polemics broke out among the three groups on the eve of the 1978 city-state elections – especially between the Green Slate and the Rainbow Slate. Each failed to clear the 5 per cent threshold necessary for winning a seat. Shortly afterward, hundreds of members of the KB and other communist groups joined the Green Slate, and over the next five years, the conservative

Green Slate and much more radical Rainbow Slate gradually fused. In 1982, the new coalition would win almost 8 per cent of the vote in Hamburg's 1982 Land elections (Fogt 1989: 93–4, 107–8, 110–11, 114–16).

The first major victory by an alternative list in a Land election occurred in Bremen. Here, several former SPD members proposed creation of an alternative list. They hoped, in part, to use the local slate to pressure the SPD into revising its environmental and social policies. The so-called Green/Rainbow Slate was ideologically eclectic and involved diverse groups whose members denounced not only ecological destruction but also capitalism, Stalinism, and the SPD's recent legal suspensions of civil rights. The slate, in the words of Markovits and Gorski (1993: 189), was 'a motley crew of environmentalists, sixty-eighters, radical leftists and disillusioned social democrats'. A few disillusioned CDU/CSU party members also joined the Green/Rainbow Slate, as did Rudi Dutschke, the former youth leader who had been shot during the years of anti-Vietnam protest and who had been vilified by the Springer press. Communist groups, however, were not welcome; and in response they created their own alternative list. To the surprise of many observers, the Bremen Green/Rainbow Slate won 5.14 per cent of the ballots cast in 1979. By crossing the 5 per cent threshold, it became the first organization in more than a decade to break the monopoly of the CDU/CSU, FDP, and SPD in the Land parliaments. Within a year, it would be cited by many founders of the federal-level Green Party as a model of how to construct an ideological heterogenous yet electorally successful alternative party.

Alternative visions of a future Green party-movement

After the 1979 victory in Bremen, there was, as Markovits and Gorski (1993: 195) aptly put it, a 'race' between right-wing and left-wing activists for influence within the emerging alternative electoral lists. Consequently, the new local parties differed greatly in terms of goals, values, and political philosophies.

In the South, many new electoral lists paradoxically tended to be conservative in their values and general world view, but radical in terms of specific policy proposals. Leaders of local lists often strongly criticized the Social Democratic party's zealous commitment to economic growth, contending that the rapidity of that economic growth had destroyed West Germany's natural environment, corrupted its cultural heritage, and compromised its national sovereignty. They contended further that petitions from citizen-action groups were being dismissed by arrogant government bureaucrats. According to many of the leaders of southern lists, because the SPD–FDP coalition government would not heed advice from the well-educated and hardworking members of the middle classes, critical problems – such as foreign workers, nuclear reactors, and the presence of foreign armies on German soil – were multiplying.

Among the conservatives, Herbert Gruhl emerged as an especially outspoken and influential activist. Gruhl led an electoral organization called Green Action Future (GAZ) and wrote the widely read *A Planet is Plundered* (a book about impending global ecological catastrophe). In his speeches and writings, he constantly decried West Germany's 'growth ideology', celebrated older values, including motherhood, and advocated development of a military sufficiently strong to resist invasion by the communist bloc. To avoid an ecological disaster, the country needed a highly disciplined culture and a centralized political order that would pursue 'an optimum of military preparedness with a minimum of consumer satisfaction and, therefore, a much smaller utilization of natural resources' (Hülsberg 1988: 87). Gruhl conceded that for the sake of achieving an environmentally sound, culturally pure, and militarily strong West Germany, an ecodictatorship might be necessary. However, the values inspiring the authoritarian regime should be neither socialist nor fascist, and neither collectivist nor private-business oriented. The values should be 'neither left nor right, but forward' (Hülsberg 1988: 125).

In the North, the local alternative electoral lists tended to reflect very different ideological predilections than did those in the South, and tended to find very different social bases of support. For example, the northern lists tended to celebrate cultural tolerance, freedom of expression, and political decentralization; the southern lists, in contrast, cultural discipline and centralized political authority. Furthermore, the new northern lists frequently proposed the replacement of West Germany's 'impersonal' system of parties and professional civil servants with a radically decentralized, 'first-person' system of local-level, direct democracy. In the North, feminists, ecological-pacifists, left-wing Social Democrats, Jusos, communist groups, radical immigrant organizations, and even some formerly apolitical spontis formed the nuclei of many local electoral coalitions. Consequently, northern lists enjoyed popular support primarily in cities such as Frankfurt, Cologne, and Berlin – where extensive networks of countercultural pubs, bookstores, and residential cooperatives existed. One particularly visible alternative list was Voters League, Nuclear Power, No Thanks! (WGA), which sought to band together all the socially disadvantaged and politically marginalized in urban areas and to create a much more egalitarian country. In contrast, in the South, the new electoral organizations were more likely to be supported by mildly conservative middle-class citizens, often living in smaller towns or the countryside and generally averse to discussing far-reaching political change.

Alongside the conservative lists in the rural South and the much more radical lists in the urban North, there appeared throughout West Germany self-described 'ecological' or 'centrist' slates, such as the Action Group for an Independent Germany (AUD), the Green List for Environmental Protection (GLU), and the Action for a Third Way (A3W). Founders of these slates viewed ecological destruction and nuclear war as imminent, the primary problems to be addressed. The centrists, wishing to change progrowth and pro-NATO policies, advocated creation of extremely broad electoral coalitions, including both Gruhl-like social conservatives *and* Dutschke-like social egalitarians and anticapitalists.

The centrists' thoughts on social problems and their strategies for change conveniently positioned them between the ideas of the northern radicals and those of the southern conservatives. For example, the centrists concurred with the radicals that the society was unjust and crisis-ridden: West Germany had become a social nightmare, with one-third of the population either unemployed or employed in underpaid, menial labour, and two-thirds needlessly consuming luxury items and plundering the earth of its resources. Even so, the centrists viewed the inequality in industrial societies as a consequence *not* of capitalism per se but of the ignorance and boorish materialism that prevailed in countries with free-market systems and also in countries with socialist economies. Humanity needed a new type of economy and culture that was neither capitalist nor socialist but a 'third way'. In describing the cultural features of their desired new order, the centrists partly agreed with the leaders of the conservative lists, who argued that there are natural limits to what people can do, that people must be circumspect whenever thinking about social change, and that people should not presume that they can alter nature harmlessly. Yet the centrists were never simply cultural conservatives because they also celebrated diversity in lifestyles, equality among all social groups, feminist values, and international peace – all of which were unappealing to most conservatives (Frankland and Schnoonmaker 1992: 105, 126–9; Hülsberg 1988: 82–4, 88, 232; Markovits and Gorski 1993: 193–5; Mewes 1983: 58–61).

As we have noted, the three types of new electoral lists were not equally strong across Germany. The differences in their regional appeal partly reflected the diverse social and economic characteristics of the Länder. In Bavaria, Baden-Württemberg, and Rhineland-Palatinate – three Länder with unemployment levels considerably below the federal average and, correspondingly, with economic growth rates considerably above the federal average – conservative lists were relatively powerful and quickly formed alliances with centrist lists, especially the GLU. To some extent, this pattern occurred in Hesse as well, although it is difficult to generalize about Hessian politics because of the significance of Frankfurt's left-alternative political traditions. In more economically troubled Länder, such as Berlin, Nordrhein-Westfalen, and Lower Saxony, strong left-alternative lists appeared and usually merged with the centrist ecology lists, forming broad 'rainbow coalitions'. In the two poorest Länder, the Saar and Schleswig-Holstein, none of the three types of new lists gained much strength, partly because of the ideological flexibility of the local SPD branches, which quickly adopted many of the themes of the ecological and left-alternative lists (Frankland and Schoonmaker 1992: 74–82; Markovits and Gorski 1993: 102, 190–8, 208–17, 219, 221, 226–9, 231, 233; Mewes 1983: 54–8).

'Ecology' provided a superficially common ground for short-lived local coalitions between Green cultural conservatives and Green ecological centrists, and between the latter and the northern Green social egalitarians. Members of all three ideological camps agreed in principle that the natural environment must be protected from the federal government's unbridled commitment to economic growth. They disagreed, however, over how best to explain the government's destructiveness and progrowth orientation. Was modern industrial capitalism at fault, as the radicals tended to think; or was West Germany's secularism at fault, as the many conservatives believed; or was the problem the hegemony of masculine values, as some centrists contended? Because of their differing answers to this question, the three groups of allies frequently proposed very different economic and cultural policies. These ideological and programmatic disagreements would contribute to intra-Green feuding and ill will for almost a decade.

Competing ideological currents within the early Greens

In early 1979, AUD, GAZ, GLU, and a diverse assortment of other nonleft environmental and ecological lists formed a federal-level electoral alliance to participate in the upcoming elections for the European parliament. The effort had been spearheaded by the federal BBU, which convened a West German environmental conference to discuss possible participation in the European Economic Community (EEC). Many left-alternative lists declined the invitation to join, partly because of their principled opposition to the free-market orientation of the EEC. As a result, the new electoral coalition, which named itself the Alternative Political Alliance – Greens (SPV-Greens), adopted a strictly anti-industrial, culturally conservative programme that criticized the current materialistic culture but not capitalism per se.

The new federal-level coalition performed respectably in the June European election, receiving 90,000 votes (slightly more than 3 per cent of the total) (Fogt 1989: 100). Encouraged by the relative success (especially given the speed with which the alliance was formed), the founders of the coalition decided to participate in the forthcoming federal parliamentary elections. The ecological centrists, however, fervently believed that the coalition would attract more than 5 per cent of the voters only if it included activists from the left-alternative lists. The centrists prevailed upon the conservatives to allow left-alternative lists to join the coalition and, furthermore, to become part of the coalition's programme commission.

Inspired in part by the Bremen Green List, several local groups with socially radical programmes, such as the Hamburg Rainbow Slate and the Berlin Alternative Slate, joined the SPV-Greens. Most conservative groups, however, steadfastly opposed the entry of left groups into the coalition, and the GAZ supported a motion at a planning conference that denied conference voting rights to all individuals who remained members of communist parties or left-alternative lists. The motion was barely defeated, 348 to 311 (Fogt 1989: 101).

From June 1979 until March 1980, conservative and left forces struggled over the fate of the fledgling federal party. At the official founding congress of the Greens Party in January 1980, the ecological centrists tried to function as peacekeepers between the conservative delegates led by Gruhl, who refused on principle to sit by any communist, and the newer alternative-list members. The conservatives quickly introduced a motion to make membership in the Greens incompatible with membership in another party. The motion, if passed and implemented, would have expelled 20 per cent of the delegates present, many of whom also belonged to communist organizations. A slight majority of the delegates approved the conservatives' motion. The representatives of the alternative lists threatened to walk out, an act that would have destroyed the party. Citing federalist principles, the centrists proposed a compromise: that each state and local organization have the right to make its own decisions about whether to permit dual-party membership, but at the federal level, no policy be adopted. All political wings found this temporary resolution satisfactory. Thus, an ideologically broad Greens Party emerged, and it extended, in the saying of the time, from 'Gruhl to Dutschke'.

Two months later, the Programme Commission for the SPV-Greens, having hammered out a statement of goals, presented it to a congress of delegates for approval. The statement reflected the changing balance of power among the ideological groups composing the Greens. During construction of the platform, representatives of openly conservative groups and representatives of radical organizations had fought endlessly. The ecological centrists more often than not allied themselves with the social radicals. As a result, the document included calls for a 35-hour workweek, the dissolution of NATO and the Warsaw Pact, the unilateral disarmament of West Germany, greater legal rights for homosexuals, and abolishment of then-current antiabortion statutes (Fogt 1989: 100–7; Hülsberg 1988: 92–7; Markovits and Gorski 1993: 195–7).

At the congress, conservative delegates were outraged by the programme's numerous nonenvironmental goals, which Gruhl called a 'socialist shopping list' (Hülsberg 1988: 95) and a 'fairy tale utopia' (Mewes 1983: 62). Many left-wing observers agreed that environmental issues were conspicuously understated. *Taz*, West Germany's major alternative newspaper, stated that the programme sounded

> more like a summary list of all the demands which the left had ever articulated during the last ten years and advocated in public than like the formulation of political goals based on ecological principles.
>
> (Fogt 1989: 106)

To maintain intraparty peace, the leaders of the Greens held another congress in June to reconsider the programme. The congress approved a more moderate version of the March programme. Conservatives were still outraged, partly because Gruhl, a cochair of the earlier Euro-election coalition, was not selected to the three-person party presidium. Feeling ideologically and organizationally outmanoeuvred, leaders of GAZ and the AUD walked out. About 1,000 conservative activists subsequently left the Green Party out of a membership of about 15,000. The desertion did not mark the end of intraparty politics, however; the remaining members held a variety of opinions on proper goals and strategies (Hülsberg 1988: 95–6; Frankland and Schoonmaker 1992: 104, 127, 129–30).

After the conservatives left the new party in 1980, four ideological currents quickly evolved. Advocates for the different currents organized themselves in semi-independent groups, such as the Green Forum, Group Z, and New Beginning '88, that held their own meetings and published their own magazines and manifestos (Frankland and Schoonmaker 1992: 110–15; Hill 1985: 37; Hülsberg 1988: 177).

One small but very vocal group of Greens advocated a position that became popularly known as 'ecolibertarianism'. Ecolibertarians adopted many of the culturally conservative ideas earlier articulated by Gruhl. Like Gruhl, they were hostile to the presence of current and former communists within the Green party-movement. Ecolibertarians, furthermore, warned other Green activists to be cautious about cooperating with the SPD, whose traditionally liberal spending policies and excessive cooperation with the United States had dangerously weakened West Germany's culture and international status. Ecolibs (a common nickname) also maintained that state economic planning and large-scale business organizations were responsible for the destruction of the environment and that a free-market system and local self-help projects would yield a much healthier society. According to ecolibertarians, the Greens, when thinking about potential legislative alliances, should consider the CDU/CSU, whose cautious outlook and Christian values naturally complemented the Greens' vision of a nonmaterialistic culture and society. Moreover, the Greens should increase their programmatic and policy appeals to farmers and other self-employed petit-bourgeois producers, whose spirit of independence dovetailed naturally with the Greens' proclaimed antihierarchical and antistate values (Frankland and Schoonmaker 1992: 89, 140; Hülsberg 1985: 24–5; Hülsberg 1988: 148–9; Markovits and Gorski 1993: 145–7).

The so-called ecosocialists constituted a second ideological current and involved many more Green activists than did ecolibertarianism. Like ecolibertarians, ecosocialists sometimes advocated building coalitions with other political parties and organized social groups. However, unlike the ecolibs, the ecosocialists viewed industrial labour and the SPD as the Greens' most promising potential allies. They contended that the industrial working class remained a powerful force for change because of its numbers, its organization, and its increasing discontent amid a stagnating and increasingly impersonal market economy. If the Greens vigorously pursued policies that benefited wage earners in concrete ways, such as passage of a mandatory 35-hour workweek and a legal ban on lockouts, then workers would feel grateful to the Greens, desert the SPD for their benefactors, and provide the Greens with sufficient electoral clout to remake German society. Therefore, one ecosocialist argued,

> The Greens must not abstain from the fight against mass unemployment and against cuts in social welfare for pensioners, young people and unemployed, but must actively join in and help to lead this fight.
>
> (Hülsberg 1988: 151)

The ecosocialists also believed that the Greens had to educate workers about the ecological dangers of current social arrangements. Workers (both employed and unemployed) are unsophisticated victims of bourgeois culture and its celebration of consumption. Tired by uncreative, repetitive labour and goaded by carefully crafted advertising, workers devour unneeded commodities – especially technological gadgetry – without concern for the waste left behind. The decentralization of modern life and increased worker participation in production decisions and community affairs would bring about a more altruistic spirit in the working class because wage earners would begin to enjoy work and to perceive how they themselves impact on their surroundings. This cognitive and moral conversion, in turn, would lead to a further transformation of politics and society, as workers began to adopt new and more humanistic and ecological values when evaluating social arrangements and acting in politics. Thus, radical decentralization and democratization of production was a necessary first step toward broader cultural and institutional transformation (Hülsberg 1988: 149–52, 189; Markovits and Gorski 1993: 147–50).

Advocates of a third ideological current were often known as realists (or realos). Realists viewed the SPD as a potential ally (at least on the national level) and, like most ecosocialists, advocated defending industrial workers' concrete interests. Realists therefore endorsed laws that increased job security, reduced the workweek, and promoted higher wages. But whereas the ecosocialists often viewed workers as a potentially revolutionary population, the realos, concurring with the New Left ideas of Herbert Marcuse, doubted that a fundamental transformation of society could be spearheaded by the proletariat. They viewed industrial workers as consumption-oriented, wage-focused, and, therefore, socially conservative. In their opinion, the more socially marginal groups in the society – such as immigrant workers, the chronically unemployed, the homeless, gays and lesbians, and women – would be more likely to support a programme of radical social change.

The realos argued that in order to mobilize marginalized populations, the Greens should adopt a strategy called radical reformism. The strategy involved winning elective offices and then skilfully using the offices to channel benefits to marginalized populations. If the legal rights and standards of living of socially marginal groups were increased through progressive legislation, these groups – whose values and lifestyles differed greatly from those celebrated by 'polite' bourgeois society – would soon culturally diversify the country and then surreptitiously and peacefully contribute to the emergence of a new society. The realos repeatedly proclaimed that a social revolution could not be forced upon unwilling West Germans but would have to arise gradually from a cultural transformation. Furthermore, such a transformation could be initiated only by groups on the fringe of bourgeois society.

The reasoning of the realos: to help socially marginal groups survive and organize, the Greens must forge alliances with other mainstream political forces wherever and whenever possible and then jointly press for enabling legislation. In the immediate circumstances, the application of a strategy of radical reformism meant that the Greens should build bridges with the SPD, for the CDU/CSU more often than not was indifferent to marginal groups and often reproved countercultural groups for their 'corrupt' values.

To cooperate legislatively with SPD, the realos posited, the Greens must eschew revolutionary rhetoric and avoid disruptive actions that might anger or embarrass SPD allies. The realos conceded that to the untrained eye such restrained political behaviour and speech might seem nonrevolutionary and a sellout of principles. Not at all. Significant change comes one small step at a time and, specifically, through the gradual construction of alternative milieus and subcultures. Openly confrontational behaviour, although perhaps attention getting, would neither truly help the marginal groups nor change the world. Therefore, as one realo leader put it, if the Greens truly wished to remake the bankrupt order, they should become 'the natural junior partner of the SPD' (Hülsberg 1985: 23; see also Hülsberg 1988: 145–6; Markovits and Gorski 1993: 142–4).

The strategy of radical reformism espoused by the realos contrasted sharply with the views of the so-called fundamentalists (fundis) who deemed electoral activity, alliance building, and legislative reform inherently futile. The West German state was controlled not through elections, but through government officials' prejudices, through special-interest lobbying, and through political constraints imposed by economic dependency on foreign powers. Because of these processes, state officials and the leaders of the SPD, the FDP, and the CDU/CSU would always seek rapid economic growth, cooperation with the United States, and export-oriented capitalism. Greens could not place their faith in alliances with the SPD, for the SPD, whatever it had been in the past, was no longer a progressive force that seriously challenged capitalism. According to one fundi theorist,

> If we want to build ourselves up to be the junior partner of the SPD then we may as well hand in our weapons now. Then we would no longer stand for the radical reversal of the capitalist industrial system, destructive on a world scale and internally destructive, but rather for some eco-reformist tinkering with the 'German model'.
>
> (Hülsberg 1988: 147)

Most fundis agreed with the realos that given industrial workers' shortsighted love of material comfort and electronic gadgetry, organized labour was an unreliable ally. But whereas the realos placed their faith in state aid to socially marginal populations, most fundis instead contended that West Germany could change only if the new social movements (that is, the new women's movement, the new peace movement, and the new antinuclear movement) taught West Germans (especially middle-class citizens) about the dangers of their cultural and economic situation. Once educated, the citizens would energetically participate in large demonstrations that pressure government officials into changing policies. Consciousness-raising activities by social movements – including mass rallies, media events, and hunger strikes – would provide the kindling for a revolutionary change, and cautious and moderate parliamentary politics would perpetuate the status quo.

The fundis argued that Greens should work alongside the new social movements and function as their legislative leg. Any Green elected to public office should use that office primarily as a bully pulpit from which to denounce the evils of the status quo (just as the new social movements used bookstores and rallies to educate about social dangers). In press releases and parliamentary speeches, Green officials should make a practice of exposing the intrigues and misconduct of the governing parties and the often unstated costs of current policies, even if the revelations jeopardize alliance building. The likely loss of legislative allies would not be of great consequence in any case, for none of the major parties is committed to changing the culture and society. Only by informing the citizenry about the daily wrongdoings of the ruling parties, would the Greens be able to change the course of West German history (Boggs 1986: 872–82; Dobson 1990: 138–9, 143–5, 166, 191; Hülsberg 1985: 11–12, 24; Hülsberg 1988: 146–8; Markovits and Gorski 1993: 119–41).

Different ideological tendencies predominated in different parts of Germany. The ecolibertarians were influential primarily in the cities and towns of Baden-Württemberg; the ecosocialists' strongholds were Berlin and Hamburg; the realos were most visible and influential in Hesse and Lower Saxony; and the fundis, while visible everywhere, were particularly strong in Frankfurt. The striking geographic concentrations of diverse Green factions have prompted some political analysts to describe the Greens as 'the most regionally diverse of West Germany's political parties' (Frankland and Schoonmaker 1992: 154; see also Scharf 1995). Leaders of the new federal-level party, in the meantime, tried to make a virtue of the obvious ideological diversity (if not confusion) by utilizing such slogans as 'Unity in Diversity' and 'Neither Right nor Left but Forward'.

Searching for a common programme

Despite profound differences in thinking among the myriad local groups that composed the Green party-movement, nationwide leaders repeatedly attempted to devise a coherent programme for change, especially on the eve of federal elections. To many observers' surprise, the federal programmes gave relatively little space to environmental issues (Frankland and Schoonmaker 1992: 127, 129; Kolinsky 1984: 304–5; Markovits and Gorski 1993: 152, 174–5, 332; Mewes 1983: 63). Instead, they addressed issues of social justice, labour rights, personal freedoms, and international peace. As the 1980 preamble to the Green party programme put it, the Greens did not see themselves as a ' "single-issue party" which concentrates exclusively on the environment', but as a party concerned with 'all essential areas of human existence in our society and in the entire world' (Schoonmaker 1988: 69).

Most of the Greens' federal programmes loosely linked arguments currently made by ecosocialists, fundis, and realos and with earlier ideas pioneered by the spontis, SDS, JUSO, and new social movements. A common theme was the need to replace modern West German 'capitalism' (broadly understood to include a mind-set oriented toward the accumulation of material resources), which encourages war, unemployment, and the rape of nature. Short-term, piecemeal, and small-scale actions, such as the development and refinement of fuel-efficient automobile engines, are, by themselves, too little and too late. What was needed was a total reorganization of West Germany's big-business and export-based economy, its growth-oriented politics, and its materialist and consumerist culture. In the words of the 1983 Green programme (Die Grünen 1983: 6), 'A radical reorganization of our short-sighted economic rationality is essential.'

According to the authors of the Greens' federal programmes, West Germans (and residents of North America and Europe in general) were destroying their habitat for two profound and analytically distinct reasons. First, modern European and Anglo-American culture, at least as far back as the Enlightenment, had celebrated humans' scientific mastery of nature and arrogantly had presumed that *Homo sapiens* has the unlimited right to consume the earth's resources. Raised in this cultural environment, Europeans and North Americans irreverently have (mis)treated nature as a convenience, rather than treasured and protected it.

Modern forms of capitalism (characterized by enormous firms, bureaucratic and impersonal modes of production, and close ties between owners of large enterprises and the state) reinforce this cultural predisposition in numerous, subtle ways. Owners of competitive big businesses, to reduce costs and increase profits, produce environmentally harmful goods and indifferently dump waste. They also try to lure people into buying more than they need. At the same time, the mind-numbing, fast-paced, and highly specialized industrial production process creates subconscious desires in wage earners to add excitement to their lives, and in consequence they consume excessive amounts of mass-produced and environmentally harmful goods. To gain even more profits, private companies lobby the state for expenditures on unneeded big-ticket items, such as motorways and airport expansions, and for international economic policies that give companies privileged access to foreign markets and allow extraction of nonreplaceable raw materials at minimal cost.

Interpreting immediate ecological problems as inextricably linked to the economic order, the Greens' federal programmes concluded that to escape the impending ecological disaster, West Germany's state-aided corporate capitalism must be destroyed. Large private enterprises should, as soon as possible, be divided into smaller units of production to be comanaged by their workers and by local communities. This could be done through various methods, including government subsidies and tax incentives for small firms. In addition, the government should redistribute unused land and abandoned plants and buildings to fledgling cooperative firms. The authors of the federal programmes argued that if small-scale and cooperative production were widespread, there would be a chance that the environmental crisis could be avoided; for such production, partly because of intimacy among producers, would serve to remind workers of their immediate impact on surrounding nature. Also, self-directed work would be more pleasurable and rewarding, reducing and perhaps eliminating workers' need for psychic compensation via the ownership of a plethora of material goods (such as plastic gadgets) of little real utility and much disutility (Capra and Spretnak 1984: 43, 83–5, 88–90, 100–1; Dobson 1990: 123, 126–7; Frankland and Schoonmaker 1992: 130, 134–5; Hülsberg 1985: 11; Hülsberg 1988: 125–6; 183–5; Markovits and Gorski 1993: 159, 166–7; Mewes 1983: 64–5; Schoonmaker 1988: 51).

The Greens' programmes further recommended that the West German central government in the short run regulate the production and sales of goods so as to prevent economically induced threats to human health and the environment. This would require in some policy areas a much more interventionist state than existed and perhaps additional government agencies. Some federal-Green programmes, for example, called for creation of a ministry of environment with powers to enforce antipollution laws on land and sea (Capra and Spretnak 1984: 35; Frankland and Schoonmaker 1992: 130; Mewes 1983: 64). Almost all Green programmes also called for closer government regulation of fishing and the chemical industries, a ban on the manufacture and export of toxic substances, greater regulation of the health-care industry, and a ban on the use of marketing techniques for unnecessary medicines and hospitalizations. Research connected to genetic engineering, regardless if publicly or privately funded, should be outlawed. Short-distance air travel, because of damage to the environment, also should be banned, and public transportation and alternatives to automobiles promoted. Government officials should lead by example during their travels and be more environmentally aware in all activities. In addition, all levels of government should vigorously promote both the manufacture of nonplastic goods and the construction of energy-efficient housing (Capra and Spretnak 1984: 91–3, 121–2; Frankland and Schoonmaker 1992: 135; Hülsberg 1988: 190, 193; Markovits and Gorski 1993: 155–6, 162, 176, 179, 203–4; Mewes 1983: 65–6).

According to most Green federal programmes, the West German government, in addition to regulating private businesses, should play a more active role in educating citizens about the products they consume. To break the hold of the print media and mass advertising over the minds of West Germans, the government should promote and protect small independent newspapers and should also strictly regulate television promotion for unhealthy products and prohibit radio advertisements for cigarettes, sweets, alcohol, pesticides, and artificial fertilizers (Capra and Spretnak 1984: 92, 122, 124; Die Grünen 1983: 11).

Although the authors of the federal programmes did not advocate the creation of common property (and in fact at times endorsed the principles of private property and of a nonregulated market economy), they did recommend that the government – to ensure that all West Germans enjoyed both a dignified standard of living and spiritually elevating work – guarantee a minimum income for the worker (and even the person out of work). They also recommended reduction of income differentials, partly on the grounds that relatively large incomes permit the purchase of wasteful consumer goods and fuel conspicuous consumption. To prevent further job losses in the private sector, the federal programmes recommended closer government regulation of labour-saving technology. They also recommended that the government legislate a shorter, 35-hour workweek and eliminate overtime, in order to facilitate job sharing. The Greens recommended, too, that the state retrain at public cost all persons who have lost jobs because of automation; trainees would receive full pay until appropriate new employment was found (Capra and Spretnak 1984: 97–8; Frankland and Schoonmaker 1992: 127, 132; Hülsberg 1985: 12; Hülsberg 1988: 125, 129–30, 193, 195; Markovits and Gorski 1993: 161, 162, 164–5, 177–8; Mewes 1983: 65).

The authors of the Greens' federal programmes acknowledged that most of the legislative proposals probably would not be passed by the existing federal and Land governments, primarily because of opposition by other parties. Consequently, they repeatedly called for radical decentralization of the political order, so that the people who suffer directly from the economic and the environmental costs of the status quo would have a larger say in the making of public policy. Ideally, public policy should be made at the town and neighbourhood levels, and each local community should decide its own service policies for the unemployed, the homeless, children and youths, the elderly, the sick, and the poor. Radical decentralization, Green programmes asserted, would result in more progressive legislation; in small communities where people know one another, environmental and human values would have greater weight in policy making than they do in bureaucratic nation-states, where the goal of large-scale economic growth constantly overrides other concerns (Capra and Spretnak 1984: 47–9, 94; Markovits and Gorski 1993: 161; Mewes 1983: 64).

Although Green programmes called for greater political and economic decentralization, they also, as we have seen, prescribed a larger role for the nation state both in regulating big business and in influencing consumer behaviour. A sceptic might ask: wouldn't this state-centred 'solution' create its own problems? After all, given the antiecological propensities of most government officials, why assume that they would change course without missing a beat? How should any errant government official be disciplined? Who should regulate the regulators?

The federal programmes' usual counterargument was that the power of an abusive centralized state could be effectively constrained through citizens' street politics (including political strikes and other nonviolent forms of protest) and through citizens' legal rights to call referenda and to initiate judicial proceedings against government officials. West Germany's current Basic Law hamstrung citizens' activities and limited their political rights. New laws were needed that would greatly expand political rights (including rights of assembly and speech) for all citizens and especially the chronically poor, foreign workers, and prisoners, who are normally defenceless before the state. Foreign workers, for example, should immediately have the right to vote in local elections and, after five years of residence, the right to vote in federal elections. Citizens should vigilantly protect current rights to demonstrate and petition, despite elites' current fears of terrorism. Concerned about the apparent misuse of judicial processes for partisan and political purposes, the federal programmes of the Greens also proposed extensive judicial and penal reforms, including the reduction of prison terms and doing away with life sentences (Capra and Spretnak 1984: 106, 114–15, 122–3; Frankland and Schoonmaker 1992: 131, 137; Hülsberg 1988: 132–3, 189; Markovits and Gorski 1993: 181–2; Mewes 1983: 62–3; Schoonmaker 1988: 52–4).

Even though the Greens' programmes emphasized domestic social and political issues, they also addressed foreign-policy issues, especially Germany's entangling military alliances. The authors of the programmes repeatedly declared that the overarching goal of foreign policy should be neither international military status nor greater access to foreign markets, but the protection of all nature (including human life). Mistrustful of nuclear weapons, the authors advocated West Germany's immediate disengagement from the Cold War, withdrawal from NATO, dismantling of the standing army, and revocation of the permission given to foreign countries to station military units on German soil. The programmes expressed profound faith in the possibility of human communities coexisting without reliance on military deterrence. In theory, if a peaceful, nonarmed community were ever invaded by another country, the 'victims' could efficiently expel the occupiers by forming local strike committees, by engaging in social ostracism, and by spontaneously practicing noncompliance in the workplace. The endless stalling at work, the daily snubbing of the occupiers and their families, the overloading of the occupiers' administrative capacities, and the creation of economic shortages and production bottlenecks would quickly force a withdrawal because of the enormous costs of staying (Capra and Spretnak 1984: 61–6, 102–3, 184–5; Frankland and Schoonmaker 1992: 130, 131–2, 136; Hülsberg 1988: 195–6; Markovits and Gorski 1993: 173; Mewes 1983: 66–7, 74–7, 84–5).

In explaining why costly wars were occurring in the late twentieth century, the federal programmes usually pointed to the United States as a culprit and interpreted its international aggressiveness as a consequence of both spiritual corruption and economic practices – in particular, its pathological culture of consumption and technology and immoderate commitment to enormous profits and high wages.

Authors of the federal programmes, especially during the last half of the 1980s, generally interpreted military actions by other nation-states, such as the Soviet Union, as acts of self-defence before the expansionist policies of the United States (although some Green theorists, such as Petra Kelly, viewed all large nation-states as inherently expansionist and therefore prone to war) (Capra and Spretnak 1984: 48, 60–2; Markovits and Gorski 1993: 169–73; Mewes 1983: 73–7, 84–5).

The federal programmes advocated that West Germany aid Third World countries in their struggles to protect their environments and indigenous traditions of production from international corporations in general and from US companies in particular. More specifically, the federal programmes recommended suspension of current international debts for Third World countries and transformation of the World Bank into a set of development funds for Africa, Asia, and Latin America. The West German government, meanwhile, should increase its aid to the Third World 'to at least 0.7% of GNP' (Die Grünen 1983: 28). Viewing many Third World governments as superpower puppets, the federal programmes also endorsed peaceful support of all national liberation movements and the 'creation of opportunities for the Third World countries to disconnect themselves from the world market, which has proved to be more of a hindrance than a help' (Die Grünen 1983: 29; see also Capra and Spretnak 1984: 63–6, 102–3; Frankland and Schoonmaker 1992: 130–1; Hülsberg 1988: 196; Markovits and Gorski 1993: 184–5; Mewes 1983: 66–7).

As the 1990s progressed, feminist themes became increasingly prominent in the federal programmes (although numerous observers, including women within the Green Party, have questioned the dedication of male members to feminist causes) (Capra and Spretnak 1984: 151–3; Kolinsky 1989). From the outset, the Greens' national programmes advocated the use of explicit quotas in all new employment and job-training programmes and equal vocational training for boys and girls. The programmes also advocated passage of novel job-protection laws that would allow men as well as women to participate in infant rearing for up to 18 months with full pay. Men's participation in child care was partly defended on pedagogic grounds. In theory, by nurturing children, men would acquire desired feminine values and outlooks – including kindness, selflessness, and a spirit of cooperation. Such cultural development would help end the predominance of capitalist values and Enlightenment thought and its hostility to nature. Further, the federal programmes advocated a richer understanding of personal rights within the family, denounced government discrimination against lesbian households and other nontraditionally structured families, and called for strictly enforced laws against marital rape (Capra and Spretnak 1984: 49–53, 108–14; Frankland and Schoonmaker 1992: 136–7, 138, 144; Markovits and Gorski 1993: 165–6, 179–81).

Electoral successes

The federal programmes were not endorsed with equal enthusiasm by all Green organizations. Many groups at the Land and local levels viewed the programmes as interesting but largely irrelevant, and as suggestive but not binding. A few Green chapters disbanded over the federal programmes' proabortion stance. Moreover, all Land organizations had their own programmes that they autonomously drafted. The 1983 programme for Hamburg Greens, for example, denounced parliamentary politics as a method for social transformation and called for greater involvement in street demonstrations, where allegedly real change could be made (Kolinsky 1984: 304; Papadakis 1984: 178–83).

The Greens' multiple programmes, aims and priorities may help explain the party-movement's success in attracting large numbers of voters, for by the mid-1980s Green slates routinely received over 5 per cent of the vote in federal elections and in elections for most Länder. As mentioned before, a local alternative slate first broke the 5 per cent barrier in the city-state of Bremen in 1979. Shortly thereafter, the Greens received respectively 5.3 per cent, 7.2 per cent, 6.5 per cent, 7.9 per cent, and 8 per cent of the votes in the Land elections in Baden-Württemberg (1980), West Berlin (1981), Lower Saxony (1982), Hamburg (1982), and Hesse (1982). The Greens captured 5.6 per cent of the vote in the 1983 federal election and became the first party in three decades to break the SPD's, FDP's, and CDU/CSU's monopoly on seats in the West German Bundestag.

After 1983 the Greens continued to perform respectably in state and federal elections, and won seats in the parliaments of all Länder except for Saarland and Schleswig-Holstein. In 1985 and 1986 the party-movement captured more than 10 per cent of the ballots cast in Land elections in Berlin and Hamburg. The zenith of the Greens' success probably occurred in 1987, when the party-movement won 8.3 per cent of the ballots cast in the federal elections, 10.2 per cent in Bremen's Land elections, and 5.9 per cent in Rhineland-Palatinate (where it gained representation in the state parliament for the first time) (Frankland 1989: 69–71; Frankland and Schoonmaker 1992: 68–71).

The Greens matched their strong showings in federal and Land elections with victories in local elections. During the early 1980s, Green candidates won seats on councils in scores of towns and districts (the jurisdictional size and administrative responsibilities of a German district are roughly comparable to those of a US or British county). These early wins encouraged individuals and groups in nearby towns to imitate and form their own 'Green' slates and other alternative lists. In Hesse, for example, the Green Party participated in only 36 local elections in 1981; in 1985 Green lists appeared in 186 of Hesse's 421 local communities (Scharf 1989: 172). In 1981 less than 2 per cent of council seats in all West German communities with over 20,000 inhabitants were held by representatives of the Green party-movement; in 1986, 7 per cent of the council seats were held by Greens (Scharf 1994: 72). By the close of the 1980s, approximately 6,000 Green activists held local-level elective offices throughout West Germany (Roth 1991: 75).

Who voted for the new party-movement? Most studies of the Green electorate have examined the social backgrounds and attitudes of voters in federal elections. Far less is known about typical Green voters in local elections.

A common finding is that people who voted for the Greens were generally younger adults. According to opinion surveys, approximately 70 per cent of Green voters were 34 or younger – an age group that accounted for only about 30 per cent of the entire electorate (Frankland and Schoonmaker 1992: 87; Hülsberg 1988: 114). Although the Greens seldom won more than 8 per cent of all ballots cast in federal elections during the 1980s, they usually received between 15 and 25 per cent of the total young-adult vote (Bürklin 1987: 113; Frankland 1989: 71–2).

Many people who voted for the Greens were well educated. According to one study, approximately 10 per cent of Green voters were professional academics, and an additional 20 per cent were college students (Hülsberg 1988: 115). Authors of another study conclude that although approximately 10 per cent of West Germany's total adult population had attended some sort of postsecondary school, more than 20 per cent of Green voters had done so (Frankland and Schoonmaker 1992: 87; see also Frankland 1989: 72; Hülsberg 1988: 114–15).

Many unemployed voters cast their ballots for Green candidates. In the words of Jens Alber (1989: 205), 'Among the unemployed, the Greens are the second strongest party, outrunning the Christian Democrats and falling short only of the Social Democrats.' Almost a fifth of all ballots for Green candidates were cast by unemployed voters (Hülsberg 1988: 113). Many of the unemployed voters were also well educated, leading some scholars to speculate that these voters may have been part of West Germany's so-called 'new poor', who despite years of higher education either could not find steady work or could only find work that was not commensurate with their skills. Again to quote Alber (1989: 205),

> Among unemployed academics voting for the Greens is found seven times more frequently than in the population. The typical supporter of the Greens, we may conclude, is young, highly trained, and unemployed or not economically active. This makes the Greens appear as a party of frustrated academic plebeians rather than as an organization of the educated new leading strata of post-industrial societies.

Many employed white-collar and middle-management workers also voted for the Greens during the 1980s. Approximately 53 per cent of all Green voters were working professionals, which is slightly higher than the proportion of working professionals in the population at large (48 per cent) (Hülsberg 1988: 115). Among major parties, only the FDP had a larger proportion of its voters come from full-time workers than did the Greens (Hülsberg 1988: 115). As one scholar puts it, the Greens did 'well in labour market segments with very low and very high job security' (Poguntke 1992a: 343).

Approximately 40 per cent of the people who cast ballots for the Greens lived in big cities (where approximately 30 per cent of the West German population lived). In addition, Green candidates received large numbers of votes in some medium-size towns (especially those with colleges) and in some rural areas affected by recent government projects, such as proposed nuclear plants and airport expansions (Frankland and Schoonmaker 1992: 76; Hülsberg 1988: 116; Rothacher 1984: 113). Eva Kolinsky (1984: 317–18), noting the Greens' ability to capitalize on local environmental issues in selected rural communities, writes that the Greens 'are not just a party for university students and critical intellectuals'. In the early 1980s the Greens managed to break into small towns, rural areas and win a more diverse group of older voters: indeed, they won about one third of their electorate in this way. Who would have thought that the Bavarian hamlet of Neufahrn near Freising would have 9.8% Green voters?

Compared to voters for the other three major established parties, significantly higher percentages of Green voters (1) had previously participated in protests and demonstrations and (2) had participated in the ecology, the antinuclear, or the peace movement. According to one public opinion survey, approximately two-thirds of self-reporting Green voters had been active in the antinuclear movement, and two-thirds in the peace movement. In contrast, less than a quarter of SPD voters and less than a seventh of all CDU/CSU voters reported supporting the antinuclear movement, and less than half of SPD voters and less than a third of CDU/CSU voters participated in the peace movement. In another survey, 18.9 per cent of the sample of Green voters stated that they had participated in at least one illegal demonstration, compared to 2.1 per cent of SPD voters, 1.9 per cent of FDP voters, and 0.2 per cent of CDU/CSU voters (Hülsberg 1988: 109; Poguntke 1992b: 251–3).

According to public-opinion surveys, people who voted for Green candidates tended to criticize current social conditions and tended to be pessimistic about current social trends. For example, one opinion survey showed that large majorities of Green voters believed that West Germany (1) was insufficiently concerned with tolerance; (2) was insufficiently concerned with social justice, and (3) was insufficiently concerned with equality between men and women, whereas less than half of those who voted for each of the other major parties held such beliefs. Another poll asked respondents if modern technology hurts more than it helps humanity. Almost four-fifths of the respondents who voted for Green candidates agreed with the statement; less than half of the sample for the entire West German population expressed comparable scepticism toward technology. In a third survey, less than half of the sample representing the entire West German population but more than 70 per cent of the sample representing Green voters said that they expected economic conditions in Germany to worsen in the immediate future (Hülsberg 1988: 110, 112–13).

Scholars, noting some of the above data about the social backgrounds and attitudes of Green voters, have developed myriad explanations for the Greens' electoral performances in the 1980s. One can discern at least three lines of argument.

First, some scholars, such as Robert Inglehart (1990) and Herbert Kitschelt (1988), have viewed the Greens' success among younger adults as a manifestation of a historically new cultural phenomenon commonly known as 'postmaterialism'. Scholars who argue along this line note that after the Second World War and the Great Depression, North American and western European societies experienced four decades of steady and rapid economic growth, during which the average standard of living dramatically rose. In theory, a new cultural orientation inadvertently spread because of the impact of successive decades of peace and prosperity on childhood experiences. Most people born after 1950 do not remember a terrifying struggle for physical survival comparable to the Great Depression or the Second World War. Freed since birth from such worries, postwar generations have acquired a distinctive outlook on life – one that emphasizes 'postmaterialist' goals, such as personal creativity and self-expression, and that de-emphasizes 'materialist' concerns, such as worldly possessions and high incomes. In the 1980s disproportionately large numbers of younger adults cast their ballots for Green candidates because, of all West German parties, the Greens most insistently demanded protection of the natural environment and most creatively called for a radically decentralized and participatory economy and polity. The Greens, in other words, endorsed a postmaterialist programme and therefore appealed to younger generations of voters with a new orientation toward life. According to postmaterialist theorists, the Greens should continue to win sizeable numbers of younger voters (1) so long as Germany's prosperity persists; (2) so long as the Greens advocate a postmaterialist agenda, and (3) so long as the other major parties remain committed to older, materialist values.

A second common argument about the Greens' electoral ascendancy can be labelled the 'labour-market' perspective and has been articulated by Jens Alber (1989), Wilhelm Bürklin (1985, 1987, 1988) and Joyce Mushaben (1984, 1985). These authors note that the West German economy struggled during the 1970s and 1980s because of sharply rising oil prices, new foreign competitors for Germany's traditional international markets, and the worldwide trade recessions of the 1970s. Unemployment correspondingly rose to record levels for the postwar period, especially among younger workers who had recently graduated from institutions of higher education and who had hoped to find well-paid jobs in the once rapidly growing service sector. To promote economic recovery, the federal government curbed its spending, which exacerbated unemployment: now many recent college graduates could not find appropriate jobs in either the private or the public sector. Angry and disillusioned, a disproportionate number of young college-educated workers cast their ballots for the Greens because, unlike the SPD, the CDU/CSU, or the FDP, the Greens openly denounced the economic status quo and recognized that the romanticized 'model economy' benefited only two-thirds of the populace while leaving the remaining third to face a bleak economic future. In the opinion of many labour-market theorists, if and when the German economy resumes its rapid rate of growth, the Greens' share of the vote will precipitously fall. Until then, the party-movement should receive a disproportionately large share of the votes cast by Germany's well-educated but often economically frustrated younger adults.

A third set of explanations for the Greens' electoral successes can be conveniently labelled 'crisis-of-modernity' theories. Writers who have contributed to this type of argument include Robyn Eckersley (1989), Andrei Markovits and Philip Gorski (1993), and Claus Offe (1987). Crisis-of-modernity theorists begin with the assumption that the modes of production and consumption typical of advanced industrialized societies do not simply reflect and generate prosperity. They also pose some serious problems, such as excessive and spirit-numbing bureaucracy at the workplace; unprecedented technological threats to the environment; new health hazards to producers and consumers; and the creation of low-skilled, dead-end, and low-paying service-sector jobs. At the same time, the production processes of advanced industrialized societies have required the rapid expansion of higher education. This turn of events has meant that many adults now have the intellectual skills to perceive the costs of modern society, to question the desirability of current social trends, and to doubt the wisdom of public policies and political leaders. To quote Eckersley (1989: 221),

> higher education not only increases an individual's ability to acquire information but also helps to cultivate the ability to think critically, question everyday assumptions, form an independent judgement and be less influenced by the judgement of others (including those of high status).

Unlike postmaterialist theorists, crisis-of-modernity theorists declare that younger adults and older adults generally hold the same fundamental values. Greater access to higher education, however, has given a large number of younger adults the ability to see how modern social trends – for example, greater bureaucracy in the workplace – contradict long-standing Western values, such as freedom and equality. Offe (1987: 88), for example, writes,

> To start with the question of 'new' values, it could very well be claimed that what is *least* new in today's social movements is their values. There is certainly nothing new in moral demands such as the dignity and autonomy of the individual, integrity of the physical conditions of life, equality and participation, and peaceful and solidaristic forms of social organization. All these values are firmly rooted in political philosophies (as well as aesthetic theories) of the last two centuries, and they are inherited from the progressive movements of both the bourgeoisie and the working class.

According to the crisis-of-modernity approach, large numbers of young, well-educated adults voted for the Greens primarily because of its telling criticisms of modern society. Older established parties, due in part to their long-standing ties to organized labour and business, have resisted addressing social problems spawned by West Germany's postwar economy, such as shortages of affordable housing in cities, the exploitation of immigrant workers, the construction of unsafe nuclear power plants, and the regimentation of the workplace. Disenchanted with the nonresponsiveness of established parties, many young and well-educated Germans have voted for the only party that has refused to interpret postwar society through rose-coloured glasses. Furthermore, according to most crisis-of-modernity theorists, many of the social problems that beset Germany are inextricably linked to the consumerist and profit-seeking spirit of German capitalism and are unlikely to disappear in the short run. The Greens therefore should continue to receive support from large numbers of well-educated voters because the social problems posed by Germany's modern economy cannot be avoided without transforming the economy in its entirety – an unlikely change, at least for the foreseeable future.

Several scholars have noted that the postmaterialist, labour-market, and crisis-of-modernity approaches rest on strikingly different assumptions about the salient characteristics of West German history and lead to different expectations about the Greens' likely electoral fortunes. Some scholars have insisted that because the approaches are so different, one cannot accept all three approaches as true but must favour one approach and dismiss the others (Bürklin 1988; Eckersley 1989; Kitschelt 1988; Offe 1987). At least one scholar, however, has maintained that each of the so-called 'competing' theoretical approaches contains a kernel of truth. They should therefore be viewed as complementary rather than competing (Kolinsky 1984). Green voters may have included: (1) many economically secure young adults with historically novel postmaterialist values; (2) many economically insecure young adults who had attended institutions of higher education and found themselves either unemployed or underemployed, and (3) many young adults who had attended institutions of higher education and who, regardless of employment histories, were unusually cognizant of how postwar economic conditions violated long-standing Western values. If, in fact, significant numbers from all three groups of young adults supported the Greens, then all three types of explanation may merit attention.

Power and discontent

The Green electoral victories, whatever their precise sociological origins, proved a bittersweet accomplishment. Having successfully run campaigns at almost every level of government, the party-movement quickly began to unravel toward the end of the 1980s, as different wings, currents, factions, and cliques disagreed about what to do. Much of the infighting can be understood as an intensification of the long-standing ideological conflict between (1) Green activists sympathetic to the realos' position of responsible participation in government, and (2) Green activists sympathetic to the fundis' call for thoroughgoing denouncement of the status quo and greater involvement in street politics.

The fundis, led by such figures as Rudolf Bahro and Jutta Ditfurth, continued to view parliamentary politics with a suspicion bordering on hostility. They maintained that having won elected office, the Greens were entering the proverbial corrupt temple where the public good was routinely sold to private interests. The fundis wanted to throw the amoral heathens (in other words, the established parties) out. Further, they feared that Green activists, if exposed to government policy making for too long, would soon become morally corrupt and indifferent to the people's needs. Bahro, for example, stated that 'political space is a trap into which life energy disappears, indeed, where it is rededicated to the spiral of death' (Dobson 1990: 139). Other Greens similarly concluded that because a person's thinking is affected by the way she or he lives, four or more years in government office would prove spiritually debilitating. Therefore, Green activists voted into office should resign after two years and allow another, noncorrupted activist to hold the office. Rotation seemed only appropriate, given the Greens' stated commitment to local-level democracy: 'Long terms would concentrate information and power, hence are in opposition to grassroots ideals' (Capra and Spretnak 1984: 41–2).

Like the fundis, the realos – such as Joschka Fischer and Otto Schily – also looked askance at established parties. The realos, however, were qualified in their suspicions and believed that some factions within the major parties were still redeemable and therefore useful for producing radical social change. In addition, they believed that through responsible, constructive, and conscientious activity in public office, they could both rapidly increase their electoral base and attract legislative allies from other parties. Patience, diligence, and hard work would allow elected Green officials to use the West German state and to remake its society. 'Verbal radicalism' would only alienate other political groups from the Greens and prevent effective coalition building.

The newly elected Green legislators entered the federal parliament with aplomb. Ignoring traditional dress codes, they dressed in blue jeans and sweaters (except for a woman delegate who wore a man's three-piece business suit). They carried large pots of flowers to their seats, a symbolic countercomment on the aesthetic and spiritual environment of the legislative institutions. At one point they wore gas masks when debating nuclear energy.

The Green legislators, although ideologically diverse, were united primarily by electoral hopes and a strong distaste for the sociopolitical status quo. In the colourful words of Fischer, the Greens at the beginning of the 1980s constituted a

peculiar union of student missionaries of world proletarian revolution with nature lovers in their knee-socks, a union which was made possible by the recognition that by working together they could make it into parliament.

(Hülsberg 1988: 140)

Although leaders of the established parties initially grumbled that their new colleagues were ill-mannered, silly, and irresponsible, the Greens quickly acquired reputations within the parliament for being remarkably hardworking and well prepared. Between 1983 and 1987, the Green caucus submitted 367 legislative proposals, 53 bills, and 87 inquiries about executive policies and behaviour (Frankland and Schoonmaker 1992: 161–2; Markovits and Gorski 1993: 220). The Greens also initiated more topical debates than did any other parliamentary group. Granted, the federal legislature approved only one of the bills – a ban on the importation of sea turtles. Nonetheless, the Green parliamentarians doggedly pursued a public investigation into the Flick financial scandal, which ultimately brought shame to many leaders of the SPD, CDU, and FDP who were involved in a complicated system of bribes and paybacks. Green parliamentarians played a key role as well in the eventual defeat of a proposed census survey that, according to a broad range of observers, would have violated personal privacy. Perhaps most important, the Greens' constant criticisms of the placement of NATO nuclear weapons on West German soil and of the construction and relicensing of nuclear-power plants (especially after the Chernobyl disaster) struck a chord among a sizeable number of German voters.

When the 1987 federal parliamentary election was held, the Greens once again emerged victorious. In fact, the percentage of voters casting ballots for the Greens jumped from 5.6 per cent in 1983 to 8.3 per cent. The number of Green activists holding seats correspondingly increased from 27 to 44.

Regardless of the established parties' unease with the appearance and novel policy positions of the Greens, the older parties were forced to admit that the upstart party had found a way to win votes. After 1987, the SPD, CDU/CSU, and FDP began to echo a number of Green positions on environmental protection, limitations on foreign military presence, and women's rights, which irritated leaders of the new party-movement. At the same time, the CDU/CSU's and SPD's duplication of Green policy proposals, such as the legalized banning of leaded petrol and opposition to Euromissiles, was a sign of the new party's impact on the evolving political culture.

Green parliamentarians were beginning to feel hamstrung by the party's lack of policy experts. Other major parties had full-time professional researchers looking into the particulars of policy proposals. The Greens were a much more amateurish group that spoke about general priorities but had little experience in designing detailed, workable legislative proposals (Kolinsky 1984: 325). The federal parliamentarians complained in their first annual report to the Green Party at large that in numerous policy areas the party had failed to clarify adequately its positions or preferences. 'We can't launch into the particulars of parliamentary work, if we don't know where we really want to go,' they wrote (Frankland and Schoonmaker 1992: 159). The parliamentarians gradually employed more assistants and began to develop policy positions independently of the Greens' Federal Executive Board, which lacked both the time and expertise to challenge their ideas.

As they acquired de facto independence and expertise in particular policy areas, the Green parliamentarians (who came from diverse social-movement and ideological backgrounds) increasingly adopted an archetypical realo view of their functions. Of course, there were some who were said to be fundis among them, and the two ideological types of Greens occasionally hurled accusations at each other and threatened to desert the party and create an organizational rival. Nonetheless, on almost all role-call votes, the fundis and realos closed ranks and voted as one unit (Frankland and Schoonmaker 1992: 161).

A much more serious fracas developed between the parliamentarians and members of the Federal Executive Board, which was composed primarily of fundis who were alarmed by the cooperative and collaborative behaviour of the Green parliamentarians. Members of the Board wanted the parliamentarians to adopt morally unambiguous positions on policy questions, to vote against legislation that directly or indirectly clashed with any principle avowed in the federal programmes, and to abide by the wishes of the Greens' social-movement allies. The parliamentarians responded that few legislative proposals unambiguously fulfilled or violated Green programmatic positions. Rather, most policies imperfectly advanced some Green goals while delaying others. In the parliamentarians' opinion, it was their responsibility to assess the details of each piece of legislation and weigh its overall value in terms of the party's declared goals and platforms. Further, the leaders of social movements and Green activists not in parliament lacked familiarity with the details of existing and proposed legislation and therefore should not direct the parliamentarians.

The Federal Executive Board and the Green parliamentarians clearly had different ideas about the purpose of law making and about intraparty accountability. Collisions were inevitable and became frequent after the 1987 federal elections, when about two-thirds of the Greens in the parliament clearly had realo leanings (Frankland

and Schoonmaker 1992: 163). Fundis charged that the realos were 'hot to govern' and had become part of the establishment, and the realos accused the fundis of 'Stalinist practices' and of political irresponsibility and immaturity (Markovits and Gorski 1993: 225–32).

Several social-movement organizations were also troubled by the realos' refusal to back unpopular legislative proposals and to defend participants in the unruly demonstrations in which violence occurred. One coalition of German feminists, for example, wanted the Green parliamentarians to introduce legislation that would ensure a two-year mandatory jail sentence for convicted rapists. The Board and the 1988 Green Party Assembly endorsed the feminists' position, and all expected the Green parliamentarians to comply with the assembly's decision. The parliamentarians, however, argued that mandatory sentences were unwise, given the questionable procedural characteristics of the legal system and also given the Greens' stated positions on the importance of protecting the rights of criminals and reducing the sentence severity. They did not support a proposal for mandatory sentencing. Fundis in the party, shocked by the parliamentarians' independent action and refusal to be directed by the movement's representative bodies, purchased advertising space to declare that the parliamentarians no longer represented the views of the Greens' rank-and-file activists (Frankland and Schoonmaker 1992: 164; Kolinsky 1989: 202–3).

Rising violence at antinuclear demonstrations was also instrumental in pushing the realos and fundis in different directions. During the mid-1980s growing numbers of antinuclear demonstrators began to throw Molotov cocktails and use slingshots when confronting police at construction sites. Police responded with water cannons and gas (which, according to law, was not to be used against civilians). Many Greens with fundi orientations publicly defended the demonstrators' use of violence. Greens with more realo tendencies, in contrast, feared a conservative backlash among the public and refrained from defending violent acts by antinuclear protesters and from denouncing police actions. The fundis, in turn, called the realos traitors to extraparliamentary movements and servants to socially conservative voters. Meanwhile, the CDU/CSU launched vicious publicity campaigns against the Greens, accusing them of being 'child murderers' (because of their periodic calls for more liberal abortion laws), 'agents of Moscow', and 'terrorists' who generated 'chaos' and cause the 'ruin of the nation' (Hülsberg 1988: 202–3; Markovits and Gorski 1993: 213). When a Frankfurt activist was killed in 1985 on an empty crossroads by police using a water gun, the fundis demanded a general government investigation of police brutality at demonstrations. The realos, however, tried to distance themselves from the controversy and not be connected in the public eye with unruly demonstrators.

During the final years of the 1980s tensions between the fundis and the realos threatened to tear the party-movement apart as advocates of the two positions virulently attacked one another in public. Many Green activists wanted to remain neutral, and some, such as pacifist Antje Vollmer, formed organizations dedicated to finding a middle ground. Most moderates, however, became deeply disillusioned by the seemingly endless factional battles. In 1987 a group of grassroots activists entered a leadership meeting and demanded an end to the back-stabbing and squabbling. 'Your quarrels truly disgust us' shouted one activist; another declared, 'Resign or we will' (Markovits and Gorski 1993: 228).

In the summer of 1988 an unexpected scandal rocked the movement. Newspaper writers discovered that a number of fundi leaders had improperly used party funds, officially earmarked for ecological and humanitarian causes, to help like-minded activists. Loans were given with little expectation of repayment and were often put to personal use. The well-documented and widely publicized findings embarrassed members of the Greens. Numerous activists who did not ally themselves with either the fundis or the realos soon resigned. Schily and a few other realo leaders left to join the SPD. Ironically, many Greens with fundi leanings also left the party and expressed anger over other factions' lack of loyalty and respect. Scholarly research has shown that the public taunting and mutual suspicions are bitter memories for numerous former Greens, who, when interviewed, looked back on their days in the party-movement with ambivalence, disappointment, and in some cases even hatred (Markovits and Gorski 1993: 229–33, 273).

While the Greens were feuding, the SPD, FDP, and CDU/CSU continued to modify their public stances on nuclear energy, women's rights, and environmental protection. The established parties, for example, no longer unabashedly proclaimed that unlimited economic growth and international cooperation with the NATO powers were always in West Germany's best interest. All three major parties began to hold policy positions pioneered by the Greens.

The juxtaposition of the two trends – (1) the 'Greening' of the West German party system and (2) the factionalism within the Green party-movement – hobbled the Green party-movement, at least at the federal level. The Greens' failure to take seriously the possibility of German reunification (in fact, some Green leaders opposed unification on grounds that it would strengthen West Germany's status quo and contribute to latent big-nation ambitions) only exacerbated their public-image problems as they entered the 1990 federal elections. Wishing to convey to voters their relative indifference to the politics of unification, the Greens adopted the counterproductive campaign slogan 'Everybody talks about Germany, we speak about the weather' (Schoonmaker and Frankland 1993: 149).

Weakened by internal acrimony and by the major parties' adoption of selected Green policy positions, the Greens failed to win 5 per cent of the ballots cast in the 1990 federal election. About 250,000 previous Green voters chose not to vote at all, and about 600,000 former Green voters cast their ballots for the SPD (Markovits and Gorski 1993: 234). Both voters and radical activists had deserted the party-movement in droves since the 1987 elections, leaving a shell of a federal-level movement that at one time had temporarily captured the imaginations of youths and had challenged the imaginations of established groups. 'The Greens knew that they were whistling in the dark during the 1990 Bundestag campaign, but they still were *not* prepared for this eviction notice from parliament' (Schoonmaker and Frankland 1993: 137).

Resurgence in the 1990s

The Greens remained visible during the early 1990s primarily in towns and cities where they won enough votes to hold local public office. Generally behaving like realos, they formed alliances with SPD, FDP, and even the CDU/CSU in order to open women's shelters, aid the homeless, regulate road construction, and locate appropriate sites for waste disposal (Scharf 1994). They also won seats in a few Land parliaments, where they again sought alliances with the major parties. According to political scientists Gene Frankland and Donald Schoonmaker (1992: 158), by 1991 Green officials in every Land 'had either participated in a coalition with the SPD or had expressed willingness to negotiate one'.

In 1991 the party-movement held a congress to determine its future. The meeting was rowdy; no faction left satisfied. The congress adopted several realo motions, such as the controversial Declaration of Neunmünster, which declared the movement's past organization as 'chaotic' and 'nondemocratic'. The fundis captured several important nationwide offices.

After the congress, some well-known fundis, such as Jutta Ditfurth, resigned and formed rival electoral organizations. According to the separatists, the realos and the centrists, such as Antje Vollmer's group, were turning the Green party-movement into a 'petty bourgeois party of careerists' (Poguntke and Schmitt-Beck 1994: 97). Truly principled Greens therefore should form a new alternative ecological party-movement that would use any government office captured in an election as a pulpit from which to educate citizens about the structural sources of their problems, about the hypocrisy of other political parties, and about the futility of half-hearted, piecemeal reform. Green citizens should be disabused of their naive faith in the progressive potential of the economic and constitutional status quo. In Ditfurth's words, Green radicals must operate

> in a consciously disillusionary manner with regard to the actual function of the parliament, continually questioning our own representative role and by means of a process of classic disillusionment reaching the point at which the citizens no longer allow themselves to be administered, but rather increasingly represent their interests themselves.
>
> (Scharf 1994: 119–20)

The splinter groups did not attract a large number of Green activists and did very poorly in local elections. Ditfurth's group, for example, won only 0.5 per cent of the vote in the 1991 Hamburg Land elections. The resignation of several prominent radical ecologists was nonetheless significant because it reinforced the party-movement's increasingly pacific and expedient approach to politics and dampened the spirited use of extraparliamentary protest and confrontational rhetoric. In the words of Christian Joppke and Andrei Markovits (1994: 236), 'The departure of the Fundis cleared the way for the Greens to establish themselves as a reform-oriented ecology party.'

Having lost several outspoken radicals, the now more ideologically moderate Greens in 1993 joined Alliance '90, an anti-Marxist, civil-rights, and environmental-protection movement that had formed in East Germany on the eve of unification. Not all Green activists were pleased. Some resigned, troubled by the movement's apparent rightward evolution (Betz 1995: 207–8; Braunthal 1995: 41–2; Joppke and Markovits 1994: 236–7; Markovits and Gorski 1993: 260–2; Schoonmaker 1995). Other long-time Green activists were pleased by the turn of events and believed that the Green party-movement was finally shedding its utopian clothing and acting responsibly in its attempts to affect social change. To borrow a phrase from one local Green faction, the party-movement was recognizing 'the realism of taking small steps' (Scharf 1994: 123).

Activists in Alliance '90, meanwhile, uneasily eyed their West German partners. The East Germans were aware of the raucous 1991 Green party congress and feared a resurgence of the Greens' anticapitalist rhetoric, 'political kindergarten' atmosphere, 'radical chic' factions, and 'extreme' socialist and feminist goals (Betz 1995: 207; Joppke and Markovits 1994: 236). Alliance '90, however, also needed an infusion of financial and organizational resources in order to compete in future federal elections. So a marriage of electoral convenience (not ideological affection) took place.

In 1994 delegates of the expanded Alliance '90/Greens movement met in Mannheim to approve a programme for the forthcoming federal election. The election programme was heavily weighted toward classic realo positions, including a qualified statement in favour of a post-election governing coalition with the SPD. The programme, despite its realo flavour, was a compromise between the movement's two wings and accordingly oscillated in the types of goals that were endorsed. To mollify the outspoken fundi minority within the party-movement, the delegates approved the inclusion of planks calling for Germany's immediate withdrawal from NATO and for a sharp reduction in the legal workweek. To mollify more numerous socially conservative members of Alliance '90/Greens, the programme no longer called for the dismantling of big business and the nation-state or for the establishment of local, highly participatory democratic communities (demands commonly found in Green programmes during the 1980s).[2]

After the Greens and Alliance '90 negotiated their common programme and launched their campaigns, some observers of German politics began to argue that the Greens had discarded almost completely their earlier radical beliefs and had been co-opted into becoming a conventional part of the German party system. Peter Pulzer (1995: 180), for instance, wrote that 'the Greens emerged more and more as pillars rather than subverters of the system'. Gerard Braunthal (1995: 41) similarly insisted that 'Having shed much of its radical image, the party was on its way to becoming the FDP of the late 1990s.' Hans-Georg Betz (1995: 217) contended that 'Yesterday's antiparty party has turned into "a normal bourgeois party".' David Kramer (1994: 231) wrote,

> Pity the fate of the graying Greens. . . . The 'anti-party' that emerged in the late 1970s and early 1980s as a synonym for youthful vigor has become just another political party – nearly as boring and encrusted as the old-line parties.

Such statements contain a kernel of truth, for the movement in general had ceased to call for a complete and immediate overhaul of the political, economic, and cultural status quo. Such broad statements also exaggerate. True, an anti-capitalist critique of Germany's environmental problems was far less prominent in Green speeches and writings. Still, compared to activists in other major parties, most Greens battled for environmental-protection measures, women's rights, and the extension of citizenship to guest workers to an unusual degree. Furthermore, the Greens' ongoing electoral campaigns and indefatigable investigations of government misdeeds had compelled Germany's major parties to adopt several Green positions or to risk losing the votes of younger German citizens. Major parties began passing laws in policy areas that no one had addressed in the glory days of the German Model. Take conservation: 'As a direct consequence of the Greens' engagement, the Federal Republic developed the strictest environmental protection laws anywhere in the world' (Joppke and Markovits 1994: 235). Green challenges in subnational elections similarly had transformed local-level policy agendas and debates. World peace, women's rights, and guest workers' treatment became common topics in town-council meetings and local elections. Thomas Scharf (1994: 112) points out, 'Even the naming of warships after towns and cities has become a contentious issue in German local politics under the influence of the Greens.'

The Greens absence from federal politics was short-lived. The party-movement soon regained its electoral momentum at the federal level (*perhaps* because of the expanded party-movement's less radical sounding programmes). The party-movement received more than 7 per cent of the ballots cast in the 1994 election for the federal parliament. The Greens also did well in the 1994 elections for the EEC parliament, winning 10.1 per cent of the vote (the movement's best ever result in a nationwide election).

The Greens were especially successful in attracting large numbers of voters in western Länder. For example, in Lower Saxony's 1994 Landstag election, the Greens attained their highest electoral success to date (7.4 per cent of the vote). The party-movement also won at least 10 per cent of the vote in elections in Bremen (1995), Hesse (1995), and Hamburg (1993).

The Greens, however, failed to make inroads in Länder that formerly had been part of the German Democratic Republic. For example, in the 1994 national election, Alliance '90/Greens received approximately 8 per cent of the vote in western Germany, but less than 4 per cent in eastern Germany. Relatively poor showings also occurred in Land elections: Alliance '90/Greens failed to clear the 5 per cent hurdle in the 1994 Land elections for Saxony and Brandenburg (whereas Alliance '90 had won 5.6 and 9.2 of the vote in each Land in 1990). By the end of 1995, members of Alliance '90/Greens held seats in only one Landstag in the former GDR (although the Greens had won seats in all but one Landstag in the former FDR).[3]

The spatial maldistribution of support for Alliance '90/Greens reignited debate within the party-movement over programmes, strategies, and tactics. The fundi minority once again asked whether diluting the movement's originally more radical demands for an immediate and far-ranging transformation of German society and politics (1) attracted significant numbers of disgruntled voters from other parties; (2) repelled significant numbers of voters dissatisfied with the status quo (such as radical feminists and former spontis), and (3) squandered opportunities to educate the electorate about social issues and alternatives. Meanwhile, a surprisingly vocal minority within the movement began criticizing its leadership for overstressing protection of the environment and civil liberties during election campaigns, when the electorate (especially voters in the economically depressed Länder of eastern Germany) seemed much more interested in 'material' problems, such as the unusually high unemployment and widespread business closings in the eastern Länder.

Despite ongoing internal disagreements over goals, strategies, and tactics, the Green party-movement has continued to receive significant percentages of the vote in federal, Land, and local elections. Some critics of the party-movement may be correct when they insist that a certain ideological 'greying' has taken place. Over time, activists with more pragmatic and incrementalist orientations have acquired a larger voice in the party-movement's policy making, and the Greens have come to resemble more a conventional party than a pathbreaking movement. Still, the Greens have retained factions and wings militantly opposed to the political and economic status quo. Furthermore, it is not beyond the realm of possibility that the party-movement's fundamentalist current may from time to time recover its early influence. If it does, then the Greens may once again significantly alter the terms of ideological debate in Germany and, in the vivid phrase of Frankland and Schoonmaker (1992: 232), add 'a dash of colour, unconventionality, and high principle' to German politics.

Notes

1. See, for example, Fogt (1989), Frankland and Schoonmaker (1992), Hill (1985), Hülsberg (1988), and Markovits and Gorski (1993).
2. Although the overall tone of the programme was nonradical, the partial concessions to the fundis generated heated debate. Several realo leaders insisted that the proposed repudiation of NATO and the advocacy of a radically shortened workweek would drive away ideologically moderate voters and thus needlessly obstruct the party-movement's effort to clear the 5 per cent hurdle (Braunthal 1995: 40–2).
3. For additional analyses of the Greens' performances in the 1993–95 elections, see Betz (1995), Braunthal (1995), Green (1995), Markovits and Dalton (1995), and Roberts (1995). For statistics on the Greens' electoral performances between 1978 and 1992, see Frankland and Schoonmaker (1992: 70–1).

Part III

Poland's Solidarity and movements against dictatorial regimes

Political-process theories of social movements emphasize how constitutional arrangements and other political conditions influence people's attempts to remake their world and redirect their histories. In competitive party systems, for example, movement leaders and activists often view elections and legislative work as appropriate tools and hence either form their own parties or try to demonstrate persuasive electoral clout.

But what happens if constitutional arrangements or other barriers preclude such legal initiatives? What happens if everyday people do not have guaranteed rights to air their discontents and to work through legalized processes toward what they believe is the public good? What happens if a government routinely represses nonelites' collective opposition to its decisions and policies?

Between 1960 and 1990 numerous social movements appeared in communist-party states, illustrating the generative capacity of movements even when constitutional arrangements and official hierarchies seem inimical to their existence. In Hungary and Czechoslovakia, for example, instances of local popular resistance, including rallies, marches, and building occupations, multiplied and became sizeable during the 1970s and the 1980s. As participation grew, demands became more socially radical and constitutionally subversive. Even in the Soviet Union – the world's first stable communist-party state – increasingly large groups challenged the regime between 1970 and its collapse in 1989 (Bernhard 1993: 9–23; Hosking 1991; Mason 1992: 24–7, 36–7).

Solidarity, in Poland, was unquestionably the largest and arguably the most internationally famous of the social movements to emerge in communist-party states during the 1970s and 1980s. In 1981, approximately 12 million people (75 per cent of the workforce) participated in the movement, despite the government's attempts to co-opt, intimidate, and coerce nonelite activists (Mason 1992: 29). The party-state, frustrated by the movement's growing popularity, instituted martial law in December 1981. Solidarity went underground, ending a period of remarkably widespread popular action. Its spirit reappeared toward the end of the 1980s, however, both in new political parties and in the cultural values of a younger generation of working-class protesters.

The following chapters look at the origins, aims, and activities of Solidarity for clues as to how a social movement emerges and develops in a dictatorial context. We will first look at the social circumstances in which Solidarity arose and consider if the movement theorists of the 1940s, 1950s, and 1960s were prophetic in identifying rapid social change as a source of widespread popular discontent. We will also note international political conditions – a factor that several political-process theories of social movements emphasize. After reviewing the sociopolitical context of Solidarity, we will look, as we did in the case of the German Greens, at the different forms of nonelite protest that preceded Solidarity and provided communication networks, activists, and ideas. Last, we will look at Solidarity's own aims and activities and at their metamorphoses over 15 years.

Chapter 5

A world to be remade: sociopolitical circumstances of Solidarity

According to the definition of 'social movement' introduced in Chapter 1, social movements involve deliberate efforts by everyday people to alter radically their social and political order. Movements are neither simply disrespectful gestures toward government authority nor simply disruptive behaviour within social institutions (even though movements sometimes manifest such characteristics). Movements entail critiques of existing social conditions, proposals for new values and institutions, and strategies for change. Consequently, the analyst cannot understand the aims and activities of a social movement ahistorically, but must become familiar with its social and political context. She or he must ask 'What is the existing order that participants in a movement wish to remake?'

In the case of Poland's Solidarity, most movement activists wished to end a dictatorial regime that was imposed by a foreign power and that was committed to rapid industrialization and economic growth via short-term sacrifices by nonelites – in particular, industrial workers, farmers, and consumers. After the Second World War a series of audacious attempts were made by the single-party Polish government to promote rapid economic development through highly authoritarian means.[1] Between 1945 and 1980 three sets of rulers tried to turn Poland into an advanced industrialized society. Historians often associate the periods with the names Stalin, Gomułka, and Gierek. The differentiation signifies in part different levels of repression and different strategies of industrialization and international trade. But in all three periods, one party – the Polish United Workers' Party (PZPR) – monopolized the official levers of power, selecting and monitoring almost all government personnel and dictating policy. By 1980 (the year Solidarity was officially founded) many Polish citizens viewed the PZPR and its 'progressive' economic policies with ambivalence, if not hostility. Food shortages were endemic, and breakneck industrialization was subjecting workers to exhausting demands and overcrowded cities. The government, despite periodic promises of administrative reform and greater civil liberties, ruled with a heavy hand throughout the four decades, outlawing numerous 'oppositional' organizations and severely restricting freedom of expression and association.

Amid these impositions, the founders of Solidarity sought a fresh start. Repeated attempts at reform from within the PZPR had been beaten back. A radical social movement seemed the only feasible response.

First attempt at economic development: Polish Stalinism (1945–56)

Like Germany, Poland emerged from the Second World War in shambles. More than a fifth of its population had died, and a third of its material wealth had been laid waste. In Warsaw, the national capital, upward of 90 per cent of the buildings had been levelled or were beyond repair. Sixty per cent of the country's schools and scientific institutes were in ruins, and the transportation system was virtually nonexistent (Ascherson 1987: 131, 139; Goodwyn 1991: 47). Lawrence Goodwyn (1991: 46) writes, 'For no nation on earth was World War II the catastrophe that it was in Poland.' In the words of Neal Ascherson (1987: 115), 'In the end it was true to say that, while no nation suffered so much, none gained so little.'

Poland's fate, like that of Germany, was meted out in treaties and agreements whose terms lay beyond most Poles' control. In summit meetings in Yalta and Teheran, the major Allied forces agreed to the Soviet Union's temporary administration of central Europe. The division of postwar responsibilities seemed militarily sensible because most central European nations had been conquered by Germany and then liberated by Soviet troops. The USSR, according to the terms laid out in various documents, would establish regimes both democratic in political procedures and 'friendly' toward itself.

Further, the Allies decided to move Poland's frontier some 100 miles westward, at the expense of prewar Germany. The externally imposed annexation benefited Poland because it thereby gained greater access to the sea as well as control of a number of industrial centres, including the shipbuilding centres of Danzig and Stettin, soon be given the Polish names of Gdańsk and Szczecin. Even so the territorial expansion posed immediate economic challenges, for the retreating German armies' scorched-earth tactics had reduced these cities to rubble. Moreover, Poland was required to cede approximately a third of its eastern region – primarily farmland – to the Soviet Union, displacing millions of its citizens.

Fearing the political consequences of even a short-term Soviet occupation of Poland, leaders of Poland's government in exile urged British and US diplomats to reconsider their foreign policy. As the expatriates saw the situation, their neighbour to the East – a traditional enemy of Poland – would always subordinate Poland's interests and needs to those of its own. A moral issue also was involved: given the enormous loss in Polish lives both off and on the battlefield, the United States and Britain, the self-proclaimed defenders of democracy, were obligated to protect the Polish people from those who in the past had been aggressors.

The Americans and the British dismissed these entreaties, deeming the Poles inflexible and lacking in political imagination; they were fretting excessively about long-past feuds. Prime Minister Winston Churchill, for example, once reproached the Polish prime minister and said of him that because he protested the Red Army's presence he ought to be committed to a lunatic asylum. 'You're a callous people who want to wreck Europe,' Churchill reportedly shouted. 'I shall leave you to your own troubles. You have only your miserable, petty, selfish interests in mind!' (Ascherson 1987: 135).

Whether Britain and the United States could, in fact, have compelled the Soviet Union to end its occupation of Poland is an unsettleable question. US, British, and French forces had fought almost exclusively in western Europe and were stationed there. To uproot the Soviet troops would have required transportation networks and personnel that were not at hand. Then there was the matter of perceived political cost. The Soviet Union, because of national-security concerns, was intent on controlling eastern Europe. Poland had been the principal route for invading armies from the West since Napoleon's time. Britain and the United States, in contrast, were nations that did not feel immediately threatened by the Soviet Union and that intensely yearned to begin economic reconstruction at home. Poland did not figure significantly in most Americans' thinking,[2] which meant that any decision to use troops to uproot the Soviets from eastern Europe and thereby risk renewed warfare would have been highly unpopular, perhaps politically suicidal. Moreover, it should be noted that many leaders in Britain and the United States initially did not anticipate aggression by the Soviet Union, which, after all, had agreed to establish freely elected governments that would be 'responsive to the will of the people'.

The Soviet Union did appear, at first, to abide by its promises, at least in Poland. Under its stewardship, a coalition government had been formed in 1945 that included representatives from all major communist and noncommunist parties, except those with ties to the Nazis. Representatives of the procommunist party, the Polish Workers' Party (PPR), held only a fifth of the coalition government's ministries – a significant number but still a minority.

The coalition government immediately pursued a number of social reforms that many Poles (especially intellectuals) believed were needed in order for the nation to overcome its long-standing economic backwardness. It divided large estates and then redistributed the smaller parcels to formerly landless peasants. Redistribution permitted more than 3 million tiny farms to be established, accounting for 75 to 85 per cent of Poland's arable land. True, many of the new holdings could not accommodate modern agricultural machinery (only 14 per cent had more than 10 hectares; more than 50 per cent had fewer than 5 hectares) (Singer 1982: 189). But the estates of conservative and nonmodernizing owners had been broken up. It was believed that social justice had been done and that greater productivity would follow.

By the end of 1946 more than 90 per cent of the country's industrial production had been nationalized. The government also had begun to construct large plants, such as a steel mill near Kraków, and helped rebuild the shipyards. These undertakings relieved severe rural overpopulation and unemployment. Between 1946 and 1950, more than 7 million peasants migrated cityward (Ascherson 1987: 141; Goodwyn 1991: 399).

Although Poles generally supported the economic reforms, many viewed the PPR and the Soviet Union askance. As a result, membership in the PPR see-sawed as Poles continued to seek out ideologically attractive affiliations. PPR membership skyrocketed from 30,000 at the beginning of 1945 to 300,000 in April. More than 200,000 then left during the next four months, as leaders of the government-in-exile returned and re-established the Poland Peasant Party and other noncommunist organizations (Ascherson 1987: 142).

The Soviet Union and the PPR feared early elections, largely because of the popularity of noncommunist parties, especially the Peasant Party. Communist leaders in both countries were apprehensive that voters might elect an anticommunist government that would ally itself with the capitalist nation-states and pose a direct military threat to the Soviet Union. In consequence the Soviets postponed the promised elections, declaring that antidemocratic forces had not yet been rooted out. In the meantime, civil war broke out in the countryside between armed bands of communists and anticommunists.

Between 1945 and 1947 the Soviet Union became more and more directly involved in Poland's domestic politics. Poland's security forces, under direction of Soviet advisers, orchestrated mob attacks on meetings of the Peasant Party, the PPR's major rival. Police arrested some of its leaders; some were kidnapped and killed under mysterious circumstances. The civil war wound down, but many villages in southeastern Poland had been levelled and many of its Ukrainians had been summarily executed or deported for forced-labour camps in the Soviet Union. Industrial workers on the Baltic coast, who had taken over the bomb-damaged factories and established local worker-run shop councils, were terrorized by the police and lost shopfloor jurisdiction to the new nationwide system of trade unions controlled by the PPR.

By the time Polish elections were held in 1947, thousands of Peasant Party activists had been jailed (including all 142 of the party's candidates for parliament). Security forces disconnected all telephones at party headquarters. The PPR, resorting to widespread fraud, won convincingly at the polls and then absorbed several smaller parties, leaving itself only two minor-party rivals. The expanded PPR renamed itself the Polish United Workers' Party (PZPR) and took an openly pro-Soviet stance. Leaders of the Peasant Party, facing a very hostile political climate, either fled from the country or withdrew from public life. The now powerful PZPR rewrote the constitution and in effect reduced the *Sejm* (parliament) to a rubber-stamp institution. By the end of 1948, democratic Poland had metamorphosed into a one-party state, purportedly ruled by an elected parliament with a couple of small opposition parties but in fact directed by the PZPR.

During the years that immediately followed the 1947 elections, several features of the de facto one-party system closely resembled those of the Soviet Union (Ascherson 1987: 137–60; Bernhard 1993: 31–6; Starski 1982: 5–28). Like the secret police in the USSR, the secret police in Poland engaged in extralegal intimidation of critics of the regime. Textbooks glorified Stalin's moral vision and political acumen, and provided a revisionist national history that stressed the accomplishments of the PZPR. Also like the Soviet Union, the new party-state sought to modernize the economy through multiyear plans that emphasized rapid development of heavy industry to the detriment of people's immediate needs. In an attempt to rationalize agricultural production, the party-state established more than 10,000 collectivized farms. It also replaced all independent trade unions with a system of licensed labour organizations that gave priority to increasing production over the protection of workers' rights. And, fearing the Catholic Church as a potential political rival, the party-state reduced its role in education and arrested prominent clerics. Finally, pro-Soviet factions within the PZPR used the secret police to purge the party of factions whose actions departed even mildly from Stalin's wishes. Among the imprisoned was Własdysław Gomułka, the former secretary of the PPR and a deputy premier in the early postwar coalition government.

In these years, Poland's industrial economy became increasingly linked to that of the Soviet Union. Poland mined coal, built ships, manufactured machine tools, and turned out much else for its political neighbour. By the early 1950s, the Soviet Union was receiving approximately a third of all Polish exports (including three-quarters of all ships built) (Kamiński 1991: 82–3; Singer 1982: 165). Many Polish workers believed these exports were being sold at ridiculously low prices, in effect, for the cost of transportation. Some analysts dispute this contention and maintain that the Soviet Union in fact propped up the Polish economy (Laba 1991: 120, 211). Whatever the accuracy of either assessment, it is clear that Poland received almost all of its natural gas and iron ore from the Soviet Union, and that the Polish party-state, increasingly lacking popular support and legitimacy, received Soviet military support as well.

Although leaders of the PZPR constantly sought to please their Stalinist allies to the East, Poland's version of Stalinism never became as brutal as the original or as brutal as Stalin wished. Aware that forced collectivization of all farmland would lead to a near-revolt, the Polish party-state only half-heartedly implemented its collectivization programme, and private farming remained widespread – in contrast to East Germany, Hungary, and Czechoslovakia, where private farming largely disappeared during the Stalinist years. Further, intraparty purges in Poland lacked the inhumanity of the purges inside the Soviet Union and in most other eastern European countries; show trials and murders of former party members did not occur. Even Gomułka, whose earlier support of Yugoslavia's Tito had enraged Joseph Stalin, was not forced to recant.

De-Stalinization under Gomułka (1956–70)

Police repression and state terror quickly subsided throughout much of eastern Europe after Stalin's death in 1953 (and especially after Nikita Khrushchev's critique of Stalin's rule in his famous 1956 speech at the Twentieth Congress of the Soviet Communist Party). Supporters of Gomułka, although they remained a minority the PZPR, gained significant influence within the party and began to advocate a 'Polish road to socialism' that would be sensitive to (1) the large number of workers employed in agricultural production (more than half the workforce in 1950 (Mason 1992: 20)); (2) the ubiquity of private farming; (3) the generalized hostility toward the Soviet Union; and (4) the institutional power and cultural influence of the Catholic Church.

The Gomułka cohort soon became known as a 'revisionist' faction. The label is somewhat misleading, however, both because the so-called revisionists differed on many specific policy issues and because they lacked a common view of how Poland should be constitutionally and economically organized. But all revisionists did agree on the following points: (1) that policy-making institutions should remain in the hands of the PZPR; (2) that socialism was workable and a noble ideal; (3) that the economy and politics of the Soviet Union misrepresented true socialism; and (4) that a genuinely socialist society should include extensive freedom of expression and assembly for everyone.[3]

While ideological debates were taking place within the PZPR, rebellions were flaring elsewhere. Farmers spontaneously disbanded the agricultural collectives and seized the holdings without waiting for government approval. In the last three months of 1956 the number of collectivized farms fell precipitously, from more than 10,000 to slightly more than 1,500 (Bernhard 1993: 34). Individual farmers once again held some three-quarters of Poland's arable land.

Urban workers also began to rebel against PZPR rule. The government's six-year plan introduced in 1950 had failed to achieve its twin goals of rapid industrial development and significant improvement in the living conditions of workers. On the contrary, real wages had dropped at an average annual rate of 3.7 per cent between 1950 and 1953 (Bernhard 1993: 35). In June 1956, as tens of thousands of workers in Poznań marched through the city's streets, they shouted 'We want to eat!' and 'we want bread for our children!' The subsequent melees, including an attack on the local security police office, brought on retaliatory police violence and eventuated in more than 70 civilian deaths. The government, worried that workers elsewhere would learn of the Poznań rebellion and take to the streets as well, acted promptly to increase real wages in Poznań and promised to consult workers during future management decision making (Goodwyn 1991: 55–80; Persky 1981: 25–9).

At roughly the same time, self-organized workers' councils began to appear in large plants throughout Poland. The councils were an initiative of plant managers and technical workers disgruntled by ill-advised, if not wholly unrealistic, production decisions made by government ministers and lower-level PZPR hacks. They wanted greater plant autonomy and managers selected on the basis of technical competence rather than political correctness. Many of the councils joined the revisionists in calling for both internal reform of the PZPR and reinstatement of Gomułka as PZPR secretary (Biezenski 1994: 63–7).

By mid-1956, the leaders of PZPR found themselves confronting defiant farmers, rebellious workers in Poznań, and increasingly vocal advocates of workers' councils. They foresaw either a general insurrection or, perhaps worse, an invasion by Soviet troops stationed on the border in case events got out of hand. The party quickly defused the situation by reinstating Gomułka as party first secretary. This was a diplomatically risky action: Gomułka, who had a history of acting independent of Soviet wishes, was not well-liked by the Kremlin elite. Nonetheless, Khrushchev chose to accept the new PZPR leader rather than invade Poland and thereby risk full-scale war.

Gomułka, who became PZPR secretary officially in October 1956, initially enjoyed widespread support from workers, who desperately needed more pay; from PZPR revisionists, who dreamt of a more democratic socialism; from nationalists, who disdained the Soviet Union; from the technical intelligentsia, who wanted economic decentralization; and from pro-Soviet PZPR leaders, who believed that a counterrevolution was in the air and that Gomułka's ascension was the sole means of continuing the party's rule. Gomułka's name quickly became associated with the notion of social and political reform via the PZPR. He spoke for roughly a year about larger political roles for noncommunist parties and groups, about a more independent and powerful Sejm, and about the legalization of intellectuals' political study clubs. Because of these and other promised reforms, he sparked enthusiasm throughout the country. Many Poles, noting Gomułka's courageous recent past, anticipated an anti-Stalinist turn.

Gomułka immediately sought to buttress his popularity by accepting the de facto decollectivization of agriculture and by permitting workers' councils to operate. By the end of 1957, almost half the large and medium-sized enterprises had elected councils that helped set production policies (Biezenski 1994: 64). He also successfully negotiated an agreement with the Soviet Union that cancelled Poland's debts and brought about compensation for the previously unusually low prices paid for raw materials and for the Soviet seizure of machinery from plants in northwestern Poland. The new government also initially reduced censorship of domestic newspapers and tolerated foreign books and music. Student clubs and cafes, avant-garde painting, journalism, and film making proliferated in 1956 and 1957. Religious education reappeared in state schools; new lay organizations emerged with their own journals; and the government relaxed its oversight of church appointments. The powers of the secret police also were curtailed, making police behaviour temporarily more predictable and legalistic.

The structure and dynamics of Poland's economy changed noticeably early in Gomułka's tenure. Factory managers enjoyed increased policy decision-making autonomy, and the party-state reduced the number of goods whose production it directly managed. Per capita gross domestic product grew at an annual rate of 6 per cent between 1950 and 1960. Between 1956 and 1958, real wages rose at an annual average rate of just below 8 per cent. Many younger agricultural workers, hungry and weary of manual labour, migrated to the industrial cities. Persons employed in agriculture dropped as a percentage of the workforce from 56 in 1950 to 39 in 1970, the last year of Gomułka's tenure (Bernhard 1993: 20, 21, 37, 220, 221).

The stunning changes caused many observers to label Gomułka's first months 'the October Revolution', for the preceding Stalinist order seemed to have been turned on its head. The PZPR enjoyed newfound popularity among intellectuals, who increasingly viewed the party as an effective tool for reforming and liberalizing Poland. Some even anticipated that the Sejm would again become a centre of open debate and policy initiatives, where groups with different values and priorities could exchange views and forge compromises in civil fashion.

From the perspective of advocates of democratization and liberty, all seemed well until mid-1957; the next two years proved disappointing. Gomułka, a committed Leninist, increasingly viewed the revisionists within the party as a thorn in his side. Their writings and speeches about freedom of speech and assembly and their support for elected workers' councils in factories threatened the party's vanguard role. At one point he declared that the 'revisionist wing must be cut out of the party' (Bernhard 1993: 221). In 1957 Gomułka moved to verify party membership and purged almost 200,000 members, many of them revisionists. At the same time, the party-state passed laws that gravely reduced the autonomy of workers' councils, rendering them, in effect, impotent before state officials (Bernhard 1993: 39; Biezenski 1994: 66).

The party-state also began to curb freedom of thought. By 1959, it was either sacking outspoken editors of student magazines or shutting down the magazines altogether. If students dared to demonstrate against the renewal of censorship (which they sometimes did), they risked being mercilessly clubbed by the police. Theatrical productions either overtly or covertly critical of the regime could not open. Religion no longer could be taught in school.

By the early 1960s the government was once again micromanaging most production and steering resources away from light industry, social services, and agriculture and into metallurgy, electronics, and machine tools. Gomułka reasoned that with a proper heavy-industry base, Poland could attract western capital and eventually western trading partners. A vibrant export sector would generate plentiful jobs and higher wages. Toward that end, workers patriotically were to lower their earning and consumption levels. Additionally, in the short run, the party-state would have to control (if not reduce) subsidies for food, housing, and other necessities that were a drain on the struggling industrial sector.

In redistributing resources among enterprises, Gomułka targeted the aviation and shipbuilding industries for closure because they lacked the technology and facilities to be internationally competitive. Ironically, those industries also employed relatively young and better-educated workers who saw economic reform as necessary but believed it was government managerial ineptitude, not technology and facilities, that was the primary impediment to international competitiveness.

Gomułka's government also tried to increase industrial output by using factory-council meetings as opportunities to exhort workers to labour longer and harder (and for less pay). At such 'consultative' meetings, government representatives typically accused workers of laziness and simultaneously announced reductions in overtime opportunities and in bonuses for reaching state-mandated quotas (Laba 1991: 16–17).

Gomułka hoped that workers' sacrifices would be short-lived and that they soon would enjoy the fruits of economic growth. Food shortages, however, were becoming a severe problem by the mid-1960s, as domestic supplies fell far behind demand. Private farmers, complaining that they already were being starved by a party-state that would not pay prices needed to cover costs, refused to expand production. They further argued that the party-state gave scarce fertilizers and tractors to collective farms, which forced private farmers to remain excessively labour-intensive and therefore inefficient.

The government announced sharp increases in the prices of basic food items in December 1970: fish by 12 per cent; pork by 17 per cent; beef by 19 per cent; lard by 33 per cent; and jam by 38 per cent, for example (Laba 1991: 19; Singer 1982: 157). The increases generated a great deal of anger among urban workers because food accounted for more than half of the average family budget and because the increases were made known on the eve of the holiday season. Moreover, the growth of real wages had declined significantly since 1959, averaging less than 2 per cent a year in the 1960s (the lowest average annual growth rate in real wages in eastern Europe) (Bernhard 1993: 221; Kamiński 1991: 129; Singer 1982: 152). Workers in numerous industrial cities, and especially in the coastal provinces, both marched on local party headquarters and called general strikes, and even briefly took control of some local government offices. The disaffected and the police suffered deaths in the resulting altercations. There were denunciations of the 'Red Bourgeoisie' (referring to the party's plant managers and the PZPR in general), and crowds sang that they would 'beat the Muscovites and hang the Magnates' (Laba 1991: 25, 82).

A frantic Gomułka entreated the Red Army to intervene. The Soviet Union, however, had other international concerns (in particular, the growing rift with the People's Republic of China), and advised him to seek a 'political' solution. In the midst of this popular revolt, Gomułka suffered a cerebral hemorrhage that partially blinded him. In his enforced absence, a majority of the Politburo expressed more freely their reservations concerning the current course of economic reform and concluded that Gomułka had become a political liability. Edward Gierek was the chosen successor.

Third attempt at affluence (1970–80)

Gomułka, it will be remembered, entered office amid showers of applause, but now he left power amid opprobrium. Naturally, Gierek wished to avoid that fate.

Gierek was acutely aware of the extent of economic dissatisfaction among workers and immediately sought to improve the government's image by travelling to local plants and speaking with representatives of factory crews. He assured them that their standards of living would rise if they became more efficient. He and other major party leaders endlessly crisscrossed the country to woo the industrial working class. Gierek himself reportedly held 187 grassroots meetings in 1971 alone (Bernhard 1993: 42).

Gierek was convinced that the PZPR's rule could be legitimized only if the workers' standards of living actually increased; material well-being would divert popular attention from potentially explosive issues, such as various personal freedoms and democracy. Workers' pacification through consumer goods would mean that PZPR authority would be unchallenged.

Gierek sought loans from Western businesses and governments (1) to raise wages, which workers then could use to purchase consumer goods, and (2) to develop internationally competitive export industries, whose profits would then pay off the loans. He reasoned that a vibrant export sector would provide new jobs and high wages to energetic and enterprising workers, whose enthusiasm and high productivity would rapidly increase the country's wealth.

There was at least one rub: Poland's 'friendly ally' might resort to invasion or some other kind of reprisal if Poland seemed too chummy with Western creditors and trading partners. To calm Soviet fears, Gierek attempted to make Poland politically more like its hegemon by adding to the constitution provisions containing phraseology such as Poland's 'unshakable fraternal bonds with the Soviet Union' and the 'leading role of the PZPR in the state'. The proposed amendments troubled a broad range of social groups, including the Catholic Church. Reformers within and outside the party protested, arguing that the amendments compromised national sovereignty and Poland's possible evolution into a more liberal democratic order. Unable to silence critics and at the same time attract western investors and creditors, Gierek reluctantly backtracked. His advisers replaced the offending phrases with more obscure and ambiguous language.

Gierek, like Gomułka, was unsympathetic toward private farmers and reserved expensive equipment and fertilizers for the collectivized operations. In 1974 the government introduced legal restrictions on the inheritance of land, which convinced many farm families that the PZPR meant to destroy the private agricultural sector through pauperization.

Gierek's export-oriented and loan-based policy initially seemed to work. Real wages rose by 40 per cent during the first five years of Gierek's rule (Ascherson 1987: 186). Between 1971 and 1975 Poland's gross national product grew at an average annual rate of 10 per cent (Fallenbuchl 1982: 6) and was the third highest growth rate in the world in 1973 (Ascherson 1987: 191). The first automobile factories opened, and privately owned cars became commonplace. With their higher wages, many middle-class Poles also bought televisions, wore foreign clothes, and even enjoyed out-of-country vacations. The daily cuisine became more expensive and elaborate, prompting the government to buy even larger quantities of food from the West and the Soviet Union, which added to the foreign debt. Health coverage and welfare services were extended to Poland's remaining private farmers, who, with more money in their pockets, began to replace their traditional thatched cottages with brick homes. Agricultural output grew by 8.4 per cent and 7.3 per cent in 1972 and 1973 (Kamiński 1991: 106). In the words of Ascherson (1987: 186), 'It was the steepest, fastest boom Poland had ever known'.

In late 1973 Poland painfully awoke from its dream of perpetual affluence. The Middle East war and formation of OPEC produced an international petroleum shortage. Western economies sputtered and, consequently, western demand for Poland's nonagricultural exports plummeted.

Meanwhile, workers, who were more economically secure than they had been in the past, increasingly called plant-level strikes whenever particular local conditions – such as safety-code violations or reductions in overtime pay – were not adequately addressed by management. The Gierek government, always wary of another popular uprising, constantly sought to placate strikers, real and potential, by raising wages and giving special access to commodities in short supply. Gradually, a set of feudal-like arrangements developed, with the government granting different economic privileges to workers in different factories in return for their declarations of political loyalty.

The patronage 'solution' carried its own dangers. Income inequalities between regions and factories increased as strategically important groups were paid off more generously than less well-organized and economically less important groups (Laba 1991: 92–3; Staniszkis 1984: 102). Moreover, because workers had more money to purchase limited goods, inflation steadily rose. Owners of private farms, whose revenues were determined by government price-control policies, discovered that their incomes were no match for the steadily upward cost of living and production. The government, however, was reluctant to increase food prices (because of the expected reaction of urban workers) or to increase subsidies to private farmers (because government funds were also immediately needed for export-industry development and for the repayment of international loans). After 1974 Polish farmers, already uneasy about their future, given the new inheritance laws, refused to increase production because revenues would not offset the entailed increased costs. Food supplies in urban areas accordingly suffered, forcing the government to spend valuable foreign exchange on agricultural imports.

Between the mounting importation of food and the dwindling international sales of manufactured goods, the economy began to stagger badly. Debts were piling up. Hard-currency foreign debt skyrocketed from $100 million in 1971 to $6 billion in 1975 (Ascherson 1987: 190).

In 1976 the government decided to raise food prices to stimulate agricultural production and thus reduce costly imports. It announced in June that the price of vegetables and poultry would rise 30 per cent, butter and cheese 60 per cent, meat 70 per cent, and sugar 100 per cent. The average family would have to spend 39 per cent more on food to maintain its current level of consumption (Bernhard 1993: 49). Outraged, workers once again closed factories and marched on local party headquarters. In some cities, they ransacked party headquarters and street fighting broke out (Bernhard 1993: 50–64; Singer 1982: 180–5; Starski 1982: 48–51). Gierek promptly cancelled the proposed price hikes. To punish workers for their insolence, however, he gave police permission to brutalize residents in cities where violent protests occurred.

Politically unable to raise food prices, the party-state tried to solve its inflation and food-shortage problems by borrowing more money from the West. By the end of 1979, foreign debt was more than $17 billion (Singer 1982: 187). Because of sagging exports, the party-state could not repay its creditors on time and asked for debt restructuring and additional long-term loans with which to help pay the interest due. At the end of 1980, foreign debt stood at $23 billion (Ascherson 1987: 197).

Economic disasters were everywhere. Dilapidated machinery led to idle factories because normally imported replacement parts were unavailable. Even the well-paid working class could not easily find food or simple household staples, such as matches and soap. The party-state, in the mistaken belief that adequate amounts of imported medicine would always be available, had neglected to develop the country's own pharmaceutical industry; remedies of all sorts were in dangerously short supply. Poles' health sharply deteriorated; the infant mortality rate soared as infectious diseases spread. Because of coal shortages, power stations could not provide sufficient energy to city dwellers for light and heat. Just a few years after its amazing economic boom, Poland 'was now entering the worst economic disaster suffered by any European country for over thirty years' (Ascherson 1987: 197).

Soviet Union and military intervention

Poland's deteriorating economy and apparent political instability troubled leaders of the Soviet Union, many of whom in the late 1970s thought seriously about armed intervention.[4] After all, Poland played several important roles in the maintenance of Soviet hegemony. Economically, Poland was part of a regional division of labour, and its economic problems rippled into neighbouring countries. Factories in East Germany, for example, relied on Polish raw materials, and their productivity suffered greatly whenever Polish workers went on strike. Poland's railways enabled troops stationed in East Germany to procure supplies from the Soviet Union, and Polish ports were valuable as navel bases should war break out between the Soviet Union and the West.

The PZPR, however, seemed incapable of passing economic policies that (1) the populace would accept and (2) would increase productivity and prosperity. Equally significant, the party's policy decisions seemed to generate waves of wildcat strikes and food riots every few years, which encouraged dissidents elsewhere in the Soviet bloc – for example, in East Germany and Czechoslovakia.

In addition, some Soviet leaders were troubled by the PZPR's periodic experiments in cultural liberalization and intraparty and intrafactory democracy. The experiments did not secure citizens' loyalty to the regime, and they set dangerous precedents before the communist world. Many communist parties were already criticizing the Soviet Union for its intraparty hierarchy and highly centralized command economy. The Italian communist party, Chinese communist party, and Yugoslav communist party depicted the Soviet experience as a lesson of what communist parties should *not* do if they wished to achieve genuine socialism. Eurocommunist leaders in western Europe contended that Poland's economic tailspin and antigovernment demonstrations illustrated the problems that occur when the Soviet Union's hierarchical practices are exported to other countries, and the eurocommunists pointed to the PZPR's half-hearted experiments in social and political reform as valuable positive lessons as to what other nations' communist parties should wholeheartedly attempt.

In the Soviet Union, the broader theme of detente arose during debates about Poland. Critics of closer relations with the West argued that Poland's economic crisis and the erosion of the PZPR's authority had been brought on by an overreliance on Western credits and subsequent indebtedness. The only solution to Poland's economic and political chaos was military intervention, for Polish citizens would never voluntarily shoulder the heavy sacrifices needed to repay Western creditors and to industrialize further.

Most members of the Soviet Politburo, however, did not favour intervention, at least for the moment. They argued that if Soviet troops invaded Poland, a quick military victory was unlikely, given the depth of Poles' hostility to the Soviet Union. Financial burdens of a full-scale war and long-term occupation precluded that option. And there was another very important consideration: Soviet intervention in Poland would probably provoke a backlash among Western powers, and the United States probably would extend the trade restrictions imposed after the Soviet invasion of Afghanistan.

Viewing Poland as a conundrum, Leonid Brezhnev and other Soviet leaders elected to wait in hopes that the PZPR could soon re-energize the economy and imitate the Soviet model of a transition to socialism.

Conclusion

By 1979 the basic materials in Poland needed to sustain its urbanized, industrial society had almost completely run out. As belts tightened, Poles looked desperately for ways to escape the downward spiral.

The government, meanwhile, faced a series of difficult trade-offs. Partly because they feared Soviet invasion, leaders of the PZPR refused either to delegate policy-making authority to plant managers and workers' councils or to privatize the economy. The only alternate way of stimulating economic growth seemed to be (1) to increase significantly the price of food and other staples (in order to curb consumer demand, encourage agricultural production, and satisfy foreign creditors), and (2) to borrow further from western financial institutions (in order to import badly needed machinery, fuel, and other raw materials). Party leaders were aware that price increases, though economically sensible and necessary to secure foreign loans, were politically risky. Strikes and other social disruptions would probably recur, and the Polish party-state, needing western loans and good will, would be hamstrung.

The Polish communists could not turn to the Soviet Union for help in either forcefully re-establishing order on the streets or reviving the economy. The Soviet economy had its own problems (especially in the agricultural sector), and the Kremlin's leaders were currently pursuing detente with the United States and would not happily risk heating up the Cold War simply for the PZPR's sake. Moreover, if the PZPR requested Soviet military aid, it would lose its modicum of legitimacy among Polish intellectuals with socialist sympathies and among middle- and lower-level party officials.

In this conjuncture of (1) yet another economic crisis after 35 years of heavy-handed PZPR rule; (2) increasing international constraints on the Polish government's ability to repress protesters, and (3) the Soviet Union's ambivalence about intervening militarily in Poland, Solidarity appeared.

Notes

1. For a highly readable introduction to Polish economic and political history, see Ascherson (1987).

2. According to Staniszkis (1984: 222), only 2 per cent of US exports were sold to eastern Europe before the Second World War, which partly explains Poland's marginality in many Americans' thinking.
3. For further discussions of the revisionists and revisionism, see Ascherson (1987: 156–7, 166–9), Bernhard (1993: 8–9, 38–41, 86–9), Karpiński (1987: 49–50), Michnik (1987: 135–48), Ost (1990: 39–53), and Singer (1982: 161–2).
4. For discussions of Soviet foreign policy and Poland in the late 1970s and early 1980s, see Anderson (1982), Bromke (1978: 38, 50–1), Goldman (1986), and Wozniuk (1986).

Chapter 6

Political antecedents

According to the first wave of social-movement theorists, social modernization creates innumerable problems – economic concentration and disruption, bureaucratic ethos and impersonal cultures, and psychological disorientation in large, rapidly growing cities – that make movement participation attractive to nonelites. The argument makes sense in the case of Poland, where economic travail favoured the formation of Solidarity. Shortages of life's necessities – on the heels of several years of remarkably rapid economic growth – generated widespread feelings of betrayal, fear, and frustration, especially in overcrowded, newly industrialized cities. Nonelites were upset over their evolving social circumstances and angry at the perceived irresponsibility of economic and political elites. According to PZPR-commissioned public opinion surveys conducted during the mid-1970s, just under half the workers in large factories deemed themselves exploited by the state, and 40 per cent favoured illegal strikes as an appropriate recourse to resolve conflicts with authorities. Moreover, polls taken in Gdańsk during December 1980 (shortly after the official registration of Solidarity) showed that on the whole, coastal workers believed that the government was corrupt, dishonest, mendacious, and incompetent (Bernhard 1993: 152; Mason 1989: 43).

After 1960, many social-movement theorists – especially those utilizing the resource-mobilization approach, the indigenous-community approach, and the autonomous popular-culture approach – have contended that individuals' discontent, sense of grievance, and beliefs about injustice cannot by themselves produce a movement (though they provide the emotional fuel that a movement needs). Movements seldom arise spontaneously from rapid social change and the privately experienced pain of individuals. Before a movement can appear, there also must have been earlier forms of nonelite protest that teach future movement participants the art of resistance – say, how to recruit allies, define common goals, sway opponents, and escape elites' punishments.

Like the Greens of West Germany and Shining Path in Peru, Solidarity appeared in an environment rich with nonelite traditions of resistance and rebellion. Previous efforts at protest and dissent, especially by industrial workers and urban intellectuals, provided Solidarity with the experienced leaders, the communication networks, and the strategic and tactical lessons necessary for its existence.

Borrowing insights and logic from resource-mobilization theories, indigenous-community theories, and autonomous popular-culture theories, this chapter examines the predecessors of Solidarity. The chapter reviews some events described in Chapter 5 (such as early experiments with factory councils and workers' resistance to state-imposed price increases), but it looks at the history of strikes and demonstrations from a different perspective – in terms of nonelites' experiences with and education in protest politics.

Traditions of proletarian resistance

The involvement of industrial workers differentiates Solidarity from the numerous social movements that appeared in communist party-states during the early 1980s. Almost 40 years of working-class struggles predated Solidarity[1] and provided it with leaders, slogans, goals, a repertoire of tactics, and tested knowledge about the regime's capacity for change.

Polish industrial workers resisted the communist-party state since its inception. During the mid-1940s, they seized factories throughout the former German coastal provinces and created independent plant councils and labour unions. Councils and local unions also developed in the mines of Silesia, in the city of Poznań (a heavy-industry centre), and in the city of Łódź (a textile centre). Workers, when managing factories and mines, tended to adopt an egalitarian approach toward wages, focused on the short-term success of the plant, and in general were interested neither in coordinating production between plants nor in working toward long-term social goals (Stefancic 1992: 2–3).

The government wished to industrialize Poland as soon as possible and after nationalizing industry in the late 1940s called for workers to labour for free on Saturdays. The government also wanted workers to accept a new compensation process, in which party-approved plant directors would use wage increases and bonuses as incentives for greater productivity and obedience to management. Workers opposed the transfer of authority from workers' councils to the new managers, refused to donate labour on Saturdays, and demanded that bonuses for nonmanual personnel (that is, managers) be eliminated. When the PZPR tried through new legislation to discipline the workers and curb the factory councils, many workers either struck or took to the streets and fought police. For example, in Łódź 6,000 workers occupied the largest enterprise in the city, while tens of thousands of workers elsewhere in the city participated in sympathy strikes. The government finally had its way and disbanded the rebellious workers' councils, but only after years of demonstrations and clashes throughout Poland (Stefancic 1992: 3–8).

The industrial calm was short-lived. Wildcat actions multiplied during the early and mid-1950s, as workers protested the government's six-year industrialization plan. From the government's perspective, the plan insured long-term prosperity and high levels of productivity for the nation; from the workers' perspective, it promoted breakneck production levels at the cost of their safety and standard of living. Miners and transport workers were especially prone to strike, and police repression followed.

Labour unrest became especially violent in the city of Poznań in 1956, when tens of thousands of workers and sympathizers took to the streets. One group marched on the local party headquarters and partly destroyed its furnishings. Another group marched on police headquarters and set fire to the dossiers they found there. The police fired on demonstrators, and between 500 and 1,000 were injured or killed, and 300 were imprisoned. At issue were not only economic demands but also political demands for the cessation of police spying, a lesser party presence, and national sovereignty. Some demonstrators sang hymns and patriotic airs. The national flag waved alongside banners calling for 'Bread and Freedom' (Persky 1981: 26–7; see also Goodwyn 1991: 55–87).

Elsewhere protest activities tended to be poorly coordinated between worker groups, and demonstrators typically dwelt on economic grievances. The lack of coordination is not entirely surprising. The government-sanctioned national trade union, after all, made little effort to spread news of the wildcat actions to workers in different enterprises, and in addition, the government censored newspapers and the electronic media. As a result, workers in different cities and even within larger plants (some of which had 10,000 and more employees) knew little about what was going on outside their immediate environments.

While the government was trying to contain public knowledge of labour unrest, the official trade union was trying to convince strikers that it could adequately defend their interests only if they returned to work. Many workers, however, perceived the union as indifferent to those interests. One Warsaw worker was succinct: '[T]he unions are a cancer on the body of the working class' (Goodwyn 1991: 71).

To re-establish the regime's legitimacy among the restive proletariat, Gomułka and other new PZPR leaders promised to be more sensitive to workers' concerns, to sack government and union officials who in the past had either mistreated or ignored workers, and to grant workers the right to form autonomous factory councils that would represent their interests before trade-union and government officials. In addition, better housing, pay raises, and greater attention to shopfloor safety codes were pledged.

Most concessions were made in plant-by-plant negotiations. The government was especially conciliatory to workers in industries with high growth potential. Because of the fragmented negotiations, workers in favoured industries began receiving significantly higher wages.

By 1958 industrial struggle was in remission, and the PZPR promulgated a law that merged the newly established workers' councils with the older official trade union. Party officials and trade-union activists soon dominated the factory councils and took power away from those who were not party members. The PZPR also tried to silence permanently the more-visible activists through incentives (new apartments, access to party stores, and so on) and through intimidation (often, beatings either in police stations or on streets by 'unknown assailants'). In some cases, managers reassigned prominent activists to distant and demeaning jobs.

The workers were quiet through most of the 1960s, even though Poland's once impressive industrial growth had slowed considerably. Gomułka, in hopes of resurrecting to the amazing double-digit growth rates of the early 1950s, shifted more and more economic resources out of social consumption (e.g. public housing and health) and into selected industries that had high growth potential. Meanwhile, the workers' standard of living fell sharply, especially during the last half of the decade. When the government proposed food price increases less than two weeks before Christmas 1970, the ensuing strikes and protest marches were even larger and more ferocious than those of 1956–57 (Goodwyn 1991: 112–28; Laba 1991: 15–82; Persky 1981: 38–44; Singer 1982: 164–80; Starski 1982: 39–42; Stefancic 1992: 21–30).

As in Poznań in 1956, workers in some cities marched on party headquarters and there were further enraged by the sumptuous lifestyles afforded party functionaries at worker expense. Gomułka became the target of their fury; in Gdańsk, some even dared to chant 'Hang Gomułka!' Party buildings occasionally went up in smoke. The police used tear gas, guns, and clubs in attempts to restore order. Almost always a protester would be seriously, if not fatally, hurt.

In Gdańsk, some protesters began to call for wage equality between party and union officials and manual workers. One group marched onto university grounds to recruit students, but very few students responded. Many among the protesters sang nationalist songs, carried nationalist symbols, and wore nationalist colours.

Shipyard workers in nearby Gdynia also went out on strike, partly in support of their Gdańsk peers. They had more on their minds than a rollback of the price increases. They wanted a wage structure such that no one in the same enterprise would be paid a wage more than double that paid to the lowest earner; at the time, the ratio between the incomes of the director and average worker was 150:1. Roman Laba (1991: 40) remarks that on the issue of compensation, 'it turned out the workers were more Communist than the Communists', for the workers were making demands 'reminiscent of English levellers'.

In both cities some industrial workers engaged in sit-down strike tactics. They correctly reasoned that the government would not want to do battle inside the yards and endanger expensive machinery. Further, the workplace was a haven of sorts against government retaliation, physical and otherwise.

On 16 December 1970, security forces encircled the occupied premises. In Gdańsk, young protesters attacked the tanks and in turn were shot at. In Gdynia, commuting workers who arrived at work were surprised by the tanks. The security forces began shooting water cannons and actual bullets into the crowd of thousands, killing at least four workers. In the street fighting that followed thousands were injured, and at least 200 were killed (Starski 1982: 41).

In another shipbuilding city – Szczecin – workers at some 90 enterprises accepted direction from a citywide strike committee, which organized security forces, interfactory communication, and medical services for wounded strikers and non-working-class supporters. In the words of one activist, the Warski Shipyards became an 'enormous Hyde park of discussion' (Laba 1991: 79). Because of the authorities' refusal to meet with workers, a series of brief general strikes were called (usually lasting less than a fortnight), during which workers' militias patrolled city streets and strikers published their own newspapers and broadcasted their own radio programmes. In retrospect, perhaps the most striking feature of Szczecin's general strikes was the demonstrators' demand for a trade union totally independent of the state and the PZPR.

The party-state responded to the multiple labour uprisings during 1970 by changing its top echelon – in particular, by replacing Gomułka with Gierek. Gierek, after a month of meetings with strike committees, retracted Gomułka's decision to raise food prices. Then, as we have seen in Chapter 5, he gambled on using western loans to build an export economy that would lead both to high wages and to sufficient profitability to enable loan repayment. Gierek won the gamble in the short run: labour quiescence.

Then came the 1973 oil crisis and world recession. Low-interest loans became unavailable, and world markets shrank. To limit domestic consumption, increase food exports, and spur private agriculture, Gierek announced on 25 June 1976 an increase in the price of key foodstuffs. The Gierek government, in effect, tried to implement Gomułka's controversial proposal of 1970. Workers again took things in their own hands.

Strikes immediately broke out at a hundred or so work sites, including about three-quarters of the largest enterprises. Few provinces were exempt (Bernhard 1993: 46–7). Many demonstrations occurred without violent incidents, but in the Warsaw suburb of Ursus workers ripped up railway tracks, stopped trains destined for the Soviet Union, and seized food from some of the cars.

In Radom, an industrial town south of Warsaw, workers lay down their tools and marched with students, housewives, and others, chanting such phrases as 'The young will not be able to live' (Bernhard 1993: 53). One crowd descended upon the local party headquarters and taunted officials there. A local party leader notable whose clothes seemed too elegant was stripped of his apparel. Barricades and bonfires appeared on several streets, and many onlookers threw their party cards into the fires. The national anthem was heard occasionally, and the national flag was flown. As occurred in other Polish cities, the regional party headquarters' accoutrements enraged the strikers to the point of setting the building ablaze. Looting in the shopping district brought out special security forces to quell the riot. Numerous women and children were hurt, and at least two people were clubbed to death. Approximately 75 police officers were wounded (Bernhard 1993: 52–9).

In other industrial towns and cities, such as Łódź and the shipbuilding centres on the coast, workers acted much less violently, though they sang subversive songs, declared that the party-state was a 'dictatorship', and shouted that the workers had been systematically brutalized. Most of these cities escaped the extensive repression that the populations of Ursus and Radom suffered. In the latter cities, thousands were detained and either jailed or fined in special misdemeanour tribunals where the right of due process was curtailed. In Ursus, for example, workers were denied counsel, and only police were admitted as witnesses. Labour activists everywhere suffered, however, as tens of thousands of demonstrators were sacked from their jobs (Bernhard 1993: 61, 64–75).

In the opinions of some scholars, such as Roman Laba (1991) and Lawrence Goodwyn (1991), the strikes of 1970 and 1976 were etched on the collective memory of Poland's proletariat. For years, workers' groups wrote letters demanding the reinstatement of coworkers who had been dismissed on grounds of illegally striking and demanding as well that they be compensated for lost wages. Workers' associations in several towns held marches and rallies to demonstrate their solidarity with local imprisoned activists. In some towns, Gdańsk for one, workers doggedly petitioned the government to construct memorials to honour workers killed in past struggles.

The ongoing warfare between workers and the party-state – especially the strike waves of 1956–58, 1970, and 1976 – played a key role in the political education of the future leaders of Solidarity. Stanisław Wądołowski, for example, participated in the Szczecin strike of 1970 and later would become the vice president of Solidarity. He declared that the street fighting affected him tremendously: 'Up until then I was not interested in politics' (Laba 1991: 64). Edmund Bałuka, a key Solidarity strategist, had been a chief negotiator during the 1970 general strikes in Szczecin and shortly afterwards participated in the official trade union until his constant questioning about possible violations of labour agreements irritated party officials. Expelled from the union, blacklisted, and fearing further reprisals, Bałuka went into exile until the leaders of Solidarity arranged for his return in 1981 (Goodwyn 1991: 126–8; Stefancic 1992: 26–8). Other future Solidarity leaders included Marian Jurczyk, another strike leader in Szczecin in 1970; Lech Sobieszek, who organized strikes in Gdańsk in 1970; and Zbigniew Bujak, who as a teenager watched his father and other factory workers strike in Ursus in 1976 (Goodwyn 1991: 32, 143, 203, 208, 236–7, 379; Touraine et al. 1983: 146–7). Future Solidarity president Lech Wałęsa also was affected by events in Gdańsk in 1970; he had been a member of the Lenin Shipyard strike committee and had helped negotiate an agreement to return to work in exchange for the establishment of a workers' council (which the government thereafter ignored). In Solidarity, Wałęsa repeatedly alluded to his experiences and warned fellow activists against being 'taken for a ride' by the state (Goodwyn 1991: 120, 127–8, 130; Pravda 1982: 182).

Although young (many of Solidarity's national and regional leaders were in only their middle and late twenties), the founders of Solidarity had been tested and were familiar with the pitfalls in negotiating with the PZPR and the government, with the effectiveness of different types of strikes (wildcat strikes, sit-ins, and general strikes), and with the emotional appeal of various kinds of demands. The movement activists would draw on this sizeable store of practical knowledge when launching Solidarity in 1980.

Intellectuals' resistance

While workers protested in the streets and in factories during the 1950s and 1960s, most politically discontented intellectuals chose to protest within the system.[2] As far back as the revisionist movement of the early 1950s, they had flirted with liberating and economically bettering society by *first* reforming the PZPR. Few questioned the notion of a vanguard party's right to mould society according to its design. The pressing question was how to clarify and improve the party's goals, not how to limit its authority. Many intellectuals, then, joined the party, to bore from within, so to speak, and to change its policies through the soft pressure of enlightened thinking and intellectual persuasion.

Revisionists shared in that political strategy for changing the society. They were not, however, of one mind in terms of the goals that they wanted the party to pursue. Some of the revisionists primarily advocated greater democratization within the party so that its policy making would be more attuned to the needs of the people. A few revisionists advocated workplace democracy and argued for creation of workers' councils that would challenge the prerogatives of government's economic planners. Other revisionists championed greater autonomy for the *Sejm* and viewed it as a potential centre for policy debate and advice.

Whatever their substantive ideas about social and political reform, all revisionists believed that Marxism could be combined with greater liberty for Polish workers, including the right to associate in factory councils. According to the revisionists, Marxist political thought, although it called for the overthrow of all exploitative conditions, did not prescribe creation of the regimented and repressive society that existed in the Soviet Union.

Gomułka's rise to power in 1956 raised the hopes of many revisionists. He permitted dissenting views to be voiced and circulated in print, and it seemed that an intellectual renaissance was occurring. Between 1956 and 1958, Polish newspapers, including the national party daily *Trybuna Ludu*, carried cautious criticisms of party-state policies and straightforward descriptions of social conditions. Publishing houses began producing translations of works by such writers as Bertrand Russell and Herbert Marcuse. A dark and foreboding quasi-fictional literature on life in Poland (including writings by 'beat' authors) flourished. Some students and younger intellectuals turned out a small biweekly, *Po Prostu* (To Put it Plainly), that covered the seamy side of Poland (corruption, poverty, government incompetence) and achieved a circulation of 90,000. Given this plethora of alternative reading materials, it seemed that free inquiry and serious critique were finally being allowed. In the opinion of most revisionists, open discussion surely would lead to the reform of party policies (Ost 1990: 39–53).

To the surprise of the revisionists, the period of widespread intellectual liberty soon ended. In 1957 the government began closing down organs of dissident opinion, such as the cheeky *Po Prostu*, and fired the entire editorial committee of *Trybuna Ludu*. Students who demonstrated in defence of their alternative paper were beaten by police. By 1962 all independent publishing houses and private discussion groups had breathed their last, including the Club of the Crooked Circle, an informal Warsaw-based seminar that had attracted many of the most prominent and influential intellectuals.

Poland's intelligentsia responded to the new censorship by writing critical 'open letters' and sending petitions to the government and the PZPR. For example, Jacek Kuroń and Karol Modzelewski, two disillusioned party activists, wrote their provocative and widely read 'Open Letter to the Party' in 1965. They described the party bureaucracy as an exploiter of working people and declared that there was no seriously 'democratic' decision making within the party. Using statistics on working-class life, Kuroń and Modzelewski (1982: 35–56) detailed at the time how the PZPR's monopoly of political and economic power had failed to improve workers' lives. On the contrary: 'The working class has been deprived of its organization, its program and its means of self-defense.' Echoing Leon Trotsky's line of argument in *The Revolution Betrayed*, the two authors also heretically interpreted the Poznań strikes and street fighting in a positive light, and referred to them as Poland's 'first anti-bureaucratic revolution'.

Kuroń and Modzelewski urged the intellectuals and workers to join forces, to turn their backs on the PZPR, and to create a new decentralized, factory-council form of socialism in which the freedom of each is a condition for the freedom of all. In such a socialist order, workers would have the right to organize any number of political parties, would enjoy freedom of speech and assembly, and would control 'trade unions absolutely independent of the state with the right to organize economic and political strikes'. Further, in a truly socialist order there would be no professionally trained security forces: 'Under a workers' democracy, political and regular (standing) armies cannot be maintained in any form.' Instead, society would protect itself through a system of popular militias under the direction of factory councils.

The government sentenced Kuroń and Modzelewski to three and a half years in prison for their Trotskyist-sounding heresies, but their writings were eagerly read by dissatisfied intellectuals. According to one student activist, after 1968 Kuroń and Modzelewski's letter 'became practically the basic reading for the student counter culture' (Starski 1982: 174–5).

In 1968 the party-state closed a production of the play *Forefathers' Eve* on grounds that it was inciting anti-Soviet feelings. The authorities had reason to be nervous. Written in the nineteenth century, the play was set during Poland's struggle against the Tsar's occupation; and its plot could be easily viewed in the 1960s as a thinly veiled critique of Poland's dependence on the Soviet Union. Angered by what they saw as unending assault on intellectual freedom, some students at Warsaw University protested the play being shut down. At one mass demonstration, police entered the campus, from which they traditionally had been prohibited, and began clubbing students. The incident set off a rash of student protests, such as sit-down strikes and marches, throughout Poland. Some students saw themselves as part of an international 'new left'; others, as Maoists. A few student leaders even adopted names such as 'The Commandos', which derived from a romanticized image of Third World guerrillas (Ost 1990: 12, 51). In the end, the Ministry of Education expelled hundreds of students from the universities, fired several professors who sympathized with them, and disbanded Warsaw University's Department of Philosophy and Sociology, a centre of student and faculty political activism.

Meanwhile, a right-wing faction of the PZPR organized an anti-Semitic pogrom. The official press identified student activists of Jewish origin and argued that Jews had organized the recent protests and, furthermore, had been the true cause of Stalinism. Jews, under threat of losing their jobs, were compelled to denounce 'Zionism' before coworkers. Thousands of Jews who received threatening leaflets and read degrading news accounts took measure of their situation and fled Poland. When Gomułka refused to discipline the anti-Semites within the PZPR, many outraged revisionists turned in their party cards (Ascherson 1987: 174–7; Ost 1990: 49–51; Singer 1982: 162–4; Weschler 1984: 16–24). Revisionism, the primary political tradition of most students, writers, teachers, and other intellectuals, died as its partisans gave up on party politics, concluding that the PZPR could not be persuaded to reform itself.

But although intellectuals turned away from party politics, they did not withdraw from politics per se. During the early 1970s a growing number of the younger ones – influenced in part by Kuroń and Modzelewski's writing – believed that desirable social change could be initiated by organized social groups, such as industrial workers and white-collar professionals, whose threats of social disruption might force the PZPR to change its ways. They believed that the state and the Communists Party were unredeemable. The police batons of 1968 had taught them never to trust the party-state, so they began to participate in the rapidly growing urban counterculture then blossoming. Student theatre groups (organized on communal-participatory principles), art centres, and coffeehouses provided a home for the new wave of political activists, many of whom wanted to organize diverse sectors of society, then build alliances among them to create a politically potent 'civil society' outside the state. One group of young activists, known as the 'Alpinists', smuggled political literature from the West through mountain passes; another group was called 'The Movement'. The government captured and tried members of both organizations in the early 1970s (Bernhard 1993: 7–9; Bromke 1978: 38; Ost 1990: 1–32; Starski 1982: 25–53).

Two other political groupings that formed during the mid-1970s were 'Fighting Poland' and the 'Polish League for Independence' (PPN), both of which called for the restoration of parliamentary politics in Poland and for Poland's independence from the Soviet Union. Both groups secretly produced subversive books, pamphlets, and leaflets and distributed them throughout cities. 'We do not conduct any other activity but writing', stated one PPN spokesperson (Zuzowski 1991: 63). The politics of both groups were essentially cultural. According to the PPN's thinking, radical ideas and exposures of brutality and corruption, once circulated, will cause people to resist the status quo in their minds. Once their thinking becomes subversive, people will not tolerate further abuses. Poles will spontaneously overthrow the regime and will resist 'the gradual sovietisation of Poland, provided one will resist in his own mind' (Zuzowski 1991: 65). Overt organization of resistance and protest is counterproductive, however, for citizens will avoid contact with self-proclaimed agitators; and once radicals identify themselves in public, they will quickly be arrested and silenced. To be effective, radicals must covertly foster what PPN activists called 'independent thinking' (in other words, not the PZPR's view of reality but Western ideas about parliamentary politics and sovereignty). Popular revolution will naturally follow (Bromke 1978: 39, 43, 46; Zuzowski 1991: 60–70).

The timing of the various forms of nonparty activism was fortuitous. The 1970s had brought a noticeable reduction in government repression as Gierek simultaneously sought to placate Western powers and smooth things over with such groups as private farmers, the increasingly resistant Catholic Church, and a restive industrial labour force. Nominally illegal publications multiplied. First came underground journals covering human rights issues; then reprints of Polish emigre writings and translations of officially forbidden western books; then oppositional tracts dealing with economics and society by intellectuals. By early 1979, approximately 100,000 underground works of one kind or another were available each month for an eager readership (Bernhard 1991: 319).

During this period the party leadership, through the government, proposed three constitutional amendments that it hoped would strengthen its legal authority. The amendments (mentioned in Chapter 5) referred to the 'leading role of the PZPR in the Polish state'; to Poland's 'unshakable fraternal bonds' with the Soviet Union; and to citizens' civil rights being conditional on their performance of social duties. The response from a broad array of intellectuals – including remaining dissident members of the party, professors, artists, doctors, and former campus 'Commandos' – was petition drives and open-letter campaigns. More than 40,000 people signed formal protests. This was the largest oppositional action by intellectuals to date. The din was sufficient to bring the party to withdraw the proposed amendments.

Church-based dissent

Members of the Catholic Church were among the organized naysayers to the 1976 constitutional changes put forth by the party-state. The clergy's opposition reflected its slow but steady estrangement from Poland's rulers.[3] Before the Second World War, the Church had supported Poland's rich and powerful, endorsed social hierarchy, and stood steadfast against the redistribution of rural wealth. Even during the first decade of the PZPR's tenure, the Church had arrived at a modus vivendi with the communists: the Church did not question the party-state's secular authority in exchange for a free rein in carrying out its spiritual charge. After the mid-1950s a more socially egalitarian and politically subversive current developed within the Church. Representatives of this new ecclesiastical viewpoint openly questioned government policies and spoke publicly of the existence the God-given rights for all humans, not least for Poland's urban workers.

The political relationship between the Church and the PZPR nonetheless remained complex during the 1950s. Many church leaders were chary of antagonizing the PZPR and permanently losing the prerogatives of religious instruction in the schools and ecclesiastic appointment, and hence regularly criticized neither the party nor the government. Indeed, some components of the Church, such as the lay group known as Pax and the so-called 'patriot priests' movement, strongly supported the PZPR and participated in the party's periodic anti-Semitic campaigns. The government, in turn, temporarily placed confiscated church-owned hospitals, nursing homes, and orphanages under the authority of the patriot priests (Nowak 1982: 5).

Still, politically rebellious church elements were growing in number and boldness. In 1953 *Tygodnik Powszechny*, a major Catholic weekly, refused to print Stalin's obituary despite pressure from the government. During the 1960s and 1970s the politico-religious group Znak published an influential public opinion journal that the party-state finally closed, held discussions of officially banned books, and allowed antiparty intellectuals to use church property for meetings. Socially oriented clerics (especially in the larger towns and cities) delivered sermons in the late 1960s and 1970s on ideas of the Second Vatican Council, on the value of inalienable rights (including the right of workers to form unions), and on human dignity as a principle in politics. Prominent church officials denounced the PZPR's anti-Semitism campaigns and the government's fierce repression of students during the late 1960s. Government authorities in several cities refused to grant building permits for new churches in working-class districts. Working-class parishioners and priests nonetheless built primitive barracks and chapels and, if priests were arrested or the authorities tore down the structures, held demonstrations and clashed with police. The Church, in short, disseminated unorthodox thoughts about public affairs and thus, according to political anthropologist Jan Kubik (1994: 116), became Poland's 'most important value-generating institution'.

During the late 1970s many church leaders were shaken by the harsh repression of workers that followed the strikes and street fighting in Ursus and Radom. In a letter to the government, the primate of Poland admonished:

> The workers who partook in the protests should have their rights and their social and professional positions restored; the injuries they suffered should be compensated; and those who have been sentenced should be amnestied.

The primate added that the government should respect the inalienable rights of all Poles and engage in a dialogue with the discontented groups (Bernhard 1993: 77).

Although the Catholic Church never advocated insurrection, it added fuel to the rising fire of economic and intellectual discontent by scheduling a visit by Pope John Paul II, a former archbishop of Kraków. The visit was to coincide with the celebration of the nine-hundredth anniversary of the martyrdom of Saint Stanisław, who died in 1079 while courageously resisting a tyrant. The party-state, believing that cooperation would earn international goodwill, gave its assent to the visit. During public addresses and masses, the pope stressed social peace but also dispensed what some activists interpreted as implicit words of support – for example, 'The future of Poland will depend on how many people are mature enough to be nonconformists' (Ash 1991: 31–2).

The visit inspired thousands of opponents of the regime, who viewed it as evidence of the latent political power of the people. The state, after all, played little or no role in organizing the huge assemblages and providing crowd control. Of the rallies, one Solidarity activist later recalled, 'We discovered an extraordinary and quite unsuspected competence *within ourselves*: we could do all kinds of things by ourselves, we didn't need the authorities' (Weschler 1984: 15). Another observer remarked that a

> whole generation . . . experienced for the first time a feeling of collective power and exaltation of which they had never dreamt. It gave them a sense of confidence, unity and strength to take up their causes even more decisively.

> (Bernhard 1993: 139)

Emergence of KOR

Prior to 1976 intellectual dissidents, rebellious workers, and religious activists had minimal contact with one another. The government's highly questionable 'legal' prosecution of workers during the summer of 1976, however, set in motion a train of events that brought the three groups closer together. To help the arrested workers, a small group of intellectuals began to arrange a transfer of money from church resources to prisoners' families. Doctors were recruited to provide free medical care to the fired workers and their families. Defence lawyers were found. The treatment accorded the imprisoned workers was monitored. Infractions of legal rights were publicized. And, professional contacts were used to organize prisoner-support committees across the country and overseas.

That autumn the supportive intellectuals published an open, signed statement in which they described themselves as the Workers' Defence Committee (or KOR), dedicated to the protection of the strikers' legal rights, not to the advocacy of illegal acts. The group numbered 14 at the time; 25 in June 1977; and in the hundreds a year later (Bernhard 1993: 76, 84, 87). As the size of group steadily grew, so did its political aims, which within 18 months of the group's founding included a request for a parliamentary investigation of the alleged torturing by police of labour activists and political prisoners. By summer 1978, KOR had established official centres in nine cities, while its calls for the parliamentary investigation of police abuses had been endorsed by scores of prominent intellectuals and church leaders (Bromke 1978: 40).

Most KOR members had histories of extensive political activism. Some had been Polish Scouts, a highly political organization, and had fought Nazis during the occupation. Some had been revisionists within the PZPR or had been involved in such 'subversive' intellectual discussion groups as the Club of the Crooked Circle during the late 1950s. Some had participated in the campus protests of 1968. Some had been part of the 1970s underground publications movement or, such as several former Alpinists, had smuggled printed political materials into and out of Poland. Some were politically oriented members of the clergy, inspired by the Second Vatican Council (Bernhard 1993: 77–80, 84–7, 104–5; Bromke 1978: 39).

Younger KOR activists (usually in their 20s and 30s) often attended workers' trials and visited workers' families, and suffered police harassment for their efforts to show public support. Many of the older KOR members (not infrequently in their 70s or 80s) enjoyed considerable national and international status, such as novelist Jerzy Andrzejewski and economist Edward Lipiński, and mobilized public opinion to protect their targeted junior peers (Bernhard 1993: 82–3, 85–7, 110–21; Persky 1981: 47–57).

The government did not appreciate KOR's technically legal tactics in defending workers, whom one party official called 'anarchists, brawlers, enemies of true working people, old malcontents, trouble-makers, drunkards, provocateurs, and hooligans' (Bernhard 1993: 67). Gierek said of KOR members in 1976: They are 'only a small group of persons of old bourgeois political orientation and incorrigible revisionists' who 'are responsible for the attempts to create disorder in Poland.

They poison national debates with their demagoguery, and try to attack the basis of our sociopolitical system and international policy. These people are in fact raising their hands against the fatherland' (Bernhard 1993: 110).

In late 1976 the government significantly increased repression of all opposition groups. Younger KOR activists underwent searches of their living quarters, detentions, and beatings. One KOR activist who was preparing a report on police brutality in Kraków was beaten to death (by government security personnel, most of his colleagues believed). Senior KOR members used their contacts with foreign organizations and notables, such as the Italian Communist Party and Willy Brandt, to mobilize pressure against the party-state. International groups soon petitioned the Polish government on behalf of the imprisoned activists, and peaceful demonstrations were held in several European capitals. Meanwhile, major cultural groups, such as the Union of Polish Writers and the Polish Academy for Sciences, declared that the activists behind bars were innocent and warned the government that groundless arrests could engender widespread defiance. Hundreds of industrial and agrarian workers in the meantime signed open letters and petitions on behalf of the prisoners. St. Martin's Church in Warsaw sponsored observance of a week-long fast to protest government repression of KOR.

The public relations crisis impelled a government reaction: the KOR activists were freed in the summer of 1977. Meanwhile, the dramatic confrontation between KOR and the party-state inspired the formation of more than a dozen new groups, each wishing to defend a specific civil or human right by engaging in legal, non-violent protest. The new groups included the Believers' Self-Defence Committee and the Christian Community of Working People, which were concerned with freedom of worship and the protection of 'illegal' chapels. Provisional Peasant Self-Defence Committees were established in at least three regions. The Polish Committee for the Defence of Life and Family was founded and petitioned the Sjem for the abolishment of currently liberal abortion laws. University students formed the Students' Solidarity Committee (SKS), which advocated greater freedom of academic speech and expression and government investigations of police brutality, and established chapters at almost every university in the country (Bernhard 1993: 131–50; Bromke 1978: 43).

Ironically, just before the prisoner release, KOR split because of differences over its raison d'etre. One faction included Kuroń and insisted that KOR now should work to protect and expand the civil liberties of *all* Poles. Adopting and modifying Kuroń and Modzelewski's original thesis, Kuroń's faction valued civil liberties for their own sake but also for their possible long-term political consequences. In theory, a general expansion of civil liberties would enable various social groups to develop particularized priorities, goals, and activities independent of the state. Society would gradually become more self-directing, and multiple autonomous groups, as they become more confident, would together be able to limit the state through legal forms of opposition and to force it to be truly responsive to the governed. KOR's task was not to tell social groups what to do but to facilitate their self-formation through development of an appropriate legal framework. KOR, moreover, should avoid overtly advocating either the removal of the PZPR from power or a major reorientation in Poland's foreign policy. Such declarations would surely provoke Soviet military intervention. KOR's goal should be politically nonthreatening, though socially radical. As social groups autonomously define and legalistically defend their interests vis-à-vis the state, a new political and economic order will naturally evolve, one that will include the establishment of independent trade unions and the easing of press censorship. The process will not involve sporadic outbursts of violence but patient use of peaceful demonstrations for limited goals. (Bernhard 1993: 88–99; Michnik and Lipski 1987; Ost 1990: 64–73). In the words of KOR activist Adam Michnik (Bromke 1978: 46):

> We realize that in Poland today the Communist party must rule, and that Poland must stay in the Soviet bloc – we just want them to rule more justly. We want a dialogue with the party, not a clash. . . .

According to another KOR activist, the organization should not promote 'revolutionary upheavals, but rather promote everyday demonstrations of civic courage' (Bromke 1978: 45).

The other KOR faction also believed that the organization should expand its agenda and defend all victims of human rights violations. But, further, KOR's agenda should be more traditionally political. It should comprise (1) the immediate restoration of a west European-style parliamentary democracy; and (2) Poland's economic and political independence from the Soviet Union. According to this faction's thinking, such political changes must accompany, if not predate, the development of civil liberties; after all, neither the PZPR nor the Soviet Union, unless checked by new political arrangements, would tolerate organized groups that can peacefully pressure the government. KOR must, therefore, include parliamentary democracy and national independence among its immediate goals. To achieve them, KOR must patiently educate Poland's citizenry as to their legal rights, social circumstances, and political options, and urge members of society to pressure the regime into changing its ways or else face organized resistance.

In spring 1977 KOR officially reorganized and renamed itself Committee for Social Self-Defence – KOR (KSS-KOR). The new organization immediately established an Intervention Bureau, which investigated cases brought to its attention. The committee also began to publish bulletins for domestic and international circulation on the day-to-day oppression of citizens.

The Movement for the Defence of Human and Civil Rights (ROPCiO), a more nationalistic organization that called for the immediate restoration both of Polish constitutional democracy and of national independence from the Soviet Union, was founded at about the same time. Some former members of the clandestine 'Movement' group of the early 1970s and some former members of KOR joined ROPCiO. A larger number of former KOR activists, however, became members of KSS-KOR.

The differences between KSS-KOR and ROPCiO were in large part ideological. Perhaps as many as half the activists in KSS-KOR were openly socialist in their thinking, and KSS-KOR contained several former members of the PZPR and even a few current PZPR members, such as Edward Lipiński. In contrast, members of ROPCiO were generally hostile toward socialist thought and especially Marxist-

Leninism. They favoured the liberal and nationalist traditions of Polish political theorizing that were popular in the interwar period. In addition, some ROPCiO members advocated the overthrow of the party-state, in contrast to the scrupulously legalistic and politically cautious methods of KSS-KOR. For example, Andrzej Czuma, an ROPCiO cofounder, argued that 'Independence and freedom are more important than life in peace and comfort. They are necessary for our [nation's] survival' (Zuzowski 1991: 75). Michnik, Kuroń, and other KSS-KOR leaders insisted that the PZPR must remain in power for the foreseeable future, or else the Soviet Union will militarily intervene.

In some cities, such as Gdańsk, KSS-KOR and ROPCiO cooperated and jointly helped launch local chapters of new social organizations, such as the Student Solidarity Committee. In many cities, however, the two groups competed and criticized each other's priorities and strategies. Most of ROPCiO's energies went into publishing periodicals for selected social groups, such as *The Farmer* (which urged peasants to continue opposing collectivization of farmland) and *Fraternity* (a paper for students associated with the SKS and other young adults). ROPCiO's major publication, *Opinion*, extensively covered domestic and international political events as well as publicized the organization's forthcoming activities, such as marches and rallies on national and religious holidays not recognized by the regime.

Ideological and strategic disputes soon split ROPCiO into smaller nationalist organizations. The Confederation for an Independent Poland (KPN) disapproved of ROPCiO's periodic collaboration with KSS-KOR and accused the latter of being a communist and pro-Soviet Trojan horse. The goal of KPN, which declared itself a 'political party', was to overthrow the PZPR through a general strike and then nonviolently implement social and political reforms, including free elections. According to the KPN's chief theoretician, 'A few days general strike in the whole country will force the authority to capitulation.' He added that the Soviet Union would be loath to intervene because 'tanks cannot influence strikers to return to work' (Zuzowski 1991: 77). In the short term, KPN intended to organize sectors of Polish society for rebellious action but without help from other opposition groups, especially KSS-KOR whose 'genealogy was shamefully infected going back straight to the Stalinist terror' (Zuzowski 1991: 78).

Another splinter of ROPCiO was the Young Poland Movement (RMP), comprised largely of recent university graduates in Gdańsk. This nationalist organization celebrated Poland's cultural and social heritage, especially catholicism. RMP activists argued that any human, in order to fully realize his or her powers, must live in an independent nation-state whose policies reflect and embody citizens' common norms. Members of the RMP admired the ideas of Roman Dmowski, an early twentieth-century political thinker who defined a 'true Pole' largely in religious terms and who celebrated the nation-state as a tool for advancing a people's collective interest. RMP activists, however, insisted that they did not embrace Dmowski's well-known racism (especially his resentment against Jews), that they were nonsectarian in their politics, and that they were willing to work with all people of 'good will' to liberate Poland from the Soviet Union. They therefore cooperated with both ROPCiO and KSS-KOR activists in Gdańsk (though some

KSS-KOR leaders expressed reservations about RMP's seemingly xenophobic and chauvinistic tendencies).

The evolution of KOR into KSS-KOR and, to a lesser extent, ROPCiO (which then splintered into other patriotic groups) coincided with the rapid evolution of the popular youth counterculture. By the close of the 1970s, the counterculture was so multifaceted and widespread that, in the opinion of historian Timothy Garton Ash (1991: 20–1), it was 'without parallel in the Soviet bloc'. Underground publishing houses produced translations of scores of anti-Stalinist books, such as George Orwell's *Animal Farm*, as well as informational booklets on how to respond to police brutality. Student groups, such as SKS, worked for curriculum reform, academic freedom, and greater student involvement in the administration of schools. In Warsaw, university faculty delivered unofficial lectures and taught clandestine seminars and classes in private homes on politically sensitive topics, such as Polish economic history. Locations changed frequently, earning the enterprise the soubriquet Flying University. As many as 100 students attended the lectures, while 'flying libraries' (sets of books banned from regular university collections) were established to help students investigate taboo subjects (Bromke 1978: 44).

The party-state reluctantly tolerated the rapidly rising tide of intellectual critique and agitation. The Gierek regime desperately needed international funds and did not want to offend potential donors. The recently signed Helsinki accords and US president Jimmy Carter's policies of linking economic support to respect for human rights further dissuaded the party-state from cracking down on the dissemination of subversive ideas. The Soviet Union, in the meantime, refrained from invading Poland both because of the current politics of detente and because of the anticipated financial costs of doing so (Bromke 1978: 48–51).

Of course, the police continued to harass politically active intellectuals (especially members of the militant-sounding KPN, which publicly advocated 'liquidating the power of the Polish United Workers' Party' (Bernhard 1993: 143). But even when arbitrarily detained, the arrestees were almost always released within 48 hours, as required by law, unless formal charges could be made that would hold up in court. Repression was comparatively mild. As Alex Pravda (1982: 192) notes:

> Whereas Polish strike leaders were typically transferred to nearby factories, their Romanian equivalents were shot. In Poland, free trade union activists were able to operate in the late 1970s, albeit under difficult conditions; in the Soviet Union, their counterparts were rounded up and placed in mental institutions.

Workers and intellectuals converge

The organizational and ideological evolution of Poland's antiregime culture during the late 1970s coincided with growing working-class anger. By 1978 resentment was once again smouldering because of growing shortages of food, because of deteriorating wage levels and working conditions, and because of new production quotas that substantially increased the length of the workday.

Until KOR's efforts in 1976 to protect labour activists from state repression, the relations between industrial workers and urban intellectuals had been cool on both sides. Polish intellectuals had a tendency to look down on workers as politically ignorant and inept. Polish workers viewed intellectuals as pampered by the regime and as patronizing toward workers.

To open further lines of communication with workers and to channel their strong feelings against the regime, KSS-KOR began publishing *Robotnik* (*The Worker*), a national newspaper with a circulation of between 30,000 and 100,000 (the highest circulation of any underground publication at that time) (Bernhard 1993: 161). Many articles were written by long-time labour activists and called for wage increases, safer working conditions, the right to strike, abolishment of privileges for party members, and an independent press. Contributors also reflected on tactics for winning strikes and covered such topics as defending leaders, creating favourable publicity, and overseeing implementation of agreements.

Most members of KSS-KOR feared the use of violence in labour struggles (partly because of a possible invasion from the Soviet Union) and repeatedly urged worker activists to explore peaceful, legalistic alternatives to street riots and wildcat strikes. They tried to convey the value of publicity networks, contacts with other social groups, and restrained, calculated protest. Partly as a result of the articles in *Robotnik* and of KSS-KOR's own behaviour, many angry worker activists came to see work stoppages and street violence as last resorts for disaffected workers. In the words of one of Solidarity's most experienced leaders, 'KOR taught the people that there are other means of arguing with the authorities than molotov cocktails' (Karabel 1993: 46).

Meanwhile, members of KSS-KOR, ROPCiO, RMP, and KPN joined shipyard workers in Gdańsk and other cities in organizing rituals to commemorate the deaths of workers in earlier struggles against the PZPR regime. In private apartments, small groups of workers and intellectuals met, planned how to demonstrate for fallen workers, and celebrated any successful liberation of worker activists from prison. During the private meetings and ceremonies, militant workers and radical intellectuals informally exchanged ideas and reflections on the relative efficacy of various types of resistance and on the desirability of a labour organization independent of government and party ties. Bonds of trust were gradually and informally built between workers and intellectuals, and also between workers from various factories (Karabel 1993: 30, 33–5, 37; Pravda 1982: 182).

It was at one of these private gatherings in Gdańsk that plans were first laid for a local strike that would culminate in the nationwide movement called Solidarity (Persky 1981: 6–8). The participants – a dozen or so local workers and intellectuals – drew on the extensive network of contacts that had been built during the past years of organizing. Demands and plans for publicity (such as informing other factories and local residents) were discussed in advance. Resources were pooled. As one scholar observes,

Of the scores of strikes that swept over Poland in the summer of 1980, the one that began in Gdańsk on August 14 was almost certainly the best planned and organized.

(Karabel 1993: 34)

Conclusion

Solidarity appeared in a time of economic crisis. It was also a time of widespread nonelite resistance to rulers. Poles in diverse sectors of society began to challenge the regime's policies and, in some cases, advocated the overthrow of the ruling party. Theories about how to change the regime – through loosely coordinated and clandestine cultural activities, through the use and expansion of civil liberties, through coordinated general strikes, through the establishment of independent trade unions, through nationalist and patriotic appeals, through the spiritual authority of Catholic leaders – multiplied. Dissidents also advocated diverse goals, including higher wages for industrial workers, fixed prices for food, higher prices for food (if one is a private farmer), improved standard of living, national independence from the Soviet Union, increased civil liberties, more urban churches, greater power for workers' commissions, and the overthrow of the PZPR.

These diverse goals and strategies (and the plethora of oppositional organizations that advanced them) provided nutrition for Poland's future, fledgling social movement. They would affect the goals, strategies, and tactics that Solidarity's leaders would consider, and would generate some of the disparate ideological currents that would gradually tear the movement apart.

Notes

1. For convenient surveys of postwar labour politics in Poland, see Goodwyn (1991), Laba (1991), and Stefancic (1992).
2. For discussions of Polish intellectuals' involvement in oppositional politics from the 1950s until 1980, see Bernhard (1993), Bromke (1978), Ost (1990), and Zuzowski (1991).
3. Nowak (1982) has written a convenient history of the evolving oppositional politics of Poland's Catholic Church from 1948 until 1981. Additional information about the Catholic Church and Polish politics may be found in Ascherson (1987), Ash (1991), Bernhard (1993), Kubik (1994), Laba (1991: 83–7, 153), Singer (1982: 189–93, 233), and Starski (1982: 30, 219–24).

Chapter 7

Discord within Solidarity

Chapter 1 introduced two slightly different lines of thinking about social movements and the formation of nonelite identity: (1) the autonomous popular-culture approach, and (2) the autonomous movement-culture approach. Both approaches emphasize the cultural dimension of movement politics. They locate movement origins primarily in people's beliefs and values and movement significance primarily in the effects on nonelites' self-understanding.

According to both lines of thinking, when apprehending public events, nonelites always rely on presumptions about their society and themselves (for example, beliefs about laws of supply and demand, justice, or feminine traits). These presumptions – actually cultural prisms, or lenses – perform important functions: they enable people to organize observations, evaluate social conditions, make predictions, and discern alternatives. Although people sometimes say that they have no theories, are unbiased, or are not committed to any cultural myth, in fact none of us experiences the world without the use of categories, concepts, and logic that enable us to make sense of what we hear, taste, touch, see, and smell.

People acquire their cultural presumptions partly by sifting, amending, modifying, and accepting or rejecting ideas propounded by economic, political, and religious leaders, and the mass media. Other influences include family, religious institutions, and schools. Elites often attempt to shape the understandings of nonelites, sometimes successfully, sometimes not.

Autonomous popular-culture theorists contend that nonelites often reconsider and modify their presumptions, their cultural lenses, in cafes, recreational clubs, sewing circles, consumer cooperatives, and other places where people talk about their lives and collectively ruminate. Nonelites bring these tested presumptions with them when they become members of a movement, where differences in presumptions often lead to disagreements over proposed courses of action. But reconciliation can occur, for example, when movement theorists and propagandists devise syncretic ideologies that splice initially logically incompatible viewpoints.

Whereas the autonomous popular-culture theorists emphasize the development of nonelites' political consciousness *prior* to their joining a social movement and subsequent intramovement ideological debate, autonomous movement-culture theorists emphasize how nonelites acquire fresh perspectives *during* movement participation. They contend that within a movement, a significant number of activists feel sufficiently safe to reject previous social orientations and create 'alternative norms' (Touraine 1981). The content of these new views is unpredictable; they are expressions of thinking freed of previous constraints; they are freewheeling intellectual moments. Social movements resemble experimental hothouses where activists daringly cultivate novel, colourful identities by cross-fertilizing different, normally separated species of beliefs. The cultural experimenters then try to convert other nonelites to these unorthodox hybrids.

This chapter recounts Solidarity's history in terms of its multiple and changing ideologies. What the outside world sometimes perceived as unity of purpose and ambitions was, on closer inspection, an endless process of negotiation and cross-fertilization among factions with different values and beliefs. During its first months, the movement lacked a coherent programme other than vague opposition to the PZPR and the demand for independent trade unions. The daring of industrial workers who launched Solidarity in August 1980 attracted individuals experimenting with very different (if not divergent) ideas about social and political change. Years later, Solidarity's most visible political leaders sought free-market reform and jettisoned other priorities. Coherence had its advantages: Solidarity's political leaders were now directing activists' energies toward one goal; and groups within the movement were less frequently working at cross-purposes. Ideological coherence also had its price: many activists, feeling that their aims were neglected, exited; and the once herculean movement quickly fragmented into numerous small and sometimes rancorous political organizations.

Confrontation in Gdańsk

In summer 1980 the Polish party-state proposed a new round of price increases. Workers once again organized local strikes and marched on party headquarters. In July alone, 81,000 workers struck in 177 enterprises (Pravda 1982: 198).

Across the country a pattern appeared. If a group of workers lost a strike and were punished, restless workers in nearby plants temporarily became more quiescent. If, on the other hand, a group won concessions (such as wage increases or, perhaps, extra provisions of meat), the news would spread, inspiring imitative behaviour in others. There was practically no coordination of worker activity. Certainly, there was little thought of overthrowing the political and economic order.

In July, shortly after the government proposal was made public, a strike called by a small group of workers at the Lenin Shipyard in Gdańsk collapsed. But the workers, with support from KSS-KOR and other local groups of intellectuals, decided to risk a second attempt at closing the yard. The earlier list of demands was revised to include reinstatement of a very popular activist, Anna Walentynowicz, who had recently been fired.

The strike at the enormous Lenin Shipyard began inauspiciously on 14 August.[1] A few onlookers joined the march, which soon lost direction and meandered through the huge worksite, at one point almost moving harmlessly outside the yard and into the streets. The director of the shipyard, a relatively popular administrator, met outdoors with the demonstrators and promised to negotiate on the workers' behalf for better wages and the reinstatement of Walentynowicz if they returned to work. The small crowd – between 100 and 1,000, no one can say for certain – had almost dispersed when Lech Wałęsa, a well-known local labour activist who formerly had worked in the yard, unexpectedly appeared on an excavator. The strike organizers had arranged for him to be present at the beginning of the strike, but he had been unable to smuggle himself into the yard until later in the morning. He shrewdly turned a scheduling 'mistake' into an opportunity, dramatically interrupting the director's argument.

A master of political drama, Wałęsa used his remarkable oratorical skills to talk the workers into occupying the yard until the matters had been completely settled with the director. His argument was persuasive to workers who had experimented with different forms of resistance over the past two decades. Only an occupation of the shipyard, he proclaimed, would effectively halt production and also protect workers from the police. Because officials would fear potential damage to the equipment, workers would gain leverage in negotiations. The assemblage rejected the director's proposal, and remaining within the shipyard, they persuaded others to participate in the strike and formed a new negotiating committee. The committee expanded the initial, almost exclusively wage-oriented, list of demands to include the reinstatement of Wałęsa and all other workers fired during the 1970s; job protection for all strikers; and family allowances comparable to those given to members of the police and secret police.

Stalemate ensued: the authorities refused to negotiate until work resumed, and the workers refused to return to their posts until their demands had been met. Every passing hour seemed to benefit the strikers because as workers elsewhere in the shipbuilding industry heard of the stand-off, they engaged in similar actions – in effect, a general strike. Information about the actions was communicated by students and other middle-class members of ROPCiO, the Young Poland Movement, and the Confederation for an Independent Poland, who served as couriers and poster makers. As workers in other local factories joined in, demands grew to include investigation of the activities of the official trade union and construction of an official memorial to honour victims of police violence during the 1970 strikes in Gdańsk.

The Strike Committee and the director signed an agreement on the afternoon of 16 August, and Wałęsa announced to the occupiers that the strike had officially ended. Some strikers pleaded with Wałęsa and their negotiators to continue the occupation because it would help workers on strike in other factories and in other cities. Some delegates from those places accused the negotiating team of betraying Poland's other workers. When the strikers began to leave the yard, they were met by outraged women at the shipyard gates who spat at them and jeered.

Sensing widespread discontent, Wałęsa suddenly turned to the remaining workers and unexpectedly called for a vote on whether to continue the strike. They voted overwhelmingly in the affirmative. Angered, the shipyard director reminded the assembly of the just-signed agreement. He was ignored. The next morning the thousands who had gone home before the vote joined the occupiers. The Strike Committee, to convey its commitment to all workers, changed its name to the City Strike Committee; later, to the Inter-Factory Strike Committee.

Over the next few days, the negotiating committee drafted a list of 21 demands, many of which went far beyond the almost purely economic demands that had been acceded to on 16 August. The new demands echoed many of the social and political proposals found in recent issues of *Robotnik* and also the demands made in the strikes of the 1970s: unprecedented political and civil rights, including the right to strike; an end to censorship; the release of all political prisoners; an end to mandatory Saturday work; a lower retirement age; and greater access to food at reasonable prices and through the use of coupons and ration cards. Perhaps the most controversial of all (and certainly the demand that most members of KSS-KOR viewed as utopian and needlessly confrontational) was for unions independent both of the state and of the PZPR. The Inter-Factory Strike Committee, furthermore, audaciously declared that Poland's workforce in toto had authorized it to negotiate on its behalf.

By the morning of 18 August (only four days after Wałęsa's appearance on the crane), workers at 40 local factories had declared occupation strikes, had endorsed the demands of the Inter-Factory Strike Committee, and had given it authority to negotiate for them. By evening, workers at 156 local factories had endorsed the 21 demands and joined in the citywide general strike. By 23 August, workers at more than 380 factories and enterprises in and around Gdańsk declared themselves part of the Inter-Factory Strike Committee.

The PZPR, discomfited by the growing power of the Gdańsk strikers and annoyed by the demand for a politically independent trade union (in effect, a repudiation of the party's claim that it adequately represented workers' true interests), launched a vicious disinformation campaign through the state-controlled media. Television, radio, and newspapers portrayed the strikers as criminals and bullies. The government also cut all communication between Gdańsk and the rest of Poland, preventing workers from telephoning sympathizers elsewhere.

Nonetheless, news of the events in Gdańsk leaked out, thanks largely to KSS-KOR's network of underground publications and to numerous middle-class couriers who produced and smuggled leaflets and posters into other factories. Regional interfactory strike committees suddenly appeared throughout Poland and were supported by various non-working-class groups. White-collar workers went out on sympathy strikes. The Catholic Church declared support for the strikers (but simultaneously urged moderation in demands and avoidance of violence). Numerous groups of intellectuals, such as KSS-KOR and ROPCiO, continued to provide favourable publicity and began to offer legal advice.

In Gdańsk, guitar-playing students, many of whom were members of the nationalistic Young Poland Movement, entered the shipyards to bolster spirits. Faculty and students at the nearby Gdańsk Polytechnic University ignored party directives and voted to support the strikers. Housewives and private farmers brought food. The Gdańsk strike, which had begun as an isolated action by manual workers for better wages, had mushroomed into a socially and politically complex phenomenon, involving diverse causes, groups, and classes.

The goals and beliefs of the strike committees were not of one cloth. Even in Gdańsk, strikers pursued a variety of short- and long-term goals, motivated by a range of moral and political visions. Some viewed themselves as traditional socialists; some as Christian humanists; some as narrowly nationalist; and some as New Left. Strikers listened to and played music of all kinds in the shipyards, including The Internationale, hymns, patriotic songs, and the Beatles' 'Yellow Submarine', among others. Despite manifestations of cultural differences, workers maintained a common front before government authorities; very few crossed the lines.

Efforts at negotiation between party-state representatives and the Gdańsk Inter-Factory Strike Committee initially failed. Before sitting down at the table, the committee insisted on the government's recognizing the workers' right to have independent trade unions; the reopening of communications between Gdańsk and the rest of Poland; the tape recording of the proceedings; and the stopping of arrests and intimidation of individuals who were disseminating posters, bulletins, and leaflets in support of the strikers. The government refused to make the concessions.

The committee meanwhile carefully avoided statements and behaviour that the party-state might construe as criminal, politically insurrectionary, or hostile to the Soviet Union. For example, it banned alcohol from the shipyards to prevent thoughtless acts of violence. The committee also produced no utopian-sounding manifesto that denied the PZPR's right to rule. And it avoided overt criticism of the Soviet Union that might provoke its military intervention.

By 29 August more than 600 factories and enterprises had been shut down and their workers had joined the Inter-Factory Strike Committee in Gdańsk. Workers at another 130 factories had gone on strike in Szczecin. Workers at the Cegielski plant in Poznań, where workers had helped topple top party leaders in 1956, threatened to go on strike should the government not accept the 21 demands of the Gdańsk committee. Delegates from one of Poland's largest coal mines arrived and reported that the miners had gone on strike to show support for the so-called Twenty-One Points and to protest the death of eight miners in a worksite accident. French and Norwegian trade unionists as well declared their solidarity with Polish workers and offered the Gdańsk strikers financial aid.

Poland's ruling elite was over a barrel; there seemed to be no satisfactory option. Hardliners within the PZPR wanted to storm the factories. General Wojciech Jaruzelski, however, was of the opinion that the hundreds of occupied factories were the equivalent of hundreds of fortified castles, and that Polish soldiers would be loath to fire on fellow citizens. Such assaults would be fruitless and could eventuate in civil war – to say nothing of putting temptation in the Soviets' way.

Another PZPR faction proposed compromise: the party-state, rather than allowing independent trade unions, would promise to reform the procedures by which workers' representatives were chosen for the official trade union. If the strikers would leave the yards, the party would cease selecting the vast majority of the official trade union's leaders and instead would hold competitive elections for the posts. The proposal was tentatively endorsed by the party leadership but failed to move the Inter-Factory Strike Committee in Gdańsk, which steadfastly insisted on an independent trade union before negotiations could begin.

The government and the PZPR, fearing the further spread of the nearly out-of-control epidemic of general strikes and occupation strikes, capitulated. The party-state reopened telephone lines between Gdańsk and the rest of Poland; police harassment of middle-class groups aiding the Gdańsk committee ceased; and, most surprisingly, the PZPR recognized workers' rights both to strike and to form an independent trade union. In effect, the PZPR agreed to stop viewing itself as the sole legitimate representative of workers' interests.

Origins of Solidarity

The Gdańsk committee never called itself 'Solidarity'. However, during the strike and negotiations, several local KSS-KOR activists described the day-to-day unfolding of events in their newsletter *Solidarity*. Jerzy Janiszewski, a graduate student with skills in graphic design, created its logo. He wished to convey the chaos, energy, and intense loyalty that he observed. The logo was simply the word *Solidarity* written in red (the traditional symbolic colour in Europe for workers' struggles) with the letters evocatively leaning against one another, as if they were a group of people engaged in helping and encouraging. One of the letters resembled a flag-waving activist – an image that, Janiszewski later stated, was intended to convey the broader, nationwide significance of the shipyard's occupation (Janiszewski 1982).

Some of the enthusiastic and unemployed in the shipyards began to produce T-shirts and posters carrying the logo. Over the next months, hundreds of organizations in Poland would adopt and modify the logo, and identify themselves as members of a nationwide 'Solidarity' movement. The symbol would appear on innumerable monuments, badges, banners, and the like, and typically would be merged with symbolic representations of particular regions, workplaces, or occupations. A range of social groups identified with the symbol, partly because it connoted mutual aid, strength through unity, and the possibility of an alternative to the current practices of state domination and citizen subordination. It bespoke a culture of defiance.

But 'Solidarity' also acquired a narrower organizational meaning; it referred specifically to a new network of local independent unions that emerged in the wake of the Gdańsk agreement. Between August and December 1980, workers in hundreds of factories, mines, and shipyards tried to organize themselves into legalized independent unions. They received almost no help from the party-state's official trade union, which deemed them illegitimate competitors for worker loyalty and relentlessly tried through judicial rulings to block their emergence. The new unions also met opposition from local party officials, who viewed the Gdańsk agreement as either nonbinding or relevant only to the shipyards along the Baltic. Workers who tried to register a union for a factory often faced threats from party officials and plant managers, and were 'mysteriously' laid off. Whenever a local union successfully registered, local party officials grudgingly (at best) gave it squalid surroundings and refused to support it with telephones, funds, cars, and so on. The fledgling locals frequently responded to party opposition with the only tools at their disposal: work stoppages and occupation strikes. Consequently, local strikes for the right to unionize multiplied between autumn 1980 and spring 1981.

Despite party-state opposition, independent unions gradually materialized, at first in Warsaw and the major seaports, and later in smaller towns, where workers were more vulnerable to police harassment and job losses. Their emergence generated debates over the desirability of establishing an umbrella organization to unite them. The Gdańsk agreement was very vague on this point, for it had been unclear whether the Inter-Factory Negotiation Committee was seeking legalization of an overarching union or multiple smaller unions. This question, in turn, was connected to numerous tactical questions about union organization (Laba 1991: 101–14; Ost 1990: 100–9). For example, should the union(s) be organized by trade or by plant? Should each plant-level union pursue its own demands and depend on its own resources during strikes? Should local unions periodically pool resources and jointly found a nationwide (or at least regionwide) organization with a modicum of control over the actions of each constituent union?

Workers' answers to these and other questions varied from city to city and from factory to factory. In Gdańsk, for example, many activists advocated development of a loosely federated system of regionally based unions. In theory, within each region, the factory-level unions would be encouraged to cooperate with one another and to submit themselves to the authority of a single regional-union committee. Each regional committee, in turn, would send delegates to a national coordinating body, which would issue general policy statements, but day-to-day policy-making authority would remain primarily at the regional-union level. Many outside Gdańsk favoured a far more centralized national-union because they feared that their local unions, even if regionally organized, would lack the experience and resources to resist pressures from the government and party. As one Solidarity activist wryly joked, for the sake of a strong ally the centralists wanted 'to accept the bondage of Gdańsk' (Drzycimski 1982: 112).

Some workers favoured a highly decentralized union structure, proposing that workers in each local factory create an independent union and decide policy questions (including strike policies) on their own. Plant-level negotiations and participatory democracy, the radical decentralists argued, would not only teach people the complexity of social and economic issues but allow people to learn to become self-reliant, independent-thinking, and politically sophisticated citizens (Ost 1988: 192–3).

On 17 September 1980, representatives from 35 coalitions of local unions and 150 individual factories met in Gdańsk to discuss the possible pooling of resources. Neither the centralists nor the decentralists could win the debate; hence a very ambiguous federalist compromise emerged. All local unions would henceforth register with the state as belonging to a unified, independent trade union called Solidarity (the name derived from the popular logo and also from the motto used by the Gdańsk strikers: 'Solidarity and Prudence'). Solidarity, however, would be composed primarily of regional coalitions whose actions would be 'coordinated' (but not controlled) by a central, national Coordination Commission that would issue broad resolutions about common policy. The regional bodies were to be responsible for interpreting and applying common union resolutions but also for supporting local-level union activities in their respective territories. Combined, the Coordination Commission and the regional bodies would constitute a federalist system of union government (although the precise powers of the Coordination Commission and also the limits to its powers were never unambiguously stated). It never was clear where authority of the national union gravitated: to the Coordination Commission, to the regional bodies, or to the local factory units? In the confusing yet telling words of Wałęsa,

> Let everybody know that Gdańsk has become the headquarters for everybody – no wait, that's wrong – that . . . a central authority has emerged in Gdańsk, though it's not really a central authority, something like it, but not that exactly.
>
> (Ost 1990: 106)

Although spokespersons at the September 1980 founding conference of Solidarity claimed that their union represented more than 3 million people from more than 3,000 factories across Poland, in reality most factories remained strikebound and lines of authority between factories were far from plain. As a national trade-union organization, Solidarity was geographically very unevenly developed. However, as a self-conscious culture of defiance, Solidarity had clearly been established and had an organizational framework separate from the state.

Most branches of the new trade union tried to develop radically democratic procedures that would ensure accountability of leaders to the led. Practices varied from place to place, but the following summary of policy-making procedures in Gdańsk's Lenin Shipyard illustrates the sorts of arrangements that local Solidarity units were exploring. Workers organized themselves into subdivisions, which elected 94 representatives to a council of delegates. Each week the council discussed constituents' concerns and complaints; final policy decisions required a three-quarters majority vote. An 11-person presidium elected by the council administered all council policies, reported all actions taken to the council at its weekly meetings, and was answerable to the council for any action taken. Members of the presidium and council were elected to two-year terms and were subject to recall at any time, and no delegate or presidium member was allowed to serve more than two consecutive terms (Weschler 1984: 39–40).

Decision-making procedures for Solidarity's regional and national-level bodies also were designed to maximize accountability to the grassroots and to prevent the emergence of a ruling clique. For example, at the first National Congress of Solidarity in September and October 1981, all policy decisions required previous consultation with local chapters. The congress even recessed for two weeks so that representatives could return home to confer with constituents and be 'instructed'. During the congress itself, every delegate had the right to enter policy debate at almost any moment. The essentially open-microphone process often generated endless wrangling and sterile discussions on seemingly trivial questions. On the other hand, the protracted debates could produce sudden, unexpected agreement on controversial matters (Ash 1991: 216–31; Sanford 1990: 1–25; Weschler 1984: 58–79).

Internal disputes over goals

From the outset, members of Solidarity were divided on short- and long-term goals. These early differences quickly proliferated during the union's 16-month youth, before the regime imposed martial law.[2] At first, members and activists simply wanted to establish a strong organization that would allow industrial workers to receive just compensation. A minority – made up primarily of white-collar workers – further argued that the new union should help create a new economic system in which elected workers' councils would make workplace policies, replacing the incompetent party functionaries who were being given management positions in exchange for party services. Still other members of Solidarity advocated that it immediately help other oppressed social groups, such as students and farmers, acquire legal rights to associate and petition the government. A tiny minority wanted to compel the PZPR to democratize Poland's political system and secure independence from the Soviet Union.

In addition to parting ways on Solidarity's goals, members disagreed from the outset on political strategy. Some believed that a duplicitous PZPR would listen only to threats, and accordingly, Solidarity must repeatedly resort to general strikes (or at least threats of strikes) to induce change. Others thought that the leadership of the PZPR contained reasonable men who would negotiate with Solidarity about significant social reform if Solidarity would help discipline the nation's workforce and prevent further strikes. To the extent that Solidarity demonstrated social responsibility and a capacity to dissuade hungry Poles from taking to the streets, it would enhance its stature in negotiations with the party-state regarding wages, the workweek, and civil rights.

Because of the proximity of the Soviet Union, a majority of the national leaders of Solidarity opposed any violent or militant action that Soviet leaders might construe as anarchistic. In the union leaders' opinions, the USSR possessed sufficient power to topple its neighbour at any moment. Interventions in Hungary in 1956 and Czechoslovakia in 1968 had amply demonstrated that the Kremlin would not tolerate any radical social or political changes in eastern Europe that might compromise its own security. Most leaders of Solidarity therefore concluded that unless the union wished to lose the modicum of legal freedoms that it had secured, it must take care not to irritate the Soviet bear.

Imitation and early militancy

Only days after the Gdańsk agreement was signed, Gierek fell ill (he suffered a heart attack) and, while hospitalized, fell from power. Leaders of the PZPR, having watched him founder with strikers and Poland's collapsing economy, concluded that he had to go. His successor, Stanisław Kania, immediately sought to incorporate Solidarity into the party-state, apparently as a consultative organization rather than as an independent union. He reasoned that by offering workers in different factories different economic incentives (wages, work-free Saturdays, and so on), the PZPR could divide the emerging trade unions. The party-state then would be able to isolate and repress any remaining Solidarity 'anarchists'.

The party-state, however, lacked the financial resources to undertake Kania's co-optive strategy. During the fall of 1980 the economy hit unprecedented lows in terms of growth rates and unprecedented highs in terms of aggregate foreign debt. Shortages of basic goods increased. Without milk, infants began to suffer malnutrition. Without oil, machines began to break down and buses stopped running. Times were becoming desperate.

Moreover, unrest seemed to be spreading rapidly across society. The courageous and successful trade-union struggles inspired other social groups to create their own independent associations. College students formed the Independent Students' Union before autumn classes resumed. Journalists and scholars set forth their own demands, including less censorship. Independent farmers began to lobby for their own freestanding, self-governing 'Rural Solidarity' trade union. Women were founding small feminist groups (Anonymous 1982; Ash 1991: 82, 110, 117–41, 144–7, 154–71, 203; Inter-University Coordinating Commission 1982; Persky 1981: 174–219; Starski 1982: 112, 115–18, 120, 122, 135–8, 147–50, 231–8; Wejnert 1988).

For 16 months the seemingly irresistible force – Solidarity and its growing number of imitators – met a seemingly unmovable wall: the intransigent PZPR. By December 1981, when the party-state finally succeed in crushing the union, the party-state still had implemented very few of the 21 points in the Gdańsk agreement. Police, for example, still harassed local-union organizers in many regions; the electronic mass media remained closed to the new union in most places; the government had yet to implement the promised five-day workweek; and promised wage increases had yet to appear.

On 3 October 1980, Solidarity flexed its nationwide organizational muscles for the first time. Workers in selected factories across Poland laid down their tools for an hour. The discipline and geographic extent of the action shocked the PZPR, and the government momentarily accelerated implementation of aspects of the Gdańsk accord.

The turnabout was short-lived. Within weeks the party and government again refused to abide by earlier agreements. The party-state, furthermore, began to water down the Gdańsk agreement's provisions for an independent trade union. During Solidarity's formal registration as a trade union, the courts altered the statutes to include a reference to the authority of the party to rule society and deleted all references to the right to strike. The tampering with union-related statutes angered the now 7 million members of Solidarity. Even workers in traditionally politically cautious regions, such as Silesia, began to call for selective strikes to compel the party-state to implement the terms of the original Gdańsk agreement.

The PZPR attempted to influence public opinion by televising old film clips of Polish–Soviet military manoeuvres. Shortly afterwards, a compromise was reached: trade union leaders agreed to accept a postponement of certain terms of the Gdańsk agreement; PZPR leaders agreed to implement more quickly some terms of the agreement that had been neglected.

Why did the party-state compromise with the union rather than engage in repression? The answer partly lies in the party-state's ongoing dread of a potential Soviet invasion in the wake of a nationwide strike. This concern was reinforced by other reasons, one being the growing popularity of Solidarity among lower- and middle-level members of the party. Some disgruntled lower-level party members had long believed that the PZPR was neglectful of workers' needs, that the party had made wrongful policy decisions (especially concerning economic reform), and that the culture of the party's top leadership was rife with corruption. Consequently, within weeks of the Gdańsk agreement, thousands of party members had joined groups that identified with the slogan 'Solidarity', including the trade union itself. Simultaneously, grassroots party activists began to hold unauthorized local meetings to discuss the need for change in the PZPR's decision-making processes and its hegemonic role in society. These meetings soon became known as the 'horizontal movement'. Many so-called horizontalists contemplated the overthrow of several 'Barons' of the PZPR and establishment of several institutional checks – such as free, secret elections for party officers and a mandatory rotation of offices among party members – on the power of the party 'establishment'. To mollify the swelling number of horizontalists, the party elders agreed to replace some unpopular bosses with new functionaries who, in theory, would be more open to the notion of independent trade unions. The elders also bit the bullet and began to negotiate with Solidarity, with whose democratic principles the participants in the horizontal movement closely identified (Ash 1991: 104–5, 179–82, 304–5; Caen 1982; Goodwyn 1991: 291–3, 306–7).

A final explanation of the government's conciliatory behaviour during the winter of 1980–81 lies in the power of Solidarity to disrupt the economy. By the end of November, it represented 10 million workers in more than 8,000 enterprises, many of them producers of primary goods, such as coal, that Poland's enterprises desperately needed.

Although the party was accommodative in the winter of 1980–81, the uppity Solidarity still rankled many party elders, who were used to being obeyed. Security forces, furthermore, viewed the new organization as a threat to established order and therefore routinely, without direction from above, invaded Solidarity headquarters and bullied organizers. Consequently, PZPR compromises were always made half-heartedly – such as that to reduce the workweek and that to eliminate Saturday work assignments – or were poorly implemented, such as the right to organize without police interference.

Bydgoszcz crisis

An incident on 19 March 1981 profoundly altered the largely moderate political style of Solidarity.[3] In the province of Bydgoszcz, a group of delegates from Rural Solidarity and Solidarity received permission to present the farmers' case before the provincial council. The chair of the council presidium assured the delegates that they would have a chance to speak at the end of the session but instead quickly closed the meeting. Angered, the delegates stayed in the hall, and 45 provincial councillors joined them.

Hundreds of plainclothes and uniformed police entered the hall, surrounding the councillors and delegates. When the delegates refused to leave, the police officers began to hit, club, and kick them; the delegates practiced nonviolent resistance. The beatings continued as the delegates were herded into the streets; several, after being systematically bludgeoned in front of shocked pedestrians, were hospitalized.

The Catholic Church issued a statement denouncing the police action. The government denied any wrongdoing, arguing that the delegates had illegally occupied a public building and that the police carried out their duty 'in a firm but not brutal manner' (Persky 1981: 204). Solidarity and Rural Solidarity demurred, insisting that the government had a duty to monitor its security forces and that the police officers must be tried and, if found guilty, punished. Workers in Bydgoszcz called two warning strikes. The party-state held its ground: such rebellious action served only to place the country in a precarious international situation.

Within Solidarity, frustration with the government had reached boiling point. Ongoing food shortages, continuing censorship of the news, and repeated violation of citizens' civil liberties (including the recent arbitrary arrests of high-profile KSS-KOR activists) had convinced many in Solidarity that continued peaceful petitioning of the party-state was futile. The organization's local and regional leaders and rank-and-file members increasingly believed that they could advance their goals only through widespread and large-scale disruptive strikes. An increasingly vocal minority further argued that the regime needed to be completely reconstituted; in particular, free elections must be held and multiple parties must compete so that the PZPR's misuse of power would end. For most of Solidarity's national leaders as well, the police brutality at Bydgoszcz was the last straw. The party-state needed to have its claws trimmed, to paraphrase Wałęsa (Persky 1981: 204). At minimum, it ought immediately to arrest all police officers involved and impose severe sanctions. Consequently, a majority of Solidarity's National Commission (the new name of what previously had been known as the Coordination Commission) voted to call an immediate nationwide general strike unless the government arrested those responsible for the Bydgoszcz attack.

A general strike probably would have taken place if not for Wałęsa, who feared (along with the PZPR) that an indefinite and probably combative general strike would set in motion a train of events that would culminate in a Soviet invasion and the end of all liberties. He proposed an alternative: a four-hour 'warning strike' that would convey simultaneously Solidarity's anger and Solidarity's respect for order and its trust in the authority of the PZPR. If the party-state did not respond positively to the warning strike, then a more serious general strike would be appropriate.

Wałęsa's proposal initially found little support within the National Commission and among Solidarity's rank and file. Indeed, many local unions were calling strikes independently of the National Commission and viewed the commission as dragging its heels. Only by threatening to resign if the national leaders of Solidarity declared a general strike, did Wałęsa succeed in toning down the proclamations made by

Solidarity's regional and national leaders. The union leadership, with limited enthusiasm, called the four-hour warning strike.

The extent and self-discipline of the warning strike impressed almost all observers, many of whom were uncertain about the capacity of the workers to act as a unit nationwide. Except for essential services and heavy-industry plants that were dangerous to stop, such as steelworks, the country came to a complete halt. In terms of participant numbers, the strike was the largest in the history of the Soviet bloc. Moreover, more than a million middle- and lower-level members of the PZPR participated in the action, despite the Politburo's explicit orders to the contrary (Ash 1991: 165).

The party-state would not acknowledge that its police may have acted criminally at Bydgoszcz or that it had improperly interpreted and implemented the terms of the Gdańsk agreement, especially those dealing with civil liberties, such as the right to associate and to engage in union organizing. Because of the party-state's firm stance, an indefinite general strike seemed imminent. Visiting observers looked on uneasily. Foreign governments advised the workers to act prudently. Representatives from the Pope urged restraint on Solidarity and warned that a general strike would lead to civil war or a Soviet invasion.

Not desirous of a showdown, Wałęsa negotiated secretly with the party-state. Many members of the National Commission wanted to participate as well, but Wałęsa declared that because of the gravity of the situation, 'democracy must be limited' (Ash 1991: 167).

On the eve of the general strike, Solidarity rescinded the order. Wałęsa had convinced the National Commission that the party-state would deliver on enough concessions that the strike was unnecessary. In particular, the party-state promised to continue investigating possible criminal behaviour at Bydgoszcz (although it carefully avoided saying that either undercover or uniformed police had in fact beaten anyone). In addition, it promised to end harassment of farm-union activists and to help draft a new trade-union law that would implement the remaining terms of the Gdańsk agreement and recognize farmers' right to unionize. Timetables, however, were never provided.

In the opinions of some scholars, Wałęsa's secret negotiations marked the beginning of severe fragmentation within the Solidarity movement (Ash 1991: 169, 171; Goodwyn 1991: 297–8; Weschler 1984: 140–1). Many activists – especially private farmers in Rural Solidarity – saw the vague terms of the agreement as a 'sell-out' (Persky 1981: 214) and a 'farce' (Ash 1991: 168); the party-state made no concrete concessions and had not even admitted that its security forces had abused their power. Some disgruntled activists argued as well that the retreat had undermined the credibility of Solidarity's commitment to people's rights and its willingness to use its ultimate weapon: the general strike.

Many union leaders also were troubled by what they deemed Wałęsa's dismissive treatment of other elected union officials. Karol Modzelewski, the highly respected coauthor of the 1965 'Open Letter to Party Members' and now the union's national press spokesperson, resigned, declaring that Solidarity had degenerated from a democratic trade union into a 'monarchic mechanism' (Persky 1981: 216). 'I think,

Lech, that if you had presented the whole problem to us, all the difficulties of the situation, we would have understood it and there wouldn't have been any criticisms', stated one member of Solidarity's National Commission. 'We should always be treated seriously' (Persky 1981: 215).

Wałęsa publicly accepted the criticisms of his style, but over the next half year worked to restructure Solidarity so that his more cooperative and noncombative style of negotiating with the regime would gain ascendancy over what he saw as the irresponsible and naive militancy of the National Commission. After the Bydgoszcz crisis, Wałęsa helped establish the Presidium, a 15- to 20-person executive committee for the National Commission. The Presidium met whenever the National Commission was not in session and, at such times, served as the union's highest internal authority. The National Commission was composed of representatives from all the regional unions plus elected representatives from the National Congress. The Presidium, in contrast, was handpicked by the president, Wałęsa, who argued that he needed a group of which he was confident. As time passed, Solidarity's national leadership increasingly bifurcated, with Wałęsa and the moderate Presidium repeatedly confronting an uneasy and at times hostile National Commission (Ost 1990: 134, 143, 245).

Internal disintegration and external defeat

The causes of the growing infighting within Solidarity cannot be reduced to Wałęsa's secretive leadership style. The movement also grew more divided over substantive questions concerning long-term social and political goals – especially the future of the economy.

The economy had turned progressively disastrous as 1981 progressed. Acute shortages of food persisted; meat was rationed and prices were doubled for many foodstuffs, but neither policy allayed hunger. For want of materials, many factories closed their doors. For want of energy, many homes were dark and, during the winter, quite cold.

During summer 1981 hunger marches, some with as many as 30,000 participants, appeared throughout the country. Local Solidarity organizations often cosponsored the marches, and local Solidarity activists helped carry them off. Very few of the marches, however, received the blessings of Solidarity's national leadership, in particular of Wałęsa and the Presidium. After all, many among them saw such demonstrations as likely to provoke a Soviet invasion because of their threatening aspect for social order.

In addition to the hunger strikes, a number of local labour groups – especially in inland factory cities, such as Łódź – initiated so-called active strikes in which workers temporarily took over factories, produced goods, and then exchanged them with consumers of their choosing. Miners, for example, might spend a Saturday working and then use the coal they brought out to buy medicine or milk. Similarly, tractor labourers might exchange their manufacture for farm-grown food. Active strikes, which first appeared in heavy-industry plants in August 1981, had spread by October to white-collar establishments, such as schools, and by November to mines in Lower Silesia. Again, Solidarity's National Commission was hesitant to endorse such anarchosyndicalist behaviour, given the tense international situation. In autumn 1981, however, the commission reluctantly acknowledged the legitimacy of active strikes, primarily in order to satisfy Solidarity's increasingly militant grassroots activists (Ash 1991: 261, 265–6, 271; Kowalewski 1982; Touraine et al. 1983: 96, 125–6, 153–4, 161).

Numerous administrators, engineers and technicians, and other white-collar workers advocated factory self-management as a solution to the economic crisis. They argued that in each factory the workers, being knowledgeable about the production process, should elect a managerial body to make binding decisions about resources, tools, output levels, and division of labour. That accomplished, the administrative inefficiencies that produced the economic crisis would end and prosperity would commence. In spring 1981 a small group of advocates met in Gdańsk and established an association called Network (shorthand for Network of Solidarity Workplace Organizations of Leading Workplaces). They then began to capture key offices within Solidarity during its summer elections. Robert Biezenski (1994: 69, 79) contends that the elections resulted in an 'oligarchic takeover of much of the Solidarity administration'. The new generation of officials saw Solidarity as a Trojan horse for advancing their programme of economic reform and opposed the union's attempts to secure a higher standard of living through more traditional local-level strikes and collective bargaining (Goodwyn 1991: 284).

Most of Solidarity's blue-collar members were lukewarm toward the white-collars' proposals for factory self-management. According to several Solidarity opinion polls taken in summer 1981, only 10 to 20 per cent of Solidarity's members thought it should be a high priority for the union (Biezenski 1994: 72; Touraine et al. 1983: 109–110, 125, 160, 163). Some labour leaders, furthermore, were apprehensive that the creation of factory-management councils might ultimately undermine Solidarity's strategy for state-imposed policies regarding working conditions, price controls, and length of the workweek. As Wałęsa had put it in 1980, 'We are not pushing our way into management . . . we're just workers. We don't want to be managers, just activists' (Biezenski 1994: 70). In the words of another Solidarity official, 'Self-management is the self-exploitation of the workers' (Touraine et al. 1983: 125).

The growing influence of Network within Solidarity also troubled leaders of the PZPR, who viewed Network's proposed factory-management councils as both an 'anarcho-syndicalist deviation' and a direct challenge to the party's prerogative of placing loyal members in factory administrative positions (Goodwyn 1991: 284–5; Singer 1982: 253). Some government leaders wondered aloud: if self-managed factories were established – with each factory deciding its own standards, product lines, and marketing policies – how would coordination of production among such autonomous, self-managed factories occur? What if, for example, shipbuilders decided to make a certain kind of tanker, and workers in steel mills decided not to produce the requisite steel plates?

The PZPR, in the meantime, went right on stonewalling Solidarity's ongoing demands for compliance with the September 1980 Gdańsk agreement. This fuelled disenchantment within Solidarity over Wałęsa's strategy of moderation and bridge building. According to one popular poster that appeared during the first anniversary of the Gdańsk agreement, 'STILL, AFTER A FULL YEAR, ONLY 2 X YES AND 19 X NO' (Weschler 1984: 58). In other words, the party had honoured only two terms of the Gdańsk agreement: (1) the legalization of an independent trade union, and (2) radio broadcasts of Sunday masses.

In the meantime, the horizontal movement within the PZPR was tactically out-flanked by party elders at the party's July 1981 Extraordinary Congress (Ash 1991: 175–90; Singer 1982: 255–60). Pro-Soviet party activists expelled pro-Solidarity reformers. In addition, right-wing Communist factions suddenly appeared with anti-Semitic creeds and rituals.

By autumn 1981 the party-state clearly had had its fill of Solidarity and its relat-ives. The constant wildcat strikes, active strikes, and hunger marches embarrassed and infuriated party leaders, who believed that Solidarity's defence (if not encour-agement) of local strikers was undermining the economy. For the first time rep-resentatives of the party-state refused to negotiate with Solidarity representatives concerning implementation of the Gdańsk agreement – a significant development, even if earlier negotiations often led to ruses and minimal concessions. Solidarity's national leadership, in turn, tried to force the PZPR to the negotiating table by call-ing another one-hour general strike in October. The party-state responded with a brief flurry of meetings with Solidarity's negotiators, and then with another suspen-sion of talks.

One winter's eve, the leaders of Solidarity experienced a crisis of confidence. Scholars interviewing Solidarity officials at that time reported a noticeable change in the activists' spirit. One international research team, for example, observed a 'feel-ing of paralysis, of having lost control of events and being at the mercy of destiny'. 'It was as though the group felt that it could not escape the course of history' (Touraine et al. 1983: 172).

Ironically, the spirit of disillusionment coincided with Solidarity's First National Congress, which by all accounts was a highly raucous affair (Ash 1991: 216–43; Singer 1982: 260–5; Sanford 1990: 1–25; Starski 1982: 150–63; Touraine et al. 1983: 139–52; Weschler 1984: 58–79). So-called fundamentalists at the congress insisted that the Gdańsk programme be implemented immediately and that the author-ity of the PZPR be challenged at every level, from factories to the Sejm. So-called pragmatists also insisted that the Gdańsk agreement be implemented, but additionally counselled patience and greater cooperation with and respectful behaviour before the party so that the Soviet Union would not be tempted to invade Poland. Pragmat-ists accused fundamentalists of secretly planning to create another political party when the primary goal of Solidarity should be to secure more bread, not to satisfy political ambitions. Fundamentalists accused pragmatists of being out of step with Solidarity's rank and file and of being naive about the PZPR's capacity for reform.

According to some sociologists, the division between pragmatists and fundament-alists reflected in part Poland's complex economic geography and workers' different experiences with the PZPR. In Gdańsk, for example, pragmatism was a significant tendency among shipyard workers, perhaps because the local party officials had in fact been cooperative and had given the union access to the daily party newspaper (Ost 1990: 137). Miners in Silesia, on the other hand, tended to be uncompromisingly hostile toward the party. Moreover, some miners (perhaps because they knew that they were using primitive tools to extract coal for export to the Soviet Union) were extremely patriotic and viewed Solidarity's proper task as freeing Poland and its natural resources from the grip of the Soviet-serving PZPR (Touraine et al. 1983: 117–27).

The conflict between the pragmatists and fundamentalists did not exhaust the variety of viewpoints present at the National Congress. Network's self-management advocates made sure their dreams of a decentralized economy were included in the agenda and were endorsed by the congress. New and diverse nationalist groups – some of whom had adopted anti-Semitic and anti-intellectual public postures – denounced Solidarity leaders who were former members of KSS-KOR (which officially dissolved itself during the congress); advocated Poland's independence from the Communist bloc; and argued that the power of the United States and West Germany would deter the Soviet Union from an invasion should Poland unilaterally insist on its sovereignty in foreign affairs. Utopian liberal democrats advocated a far-reaching constitutional transformation of Poland, including creation of a genuinely representative parliament, a judiciary independent of PZPR influence, and free elections. More cautious political reformers simply asked that Solidarity defend civil liberties more vigilantly and continue to encourage 'civil society'. Enthusiastic advocates of the immediate introduction of a free market were present, as were advocates of more gradual market reform. There were even numerous pleaders for a new type of controlled economy, in which representatives of diverse economic interests would form a council of producers that would help the PZPR make policy.

Not surprisingly, Solidarity's first official programme was not very coherent. It can perhaps be described as a quilt of clashing colours. Almost all factions at the congress had their ideas mentioned. The result was an often inconsistent-sounding document, which noted in passing that 'Solidarity embraces many social currents' (Solidarity National Congress 1982: 205).

The programme emphasized that the goal of Solidarity was not merely to end abuses by the party-state but 'to rebuild a just Poland', to spawn a 'national renewal', and to promote 'the moral rebirth of the people' (Solidarity National Congress 1982: 206). Among the defining features of the rebirth was a greater spirit of initiative among citizens and a steadfast refusal to defer to the PZPR. In addition, 'moral rebirth' involved a revival of Christian ethics and of working-class democratic traditions. The ethics and traditions involved 'a true socialization of our government and state administration' and 'a just distribution of the nation's material and spiritual wealth' (Solidarity National Congress 1982: 206).

Regarding international relations, the programme declared that Solidarity was committed to a 'strengthening of the sovereignty of our nation and state' and to 'freedom and total independence'. However, the programme also stated that Solidarity desired both peace and the preservation of current international alliances:

'Indeed, we seek to provide more solid guarantees for those alliances.' Thus were commended both greater national independence *and* apparently closer ties with the Soviet bloc in the space of less than two pages (Solidarity National Congress 1982: 206–7).

The economic order endorsed by the programme was also incongruous. The programme called for a 'new economic and social system to combine planning, autonomy and the market', but the practical meaning of the terminology was unclear. Was the union saying that it was in favour of an economy based primarily on free-market principles, or of more extensive government intervention? Different parts of the programme supported each position. According to some sections, Solidarity intended to abolish all 'bureaucratic barriers' to market exchange and to support antimonopoly legislation. Other sections called for not less but more efficient government involvement in the distribution of goods and services – in particular, for a new system of government food rationing that 'ensures that every citizen has the minimum necessary' and for the government's immediate provision of 'essential consumer items', such as clothing, shelter, education, and health. In addition, 'We demand a *major increase* in social welfare' (italics added) that includes 'a special fund to restrain retail price rises on certain goods and services (milk, schoolbooks, children's clothing, etc.)' (Solidarity National Congress 1982: 208–13).

Elsewhere, the document endorsed three distinct and arguably contradictory images of economic policy making. One section called for the creation of factory management councils that would not be dependent on government ministries for decisions on production goals and methods. But another section called for creation of a social council for the national economy that would make economic plans and design appropriate legislation. Yet another section called for the use of referenda on basic economic policy questions, such as the continued use of ration cards for major consumer items, so that 'society' could decide on how the economy is organized. Somehow, factory independence, government planning, and popular referenda were to be combined into a single, workable, and efficient economic system (Solidarity National Congress 1982: 211–14). Private commercial farming was also endorsed ('because private farms are more efficient than socialized ones'). But this apparently straightforward endorsement of free-market economics soon was contradicted, because the programme also endorsed the union's influence on the state in creating nationwide policies that would reduce income inequalities between regions and enterprises (Ash 1991: 236; Solidarity National Congress 1982: 210, 212).

In contrast to the confusing and seemingly inconsistent array of market and nonmarket principles presented in the economic sections of the First National Congress programme, the political sections provided a more or less coherent picture. The congress proposed establishment of a federated system of rule, with extensive civil liberties, an independent constitutional court, and elected regional and national legislatures. It was proposing, in short, a decentralized western-style liberal democracy akin to West Germany's federal system.

The bitter aftertaste of the Bydgoszcz struggle was apparent in many of the political proposals of the programme. Despite the pragmatists' efforts to tone down antiparty rhetoric and avoid unnecessary confrontation, the programme seethed with antiparty sentiment. The country's economic problems were laid squarely at the feet of the PZPR: 'continual party inference in the functioning of enterprises is the main reason for the present crisis of the Polish economy' (Solidarity National Congress 1982: 214). The document not only explicitly denounced the police brutality at Bydgoszcz, as well as at earlier strikes during the 1950s, 1960s, and 1970s, but called for the prosecution of all members of security forces who violated the law. In addition, the programme proposed that criminal proceedings be instituted against all politicians 'who, by their actions between 1970 and 1980, have brought the country to economic ruin', sparing 'no one, including those who occupy the highest functions in the party and government'. Solidarity would 'insist categorically on this point. If legal proceedings have not begun by December 1, the national committee will convene a people's tribunal to hold a public trial and render a verdict' (Solidarity National Congress 1982: 217).

Dissatisfaction with Wałęsa's private style of negotiating was also evident in the programme's proposals for future intramovement decision making. Henceforth, all negotiations with the party-state were to be conducted openly, and union leaders were to consult regularly with members before *and* during negotiations. To facilitate grassroots communication with leaders, a system of polling should be instituted that would allow leaders to discover what members are thinking before union–government negotiations begin. The programme also stated that although negotiations would be Solidarity's principal means of influencing the party-state, demonstrations, strikes, and boycotts could be used if and when demands fell on deaf ears, or if and when the party-state failed to carry out promises (Solidarity National Congress 1982: 222–4).

The programme closed on a dark note. It warned that Poland confronted an impending economic 'catastrophe' that threatened the 'survival of society'. An anticrisis coalition should be formed of Solidarity and the party-state – a coalition that would involve 'collaboration between the state power and society for a radical change in the existing economic order'. But this prescription jarred with much of the document's analysis of the PZPR; after all, if the party was as corrupt, inept, and intransigent as the programme repeatedly stated, what hope was there for a meaningful union–party agreement (Solidarity National Congress 1982: 206, 208, 214, 217, 224–5)?

The programme's utopian vision and often combative rhetoric reflected the radical, subversive, and aggressive spirit that pervaded the congress' discussions and that was made real by almost all of its actions – for example, an audacious resolution denouncing the 'selfish interests of the bureaucratic apparatus of the Party-state' (Touraine et al. 1983: 140). The congress passed a motion demanding elections to Regional Councils and the Sejm. Additionally, the congress challenged the government either to hold a referendum on Solidarity's factory self-management proposal or to expect Solidarity to hold one.

Perhaps the greatest act of bravado at the congress was passage of a letter 'to the working people of Albania, Bulgaria, Czechoslovakia, the German Democratic Republic, Rumania, Hungary, and all the nations of the Soviet Union'. The union declared its commitment 'to improve the condition of all working people' and promised to work with labourers in other Communist countries 'who have decided to embark on the difficult road for the free trade-union movement. We believe that it shall not be long before our representatives meet yours to exchange experiences' (Ash 1991: 221; see also Weschler 1984: 72). Fears of Soviet intervention clearly had been overridden.

The Soviet Union described Solidarity's Congress as an 'anti-socialist and anti-Soviet orgy' (Touraine et al. 1983: 140). Though an exaggeration of facts, the statement contained a kernel of truth. The congress did openly challenge the legitimacy of the PZPR, the Soviet Union, and the Leninist notion of a single party-state with a command economy.

Wałęsa and other national leaders of Solidarity who shared his pragmatic orientation were shocked at the turn of events. At one point Wałęsa reportedly declared, 'I'm just sitting here trying to figure out what it is you guys ate today that makes you talk like you do' (Ost 1990: 145).

The daring of the congress contrasted with the silence in the streets. Grassroots support of and confidence in Solidarity was clearly waning as widespread hunger persisted. By winter 1981, nightmarish conditions prevailed. Ration cards, which in the best of times could not assure very much, were no longer honoured. In some regions, grassroots meetings organized by Solidarity no longer attracted scores of participants but less than handfuls (Ost 1988: 200; Ost 1990: 142, 147). According to 1981 opinion polls, many people began to view Solidarity as no better than the government in terms of solving the immediate economic crisis (Ost 1988: 200).

To retain the loyalty of its membership, Solidarity had to appear an effective actor capable of changing social circumstances, not a meek, impotent negotiator with the party-state. Wałęsa believed that if workers had a greater voice in the making of economic policy, a way out of the depression could be discovered. Hence, he and some other pragmatists proposed that the government include Solidarity in the drafting of all measures involving labour conditions, wages, and work rules (Ash 1991: 200–15; Ost 1990: 113–48). In exchange, Wałęsa promised that Solidarity would put limits on the demands of the workers and even would help discipline the workforce by compelling some givebacks (such as work-free Saturdays) and preventing further strikes and other disruptions of production. But if the government wanted social peace, it would have to pay the price and regularly include Solidarity in the economic policy making.

The government coyly hinted that if Solidarity helped legitimize the party's monopoly of political power and helped implement necessary limits on wages and increases in prices, then the government would permit Solidarity to have a limited voice in the design of economic policy. Some officers in the trade union saw cooperation as the only way to save the economy and agreed that if Poland was to survive in the long term its workers would have to tighten their belts in the short term. Others, however, viewed the government's offer before the trade union as a transparent suggestion that Solidarity betray its loyal workers.

When the Solidarity activists who favoured cooperation with the government asked the government to specify the types of policy input the trade union would obtain, silence was the response. The PZPR, it increasingly seemed, was willing to let economic chaos proceed. Then, if and when the workers lashed out through riots, the party would allow the military to come to the country's rescue (Ash 1991: 200–10, 244–57, 266–9; Ost 1990: 113–48).

The last months of 1981 were a period of confusion for Solidarity's leaders. After the congress had completed drafting and approving its programme, wildcat strikes, involving several hundreds of thousands of workers, exploded throughout Poland. Wałęsa and other activists from the Gdańsk region attempted to talk workers out of uncoordinated acts of resistance and into preserving the union's reputation for self-discipline, but most strikers refused to return to work. Further, students, angry over political appointments to educational offices, went on strike in early December and closed 70 of Poland's 104 institutions of higher learning. Solidarity's pragmatists, in the meantime, failed to overcome the stony silence of the PZPR, which refused to treat Solidarity as an equal in economic policy making but nonetheless wanted Solidarity to help implement the party's austerity policies.

In mid-December the newest party secretary of the PZPR, General Wojciech Jaruzelski, was encouraged by the Soviet Union to declare martial law. The Polish military closed down Solidarity's regional and national headquarters, banned its publications, and arrested hundreds of its activists (including almost all of the National Commission and most former members of KOR). Local groups, especially students and miners, tried to resist the soldiers, but resistance was uncoordinated, and the military won easily. The once-mighty Solidarity – more than 10 million members – was reduced to small local resistance groups putting out clandestine publications and endlessly feuding over goals and tactics (Łopiński et al. 1990; Ost 1990: 149–60; Weschler 1984: 147–96).

Years of repression (1981–85)

The first year of martial law was harrowing for members of Solidarity and other oppositional groups.[4] The military government set up 78 internment camps, where it detained at least 10,000 individuals without formal charges and jailed thousands more for illegally demonstrating, distributing leaflets, and hiding banned literature. Martial law decrees imposed strict curfews, instituted summary courts, suspended private mail and telephone service, and militarized key industries.

Jaruzelski's government was hardly a front for the PZPR. The military blamed Poland's economic and political disorder not only on Solidarity's disorderly behaviour and combative rhetoric but also on the PZPR's corruption and incompetence. Former party personages, such as Gierek, were arrested. By the time the military transferred political authority back to civilians in 1983, it had sacked more than 600 party-appointed directors of major enterprises and filled 80 per cent of the PZPR's posts with new faces (Brown 1991: 78; Weschler 1984: 199).

Although reliable statistics on government violence towards citizens thus far have been impossible to collect, it appears that the military regime engaged in far less killing than occurred in the most notorious dictatorships of the twentieth century. Still, people were afraid, and for good reason. To be arrested frequently meant arbitrary beatings while in jail (especially if the arrestee was of working-class background and lacked the international contacts that many highly visible intellectuals had cultivated). In addition, to be arrested meant not only temporary loss of income but, upon release, loss of one's current job and assignment to lowest-paying positions, with no promotion for at least a year. Finally, before a prisoner could be released for good behaviour, he or she had to sign a loyalty oath and attend a reaccreditation hearing. Both procedures were personally demeaning, requiring public denunciation of previous allies and political beliefs.

The chief military prosecutor tried to split Solidarity by arguing that the movement was primarily constituted of well-intentioned and hardworking citizens who had been misled by opportunistic intellectuals associated with KOR – the very same power-hungry cohort that had masterminded the strikes in 1980 and 1981, which had wreaked havoc with the economy and brought on hard times. At one point, to undermine the popularity of Solidarity's leadership, military officials maintained that KOR was ideologically and organizationally connected to Italy's notoriously violent Red Brigades.

Most industrial and agrarian workers did not buy the argument that KOR had bamboozled them. Opinion polls revealed growing working-class disenchantment with Solidarity, partly because of its confused responses to the coup. Workers, however, remained angry first and foremost with the PZPR, on whose shoulders they placed primary responsibility for economic conditions (Mason 1983).

The military government also tried to dilute Solidarity's appeal in 1982 by creating a new, semiautonomous union, the National Federation of Trade Unions (OPZZ), which in theory would represent workers' interests before government officials. What was left of Solidarity's leadership issued statements from underground urging workers not to join the OPZZ. Initially, many did not, but as time passed Solidarity became less relevant to day-to-day struggles for economic survival. Moreover, the OPZZ proved to be a relatively conscientious defender of workers' interests at worksites, a generous dispenser of patronage, and a more autonomous agency than had been anticipated. By 1984, 4 million workers had joined the new union (Brown 1988: 192). By the time Solidarity was relegalized in 1989, membership stood at approximately 6 million, easily surpassing Solidarity's 1.5 million members (Bernhard 1990: 333–5).

The Polish economy, meanwhile, continued flirting with disaster. In 1981, on the eve of the military coup, gross domestic output declined 13 per cent. In 1982, after the Military Council of National Salvation had ruled Poland for a year, the economy shrank another 8 per cent. According to the government's own statistics, 30 per cent of all workers were living below the poverty line (Weschler 1984: 108). The regime tried to stimulate economic growth by raising the artificially low prices, by decentralizing authority over production goals to enterprises, and by legalizing workers' councils (one of Network's goals), which were to comanage worksites. The measures were unavailing.

Solidarity was uncertain how to respond to the military dictatorship. Prior to the coup, the movement had almost always denounced physical violence and sought to increase communication with the regime, bargaining for expansions of citizens' rights through a mixture of dialogue and strike threats. What should be done when the regime outlaws discussion, public assembly, and legal petitioning?

About five months into martial law, a few regional leaders who had escaped to the underground and lived with false identities formed a leadership group, the Temporary Coordinating Commission (TKK). The TKK for the most part disregarded local activists' calls for large-scale demonstrations against the regime, counselled moderation and patience, and condemned political violence. It urged activists to produce and distribute clandestine literature that would sustain pride and courage, and viewed repression as likely to persist into the foreseeable future. Politically motivated strikes would not topple the regime but only lead to needless suffering, especially because Western powers were not about to intervene militarily and free Poland from its military rulers and from the Soviet Union.

Most Solidarity activists who had eluded the police agreed with the TKK's advice. As early as summer 1982 more than 250 periodicals were being printed, with press runs as high as 30,000 (Weschler 1984: 149). Illegal pamphlets, handbills, bulletins, journals, booklets, and the like appeared everywhere and, reflecting the ideological heterogeneity of Solidarity, criticized the government's policies from diverse perspectives (nationalist, liberal, social democratic, Christian, anarchist, etc.).

Polish workers were becoming impatient, however, especially as the government was raising prices on necessities. Demonstrations and street battles exploded here and there but usually lacked support from Solidarity's leadership and were easily repressed. A few illegal Solidarity cells existed in larger factories, but as one activist put it, these cells were 'so deeply underground that many workers didn't even know they existed' (Ost 1990: 208).

From their cell blocks and hideaways pragmatists and fundamentalists in Solidarity continued to criticize one another's ideas. Pragmatists such as Wałęsa (who had been released after a year in jail but who remained under constant police surveillance) accused fundamentalists of irresponsibly provoking martial law through rhetorical bluster. Fundamentalists accused pragmatists of naively trusting the PZPR and therefore failing to prepare Polish citizens for armed struggle. The security forces, apparently without the pragmatists' foreknowledge, covertly aided them by selectively arresting activists known to advocate protest and confrontation (Ost 1989: 76; 1990: 191).

From his jail cell, Kuroń provocatively called on Solidarity in February 1982 to organize a disciplined nationwide general strike that would force the government to grant liberties and end martial law. He acknowledged that violence might erupt during the strike but insisted that

> No program can be built on the hope that the generals and the secretaries will voluntarily agree to a compromise. . . . It has to be assumed that violence retreats only before violence.
>
> (Weschler 1984: 154)

The TKK and other Solidarity leaders, such as those belonging to the Polish Academy of Sciences, strongly disagreed with Kuroń and insisted that the best strategy was to foster a loose coalition of underground presses while petitioning the PZPR and the military for peaceful conciliation. In the words of one, Solidarity must patiently pursue 'the long march' (Ost 1990: 152). In the words of another,

> It is necessary to have a sense of reality. A belief that a general strike would immediately force the authorities to make concessions or would lead in two or three days to a change of government has nothing to do with reality. . . . A bloody confrontation will certainly lower resistance: cowards will break down, the best will die or land in prison, the rest will give up or resort to terrorism. . . . We have to tell the people the truth: no spontaneous or organized strike will bring about independent free unions.
>
> (Weschler 1984: 155)

Military rule formally ended on 22 July 1983. Authority returned to the Sjem, which the PZPR monopolized, permitting a modicum of participation by ancillary parties. Many observers, Lawrence Weschler (1984: 194) among them, judged the regime's liberalization a charade because of continuing restrictions on civil liberties. New laws permitted managers to lengthen workweeks without extra pay whenever production quotas were not met. Students could be expelled if they participated in organizations not approved by the regime. The Solidarity trade union, which had been merely suspended at the onset of martial law and officially delegalized eight months later, remained officially illegal, and hundreds of Solidarity officials remained incarcerated. Remnants of martial law included the admissibility in court of evidence obtained through wiretaps, the dismissal of a worker who 'sows disorder', and the banning of almost all professional organizations whose members frequently criticized the regime, including the actors' union, the Polish Journalists' Association, and the writers' union. Before a group of reporters, Wałęsa declared, 'I would rather have martial law than this' (Weschler 1984: 195).

Liberalization (1986–89)

The year 1986 was a watershed for Solidarity and the Polish regime. The government granted full amnesty in the autumn to all 225 political prisoners (including key figures within Solidarity). At the PZPR's Tenth Party Congress in July, Jaruzelski, who held the party's top leadership position, called for economic reform by means of 'market socialism', that is further decentralization of economic decision making, deregulation of prices, and increasing reliance on market dynamics to determine allocation of scarce resources. At the end of 1986, to help plan the reorganization of the economy and then to disseminate information about forthcoming reforms, Jaruzelski created the Social Consultative Council with members from key nonparty constituencies, such as the Catholic Church, OPZZ, and the intellectual community.

These changes in PZPR policy occurred partly because of new international circumstances.[5] Conservative Soviet leader Leonid Brezhnev, who had pressured Jaruzelski to quell Solidarity in 1981, died in 1982. A few years later, Mikhail

Gorbachev became the Soviet Union's highest ranking Communist official. Believing that traditional trade relations with Eastern bloc countries were draining the Soviet Union of its economic resources, Gorbachev encouraged Poland and the others to become more involved in world trade and less economically tied to the USSR. Believing, too, that those countries could develop extensive trade relations with the West only if they improved their record on civil liberties, he urged them to do so. And during the mid-1980s Gorbachev gave his blessing to Jaruzelski's efforts to grant amnesty to remaining Solidarity prisoners despite demands by the PZPR's hardliners for a crackdown on all counterrevolutionaries.

Gorbachev's policies toward Poland were certainly uncharacteristic for a Soviet leader. The pro-Soviet PZPR hardliners, who for decades had blocked proposed social and political reform through warnings of a possible Soviet invasion in reaction thereto, were suddenly toothless. The more liberal Marxists within the PZPR, who for decades had advocated some degree of trade-union pluralism and multiparty pluralism, were suddenly on the offensive. Through astute coalition building and careful replacement of key committee members, the reformers quickly became the single most powerful group within the PZPR. They directed the government to relax censorship and establish an ombudsperson office to protect civil liberties. They helped legislate a series of economic reforms, making it easier for citizens (usually party members) to start private businesses, acquire foreign exchange, and import overseas investment capital. Also, in hopes of stimulating greater agricultural production, they sharply raised food prices on 1 February 1988. As we shall see, this action fed another outbreak of labour unrest, which would have great consequence for Polish constitutional history.[6]

Between 1986 and 1988 some local and regional workers' associations tried (without success) to register themselves under the title Solidarity. Solidarity's national leadership (in 1987 the TKK and Wałęsa's handpicked advisers formed a new leadership body called the National Executive Commission (KKW)) ignored these grassroots efforts to resurrect a federated Solidarity union. In the words of political scientist David Ost (1990: 164–5), 'most Solidarity leaders did not want to get bogged down in union work per se. They were after bigger game.' They wanted a market economy.

By 1988 most of Solidarity's national leaders were extolling free-market economies and had jettisoned earlier goals of factory councils, a powerful trade union that would help the state make economic policies, and other visions of an alternative to both the Soviet command-economy and Western capitalism. They declared that private ownership of commercial property, deregulation of wages and prices, and free trade promoted individuality while reducing the state's intrusion into people's lives. A more laissez-faire system would also, they argued, quickly end Poland's ten-year economic recession (Millard 1994: 174–8; Ost 1989: 71–80).

Possible explanations for the ideological conversion of so many of Solidarity's most visible national leaders are legion. Some scholars, especially those who are critical of capitalist economics, argue that Solidarity's leaders were following Polish intellectual fashion (Ost 1989; 1990: 165–9). They believe that during the mid-1980s almost every well-educated Pole fantasized about the virtues and benefits of liberal economics and overlooked the costs. Solidarity was riding the wave of a new dogma. Other scholars, often those sympathetic to capitalist economics, believe that the leaders' interest in free-market economics was evidence of their maturity and pragmatism, their rejection of socialist dogmatism and utopianism, and their respect for historical demonstrations of capitalism's superiority to other modes of production (Sachs 1993). In the words of one Solidarity leader, 'We know what works in the world, and we know what doesn't, and we want what works. . . . We don't need to rediscover America' (Weschler 1989: 103). Still other scholars believe that many Solidarity leaders' ardent advocacy of market reform reflected changes in their life experiences. Many had been arrested and, once released, were prohibited from working in state-owned enterprises. To survive, they formed independent businesses during the 1980s. Rewarded for their own entrepreneurial skills and constantly thinking about market conditions, they were gradually transformed into bourgeois theorists. They were no longer concerned with economic equality as a summum bonum and no longer viewed the state as the proper guardian of the poor. For them, market competition justly rewarded the creative and hardworking and justly punished the indolent and incompetent (Weschler 1989: 82, 84, 99–102; Zubek 1991a: 358–9).

Not all Solidarity activists were free-market converts; a plethora of nonmarket ideas also commanded loyalty, especially at the local and regional levels. One leader in 1988 compared the movement to 'a fresco – it has everything in it' (Weschler 1988: 64). An American journalist interviewed members and concluded that the movement 'runs the gamut from proponents of Milton Friedman to disciples of the young Marx' (Weschler 1988: 66).

Troubled by the national leadership's advocacy of market reform, several veteran Solidarity labour activists, who in 1981 were elected to the National Commission, requested a meeting of that body to discuss the leaders' new political agenda. Wałęsa, his allies, and the TKK refused to convene another rambunctious gathering that might include obstreperous fundamentalists. Frustrated, several battle-hardened activists (including the three principal challengers of Wałęsa in his successful bid for the presidency of the Solidarity trade union in 1981) withdrew from Wałęsa's increasingly market-oriented Solidarity and established their own rival labour organizations, among which were those evocatively named Workers Group, Fighting Solidarity, and Solidarity '80 (Bernhard 1990: 335; Ost 1989: 71, 86; Ost 1990: 169).

While Solidarity was undergoing an internal ideological struggle, the Polish economy staggered on. The gross national product, which grew at an average annual rate of 1.2 per cent between 1981 and 1985, grew at merely 1.5 per cent during 1986–88 (Mason 1992: 32). Despite the new directions in PZPR economic policies, inflation reached an annual rate of 64 per cent in 1988 (Ash 1993: 42). Food and other necessities were in short supply. Average meat consumption in 1987 was almost 15 per cent below its already low 1980 level (Weschler 1988: 52). Queues formed outside empty stores. Plants sat silent because of shortages of raw material and spare parts. In 1987 more than 60 per cent of industrial capacity lay unused (Brown 1991: 81).

Neither the PZPR reformers nor Solidarity leaders had anticipated the waves of wildcat strikes that appeared in summer 1988. According to Lawrence Weschler (1988: 48),

> the truth was that Solidarity's underground national leadership had not called any of these strikes and really wanted nothing to do with them. As far as most of the national Solidarity leaders were concerned, this was the wrong time for a strike. . . . These strikes seemed to be bubbling up of their own accord.

The demands of strikers quickly grew from wage hikes (to compensate for the price increases in February) to the legalization of Solidarity, even though the national leadership was not pressing for the latter. Only a few strikes were led by veteran Solidarity labour activists. Sometimes post-Solidarity groups, such as Solidarity '80, helped organize the uprisings and, to Wałęsa's chagrin, declared themselves the genuine descendants of pre-martial-law Solidarity. Some were led and supported by the OPZZ, which, competing with Solidarity and post-Solidarity groups for members, loudly defended workers' wages, safety, and other rights before state authorities. But most were launched by unaffiliated younger workers who had never had contact with Solidarity's underground cells and who often viewed Solidarity's leaders as out of touch with current suffering (Błaszkiewicz et al. 1994; Ost 1989: 80–4; Ost 1990: 182, 207–9; Weschler 1988; Zubek 1991a: 359; Zubek 1991b: 72).

The waves of economic protest overlapped with the rise of a new youth counter-culture after 1986. These young adults (some of whom had been active in the Solidarity student movement of 1980–81) disapproved of all current authority – religious, political, and trade union – and celebrated nonconformity for its own sake. Several leading activists in the so-called New Culture Movement/Orange Alternative, for example, had participated in Solidarity during 1980–81 but no longer supported Solidarity, the OPZZ, or semi-illegal strike committees. Instead, the Orange Alternative organized unorthodox street protests (or 'happenings'), such as public gatherings of citizens dressed as Santa Clauses in shackles, to denounce the commercialization of Polish culture and illustrate the implications of the regime's economic policies for an increasingly poor working class; 'patriotic' marches on national holidays with banners calling for shorter workweeks 'on behalf of' security police; and public 'funerals' for toilet paper and sanitary napkins, to highlight how a socialist regime had made it difficult for citizens to acquire even simple necessities (Anonymous 1988; Błaszkiewicz et al. 1994: 131–4; Staniszkis 1989: 46–9).

The strikes and happenings troubled leaders of the PZPR, who could conceive of no solution to Poland's economic malaise and social breakdown short of further market reform. Desperate to retain political power, the PZPR decided, after intense debate, to invite Solidarity's more moderate leaders to become part of a new constitutional order. During initial probes between representatives of the PZPR and Solidarity, the party implied that it might legalize Solidarity's trade union, increase its access to the news media, reduce censorship, and democratize some political institutions in exchange for Solidarity's help in quieting striking workers and reconciling them to the need for short-term sacrifice during the implementation of future market reforms. In general, Solidarity's national leaders were not averse to working with the party-state (indeed, most pragmatists had advocated closer cooperation with the regime since the movement's inception). They also agreed in general that the creation of a market economy was a prerequisite for Poland's stability and growth. Some veteran labour activists, however, believed that the PZPR could not be trusted and feared that Solidarity was more than ever betraying its original pro-labour orientation (Brown 1991: 90; Millard 1994: 57–8, 135; Staniszkis 1989: 37, 40–2).

During the summer and fall of 1988, while Solidarity and the PZPR were exploring possibilities for imminent power sharing, Wałęsa travelled to sites of labour unrest. There, he argued that by returning to work and temporarily accepting low wages, striking workers could facilitate long-term economic reforms that would benefit all Poles. Immediate wage increases without the reforms would only perpetuate the economic free-fall. Some strikers jeered and accused Wałęsa of selling out. A majority, however, trusted him and resumed work (Ost 1990: 182–4, 209–10; Zubek 1991b: 71).

During winter and spring 1989 teams representing Solidarity and the PZPR negotiated a transition to a more pluralistic, democratic, and market-oriented society.[7] The negotiators agreed that if Solidarity helped contain labour militancy, the party would create a new Polish parliament with two chambers (a Senate and the Sjem). Elections would be a compromise between a wholly free process and a wholly prearranged one. All registered parties could run candidates for the slightly less powerful Senate. Elections for the Sjem, however, would be only partly free, to ensure the legislative superiority of the PZPR; 35 per cent of its seats would be contestable by all parties. The remaining seats would be contestable only by candidates affiliated with either the PZPR or its long-standing allies (the Democratic Party, the United Peasant Party, and Pax).

The negotiating teams also agreed to establish a new executive officer (the president) with power to nominate prime ministers for the parliament and with primary responsibility for conducting foreign policy. The negotiating teams concurred on a number of economic issues as well. Henceforth, average real wages would not fall more than 20 per cent behind the annual inflation rate. Social services, including health and education, would be protected from future budget cuts. Last but not least, the development of producer cooperatives would be a primary goal in future privatization programmes.

Solidarity as a party-movement

Elections for the new parliament were held in June 1989. The party-state wanted them held as soon as possible because Solidarity would thereby lack time to prepare a campaign (or even select candidates, given the movement's very recent relegalization on 17 April 1988 and its nonexistence in many locales). The PZPR, meanwhile, could count on its extensive organizational networks, financial resources, and monopoly over the news media.

In response to adverse political conditions, Wałęsa deftly created a nationwide coalition called Citizens' Committees, or KO, that united locally well known dissidents, often intellectuals and other middle-class professionals with previous ties to Solidarity. With the help of local clergy, who during sermons would urge parishioners to vote for KO candidates; international radio stations, such as Radio Free Europe, that would broadcast endorsements; members of Poland's art community, who designed eye-catching posters; and Solidarity's pre-existing underground press, a colourful anti-PZPR campaign was launched.

To almost everyone's surprise, KO candidates won all but one of the Senate seats *and* all 162 of its allotted maximum in the lower chamber. They beat not only PZPR opponents but candidates from the OPZZ and other non-Solidarity organizations. Even in the more prearranged contests, the PZPR did poorly, sometimes losing to candidates sponsored by the Democratic Party, the United Peasant Party, or Pax. In contests where PZPR candidates ran against only each other (the PZPR did not limit itself to one candidate per district), those known to sympathize openly with Solidarity generally defeated hardliners.[8]

Shortly after the election, members of the United Peasant Party and Democratic Party, eyeing prospects for future elections, distanced themselves from the Communists by announcing that they would not vote for the PZPR's candidate for the presidency. Wałęsa again showed his political dexterity by meeting secretly with the former PZPR allies and arranging for their inclusion in a proposed Solidarity-led government coalition. Wałęsa's secret negotiations caught many KO members off guard, especially because he himself had not run for office and was not an official member of the parliament. His promises of senior cabinet posts to the two parties also troubled some of Solidarity's elected officials – for example, those who belonged to Rural Solidarity and had expected to lead the ministry of agriculture. The KO parliamentarians were further miffed when Wałęsa insisted that his personal friend, the colourless Catholic journalist Tadeusz Mazowieck, be prime minister instead of the parliamentarians' favourite, the astute and eloquent Bronislaw Geremek, whom Wałęsa increasingly feared as a rival. The parliamentarians nonetheless accepted Wałęsa's fait accompli (Weschler 1989: 68–70).

In autumn 1989 the members of the new government were announced. It was a broad coalition, including PZPR leaders in sensitive foreign-policy ministries, members of the United Peasant Party in the ministry of agriculture, and members of Solidarity who strongly advocated free-market economics in the ministries of finance, industry, and housing. Twelve ministries (including the premiership) were headed by members of Solidarity, two by the Democratic Party, three by the United Peasant Party, and three by the PZPR. For the first time in four decades, a predominantly non-Communist government ruled Poland.

Embarrassed and deflated by the election results and further weakened by lingering anger over recent liberalization policies, the PZPR officially disbanded in January 1990. Those who had favoured political and economic reform in the past founded a new party called the Social Democracy of the Polish Republic (SdRP). Many hitherto hardliners were uncertain how to participate effectively in the new electoral system and haplessly formed and destroyed tiny political organizations.

Some former Communists withdrew from politics altogether and entered the business world, such as former regime news journalist, Tadeusz Zakrzewski, who became a public relations director for Mercedes-Benz (Brown 1991: 94–5; Weschler 1992: 42, 57–9; Zubek 1995: 280–5).

The new Solidarity-led parliamentary government accelerated the promarket reforms begun by PZPR and ignored the agreements over wage increases and worker self-management made by Solidarity and PZPR negotiators in early 1989. The government had turned for advice to a wunderkind economist from Harvard University, Jeffrey Sachs, who was an ardent advocate of free trade and corporate forms of capitalism and an indefatigable critic of producer cooperatives, which he once had called 'pernicious'. Sachs argued that gradual economic reform was out of the question. Poland had severe economic problems (for example, outmoded machinery, food shortages, hyperinflation, heavy foreign debt, and excessively high wages) and obvious economic advantages (for example, proximity to western European markets and untapped opportunities in the retail sector). Given these circumstances, price deregulation, privatization, and free trade must be pursued as soon as possible. Otherwise, Sachs warned, Poland's careening economy would generate so much political instability that its democratic experiment would fail (Millard 1994: 76, 174–6; Sachs 1993; Weschler 1989: 84–94).

The government's enthusiastic pursuit of a free-market order perturbed many members of the recently legalized Solidarity trade union. The union's newspaper contended that recent application of Sach's ideas in Bolivia had produced economic chaos (including the closing of 75 per cent of the mines) and dramatically increased unemployment (Ost 1990: 221). The union's executive, fearing the growing independence of Solidarity's parliamentarians from Solidarity's working-class constituencies, voted to have the union become Solidarity's primary tool for candidate selection and voter mobilization and to disband the largely middle-class Citizens' Committees. Solidarity's parliamentarians ignored the vote.

In January 1990 Poland became the first country in eastern Europe to legislate so-called shock therapy – that is, a set of radical free-market reforms designed to cure the economy of excessive nationalization and planning and to base production and distribution decisions on personal calculations of self-interest and unregulated market incentives. The government dismantled price controls in several sectors (for example, in energy), eliminated several subsidies and favourable credit programmes for state firms, and significantly relaxed previous restrictions on free trade. More than 100,000 small state enterprises (such as restaurants and stores) were either sold to private investors (often former state-employed managers and directors) or were liquidated. Upwards of 500,000 new private small businesses appeared (Mason 1992: 123). By September 1991, 75 per cent of all retail business was in private hands (Curry 1992: 387).

The economy did not initially flourish. The United Nations, in fact, demoted Poland's economy in 1990 by reclassifying it from Group B (a developed economy) to Group C (a developing economy) (Bernhard 1990: 324). The gross national product shrank 11.6 per cent in 1990 and another 8 to 10 per cent in 1991 (Curry 1992: 387). Total annual industrial production fell 23 per cent in 1990, and total agricultural production dropped almost 40 per cent between May 1989 and May 1990 (Bernhard 1990: 326; Mason 1992: 93). While overall production contracted, the official unemployment rate rose from nil in 1989 to 6.3 per cent in 1990 to 11.8 per cent in 1991 (Kramer 1995: 80). In cities heavily dependent on state-owned factories, such as Łódź (one of Poland's textile centres), official unemployment soared beyond 20 per cent (Kramer 1995: 84). Price deregulation raised the already high annual rate of inflation to 800 per cent in 1990 (Mason 1992: 94). Food prices rose 978 per cent in 1989 alone (Bernhard 1990: 325).

The government's refusal to raise wages meant that the average real wage in industry fell 32 per cent in 1990 (Kramer 1995: 80, 89). That year, average real household income for the nation as a whole fell nearly a third (Ash 1991: 365; Mason 1992: 93). Sometimes workers sardonically joked about the supposed benefits of economic reform: 'First World prices at Third World wages' (Weschler 1990: 87).

The short-term economic dislocations – generated by the combination of price deregulation, privatization of overstaffed state companies (and concomitant lay-offs from the white elephants), wage freezes, and the flooding of Polish markets with cheap imports – proved much more severe than advocates of market reform had advertised. Spokespersons for the Solidarity-led government had predicted a temporary decrease in industrial productivity in 1990 of 5 per cent, not 20 per cent. The government also had vastly underestimated the first year's inflation rate, predicting that it would not exceed 100 per cent; in fact, it easily exceeded 500 per cent (Millard 1994: 81; Weschler 1990: 88).

Divided over the reasonableness of continued free-market reform, the Solidarity movement rapidly splintered into rival profarmer, proworker, and promarket factions (Bernhard 1990: 325; Millard 1994). Profarmer activists wanted higher tariffs to slow the influx of cheap food, removal of all remaining price controls on food so that farming would again be profitable, and government subsidies to help small farmers procure the expensive chemicals and machinery necessary to become internationally competitive (Bernhard 1990: 324; Zubek 1991b: 80–1). Solidarity's prolabour activists pleaded for indexing wages to the remarkably high inflation rates; price controls (especially on food); job protection (especially in the nationalized firms about to be sold to private investors); more government-subsidized housing for urban workers (apartments were so scarce in some cities that waiting lists exceeded 50 years); more worker-managed cooperatives; and larger government expenditures on health, education, and unemployment compensation (Ost 1990: 210–11, 214; Zubek 1992: 585–9).

Many profarmer and prolabour activists either organized official factions within Solidarity, such as the Solidarity Peasant Party and the Group for Defending the Interests of Working People, or left Solidarity altogether and formed rival political parties, such as the Polish Socialist Party. In response, promarket advocates organized their own factions, such as the Christian National Union, to defeat the 'Reds and the Pinks' within Solidarity (Millard 1994: 132). Meanwhile, disgruntled agricultural and industrial producers protested outside parliament, where antigovernment hunger strikes, transportation general strikes, and road blockades suddenly appeared (Bernhard 1990: 326–7; Kramer 1995: 91–8; Zubek 1991b: 80–1; Zubek 1992: 594–5).

The organizational break-up of Solidarity was painful. 'For thousands of individual men and women, Solidarity was a part of their identity, of their emotional life,' writes historian Timothy Garton Ash (1991: 368). 'There was no mistaking the genuine pain, sorrow, and often bitterness felt at the parting of ways with former comrades.'

Somewhat surprisingly, the growing unrest over free-market reform failed to unite the KO's free-market advocates in parliament behind a single leader. On the contrary, the parliamentarians associated with the Solidarity movement became divided between Wałęsa's followers (who supported his half-hidden aspirations for the presidency; at this time Wałęsa was president of the Solidarity trade union but held no government post) and anti-Wałęsa parliamentarians (who found Wałęsa's earthy language and manipulative style of personal politics anathema, especially compared to the urbane, eloquent, and highly principled political style of Yugoslavia's new president, Václav Havel). The favourable and unfavourable assessments of Wałęsa's leadership style were reinforced in some cases by subtle differences in capitalist economic philosophy. Many of Wałęsa's supporters shared his well-known admiration for Margaret Thatcher and her economic vision for Great Britain (that is, a minuscule nationalized sector, a bureaucratically trim government providing minimal public services, and reliance on the market for impartial allocation of resources and jobs, and reasonable decisions about welfare). Several of Wałęsa's opponents (many of whom were former KOR activists) favoured a more Sweden-like social-welfare order, in which the state plays a larger role in distributing income and protecting the economically unfortunate.

The two parliamentary factions fought bitterly for control over Solidarity's Citizen Committees, which had effectively mobilized voters in 1989. Wałęsa's side won and dismantled local branches sympathetic to his rivals.

After Wałęsa announced his intention to run for president in 1990, mudslinging broke out. Anti-Wałęsa free marketeers accused him of being clownish, uncouth, intellectually inept, and a potential ultranationalist and religious extremist. Wałęsa responded with red-baiting (noting the former revisionist background and PZPR-participation of many older Solidarity leaders), calling his opponents 'pinkos' and cryptocommunists, and at one point making anti-Semitic remarks about his rivals.[9]

Wałęsa, partly because he received support from peasant organizations angered by what they perceived as the Mazowieck government's antifarmer policies, easily defeating Mazowieck for the presidency. Mazowieck's supporters then organized a new party called the Democratic Union (UD) that mildly opposed Wałęsa's leadership and advocated a vaguely modified free-market economy. The pro-Wałęsa and anti-Wałęsa groups disagreed on ministerial appointments, viewing each other's nominees as incompetent for the sorts of economic policies that needed to be made.

In autumn 1991 the second parliamentary elections were held, with a purely proportional system of representation as the format. There were signs – for example, results from the government's Centre for Public Opinion Studies (Marody 1995: 266) – that voters were tiring of economic change and of political bickering among non-Communists. Turnout on election day was barely above 40 per cent (20 per-centage points below the voter turnout in 1989). The Solidarity movement by this time had fragmented into dozens of post-Solidarity parties, each addressing distinctive constituencies. Twenty-nine parties won seats. The two largest, the post-Solidarity UD and the post-Communist SdRP, each received approximately 12 per cent of the seats in the Sjem; the others received far less than 10 per cent of all ballots cast and therefore far less than 10 per cent of the seats. The following sample of party names illustrates the variegated interests and priorities now represented: Catholic Election Action, Peasant Party – Programmatic Alliance, Peasant Accord, Solidarity, Labour Solidarity, Solidarity '80, German Minority, Movement for Silesian Autonomy, Great Poland and Poland, Friends of Beer, Women Against Life's Hardship, Union of Political Realism, and Party X.[10]

The election results stunned both Wałęsa and the leaders of the UD. Wałęsa had not openly endorsed any party because he wished to play the role of a nonpartisan leader of all Poles, but he had not anticipated dealing with such a fissiparous parliament in which only short-lived governing coalitions, combining a half-dozen parties with incredibly diverse policy agendas, could be formed. Frustrated by the very short life spans of the ministerial governments he nominated, Wałęsa increasingly described Poland's parliamentary politics as anarchistic and irresponsible, adding that the predominance of organized special interests prevented him from shepherding legislation through that reflected the real will of the people. Accordingly, he advocated constitutional amendments that would give the president (in other words, Wałęsa) sufficient power to override a divided and stalemated parliament (Holc 1995: 71, 75–7; Millard 1994: 89–90, 96, 146–66).

The leaders of the UD were likewise stunned by the election results. The UD was the largest single party in the Sjem, capturing slightly more than 12 per cent of the chamber's seats. Its leadership, however, had hoped to win at least 25 per cent of the vote and to become the centerpiece of a governing coalition. After all, the party contained many of the most famous intellectuals associated with Solidarity between 1980 and 1989, and they were the undisputed heirs to the courageously defiant organization before martial law. The populace, surely, would look with favour on such principled and steadfast opponents to communism. But the UD's grand expectations went unfulfilled: most voters cast ballots for other candidates. Furthermore, other parliamentary parties were hesitant to form a coalition with the UD partly because of its apparent intolerance of other interests and viewpoints (a perception fuelled in part by the UD's combative election campaign) and partly because its small number of parliamentarians made it expendable in a coalition government.

The SdRP (the only other party in the Sjem controlling more than 10 per cent of the seats) was also ostracized because of its members' Communist affiliations. Non-Communist parties were very reluctant to cooperate with the former PZPR members, partly because of memories of earlier decades of repression and partly because of fears of an electoral backlash.

In effect, there was no major party commanding at least a quarter of the legislative votes and available to lead a coalition government. Rather, unstable governing coalitions of very small parties with little programmatic common ground were formed.

The promarket reforms of 1990, meanwhile, seemed to be producing some positive results. The gross national product grew 1.5 per cent in 1992 and 4.5 per cent in 1993, after more than a decade of negative and near-zero annual growth rates. International corporations such as Fiat and Levi Strauss were investing in plants. The annual inflation (though still high by western European standards) dropped to less than 50 per cent in 1992. Statistics also indicated a rising standard of living. Per capita annual consumption of meat and fruit, for example, rose between 1988 and 1991, as did per capita ownership of automobiles, radios, and televisions (Kramer 1995: 80, 102–3; Sachs 1993: 69–71).

Despite these positive signs, there remained reason to worry. The official unemployment level rose to the mid-teens in 1992 and 1993. Well over 2 million workers were on the dole (Kramer 1995: 80; Millard 1994: 111). High prices and frozen wages meant consumer belt-tightening, which in turn meant reduced sales for many retailers, service-sector companies, and light industries. Caught between low consumer demand and the flooding of the domestic market with cheaper imports, Poland's textile industry was almost completely destroyed (Weschler 1990: 88, 95–6; 1992: 64). Farmers' standards of living declined, according to diverse measurements (for example, farmers' per capita annual consumption of meats and fruit (Sachs 1993: 70, 77)). Approximately 300,000 peasants joined in a new radical organization called Self-Defence blocked roads, occupied government buildings, and demanded suspensions of debt repayments (Millard 1994: 98, 108). Rumours of growing inequality in wealth and income spread (Bernhard 1990: 329; Curry 1992: 338; Kramer 1995: 78, 81). The nouveau riche, unlike the less visible PZPR members during the Communists' rule, flaunted their lifestyles in public. One journalist noted

> widespread and growing resentment over an obviously increasing polarization of wealth. . . . [T]here is a new, ostentatious cult of wealth, which seriously grates on the many more who are not doing so well.
>
> (Weschler 1992: 57)

Industrial workers, meanwhile, manifested their discontent in strikes and other industrial actions, which were gradually increasing in number and size (Kramer 1995: 91–2, 102; Millard 1994: 98, 108). Even the Solidarity trade union now regularly denounced the government's commitment to capitalism (Kramer 1995: 95, 102–4; Millard 1994: 89, 92; Zubek 1995: 297). Opinion polls between 1990 and 1992 also evidenced widespread popular disillusionment with the economy and with recent free-market reforms (Kramer 1995: 99; Marody 1995: 266). For example, in a government survey taken in May 1992, 57 per cent of the respondents said the economy was weaker than it had been at the end of the Communist rule, and 87 per cent expected the economy to worsen over the next few years (Curry 1992: 386).

In September 1993 another parliamentary election was held under rules once again changed. This time candidates had to receive at least 5 per cent of the ballots cast in a district to earn a seat. Turnout was modest: slightly more than half of all eligible voters cast their ballots. Voters turned away in droves from candidates sponsored by the Solidarity family of parties. For the first time, Solidarity and post-Solidarity parties failed to capture together at least half of the ballots cast. The Union of the Democratic Left (an electoral coalition led by the post-Communist SdRP) and the Polish Peasant Party (a reincarnation of the PZPR's traditional ancillary party, the United Peasant Party) were the two most successful vote getters and jointly controlled a majority within the Sjem. Solidarity and post-Solidarity parties had been ousted by former Communists. In the opinion of one social scientist, parties tied to the Solidarity movement were partly responsible for their own demise. They were so vicious to one another during the campaign that the outcome was a foregone conclusion: 'the post-communist left had victory delivered to it on a silver platter' (Zubek 1995: 299).[11]

For Solidarity, the worst was yet to come. In 1995 several post-Solidarity parties, including those headed by Kuroń and other former KOR activists, refused to endorse Wałęsa during the runoff presidential election, either out of personal animosity (Wałęsa had adopted an extremely combative leadership style vis-à-vis his former comrades) or out of discomfort with his laissez-faire orientation in economic policy. Wałęsa failed to win majorities in a number of traditionally pro-Solidarity districts, especially in blue-collar areas dominated by government-owned enterprises specializing in mining and heavy industry (Taras 1996: 125, 127–8). Wałęsa also failed to win over younger voters, many of whom saw Solidarity's mobilizations in 1980–81 and the PZPR's rule as part of the distant past. To the chagrin of Wałęsa and other veteran activists who had led Solidarity in 1980–81, a former PZPR leader with extraordinary public-relations skills, Aleksander Kwaśniewski, won the election.[12] Ash writes (1995: 10),

> this was an astonishing result. Six years after the end of communism, the country which had the strongest anti-communist opposition and the weakest communist party in the Soviet bloc has both a government led by former communists and a president who is one. Anyone who had predicted this in the autumn of 1989 would have been laughed out of the room.

By the mid-1990s Solidarity and post-Solidarity leaders were once again on the outside looking in. But unlike the glory days of 1980–81, Solidarity was now ideologically polarized and organizationally disunited. Its prospects looked bleak.

Conclusion

The ideological story of Solidarity before martial law matches many generalizations about social movements made by autonomous popular-culture theorists. Activists from different social and political milieus joined the movement, bringing with them heterogenous opinions about political strategies and social goals. The movement's official ideology was inelegantly patched together during a raucous convention. Leaders, followers, and factions, informed by diverse beliefs, often moved at cross-purposes.

During the mid-1980s, a more ideologically coherent Solidarity evolved. Imprisonment prevented fundamentalists from directing the movement, and labour organizers had to be chary while avoiding arrest at the workplace. In these adverse political circumstances, pragmatists monopolized national leadership posts. As autonomous movement-culture theorists would anticipate, novel beliefs were embraced by Solidarity's national leaders – beliefs about the desirability of a free market, private property, and unrestricted international trade that many of them did not hold before martial law. As David Ost (1989: 85) notes, their ideological commitment did not automatically trickle down to the movement's regional and local levels: 'the problem is Solidarity now has a leadership that supports economic reform and a rank-and-file that opposes it'.

After 1989 the movement organizationally splintered, partly because of growing disagreements over social and economic goals. Solidarity's parliamentarians pursued programmes of radical economic reform; disenchanted agrarian and proletarian groups launched competing political organizations. By 1995 the decimated movement controlled neither the parliament nor the presidency – an amazing reversal from its landslide victory in 1989.

Solidarity's ideological evolution resembled and differed from that of the West German Greens. Both movements at first combined disparate ideological traditions (although activists in both movements called for 'freedom' from what they viewed as an oppressive social and political order). The Greens' initial amalgam included ecological reasoning, Marxism, libertarianism, pacifism, feminism, and the spontis' and squatters' avant-garde, countercultural, and semianarchistic pastiche. Solidarity's initial amalgam included the Network's theories of producer cooperatives, working-class theories of trade-union independence, ROPCiO's calls for national independence from the Soviet Union, and KOR's vision of extensive civil liberties and rule of law.

Both movements' ideologies metamorphosed in roughly a decade. In Germany, environmental concerns and orthodox parliamentary coalition building became hallmarks of the once economically decentralist and semianarchistic Greens. After martial law, Solidarity's national leadership vigorously advocated market reform. True, the movement's 1981 programme contained occasional references to the desirability of a market economy, but this was not a salient theme prior to 1985.

In both cases, ideological differences of opinion became more divisive after the movements, through elections, gained access to governmental institutions. Once movement representatives held positions of authority, previously largely theoretical disagreements over goals and priorities took on additional practical implications. In both cases, leaders of the dominant ideological factions steadfastly acted on their beliefs, while ideological losers often bitterly resigned.

The ideas and actions of both movements shaped the broader political culture of their respective countries. In Germany, ecology and feminism became part of mainstream political discourse by the beginning of the 1990s. Solidarity likewise disseminated free-market theory among Poland's political classes between 1986 and 1991 and through its legislative actions created a range of economic expectations, institutions, and practices (free trade, private enterprise, and shock treatment) that would shape Polish politics for the remainder of the twentieth century.

One striking difference between the Greens and Solidarity is the latter movement's greater ideological disjointedness. The realo tradition was always a central component of the Greens' syncretic ideology. Thus, there is an element of ideological continuity in the case of the German Greens that is absent when one looks at the beliefs of Solidarity's national leaders between 1981 to 1990. Many national leaders of Solidarity suddenly followed a new ideological fashion and jettisoned almost all of the movement's early dominant ideas, such as workers' comanagement. Why?

Part of the explanation may lie in Poland's nondemocratic political circumstances, especially before 1986. Repression silenced many factions within Solidarity (especially prolabour groups and the fundamentalists). Also recall that the government systematically repressed more radical factions within Solidarity in the hope of allowing the more collaborative elements to control the movement. These political conditions enabled the national leadership to move in new ideological directions without feeling overly constrained by oppositional groups. The more ideologically conservative groups in Solidarity, prevented from meeting publicly, could only look on in frustration as national spokespersons adopted a new rhetoric.

This contrast between Solidarity and the German Greens suggests a pair of hypotheses that might be applicable to other movements. First, social movements that emerge in despotic orders have a greater likelihood of undergoing root-and-branch ideological transformations and, therefore, becoming exposed to broad swings in nonelite popularity. Second, movements that emerge in liberal constitutional orders, that are not systematically repressed by the state, and that engage in electoral politics, have a greater likelihood of undergoing incremental (as opposed to radical) ideological change and, therefore, having a more constant level of popular support. The broader generalization lying behind these propositions can be summarized as follows: to forecast the organizational unity of a social movement and the durability of its popular support, one must attend not only to the diverse beliefs that its activists hold but to the constitutional circumstances in which its factions jostle.

Notes

1. For descriptions of the Gdańsk strike, see Ash (1991: 41–72), Goodwyn (1991), Persky (1981: 3–24, 58–135), Singer (1982: 217–31), and Starski (1982: 57–92).
2. For detailed descriptions of both the diverse social and political viewpoints within the trade union and the recurrent conflicts between proponents of the different viewpoints, see Ash (1991: 73–272), Starski (1982: 199–217, 247–48), and Touraine et al. (1983).
3. For further descriptions of the Bydgoszcz crisis, see Ash (1991: 154–74), Goodwyn (1991: 293–8), and Persky (1981: 197–214).
4. More information about Poland's martial law and its impact on Solidarity may be found in Łopiński, et al. (1990), Millard (1994: 18–23), Ost (1990: 149–60), and Weschler (1984: 97–204, 225–32).
5. For discussions of the implications of the Soviet Union's changing foreign policy for the liberalization of Poland's communist regime, see Brown (1991: 74–86), Mason (1992: 43–56), and Ost (1990: 192–5).
6. For more details on the PZPR's reform initiatives in the late 1980s, see Brown (1991: 83–6) and Ost (1990: 160–3, 169–82).

7. For additional information on the roundtable negotiations, see Kowalik (1994: 136–7), Millard (1994: 56–63), Ost (1990: 206–7, 211–12), and Zubek (1991a: 359–65).
8. More information on the 1989 election may be found in Ash (1993: 25–46), Millard (1994: 64–70), and Zubek (1991a: 361–76).
9. For further information on the presidential campaign of 1990, see Millard (1994: 84, 119–32), Weschler (1990: 120–36), and Zubek (1991b; 1992).
10. For more information on the 1991 parliamentary election and parliamentary politics between 1991 and 1993, see Millard (1994: 92–3, 132–40), Weschler (1992: 73–7), and Zubek (1993).
11. Analyses of the 1993 parliamentary election may be found in Marody (1995), Millard (1994: 140–3), Wade et al. (1995), and Zubek (1995).
12. Some early analyses of the 1995 presidential election may be found in Ash (1995) and Taras (1996).

Part IV

Peru's Shining Path and agrarian-based movements

Thus far, we have looked at two social movements in highly industrialized settings with large metropolitan populations and nationwide systems of communication and transportation. Although the West German Greens and Poland's Solidarity emerged in very different political contexts – a liberal democracy with regularly held competitive elections and a communist-ruled state with minimal legal rights to contest government decisions – both movements shared a largely nonagrarian social backdrop and in each country agrarian production had become largely mechanized by the 1980s. These environments seem to have profoundly affected the resources, tactics, and goals of both Germany's Greens and Poland's Solidarity. It is difficult to imagine the Green party existing independently of urban settings – especially university towns and cities with sizeable youth ghettos – or Solidarity appearing independently of radios and newsletters, gigantic factories, and large working-class neighbourhoods. To some extent, each movement was a by-product of its largely nonagrarian economic environment.

Some scholars, such as Barry Adam (1987), Sidney Tarrow (1994), and Charles Tilly (1978), have suggested that urban settings, industrial production, and modern mass media are critical, if not necessary, preconditions for the emergence of national social movements. They credit cities' cultural networks (newspapers, radios, coffeehouses, political bars, and the like) with facilitating the discussion of public events and the discovery of common concerns among people who do not work and live next to one another. In addition, because of population density and the constant social interaction, fledgling movements have a better chance of attracting activists and of organizing huge demonstrations because attendance at such events entails neither high transportation costs nor great expenditures of time. Similarly, subversive ideas can be easily communicated (for example, through pamphleting outside plant gates and through well-placed posters), and knowledge about the successful tactics of other groups can be circulated, thanks to myriad meeting places and metropolitan news media.

Social movements, however, sometimes appear in countries with relatively small industrialized sectors, and they sometimes involve large numbers of rural people. For example, Peru's Shining Path (Sendero Luminoso) movement was contemporaneous with the Green movement and the Solidarity movement. Unlike them, its primary theatre of action was an impoverished region – the southern Andes – where paved roads were novelties, where few households had indoor plumbing (much less television), where literacy was uncommon, and where tiny villages often viewed each other antagonistically as territorial expansionists. Granted, the Shining Path movement quickly attracted members and sympathizers throughout Peru, yet its spiritual and organizational centre remained the economically stunted southern Andes.

Let us look more closely at this initially and primarily nonurban movement and search for clues as to how social movements emerge and develop in countries with partial urban development and industrialization and with relatively large proportions of the population engaged in nonmechanized and noncommercial agriculture. How do radical nonelite politics evolve in such economic conditions?

A world to be remade: sociopolitical circumstances of Shining Path

First- and second-generation social-movement theorists posited that social conditions can facilitate the appearance of social movements in two distinguishable ways. According to the second-generation writers, local social institutions and traditions of protest can facilitate the emergence of social movements by providing resources (say, models of resistance and communication networks) that increase a movement's likelihood of success. Neighbourhood churches, for example, can provide meeting places, tested leaders, and emotive symbols of solidarity with which to mobilize a discontented cohort. According to first-generation theorists, elements of modernization – such as rapid industrialization and the corresponding deterioration in the economic security and social status of traditional middle classes – facilitate the formation of movements partly by posing unprecedented large-scale problems that people believe (1) need to be addressed immediately and (2) can be solved only through a societal restructuring. Movements thus are consequences of dramatic, large-scale social changes.

In the next chapter we will look at how local social institutions and traditions of protest affected people's receptiveness to Shining Path and provided its leaders with valuable resources. In this chapter we will look at Shining Path's broader social and political context – in particular, at Peru's economic history and geography.

To anticipate some of our findings, Shining Path appeared during a long-term contraction in Peru's economy that began in the mid-1970s and continued through the early 1990s. During these two decades, per capita gross domestic product declined at an average annual rate of 2.16 per cent, real wages at 3.89 per cent. The annual inflation rate averaged 293.5 per cent and at times exceeded 1,000 per cent (Gonzales de Olarte 1994: 160).

These turbulent economic conditions resembled many of those that early social-movement theorists had posited as crucial in the fomenting of a social movement. According to Seymour Martin Lipset (1950), for example, widespread and sharp economic contractions can prompt many people to join a radical movement because they want something to be done and there are no obvious short-term or nonradical alternatives. James Scott (1976), who is not a classical modernization theorist but who sometimes investigates the political consequences of macroeconomic change, has also concluded that when modernization disrupts a nation's traditional economic practices and generates a subsistence crisis, a social movement is more likely to occur.

Many specialists in Peruvian politics have echoed Lipset's and Scott's lines of argument and have concluded that the country's severe depression in the late 1970s and 1980s spawned popular support for Shining Path and its guerrilla activities. '[H]ow important is a crisis of subsistence to peasant revolt?', asks Cynthia McClintock (1984: 49). 'I will argue that in the Peruvian case, it has been outstandingly important.' In the words of John Sheahan (1994: 19),

> there is a strong sense among young people that there is no future in the society and that the only alternative is to leave. We see people leaving the society both physically and by joining the violent organizations that are attempting to tear the society apart. It is safe to presume that an economy that is perpetually in decline and that fails to offer any evident future to its youth is going to face a lot of violence.

Given frequent scholarly arguments about the centrality of rapid economic and social change both to the emergence of social movements in general and to the emergence of Shining Path in particular, it behoves us to become familiar with the evolution of Peru's economy, with patterns of poverty in the country, and with the frustration, resentment, and desperation generated thereby.

Early capitalist development in Peru

Latin America historians concur in the notion that Peru, after winning independence from Spain in 1821, underwent a process of capitalist development unique in Latin American history.[1] Other countries of the region sooner or later experimented with high tariffs and nationalist programmes of industrialization. Peru's governments, however, have been far more consistently committed to an export-based strategy of economic development. Historians Thomas Skidmore and Peter Smith (1992: 193, 197) write that Peru's

> Policymakers have almost always focused on the international market, not domestic demand. . . . [Even after the Depression and World War II] – in contrast to their counterparts in Argentina, Mexico, and Brazil – national policymakers did not even try to embark on a sustained program of import-substitution industrialization. When opportunity beckoned in the late 1940s they turned instead to a tried-and-true strategy: export-led growth with ample room for foreign investment and integration of Peru's economy with the international economy, above all the U.S. economy.

Aníbal Quijano Obregón (1968: 291–2) similarly has argued that 'the whole history of the development of this [Peruvian] society can be considered largely as the history of successive modifications of this relationship of dependency'.

Peru's initial integration into the world capitalist economy involved the exportation between 1840 and 1870 of guano, a valuable seabird dung used as fertilizer by commercial farmers. The government shrewdly sold guano found on publicly owned land to European merchants, who set up a thriving worldwide market in the product. The government used its profits to establish a standing army and a bureaucracy, to develop public education, and to abolish plantation slavery (through compensation to slave owners). Treating guano as an inexhaustible resource, the government also pledged future profits from its sale to foreigners as collateral for loans with which to build ports and railways.

A culture of consumption rapidly took root along the coast, where a small number of speculators prospered from guano and, later, sugar and nitrates exports. One Peruvian writer in the 1800s uncomfortably observed that among the coastal landowners, 'popular imagination endowed fantastic proportions to the improvisation of fortunes. . . . For the first time money emerged as the exclusive social value' (Skidmore and Smith 1992: 193).

The highly profitable guano trade soon proved to be a double-edged sword. First of all, it exacerbated the already geographically skewed evolution of Peru's national economy. Almost all commercial activity in colonial Peru had taken place along its arid coastal belt, which accounts at most for only 15 per cent of Peru's present area. Some fief-like estates and a few mines had developed in the mountains and depended on slavery to yield livelihoods for the Spanish invaders. The owners, however, seldom sought to increase profits through investment in machinery, buildings, and improved agricultural practices; they simply indulged in the lavish lifestyles afforded by the wealth produced by Indian labourers. Even those few landowners who wanted to act in a more rational capitalistic fashion found commercial agriculture a daunting undertaking because of the prohibitive costs of sending their crops to markets in western Europe and North America. In addition, anti-Indian prejudice – inherited from the earliest colonists and reinforced by an ongoing need to rationalize the mistreatment of indigenous peoples – dissuaded many early nineteenth-century landowners from risking capital and employing purported 'brutes' to (mis)handle expensive machinery.[2]

Second, its dependence on guano trade rendered the government extremely vulnerable to downturns in international business. The government derived about 80 per cent of its revenues from guano exports, and it viewed loans based on future sales as a convenient method to finance public services (read: to secure popular support without high taxes; in fact, the government did not directly levy taxes until the 1960s) (Rudolph 1992: 146; Skidmore and Smith 1992: 190). It was not the most stable of economic bases upon which to rest political legitimacy.

A worldwide recession late in the nineteenth century tumbled guano prices and profits. Government revenues plunged precipitously, and interest payments on outstanding foreign loans could not be met. Public works and the modestly sized bureaucracy soon became unaffordable. The government responded with draconian measures – for example, downsizing the military by three-quarters (Rudolph 1992: 29).

The economic crisis overlapped a war with Chile over ownership of nitrate mines on Peru's southern frontier, which the Peruvians lost badly. Chilean forces raided Peru's ports with impunity and at one point even occupied Lima, the capital. By the mid-1880s the once-modest state apparatus was in shambles.

At the close of the 1880s Peruvians faced a bleak political and economic future. The country was unable to earn sufficient foreign exchange to meet loan obligations, and guano deposits were nearly exhausted. There were valuable mineral deposits in the mountainous interior, but European and US companies were reluctant to finance their extraction without being given special compensation because of the high cost of shipping around the dangerous Horn at the southern tip of the continent. (The Panama Canal had yet to be built.)

Salvation arrived from overseas. British investors offered to cancel Peru's entire foreign debt in exchange for long-term control of future guano exports, the railway system, and large tracts of ore-bearing land. The Peruvian Congress reluctantly agreed in 1889 to the highly controversial 'Grace Contract'.

At first, the contract did not seem to be a sell-out. The short-term infusion of British capital allowed a railroad to be built in the department of Junín, where mineral deposits awaited extraction. Mining profits helped spur another period of prosperity, guided largely by international demand for certain highly valuable raw materials. Commerce very soon was once again growing at a respectable clip. Gigantic sugar enterprises with highly mechanized mills and irrigated cotton plantations appeared on the northern coast. Coastal plantations utilized tens of thousands of workers, including sharecroppers of African descent, Chinese indentured labourers, and indebted Indians from the interior. In the central mountains, enormous farms (owned primarily by very wealthy Peruvians) raised sheep and produced wool for export. Smaller farms raised diverse cash crops for sale in the coastal cities. Foreign investors purchased oil fields in the North and held mineral rights in the northern and central mountains. US investors financed vast mining operations for copper, silver, lead, and zinc. On the eastern slopes of the Andes, both foreign and domestic adventurers established rubber plantations, which initially relied to some extent on coerced and unsalaried labour, including debt peonage, to compel Amazonian Indians to participate in a short-lived boom.

Attracted by the government's generous taxation and profit-remittance schemes, foreign investors soon dominated the Peruvian economy. International investors controlled more than 450 of the 542 largest commercial and manufacturing firms in Lima (Rudolph 1992: 34). By 1919 they controlled upwards of 90 per cent of the mining industry, 80 per cent of sugar production, and 75 per cent of textile production (Poole and Rénique 1992: 104). For the next four decades Peru, whose access to foreign markets dramatically increased with completion of the Panama Canal, continued to be a haven for foreign investors, who, by the 1960s, owned 80 per cent of the oil industry and nearly all of the major telephone, electricity, banking, and railway companies (Rudolph 1992: 55).

Not surprisingly, many smaller domestic manufacturers felt unfairly disadvantaged by the government's ever-lenient free-trade and foreign-investment policies. Couching their arguments in patriotic language about national interest and political independence, they contended as early as the 1920s that foreign interests were monopolizing the most profitable sectors of the economy and setting unreasonably high prices for raw materials, which made adequate profit margins hard to come by. Other middle-class groups – in particular, intellectuals – soon joined in the nationalistic chorus against what they described as foreign (and especially Yankee) 'imperialism'.[3]

Most of Peru's wealthiest capitalists, who increasingly held investments in multiple rural and urban companies, disagreed with the naysayers and saw the country's involvement in the world capitalist system as a boon for everyone. After all, during the first two-thirds of the century, Peru had recorded relatively stable levels of economic growth, as measured by the nation's total output of goods and services. As we shall see, the steady growth in aggregate productivity coincided with strikingly high degrees of inequality. Total output, nonetheless, grew so impressively from year to year that many national and international capitalists came to view the Peruvian economy as one of the most successful in the western hemisphere. Even the most radical critics of Peru's economic order were conceding by the late 1960s that Peru was one of the most rapidly industrializing countries in the hemisphere and that its economic growth rates during the second third of the twentieth century may have been second only to those of Mexico (Pastor and Wise 1992: 83; Quijano Obregón 1968: 326).

Failure of populist politics

Wanting to sustain and, if possible, accelerate economic growth, successive Peruvian governments during the twentieth century sought additional low-interest loans from international banks and development organizations, such as the Alliance for Progress. Government leaders deemed the loans low-risk resources with which to develop the economic infrastructure – such as highways, railways, utilities, and ports – and thus coax further private investment. They also believed that domestic taxes could not be relied upon to finance economy-stimulating public works, in part because the private banks and individuals who collected taxes for the government were notoriously corrupt and skimmed large amounts through 'service' charges. Domestic taxes, in addition, reduced the profit margins of private firms and thereby reduced funds available for private investment and business expansions. In sum, foreign loans came to be the politically acceptable, economically shrewd, and administratively effective means of choice for underwriting necessary public works. The government's ongoing preference for loans had predictable consequences: in 1919, foreign debt was approximately $10 million; in 1930, in excess of $100 million; and in 1968, $750 million (Rudolph 1992: 37, 50).

The government used the hefty international loans to stimulate economic growth indirectly, through roads, railway systems, and other transportation and communication projects. It also used the loans to expand the state's minuscule bureaucracies (such as its small departments of statistics, industry, and Indian affairs) and to fortify the military.

Government leaders with so-called populist agendas periodically proposed using borrowed money to improve the condition of the rural poor (Skidmore and Smith 1992: 201–13; Stein 1980). They argued that economic growth had thus far bypassed the majority of Peruvians, who lived in the Andes. The enormous and expanding cattle and sheep ranches in the central Andes, for example, had taken over villages' and smallholders' lands at the expense of indigenous forms of agriculture, such as communal herding and planting. Livelihoods in the mountains were steadily disappearing at a time when Peru had one of the highest population growth rates in the hemisphere. The populists, who advocated smaller farms and better employment training for peasants, maintained that because the rulers of Peru had failed to address the economic suffering of poorer classes, social conflict was spreading. Land invasions and general strikes were becoming more frequent occurrences in the highlands.

Being liberal reformers and not socialists, the populists avoided calls for the expropriation of land (which Peru's Marxists advocated) and instead proposed using a portion of the public purse to reconcile mine workers and peasants to the new economic order through public education programmes, through humanitarian labour laws that would be conscientiously monitored, through modest public housing projects, and through ambitious road construction programmes that would bring fresh business and employment opportunities to the mountains and eastern jungles. They asserted that new roads and a literate Indian workforce would make the mountains and jungle areas more attractive to investors (both domestic and foreign) and thus would lead to job opportunities, a higher standard of living, and possibly even perpetual prosperity.

The conservative business interests, however, viewed most public works projects and educational experiments in the countryside as unnecessary and wasteful. They argued that the government should invest primarily in sectors of the economy that had already proved themselves either to be highly profitable or to have significant growth potential. Sugar plantations, cattle ranches, and mines, in other words, should be helped. As such export industries prospered, wealth would trickle down to other classes. The coastal capitalists and mountain landlords wielded considerable clout within the Congress and the military and regularly defeated the legislative proposals of the populists, who wished to rechannel money borrowed from abroad.

Peru's constitutional traditions further limited the political power of the populists because until 1980 constitutions did not extend suffrage to illiterates, who made up the vast majority of the rural poor. On the few occasions when a populist was elected president and seemed to be on the verge both of using public funds to aid the poorer classes and having legislation passed that might threaten the prerogatives of the rich (such as humanitarian labour laws and minimum-wage statutes), a coup typically occurred (for example, in 1948) or the legislation was skilfully emasculated in the capitalist-dominated Congress (for example, between 1963 and 1968). Populist leaders, in short, were seldom able to elevate the condition of the vast majority of Peruvians.

Acute economic inequality persisted in Peru, despite impressive economic growth rates. By the mid-1960s, less than 2 per cent of income-earning Peruvians received 45 per cent of the aggregate national aggregate income (Quijano Obregón 1968: 326). In addition, less than 1 per cent of the rural population owned almost 80 per cent of all commercial farmland. According to an international team of social scientists who statistically analyzed economic inequality in 51 nation-states during the late 1960s, Peru was the most economically inegalitarian (Handelman 1975: 24; McClintock 1984: 64).

Failed revolution from above

Immediately after the Second World War inequality seemed the fate of most Latin American countries. In 1959, however, a small group of conspirators successfully toppled a notoriously brutal dictatorship in Cuba and then repelled a counter-revolutionary invasion that was financially backed and militarily orchestrated by the United States, which feared the Soviet Union's involvement in the New World. The Cuban revolution caught most of the political leaders of the western hemisphere off guard. Incumbent governments trembled; young radicals were inspired.

In 1968 the Peruvian military, both fearful of a Cuba-inspired revolution and insulted by Peru's seemingly endless concessions to foreign investors (especially Standard Oil, ITT, and Chase Manhattan Bank), overthrew the elected government and for the next dozen years directly ruled Peru. The leaders of the coup promised that they would defeat the consumer-oriented and nonproductive oligarchy and create an economy that would be 'neither capitalist nor communist' but would resemble the ethos of the armed forces in its enthusiasm, fairness, and opportunities for social advancement.[4]

The self-defined Revolutionary Government of the Armed Forces attempted to transform the economy in several ways. First, believing that previous governments had too often been the handmaiden of internationalist capitalists, it seized holdings from more than a dozen large foreign-owned firms (including Standard Oil) and nationalized mainly foreign-controlled banks. The Revolutionary Government also nationalized the electricity and telephone systems, airports, and railways. To some extent, the government encouraged foreign investment in the manufacturing, mining, and oil industries but imposed relatively strict guidelines to prevent international corporations from undermining Peruvian prosperity. For instance, it insisted that foreign-owned companies sell raw materials at a discount to state-run enterprises and domestic manufacturers, and limited the amount of stock foreigners could own in nominally Peruvian enterprises. To protect the modest manufacturing sector and encourage its growth, the government also dramatically raised tariffs.

The new government, besides wresting control of the economy from foreign investors and international market pressures, sought to improve the workers' standard of living by expanding existing public health, education, and social security programmes, which previously had been among the least funded and developed in Latin America. It imposed price ceilings on consumer goods – especially food and transportation.

The Revolutionary Government also tried to increase workers' rights. An employment-stability law prevented employers from dismissing employees who had been on the job for at least three months. Producer cooperatives in which employees owned stock and, through elected representatives, helped make management decisions were encouraged.

Perhaps the military government's most controversial action was its attempt to defuse rural discontent by land redistribution. The 1969 Agrarian Reform Law, which numerous scholars have termed one of the most radical land reforms in the history of Latin America, affected about 40 per cent of all farmland. The government transferred ownership of almost all large coastal estates – including the highly profitable sugar plantations – to their employees, who were to manage the enterprises by means of producer cooperatives.

During the first six years of the military's rule, the total output of the economy grew impressively at an average annual rate of more than 6 per cent. The Revolutionary Government, confident that prosperity would continue, sought low-interest loans to help finance new public-works projects. Accordingly, foreign debt quadrupled between 1968 and 1975, reaching $3 billion in 1975. The government believed that it could easily pay off its new loans through the country's sales on foreign markets of metals, sugar, wool, and fishmeal. The export sector collapsed, however, as international prices for petroleum, sugar, and copper plummeted during the late 1970s. Public and private industries in Peru failed to earn sufficient profits and foreign exchange to service the country's enormous foreign debt. Economic growth correspondingly slowed because businesses could not move inventories and could not find the foreign exchange needed to import parts and machinery.

The military government reacted to the sudden economic recession by reversing many of its earlier reforms. It reduced consumer subsidies for transportation, food, and utilities. It courted foreign investors through more lenient regulations on profit remittance. It amended the once-radical job-security law; workers now had to be employed for three years (instead of three months) before they could secure tenure.

The ailing economy did not respond to the more laissez-faire policies. Businesses did not greatly increase production, and joblessness remained high. Many companies in the export sector went bankrupt. Meanwhile, the Revolutionary Government, needing to import food and other consumer goods in order to quell growing social unrest in the cities, took out additional loans and thus exacerbated the debt crisis and fuelled inflation. By 1980 foreign debt exceeded $9 billion.

The working classes were especially hard hit by the recession. By the late 1970s between 50 and 60 per cent of the workforce could not find permanent employment (Palmer 1990: 5). Between 1973 and 1978, real income of the urban workforce fell 40 per cent (Skidmore and Smith 1992: 217). According to David Werlich (1984: 78), the sharply declining real wages 'translated into widespread malnutrition, dramatic increases in poverty-related diseases and a sharp rise in the rate of infant mortality.'

Three failed searches for prosperity

The economic crisis worsened during the late 1970s, and protest actions multiplied in the cities and countryside. The now dismayed and disillusioned Revolutionary Government responded by relinquishing power to civilian politicians.

In 1980, Fernando Belaúnde Terry, a relatively conservative candidate committed to international trade, won the first postmilitary presidential election. During the campaign, Belaúnde had courted both big-business owners on the coast and the upwardly mobile middle-class in the economically backward mountains and jungles. He had pledged to the former constituency that he would resurrect the export sector through a mixture of radical free-market and free-trade policies, and had told owners of small businesses that he would initiate grandiose economic development projects in the mountains and eastern jungles. Belaúnde contended that highway construction, coupled with irrigation and energy projects, would generate temporary jobs for the unemployed and underemployed and, in the long run, encourage sufficient capital investment to create a million well-paying, permanent jobs in the countryside.

Belaúnde tried to carry out his promises and quickly tore down tariff walls, ended government subsidies to infant industries, and deregulated the prices of gasoline, food, and public services. His government also launched the promised irrigation, education, and highway undertakings in the mountains and jungles.

The envisaged miracle never materialized.[5] Domestic industrialists and manufacturers feared Belaúnde's radical trade liberalization policies and the possibility of increased foreign competition, and therefore did not expand production facilities, as it had been anticipated they would. Indeed, several textile and automobile-assembly plants significantly *reduced* production because their owners foresaw foreign competition, and as a result thousands of workers lost their jobs. Meanwhile, sharp declines in international demand for petroleum, copper, and fishmeal continued to have doleful effects on the export-based economy. International prices of raw materials dropped to their lowest point since the Great Depression. Memories of the 1968 coup also played a role in the continued economic downturn. Belaúnde, haunted by the prospects of another military takeover, spent incredibly large sums for weapons, such as $870 million for 26 state-of-the-art jet fighters, that the military requested (Rudolph 1992: 83). Needless to say, the drain on the public coffers exacerbated the government's debt problems and indirectly led to further borrowing from international lenders.

These and other problems (including unusual weather patterns that brought the fishing industry to its knees, destroyed cash crops, washed away roads, and ruined irrigation systems) contributed to five years of unprecedented economic disaster for Peru. The economy, after having grown at a respectable 4.2 per cent in 1980, stalled in 1982, when a mere 0.8 per cent growth was recorded, and then contracted by almost 12 per cent in 1983. Between 1980 and 1982 manufacturing output declined 20 per cent; by 1985, 60 per cent of industrial capacity was idle. Average real wages, meanwhile, dropped 35 per cent between 1980 and 1985, and by the end of Belaúnde's five-year term, were only slightly more than a third of what they had been in 1973. Underemployment (in which people seek full-time permanent work but find only part-time and low-paying temporary jobs) rose from 51 per cent of the urban workforce in 1980 to 57 per cent in 1985, and urban joblessness rose from 11 per cent in 1980 to 16 per cent in 1985 (Dietz 1986–87: 142; Pastor and Wise 1992: 94; Poole and Rénique 1992: 125; Rudolph 1992: 82, 101).

In 1985 disgruntled Peruvians elected as president a self-styled economic reformer and leader of the American Revolutionary Popular Alliance (APRA), Alan García. García advocated so-called heterodox economic theories and argued that business activity could be stimulated by simultaneously (1) protecting indigenous businesses from foreign competition, and (2) increasing the purchasing power of middle- and lower-income Peruvians through tax reductions, wage increases, and a higher minimum wage.[6]

Once in office, García quickly acted on his convictions. He banned the importation of more than 200 products, quickly cut payroll and sales taxes, and raised minimum wages. He also attempted to encourage agricultural production by dismantling 600 inefficient cooperatives established by the military regime and by parcelling out the cooperatives' holdings among private farmers.

To increase the foreign exchange needed for the importation of machinery by domestic businesses, García announced that Peru would limit its debt service payments to 10 per cent of its annual export earnings (full debt service in 1985 would have consumed about 60 per cent of the $3 billion annual export earnings). He pressed other Latin American presidents to join him in demanding more lenient debt repayment schedules. In a major speech before the United Nations General Assembly, García referred to the schedules imposed by international lenders, such as the International Monetary Fund, as veiled imperialism. To increase Peru's foreign-exchange reserves further, he drastically cut back military armament purchases and urged other Latin American countries to adopt a multilateral arms reduction treaty, including a regionwide freeze on the purchase of weapons.

At first, García's policies seemed to rejuvenate the economy. In 1985 the annual inflation rate dropped 100 points, to 158 per cent; in 1986 it fell to 63 per cent. The nation's aggregate output rose 8.5 per cent in 1986 (the fastest GDP growth in Latin America for that year) and another 6.9 per cent in 1987. Real wages went up by at least 7 per cent in 1986. Even total agricultural production, which for more than a decade had slumped as new investment went into other sectors of the economy, rose 3.6 per cent in 1986 (Rudolph 1992: 132; Werlich 1988: 14).

The rosy statistics hid deep-seated economic problems. Even though previously underutilized factories were humming at close to full capacity by 1987, private investment in *new* enterprises was lagging. Unless new factories and new jobs soon appeared, Peru's seemingly booming economy soon would stagnate. In addition, a serious food crisis was brewing. Farmers, frustrated by the low prices set by the government for their goods, refused to increase production; food shortages materialized in the cities. The shortages, in turn, were quietly contributing to inflation, which soon exceeded 100 per cent a year and discouraged private investors from launching new enterprises.

To stimulate business investment, García allowed prices for certain key agricultural commodities to rise (which, in theory, would increase profit margins and thus further induce private investment in greater production), but he also capped wages to contain inflation. As a result, workers' real income began to decline dramatically after 1986. Workers, understandably, demanded wage increases to parallel the rapidly rising cost of living, but García stood steadfast against such a course, insisting that austerity measures were needed in the short run to achieve his purpose. In 1987 Peru's unions would call their first general strike against García's administration.

García, seeking to stimulate further economic growth without antagonizing organized labour, decided to increase the state's role in channelling private investment. In 1986 he shocked both his supporters and his adversaries by announcing a plan to nationalize private banks and insurance companies. He argued that Peru's financial institutions were not investing enough of their profits in either domestic companies or government securities but, in fact, were encouraging the flight of investment capital. He also argued that bank nationalization would ultimately lead to fairer lending policies because smaller investors would be able to secure loans at rates normally reserved for larger corporations.

Although García may have intended to reassure and inspire Peru's petit bourgeoisie, his proposal for the banks alarmed the middle classes and marked what Pastor and Wise (1992: 104) call 'the beginning of a war with private capital'. Spokespersons for big business, which had been made uneasy by García's wage policies and opposition to free trade, argued that the presidency was threatening to all property owners – including middle-class entrepreneurs and street vendors. Middle-class Peruvians, already unnerved by triple-digit inflation, believed that the proposed seizure of the banks was representative of the García regime's secret agenda to take over all private property. The socially conservative print media meanwhile carried allegations that the proposal revealed the government's intention to establish a proletarian dictatorship.

The government quickly backed away from the proposals; the banks and insurance companies were secure. Nonetheless, the political damage had been done. Business owners, always somewhat chary about risking capital, now became extremely reluctant. The economy continued to contract.

The effects of García's bank-nationalization blunder were compounded by the international financial community's cool response to his radical rhetoric about foreign-debt servicing. The United States pressured international lenders to offer loans on more attractive terms to poorer nations, who eagerly seized the new credit opportunities. Having lost his Third World allies, García had to face an irritated international financial community alone. Angry at García's impudence and fearful that his unilateral reduction in debt repayments might serve to inspire other indebted countries, that community chose not to extend Peru's credit line.

Peru's economy deteriorated badly during the last three years of García's rule. In the words of Skidmore and Smith (1992: 220), 'Peru suddenly turned in Latin America's economic basketcase.' Between 1987 and 1989, the annual gross domestic product declined 28 per cent. The annual inflation rate skyrocketed to 1,722 per cent in 1988 and then to 2,778 per cent in 1989. Average real salaries declined by more than half between 1985 and 1990. Then, the worst drought in 30 years destroyed 100,000 hectares of crops in the Andes. Hundreds of thousands of rural Peruvians migrated citywards and soon exhausted the always limited urban resources, including medical services and drinking water (Poole and Rénique 1992: 134; Rudolph 1992: 132–4; Skidmore and Smith 1992: 220; Werlich 1991: 62).

In 1990 a majority of restless and angry voters rejected the major parties' presidential candidates and instead installed as the country's top executive Alberto Fujimori, a political neophyte, an engineering professor, and a television talk-show host. Fujimori won partly because low-income voters were divided among at least three 'left-wing' candidates and partly because the primary conservative candidate, Mario Vargas Llosa, had advocated a radical programme of price deregulation, wage controls, and free trade that many believed would eventuate in drastic price increases, numerous bankruptcies, and widespread joblessness in the short run. Fujimori argued that Vargas's programme was far too extreme and proposed a more spiritual and scientific programme of economic recovery involving, in the words of his campaign slogan, 'Honesty, Hard Work and Technology'.[7]

Once in office, Fujimori faced the daunting task of repairing an economy that according to international economic observers could not meet the nutritional needs of almost a third of the populace (Rudolph 1992: 145). Fujimori concluded that it would take more international loans to pull Peru out of its downward spiral and accepted the International Monetary Fund's loan requirements. He set about privatizing state enterprises, dismantling tariff barriers, eliminating price controls on necessities, and slashing public expenditures on social welfare. The press dubbed his free-market and free-trade policies 'Fujishock', and called attention to how they contradicted his earlier calls for policy moderation. Within weeks of the inauguration prices for food, petrol, and water exploded upward. For example, in one day, the cost of petrol soared 3,000 per cent and electric rates quintupled (Werlich 1991: 82). By 1992 the government had sold its petrol stations, airline, and a mining company to private investors, and was attempting to sell its electricity company and a publicly owned bank. Because of budget constraints, salaries for nurses and teachers were frozen (which meant that real wages fell sharply), and tens of thousands of these professionals emigrated.

Fujimori's free-market and free-trade policies did not lead to immediate economic recovery (and whether they will do so in the long run remains unclear).[8] The government's closing of national development banks and the deregulation of interest rates resulted in more expensive loans and in widespread bankruptcies both in commercial farming and in small- and medium-sized businesses. The gross national product contracted 4.5 per cent in 1990, expanded 2.1 per cent in 1991, and then contracted 2.8 per cent in 1992. The total number of workers employed in the manufacturing sector decreased by a fifth between 1990 and 1992. By the early 1990s more than 90 per cent of the workforce could not find employment, held temporary jobs, or worked at marginal pursuits, such as street vending. A quarter of all Peruvians suffered chronic malnutrition; more than half lived in conditions that met the United Nations' statistical criteria of 'absolute poverty' (Gonzales de Olarte 1993: 63–4; Poole and Rénique 1992: 22–3).

Diverse economic conditions in the countryside

The once-prosperous Peruvian economy had unravelled between the beginning of the revolutionary military regime in 1968 and the election of Fujimori in 1990.

Although the overall economy stumbled during these two and a half decades, the rural economy was particularly hard hit. By almost any standard measure of prosperity, the countryside fell considerably short of the cities. During the early 1970s, for example, per capita income on the urbanized coast was two to three times higher. During the late 1970s, life expectancy in the countryside was on average 20 years shorter than in Lima. Whereas 85 per cent of all permanent housing in Lima received sewage services, electricity, and potable water during the 1970s, less than 10 per cent of the homes in the mountainous department of Ayacucho had such basic amenities. During the 1970s, 73 per cent of all doctors in Peru resided and worked in Lima (about one doctor for every 500 residents). In contrast, there were fewer than 30 doctors in two of the poorest mountain provinces (one doctor for every 29,000 residents) (Gianotten et al. 1985: 184; Handelman 1975: 19–21; McClintock 1989: 66; Rudolph 1992: 9).

Economic conditions also varied considerably *within* rural Peru. One can identify at least four major rural regions, each with distinctive agricultural methods and a distinctive standard of living.

Coast

Almost all of Peru's major cities and almost all of its enormous sugar and cotton plantations are found in the 20-mile-wide flat and dry coastal region. In the North, expensively irrigated plantations employ tens of thousands of low-skilled workers, most of whom live either on the plantation (usually as full members of the co-operatives) or in small nearby villages (usually temporary employees who are not allowed to be cooperatives' members). Because of most plantations' relative prosperity, the standard of living of full members tends to be noticeably higher than that of agrarian populations elsewhere in Peru. Not surprisingly, temporary plantation workers do not enjoy the same wage levels as do full cooperative members; but even their average yearly income tends to be higher than the national norm for agricultural workers. Despite the relative high standard of living found on the coast, there tends to be social restlessness and conflicts of interest between the full members of the cooperatives, who wish to protect their enterprises' profitability and minimize costs, and the *comuneros*, or residents of the neighbouring peasant villages, who feel underpaid and threatened by the expansionist tendencies of the mechanized and generally profitable cooperatives (Rudolf 1992: 63).

Northern and central Andes

Immediately East of the coastline stand the towering Andean mountains, where a majority of Peruvians lived until the 1970s, when the country's demographic centre of gravity shifted to the increasingly urbanized coast. Uneven terrain postponed mechanized commercial farming in the central and northern Andes until after 1920. Thereafter, metals, wool, dairy products and other foodstuffs flowed to Lima. In particular, mining flourished in the central Andes, while dairy farms prospered in the North. Before 1950 many commercial farms recruited labour through debt bondage and occasionally outright kidnapping and slavery. However, peasants sometimes voluntarily worked part-time in the large haciendas and local mines, and hoped to put aside sufficient funds to open their own small businesses or commercial farms (Brown and Fernández 1991: 54–78; McClintock 1987: 237–40).

Compared to northern Andeans, central Andeans have generally been more prosperous and materially comfortable, partly because of the availability of part-time work in nearby mines and partly because of the proximity of Lima's markets for peasant-grown cash crops. Per capita farm income in the central region is about 40 per cent greater than per capita farm income in the northern mountains (McClintock 1989: 67).

After the early 1970s, the economy of the central Andes significantly contracted, largely because of sharply declining world demand for Peruvian metals. Many mines closed, and those that remained open laid off thousands of part-time workers. Males increasingly travelled to Lima for work but found few jobs because economic conditions there were no better.

Southern Andes

The economy of the southern Andes has been much less mechanized and diversified than elsewhere in the mountains. Most farmland is windswept, rocky, and arid. Until the early 1960s the vast majority of farmers relied on hand tools. Until very recently, the small yields have primarily been used for family consumption, not the market.

With the exception of Cuzco department, which has benefited from a relatively prosperous tourist industry, the standard of living in the southern Andes has been well below that of the central and northern Andes (McClintock 1989: 67–8). About two-thirds of the peasants lived during the 1970s in small villages that lacked the amenities found in other parts of Peru. During the 1960s and 1970s the mean farm income in the southern highlands was a third of the mean farm income in the central and northern highlands (McClintock 1989: 66). Cynthia McClintock (1984: 59) writes, 'Peru's southern highlands are a region in a Third-World country where poverty is at Fourth-World levels.'

Ayacucho – a severely impoverished department in the southern Andes – deserves special mention because of the persistence of poverty despite signs of economic modernization. The department enjoyed its first all-weather road in the mid-1960s, and telephones were installed in the capital city (also named Ayacucho) in 1964. In 1959, the Peruvian government reopened the National University of San Cristóbal de Huamanga in Ayacucho city. The university's primary mission was similar to that of US land grant institutions: the dissemination of modern agricultural techniques and business practices to the local population. In the words of the university's first rector, 'we are preparing our students to bring about the socioeconomic development of our area' (Palmer 1986: 135). The government also tried to familiarize locals with the notion of wage labour by means of a variety of 'self-help' charity programmes, such as Food for Peace, which gave youths cash and food in exchange for their work.

Within 15 years after the opening of the university, Ayacucho department had noticeably changed. The newly built 'Highway of the Liberators' rendered the department more accessible to outsiders, and roughly 30,000 families had immigrated in search of economic opportunities. The new university brought Ayacucho city an average annual growth rate of 4.5 per cent between 1961 and 1972. A new electrical system in the city contributed to the proliferation of television sets during the mid-1970s. Partly because of the opening of elementary and secondary schools, adult literacy rose from slightly over 20 per cent in 1961 to slightly over 55 per cent a decade later (McClintock 1989: 72; Poole and Rénique 1992: 34).

Hard times persisted, however. Despite the bustle of Ayacucho city, in 1972 only 5.5 per cent of all households in the department had electricity; and only 6.6 per cent had drinking water. The department's infant mortality rate in the 1970s was among the world's highest. Per capita real income *declined by a third* between 1961 and 1979 as high inflation and unpredictable government price controls on foodstuffs wreaked havoc even as commercialism took hold. Even by 1981, only 7 per cent of the department's households had running water, and only 14 per cent had electricity (Harding 1987: 187; McClintock 1984: 59–61; McClintock 1989: 68; Palmer 1986: 134, 139; Poole and Rénique 1992: 36).

Jungles

Just to the East of the Andes are Peru's jungles and the Amazon basin, which in terms of surface area, are the largest of the country's three major land formations (the coast and the Andes being the other two). The jungles are not densely populated, containing less than 10 per cent of Peru's total population. In the colonial period, Christian missionaries attempted to convert the multiple indigenous and seminomadic peoples; but the Spanish rulers were generally indifferent to the region's economic possibilities and focused their energies on the coast.

At the end of the nineteenth century, British capitalists established a coffee plantation system and gained a marketing monopoly. Rubber tapping, which began in the 1870s, was a short-lived industry that led to a boom in the town of Iquitos. Indians were forced, through debt servitude and by threats of flogging, beheading or other physical punishments, to engage in the tedious and lonely labour (Brown and Fernández 1991: 57–60). Despite these and other attempts to develop commerce by exploiting human and natural resources, the region's economy remained strikingly backward – until, that is, the cocaine industry exploded in the 1980s. Even then, the region was singularly lacking in infrastructure, commerce, and the presence of government officials, agencies, and services.

Conclusion

To some extent, the economic situation of Peru in the 1980s resembled those of West Germany and Poland. Years of impressive rates of growth had suddenly ended, and older policy formulas for economic success no longer seemed to work. But the situation in Peru was much more desperate. Regional economic inequality was considerably higher; the average annual growth rate during the 1980s and first half of the 1990s was negative; and the median standard of living was much lower.

Peru, after being widely viewed in the mid-twentieth century as an economic success story, suddenly in the early 1980s became one of the poorest countries in Latin America. Between 1975 and 1990 exports plummeted, joblessness spread, and hyperinflation became a normal feature of everyday life. By the mid-1980s average income levels were far behind those of Argentina, Brazil, and Chile. Perhaps most important, subsistence itself became an issue. Life expectancy was much lower than in all other Latin American countries, save Bolivia and Haiti. The annual incidence of chronic malnutrition jumped from 985,700 to 5,753,600 cases between 1970 and 1990. And the caloric intake of many Peruvians (especially in the countryside) fell far below international malnutrition levels (McClintock 1989: 68; Poole and Rénique 1992: 22–3; Rudolph 1992: 8; Skidmore and Smith 1992: 408).

Moreover, since 1968 a succession of military and civilian leaders tried alternately to break with Peru's economic past and to return to its traditional reliance on both export industries and foreign loans. Each attempt to cure or at least ameliorate Peru's economic distress ended in greater unemployment, a higher cost of living, lower production levels, and added indebtedness. According to many scholarly observers, a growing number of Peruvians believed during the 1980s that the time for moderate steps had passed and that a radically different political and economic order was needed (Graham 1994a: 74–7; Graham 1994b: 3, 14; Rudolph 1992: 1–2, 144–6, 151–2; Taylor 1993: 174).

In this challenging economic environment, Shining Path appeared and attempted to mobilize an insurrection against the status quo.

Notes

1. For interpretations of Peru's distinctive economic history and its consequences for politics, see Mariátegui (1970), Rudolph (1992), and Skidmore and Smith (1992: 185–220).
2. Some terse and very readable introductions to the problem of racism in Peru may be found in Brown and Fernández (1991) and Rudolph (1992), especially chapters 1 and 2.
3. For an excellent example of early anti-imperialist literature and rhetoric in Peru, see Mariátegui (1970), originally published in 1928 and considered by many to be a classic in Latin American social theory.
4. For descriptions and analyses of the military coup and subsequent revolutionary regime, see McClintock (1981), Rudolph (1992: 53–76), and Stepan (1978).
5. Convenient chronologies and analyses of Belaúnde's economic policies may be found in Pastor and Wise (1992), Rudolph (1992: 77–99), and Werlich (1984).
6. For discussions of García's economic policies, see Crabtree (1992), Pastor and Wise (1992), Rudolph (1992: 101–50), and Wise (1986).
7. For descriptions and analyses of Fujimori's economic programmes and beliefs, see Andreas and Sharpe (1992), Gonzales de Olarte (1993), McClintock (1993), and Werlich (1991).
8. See, for example, the exchange between Sheahan (1994: 187–93) and Velarde (1994: 139–54).

Chapter 9

Political antecedents

As we have seen, many social-movement theorists during the past two decades have emphasized how oppositional groups contribute resources, goals, and strategies to later social movements. Antecedent parties, movements, and traditions of protest provide meeting places, experienced activists, communication networks, and pioneer tactics and strategies that later movement activists emulate, modify, or, in some cases, intentionally avoid.

Long before guerrillas belonging to Shining Path attempted their first known armed action in May 1980, several political parties, unions, and other social organizations had attempted a transformative role. Some developed critiques of Peru's distinctively dependent capitalist economy, which they juxtaposed to ideas about the natural communalism of Andean Indians. Others found inspiration in the hard-work ethos of the urban middle classes and in the promise of technology. Some experimented with electoral politics, some with guerrilla warfare. Some were advocates of producer cooperatives and shantytown self-rule and distrustfully eyed the government. From such diverse ideas, dreams, and experiences, Shining Path was born.

Radical parties

Peru's first mass-based radical party appeared during the 1920s. Its founders, many of whom were former student activists who had been sent to prison or into exile for political agitation and who were fearful of alienating middle-class voters, avoided using the adjective 'socialist' in their party's name and instead called themselves the American Revolutionary Popular Alliance (Alianza Popular Revolucionaria Americana, or APRA).

The so-called Apristas contended that unless the government pursued a radically new set of economic policies, Peru was destined to remain a second-rate world power, subject to the arbitrary will of the United States and western Europe – as would every other Latin American state. The current economic travails derived from Peru's history. The Spaniards had put in place a system of economically conservative aristocratic privilege. Large landowners complacently relied on labour-intensive methods at the expense of native peoples, including their enslavement. Subsequent patterns of foreign investment (for example, in the sugar, coffee, and rubber industries) reinforced this pattern of concentrated landed wealth, ruthless exploitation, and widespread poverty and degradation in what was passed off as economic development.

APRA's most influential theorist, Víctor Raúl Haya de la Torre, believed that all Latin American countries had to restructure their national economies to achieve sovereignty and economic justice. Hence, Apristas ambitiously saw their mission as redemptive in regard to not only their own country but others as well. They called for:

(1) immediate and steadfast opposition to continued US presence in Peru's economy;
(2) promotion of the economic and political unity of Latin America and international control of the Panama Canal;
(3) development of agricultural cooperatives;
(4) nationalization of land and key industries, whose policies would be determined by a national economic council made up of representatives of labour, management, the professional classes, and government;
(5) extension of political freedoms and government-protected human rights, including regulations concerning child labour, workday length, and independent trade unions; and
(6) promotion of Indian values and social and economic institutions.

APRA attracted a significant following among Peruvian intellectuals and wage-workers, especially on the northern coast, where the foreign-controlled sugar industry predominated. APRA-sponsored unions soon became the primary representatives of wageworkers in struggles with management. The party, however, was never simply a proletariat oriented entity. Many of its leaders viewed the middle classes (both salaried professionals, and small farmers and business owners) as unjustly shackled by the country's extensive involvement with foreign markets and unusual openness to foreign investment. In the words of Haya de la Torre,

> It is the middle group that is being pushed to ruination by the process of imperialism. . . . The great foreign firms extract our wealth and then sell it outside our country. Consequently, there is no opportunity for our middle class. This, then, is the abused class that will lead the revolution.
>
> (Skidmore and Smith 1992: 206–7)

The middle class not only was angry but had the training needed to promote economic growth. At least half of all public offices should be filled by intellectuals; the remainder by people with working-class backgrounds (Stokes 1995: 20–1).

> We want a state in which the technician and the expert direct state activities in order to put them on the correct path of solving our great problems. We propose the organization of a technical state; we propose moving toward a functional democracy.
>
> (Haya de la Torre 1995: 243)

APRA initially hoped to use the ballot box to win control of the state and then legislatively redirect Peru from export dependency toward a more scientifically informed and independent economic order. Partly because of the impact of the 1930s worldwide depression on export earnings, many Peruvians were receptive to the Apristas' denunciations of imperialism. In the heated 1931 presidential election, Haya de la Torre won large numbers of votes in the sugar-producing areas around the city of Trujillo and in Lima. The party lost the election, although almost all scholars today accept its leaders' contention of massive fraud by government officials (Rudolph 1992: 39).

After the election the wary president closed APRA's offices and deported Haya de la Torre and APRA's representatives in Congress. A small group of APRA militants angered by the government's high-handedness and repeated violations of the constitution tried to assassinate the president in 1932. Another group launched an unsuccessful insurrection in Trujillo that ended in their brutally murdering some 50 prisoners, including 10 military officers and 15 policemen. A year later the Peruvian president fell to Aprista assassins.

The armed forces – especially after the Trujillo uprising and the assassination – increasingly viewed APRA as a dangerous, extremist organization that must never come to power. In the late 1930s the government (with the military's blessings) annulled congressional elections that had been won by Apristas. In 1948 APRA was officially prohibited from running candidates for public office. For the next eight years, a socially conservative dictatorship promoted free trade and courted international investors.

Despite legal prohibitions and the periodic jailing of known APRA activists, the party remained popular within labour circles, which compelled the government to become less repressive. It slowly reconciled with APRA, implicitly offering full legal rights if the party would tone down its radical rhetoric and become more conservative in its policy positions. During the late 1950s the APRA leadership bit the political bullet and agreed to support a conservative presidential candidate in exchange for increased government tolerance of APRA electoral activities.

Peruvian Marxists were divided from the beginning on how to relate to both APRA and the non-Marxist yet somewhat socialist-sounding ideas of Haya de la Torre. During the early 1920s, before APRA had been formally established, Haya de la Torre had built popular organizations in several labour strongholds. He was interested enough in communism to have visited the Soviet Union (although he afterward concluded that the Soviet experience was not relevant to Latin America). Attracted by his energy and assertiveness, many of his Marxist compatriots initially viewed him as a potential ally, even though they were openly critical of his theory about the revolutionary potential of the middle classes. For almost a decade, then, Peru's Marxists and Apristas worked side by side. The marriage of convenience suddenly ended around 1928, largely because of disagreements over revolutionary strategy.

Most of the Marxists believed that peasants and the urban proletariat should be the primary targets of organizational activities; it was these classes that had (in theory) an objective interest in transforming the social and political order. Haya de la Torre, in contrast, adopted a more populist position and contended all nonwealthy classes in Peru, including the urban petit bourgeoisie, desired radical social and political change. The Marxists found his argument hard to swallow. In the words of one activist:

> To imagine that a feeling of revolutionary nationalism will develop among the middle and upper classes . . . would be a serious mistake. The creole aristocracy and bourgeoisie do not feel a bond of solidarity with the common people by ties of common history and culture. In Peru, white aristocrats and the bourgeoisie look down on popular traditions, on national traditions. They feel themselves before anything else to be white.
>
> (Mariátegui 1995: 231)

Further, the Marxists believed that APRA should openly endorse socialism as its goal. Haya de la Torre, in contrast, stood fast against the word *socialism* on political grounds. He believed that it frightened the middle classes and that social transformation would be brought about by language that didn't raise a red flag, so to speak. Increasingly unsettled by the proletarian and peasant orientation of the Marxists, Haya de la Torre told Peru's José Carlos Mariátegui, one of the most creative and influential Latin American Marxists of the twentieth century,

> You are doing a great deal of damage because of your lack of calm and your eagerness always to appear European within the terminology of Europe. . . . We shall accomplish the revolution without mentioning 'socialism' and by distributing land and fighting imperialism.
>
> (Rudolph 1992: 38)

Immediately following the bitter separation in the late 1920s of the Apristas and Marxists, Mariátegui set up a separate socialist party and also a socialist trade-union alliance known as the CGTP (General Confederation of Peruvian Workers). The government harshly repressed the new Marxist organizations because of their involvement in numerous strikes. Driven underground during the 1930s and angered by the elites' endless use of electoral fraud and military intervention to prevent social change, the Marxists temporarily turned from electoral politics to social agitation, running educational centres, publishing muckraking newspapers, and organizing local strikes.

The ideological trajectories of APRA and of the rapidly fragmenting Marxist movement increasingly diverged between 1940 and 1980. APRA's leaders, hungry for political power and viewing the state as an ideal tool for reform, began to avoid discussions of social revolution. They even replaced the party's once-strident anti-US rhetoric with attacks on communism, which led to growing dissent from within the party's more radical ranks. Haya de la Torre, still hopeful of capturing the presidency, led the party's march to the right and at one point adopted the strikingly conservative slogan 'We do not want to take away the wealth of those who have it' (G. Smith 1989: 185). In his reckoning, moderate rhetoric would secure votes for APRA, enabling it to capture key elected offices in the short run and to reform the economy in the long run.

Meanwhile, the fragmentation of the international communist movement into Trotskyist, Maoist, Stalinist, and Fidelista currents, and then into innumerable smaller factions was replicated within Peru, where a half dozen self-defined 'Marxist' and 'Communist' organizations appeared during the 1960s and early 1970s. Despite this fissuring, the primary communist-affiliated trade union, the CGTP, remained highly popular among workers and continued to evolve organizationally. In fact, during the late 1960s and early 1970s the CGTP surpassed the APRA-affiliated union, the CTP (Confederation of Peruvian Workers), in terms of numbers of locals.

Ironically, the Communists' ascension in the world of organized labour occurred primarily during the twelve-year military regime. The military government, intensely hostile to APRA, decided to throw its support behind communist unions, and thus produce an organizational counterweight to the CTP. Unions, protected by a government that sought class reconciliation, appeared in previously nonorganized sectors of the economy and in small and medium-sized enterprises. In seven years, the total number of unions almost doubled: 2,297 in 1968, 4,172 in mid-1975. The government hoped to oversee, contain, and channel labour mobilization through its SINAMOS (an anacronym for National System of Support for Social Mobilization). SINAMOS fell short of these goals, partly because the regime's labour policies became more conservative after 1975 and the newly unionized working class refused to accept quietly reductions in legal rights, job security, and real wages. In 1977 Peru's first nationwide general strike occurred, to be followed by more in 1978 and 1979. Not only unionized workers but also students, peasants, women's organizations, and shantytown organizations demonstrated. The frequency of plant-level strikes also rose to an all-time high by the end of the 1970s, triple the rate of the previous decade. More than a million workers took to the streets in 1978 alone. Labour organizations demonstrated against government policies in the traditionally tumultuous northern coast and Lima metropolitan area, and also in provincial towns, such as Arequipa, Cuzco, and Huancayo as well, where organized labour protests once had been a rarity (Mauceri 1995: 15; Stephens 1983: 57–79; Stokes 1995: 45).

The Maoist and Trotskyist labour organizations enjoyed an unusual amount of popular support during the 1970s, especially among lower-income white-collar professionals such as teachers in primary and secondary schools. The military government's policies with respect to primary and secondary education had angered many of the teachers at these levels, who were underpaid and untenured, and were being assigned to grossly underfunded and isolated rural schools. Parents, too, especially in the countryside, where education was viewed as a means of social advancement, were incensed by the government's periodic attempts to raise tuition either for all students or for students who had failed a course. In such a climate, many teachers, when considering political options, saw APRA as impotent and the conventional communist union, the CGTP, as excessively conciliatory toward the military government (especially during the first seven years of the regime). The openly confrontational Maoists seemed the most appropriate union option. Later, Shining Path would recruit activists from this cohort (Angell 1981).

The regime, however, did promote a new educational philosophy. Previously, the curriculum of primary and secondary schools had been geared toward the oligarchy and coastal middle classes, whose children had been taught the desirability of economic inequality, while children of wageworkers and peasants were taught deference and the inevitability of hierarchy, if they were lucky enough to have access to a nearby school. The military government attempted to combat this conservative view of the world by expanding the number of primary and secondary schools (especially in the mountains and jungles) and centres of higher education, and using history texts that highlighted and questioned the consequences of the country's colonial past, free-trade orientation, and enduring glaring economic disparities (Stokes 1995: 38, 73–4, 85, 92, 159).

After the military government relinquished its power in 1980, most Marxists publicly endorsed an electoral road to social revolution, believing that a majority would support an openly radical party. After all, the constitutional reforms of 1980 had lowered the voting age to 18, and for the first time ever illiterates had the right to vote. Moreover, CGTP activists had acquired a measure of goodwill from diverse low-income groups who were grateful for the activists' involvement in land invasions, shantytown politics, and labour mobilizations. The time seemed right for a peaceful, legal, electoral march to socialism.

The Marxists, however, were divided by strategic disagreements over; (1) whether revolutionary parties should court middle-class voters during the campaign, and (2) whether the postmilitary democratic regime was stable enough to institute significant social and economic reform (Taylor 1990). Broadly speaking, two camps evolved. Some Marxist parties (and major factions within parties) advocated a strictly legalistic road to socialism and argued that only by forging an alliance with the middle class could wageworkers and peasants capture a majority of seats in Congress and then gradually legislate the abolishment of mass poverty. According to this classical social democratic line of argument, radicals should be cautious and pragmatic and not encourage lower-class strikes, land invasions, and other types of tumult that might frighten off middle-class voters and induce the military to overthrow the newly established democratic political order.

Other Marxists maintained that electoral victories alone would never yield enough political clout to transform the society. The government bureaucracy was riddled with corruption and overwhelmingly committed to the status quo. Advocates of a combined legislative-and-extralegislative strategy insisted that ongoing bribery by large companies and wealthy individuals of underpaid judges and other public officials had the effect of perpetuating the oppression of the poor. Progressive legislation would be enacted *and* implemented only if the poor, through large boycotts, embarrassing demonstrations, general strikes, and disruptive street politics, so demanded. Furthermore, the middle classes were so afraid of losing entirely their rapidly disappearing wealth and diminishing incomes that they themselves would never become willing supporters of any serious programme of economic redistribution. Radicals therefore should not waste time in seeking broad, inter-class electoral coalitions; instead they should nurture strong and militant worker, neighbourhood, and peasant organizations with the capacity to pressure the government through disruptive actions as well as voting.

Because of irreconcilable strategic differences among the Marxists and because of personal rivalries among left-wing candidates (Marxist and non-Marxist), the myriad organizations of the Left seldom made common cause after a short-lived 1980 alliance – the so-called United Left (or IU). After that, fragments of the Left ran competing slates in national elections and in most municipal ones. Organizationally divided, the Left suffered several embarrassing defeats, and the total number of votes won by Left parties and coalitions significantly declined between 1980 and 1990. A vast majority of Peruvians (including the poor) decided not to waste their votes on such obviously unstable electoral options. Instead, voters dissatisfied with the social and economic status quo cast their ballots either for non-Marxist APRA candidates, such as García in the 1985 presidential elections, or for candidates with no party affiliation or political record, such as Fujimori in 1990. Only in local elections in the largest coastal cities did Marxist parties forge relatively harmonious and durable coalitions, and there they often won decisively, especially in poorer districts (Dietz 1986–87; Taylor 1990).

Evolution of peasant politics

After the Second World War, the conditions of peasants and farmworkers steadily deteriorated. Owners of haciendas became more and more commercial in their thinking, and their operations more mechanized and capital intensive. The number of jobs diminished, and landowners steadily encroached on villages' common lands. Inequality in land ownership thus persisted and even intensified. In 1963, 0.1 per cent of Peru's population controlled more than 60 per cent of land under cultivation (Campbell 1973: 45).

During the late 1950s and early 1960s land invasions and labour strikes spontaneously broke out throughout the Andes and in the sugar haciendas along the central and northern coast. Between 1959 and 1963 approximately 300,000 peasants seized hundreds of private estates in southern Peru alone, while sharecroppers and tenant farmers set up their own unions (Campbell 1973: 45; Poole and Rénique 1992: 113). Villagers in the central Andes seized grazing land from large ranches throughout the 1950s and 1960s. When hacienda owners pressured reluctant and resource-poor government officials into evicting the peasants, the arrival of police sometimes meant violence; but sometimes a modus vivendi ensued between the elusive peasants (who would lead their animals to pasture at odd hours and at disparate points along ranch boundaries) and the outnumbered and weary forces of order (Poole and Rénique 1992: 113; G. Smith 1989: 212). In the North, newly established agrarian unions involving wageworkers, serfs, and semiserfs repeatedly called general strikes, which sometimes lasted as long as two months. Some of these actions yielded stunning benefits for workers; others, such as those of the sugarcane workers, ended with brutal repression.

Landowners despaired for social order and civilization; they saw barbaric communism and anarchism on the horizon. Their anxiety is understandable, for as some scholars have noted, 'Between 1956 and 1964, Peru witnessed the largest peasant movements in South America' (Starn et al. 1995: 255). Few participants in land invasions and rural strikes, however, were motivated by either revolutionary class consciousness or a desire to restructure the economy; many simply wished to supplement their own smallholdings and were hostile to the idea of sharing seized land. Moreover, many of those who seized land saw themselves not as trespassers but as the actual owners of land now regained. Most invasion campaigns therefore coincided with ongoing attempts to secure legal transfers of titles from the state. Strikers in the northern haciendas similarly had limited goals – primarily to preserve jobs and improve wages – and did not advocate the socialization of property or production. What the landowners saw as imminent anarchism and communism, the landless and relatively landless saw as attempts to conserve and, in some cases, legally reclaim (G. Smith 1989: 169–236).

Regardless of the peasants' and farmworkers' nonrevolutionary aspirations, their open defiance of large property owners and security forces inspired many radicals – in the afterglow of the Cuban revolution – to believe that a social revolution was also imminent in Peru. The Trotskyist Hugo Blanco, for example, threw himself into the exhausting tasks of helping to organize land seizures in the southern Andes and of helping farmworkers think about their political options. A university graduate educated in Argentina, Blanco became a subtenant farmer in 1958 and was zealous in constructing grassroots institutions such as schools and defensive militias. He opposed open armed insurrection against the state, advocating instead creation of a 'dual-power' pattern of authority in which local farmworkers provided their own public services and relied on community notions of justice instead of passively obeying bourgeois law. By ignoring the state and its notions of economic development, Blanco hoped to foster a more ambitious political and economic agenda among the tumultuous but not yet revolutionary rural masses (Brown and Fernández 1991: 85–8; Campbell 1973: 45–70).

Many other radicals, however, saw in the rural rebellions possible widespread support for a Cuban-like guerrilla movement. Some younger members of APRA, for example, had been frustrated by the party's increasingly conservative rhetoric during the 1950s and inspired by Castro's successful insurrection. They left APRA during the early 1960s and formed MIR (Movement of the Revolutionary Left), declaring that APRA's moderate electoral strategy could not work but that favourable conditions existed for a rural insurrection. Leaders of MIR established rural guerrilla units during the mid-1960s. MIR's agenda included: immediate dissolution of Congress (an institution they deemed the instrument of Peru's export-oriented capitalists); liquidation of all large estates; transfer of urban and rural land (except for plots worked by independent farmers and the homes and business sites of mid-size and small property owners) to the poor and landless; and abrogation of all treaties and trade agreements that compromised national sovereignty. Unlike Blanco, most MIR activists did not take time to master indigenous Andean languages and did not spend years working alongside peasants and earning their trust. MIR activists, rather, viewed themselves as members of an intellectual vanguard with superior political knowledge whose task it was to liberate peasants from conventional ways of thought. They even self-consciously dressed differently from local peasants:

black jackets, jeans, and high-top boots. Further, the mobile guerrilla strategies used by Castro and formalized by Ernesto 'Che' Guevarra and Regis Debray were not adopted. MIR guerrillas settled in permanent 'security zones' (Brown and Fernández 1991: 79–140; Campbell 1973: 51–7; Petras 1968: 345–50, 362–6).

During the mid-1960s a few smallish Marxist organizations also tried to establish guerrilla units in the Andes. The largest Marxist party, the Communist Party of Peru (PCP), constantly argued that guerrilla violence was a counterproductive shortcut to revolution; it provoked only repression of nonviolent organizing activities in the cities. Some activists within the PCP, however, found the party's patient neighbourhood and factory agitation too moderate and uninspired and soon resigned from the party to form Peru's first significant Marxist rural guerrilla organization, the ELN (National Liberation Army).

Although the ELN and MIR were contemporaries, the two groups of guerrillas distrusted each other and did not coordinate their activities even when hounded by the military. Like the MIR, the ELN also failed to secure peasant trust through familiarity with and participation in peasants' lives. Peasants wanted to pursue agrarian reform by means of local-level land recuperation and hence spurned the guerrillas' importuning for more radical projects and goals. By 1966 the Peruvian military – well armed with helicopters, napalm, and infrared technology – routed both socially isolated guerrilla organizations (Campbell 1973: 56–7).

In the course of eliminating the ELN and MIR, many military officers were profoundly affected by the rural poverty they observed, for them a revelation. Their compassion for the land-poor and landless and their fears of a future popularly supported insurrection led them to the conclusion that a Cuban-style revolution could eventuate from civilian governments' ongoing imperviousness to human despair. As a result, when the military took over the reins of government in the late 1960s, redistribution of rural property became one of the government's goals. In the words of General Juan Velasco: 'We are not alone. In the work of the agrarian reform, we have at our side peasants, workers, students, the immense majority of intellectuals, priests, industrialists, and Peruvian professionals. And this is what counts. These are the authentic people of our motherland.' Velasco's 'authentic people', it is worth noting, did not include the oligarchy,

> a privileged group of political elites and economic monopolies . . . which will see its antipatriotic dominance of Peru in jeopardy. We do not fear them. To this oligarchy we say that we are determined to use all the energy necessary to crush any sabotage of the new [Agrarian Reform L]aw and any attempt to subvert public order.
>
> (Velasco 1995: 268)

To help the rural poor, the military handed over hundreds of large estates to their former employees, who were to run the property as jointly owned and jointly managed cooperatives. The military also limited the size of all private holdings, for 'land must be for those who work it and not for those who charge rent without tilling' (Velasco 1995: 267). In theory, the property would be well used because of workers' pride and concern with profitability, and rural discontent would subside.

'Robust agricultural production' would ensue and 'benefit not the few but society as a whole' (Velasco 1995: 266).

The experiments in cooperative production fell far short of the officers' expectations. Estate owners sold machinery and choice parcels to private investors before the Revolutionary Government of the Armed Forces could legally expropriate their properties. Many of the new cooperatives, furthermore, lacked cash for badly needed machinery, fertilizer, and seed, and went deeply into debt. In addition, new forms of rural class tension appeared as cooperatives hired landless peasants and residents of nearby impoverished villages for part-time work at very low wages, and as cooperatives tried to expand holdings at nearby villages' and small farmers' expense.

Peasant unions quickly shifted their targets from the former estate owners to the new cooperatives and sought to protect both peasants and villages from the cooperatives' employment policies and attempts to encroach on peasants' lands. When the Revolutionary Government in the late 1970s began to reverse its earlier economic reforms and dismantle agrarian and factory cooperatives, several peasant unions organized land invasions, seized unused cooperative property, and not infrequently divided the land into individualized private holdings (Petras and Havens 1981a: 223–34).

By the time the military returned to the barracks and civilian parties were once again in charge of government, peasants' views of the legitimacy of the state and the sanctity of existing property relations were at a nadir. Although there is little evidence that the peasants had become advocates of a wholesale transformation of society or proponents of a return to a mythic Peruvian past of communal production and common landholding, many scholars believe that the peasants had developed greater awareness and greater distrust of their broader political context (Petras and Havens 1981a: 229–36). They were not only land hungry, often unionized, and often experienced in labour struggles, but viewed the state as a primary cause of their poverty. Political scientist Cynthia McClintock (1989: 76) after informally surveying peasants in the 1980s, noted that both Andean and coastal peasants were unusually politically enraged compared to earlier times: 'More than ever before, peasants and students blamed their abject poverty on the government.' According to one peasant respondent, 'There's no help from the government. . . . Here, they've always forgotten us. There's no help. Exactly the opposite. . . . They're killing the poor people.'

Urban squatters and changing shantytown politics

Between 1960 and 1980, acts of political protest multiplied in not only the countryside and factories but also the cities and working-class suburbs. The cities had grown rapidly during the second half of the twentieth century. Metropolitan Lima, for example, had 645,000 inhabitants in 1940, 7 million in 1990. One-third of Peru's total population could be classified as urban in 1940; two-thirds in 1980 (Rudolph 1992: 7, 24).

Many of the new urban dwellers were former peasants who hoped to find well-paid jobs, comfortable homes, and abundant food. Jobs were relatively plentiful between 1945 and 1975, and before 1970 the standard of living in the cities was slowly yet steadily rising. Housing, however, seldom met the newcomers' needs, and many were shocked to find themselves employed but homeless.

As early as 1946 small groups of newcomers seized unused property in well-planned land invasions and built temporary homes of tin and mud. In 1956, about 10 per cent of Lima's populace lived in these squatter communities; the proportion was about 25 per cent in 1970 and 40 per cent in the 1980s (Rudolph 1992: 15; Stepan 1978: 160). The settlements did not always remain impoverished. Villa El Salvador in Lima, for example, soon had brick and stone dwellings, and within decades a majority of the dwellings had running water (Carlessi 1989: 15–16). Especially after 1960 many of the settlements received funds from international organizations, such as the Catholic Church and the United Nations, that financed a wide range of services, including schools, music halls, libraries, and medical centres.

The Catholic Church – divided between traditionalists, who urged the poor to accept their place in society, and liberation theologists, who advocated social equality on earth and the right of the poor to a larger portion of society's wealth – was especially active in aiding community institutions. After 1968 socially radical clerics entered shantytowns in large numbers and helped establish dining halls and medical centres, and even top ecclesiastical figures intervened on the squatters' behalf when police threatened evictions (Blondet 1995: 275–6; Stokes 1995: 19, 39–40, 72–3, 107).

Before 1968 most immigrant settlements elected community representatives who would lobby for outside funds. The representatives were seldom chosen on the basis of ideology or party affiliation but were largely chosen for reputed effectiveness in dealing with national and international funding agencies. Thus, whenever the national government changed, the representatives would also change. As a result, the settlements lacked durable ideological orientations and partisan loyalties. According to urban sociologist Manuel Castells (1983: 193),

> The picture of the Liman squatters' movement appears as one of a manipulated mob, changing from one political ideology to another in exchange for the delivery (or promise) of land, housing, and services. And this was, to a large extent, the case . . . [T]he behaviour of the squatters was not cynical or apolitical, but, on the contrary, deeply realistic, and displayed an awareness of the political situation and how their hard-pressed demands could be obtained.

The 1968 military government sought support from the squatters, partly because the officers feared that the overcrowded shantytowns might become a hothouse for insurrectionary movements. The legality of the residents' claims to the land was quickly recognized (a policy that squatters naturally welcomed), and the settlements were renamed '*pueblos jovenes*' (new towns). The Revolutionary Government of the Armed Forces also offered to cover part of the cost of public services if each settlement rank ordered its needs (say, of paved streets, water provisions, and electricity) and made a downpayment covering part of the costs (Stepan 1978: 158–89).

Partially to localize grievances and prevent possible cross-settlement alliances, the government institutionalized a system of grassroots democracy in which heads of families in each block elected a representative, who with similar representatives within an urban zone would pick a spokesman to petition the state for zone services. Government policies prohibited election of a block representative who either (1) lacked a recognized occupation or (2) had a police record suggestive of a 'subversive' political background. These moves, which were intended to screen out full-time labour organizers and left-party militants, reinforced the long-standing clientelistic relationship between the settlements and the government. Squatter leaders, consequently, seldom developed ties with either translocal unions or parties that had broader agendas for political and social change. Furthermore, the size of the block electorates (rarely were there more than 50 voters in a block election) ensured that the candidates' personal characteristics and provincial ties would largely determine the outcome of elections and that ideological and partisan affiliations would not play a significant role.

The nonpartisan and provincial spirit of settlement politics changed somewhat in the late 1970s, when the Revolutionary Government decided to reverse its highly decentralist urban policies and to integrate urban neighbourhoods into larger municipal governments. It also proposed reducing services and thereby lessen public expenditures and the public debt – this to help usher in a period of prosperity. The imminent loss of political power brought neighbourhoods in the settlements to organize street protests, erect barricades, engage in street battles, and for the first time cooperate with oppositional parties and participate in trade union general strikes. In 1979 squatter settlements in metropolitan Lima established a citywide political alliance. In 1980 pueblos jovenes throughout Peru sent representatives to the founding meeting of a nationwide organization, the General Confederation of City-Dwellers (Carlessi 1989: 16–17).

The new alliances were short-lived. Unfamiliar with one another's needs and values, individual settlements could not settle on a common goal or programme beyond resisting the military government's proposals for large, centralized municipal governments. Once the government backed down from that objective, the alliances lost their raison d'etre and commanded little loyalty and few resources.

After democratic elections were reinstituted in 1980, some Marxist parties tried to use the alliances as organizational resources for left-wing candidates, but as we have seen, the Marxists were hardly a homogenous group. Disagreements over ideologies and over public-service priorities split the always fragile electoral coalitions over and over again. Those settlers who at first tended to support the United Left candidates quickly became disillusioned with the Marxists' infighting and policy ineffectiveness and began to cooperate with other parties and work with nonelectoral organizations, such as the Catholic Church and even Shining Path (Cameron 1991: 293–313; Dietz 1986–87: 153–9; Stokes 1995: 49–51, 53–5). Soon, experienced neighbourhood activists returned to their former habits and re-established the politics of patronage, of charity, and of nonpartisan projects, such as free-milk programmes for children, public soup kitchens for the indigent, citizen police patrols, and local cultural clubs.[1]

However, Peru's economic crisis was leaving its mark on the squatter communities, which could no longer acquire the amounts of external funding needed to support public services from straitened governments. The shantytowns increasingly undertook projects designed not so much to enrich life as to ensure the residents' physical survival, such as the administration of free-milk programmes and collectively run soup kitchens.

Meanwhile, refugees still streamed toward the cities. Declining job opportunities in the Andes and the escalating war between Shining Path and the military had made life in the hinterland, always on the edge of subsistence, unbearable. The cities, however, were no longer a haven because of their grossly inadequate infrastructures and declining state aid. Ill-housed, ill-fed, and disillusioned, many new migrants were receptive when Shining Path activists came to their doors offering aid of one sort or another (Poole and Rénique 1992: 40, 84–95).

The state's curtailments in funding services weakened the legitimacy of many of the older neighbourhood leaders, who continued to advocate peaceful petitioning of government rather than street protests. A younger generation of leaders appeared, more ambitious for social change, more global in policy demands (including an end to Peru's international economic dependency), and more confrontationalist in rhetoric (Petras and Havens 1981b: 248; Stokes 1991b: 75–101; Stokes 1995: 61–83). Despite their frequent lack of formal training in Marxism, Leninism or other radical political philosophies, the new leaders openly advocated a radical transformation of the society. A washerwoman and activist in an urban mothers' club declared: 'our objective is that there should be a new society, a change. . . . We hope that there will be a change like this: either we all eat or no one eats' (Stokes 1995: 74).

Conclusion

The 1960s and 1970s were decades of protest in Peru, as well as years of hunger. Land invasions, labour mobilizations, and ebbs and flows of shantytown militancy were parts of a tumultuous political landscape. APRA, Marxist parties, and rural guerrilla organizations attempted to channel popular discontent and local protests into organized actions for radical change, but the radicals' popularity was mixed, at best. The sectarianism of Peru's Marxists frustrated the urban poor, and the rural guerrillas' refusal to familiarize themselves with the customs and values of the countryside (the Trotskyist Hugo Blanco being a notable exception) alienated peasants.

Many Shining Path activists were aware of ongoing protests and oppositional programmes. As we will see in the next chapter, a good number of its activists had participated in land invasions, labour demonstrations, or other forms of Left politics. When deciding what to do, they drew upon their own experience and that of other parties, and studied past mistakes and victories. In a sense, the movement was a recapitulation of Peru's oppositional traditions, which provided warnings, lessons, and inspiration.

Note

1. This is not to deny that radicals attempted to organize members of pueblos jovenes into more radical movements. But by and large the efforts failed to bear fruit. For observations on the extent of clientelism in the urban squatter communities, see Stokes (1991a; 1991b; 1995) and Petras and Havens (1981b).

Chapter 10

Diverse directions along the Shining Path

The year 1980 was seminal in Peru's political history. Citizens elected a president for the first time in more than a decade. The drafters of the new constitution allowed illiterate citizens and 18-year-olds to vote for the first time ever. And the new social movement known as Shining Path held a rare plenum of its Central Committee that, among other things, adopted the slogan 'Initiate the armed struggle'.

Shining Path's first armed action was brief, local, and certainly not bloody. On the eve of the 1980 presidential election, a small group of its young activists, masked and carrying two malfunctioning pistols, broke into an election office in the remote mountain town of Chuschi in the department of Ayacucho. They seized unmarked ballots and unused ballot boxes, took them into a public plaza and burned them, and then fled. The next day replacement ballots arrived, and the election proceeded without further disturbance (Isbell 1992: 65; Poole and Rénique 1992: 57–8).

Identity-formation theorists presume that nonelites create their own beliefs, which in turn shape their activities. Nonelites who join a movement bring beliefs developed in other social contexts, such as workplaces and churches, with them. They also develop new political beliefs while participating in the movement. Movement leaders try to weave the diverse and often incompatible beliefs into a relatively coherent creed. Because members are constantly creating new ideas and because newcomers to a movement bring novel beliefs with them, the ideological mix constantly changes.

This chapter explores the activities and ideological evolution of Shining Path from 1980 to the mid-1990s. As we shall see, Shining Path's ideology was characterized by some enduring themes about imperialism, the need for an interclass alliance among the nonrich, and violence as a political tactic. But the movement's ideology was not a simple, direct 'line' nor a completed, detailed 'blueprint'. For example, although the vast majority of Shining Path activists agreed that some illegal force was needed to reconstruct Peruvian society and redistribute economic resources and political rights, they continually disagreed about the appropriateness of specific forms of violence – for example, assassination of civilians versus industrial sabotage – and about the proper ratio of violent to nonviolent forms of struggle.

The rub was how to combine politically necessary violence with equally important nonviolent tactics. And the diversity of opinions fostered factional rivalries as well as a host of movement activities.

Origins and early ideology

A coterie of radical university professors and students had formed Shining Path about a decade before the attack in Chuschi. Known officially as the Communist Party of Peru – Shining Path (or PCP-SL), it seemed to be just another local splinter group within the constantly expanding universe of Marxist parties. Many members recently had been active in rural protests or in efforts to help the local urban poor. The name derived from the name of a student publication, *Along the Shining Path of Mariátegui*, whose own name derived from the novel applications of Marxist ideas to Andean economic and cultural history by José Mariátegui, Peru's renowned Marxist of the early twentieth century.

The most visible and perhaps the most notorious leader of Shining Path was Abimael Guzmán Reynoso. Born in 1934, he was the illegitimate son of a prosperous import wholesaler. When Guzmán was 12 years old, his mother died. Shortly thereafter he moved in with his father, and they travelled to various city-ports, living in relative comfort. In a 1986 interview, Guzmán recalled how, as a teenager, he observed street battles between poor people and government forces:

> I saw the fighting spirit of the people. . . . And I saw how they fought the army, forcing them to retreat to their barracks. And how forces had to be brought in from other places in order to crush the people. This is an event that, I'd say, has been imprinted quite vividly in my memory. Because of that, after having come to understand Lenin, I understood how the people, our class, when they take to the streets and march, can make the reactionaries tremble, despite all their power.
>
> (Guzmán 1988: 99)

Guzmán also recalled being excited about the Second World War, hearing news on the radio about faraway bombings and meetings of the 'big five' Allied leaders (including Stalin), and celebrating the war's end.

> I'd say these events left their mark on me, and impressed upon me in an elemental and confused way the idea of power, of the masses, and of the capacity of war to transform things.
>
> (Guzmán 1988: 100)

Guzmán attended an exclusive Catholic high school and excelled academically. Towards the end of his studies, he formed a discussion group with some classmates, who debated 'all kinds' of political ideas (Guzmán 1988: 100) and who were especially curious about the costs and shortcomings of Peru's economy.

He first seriously studied political theory in college, where he also observed firsthand confrontations between Apristas and communists. He read many biographies and developed a lifelong love for novels and plays, having discovered valuable political lessons in the writings of Thomas Mann and William Shakespeare. A classmate lent him Lenin's *One Step Forward, Two Steps Back*, which was Guzmán's first Marxist book. Meanwhile, instructors exposed him to European analytic philosophy, to the natural sciences (physics became one of his favourite subjects), and to socialist-realist theories about revolutionary art. To meet a course requirement, Guzmán collected census information in Arequipa city following a major earthquake; once again, direct observations of Peru's poor profoundly affected him (Gorriti 1992: 152–3; Guzmán 1988: 100, 103–4; Strong 1992: 4–9).

In college, Guzmán became increasingly interested in the Bolshevik revolution and admired Stalin's ideas, nerve, and perseverance. Toward the end of the 1950s, Guzmán underwent a political conversion. Having been a social democrat for most of his early adult years, he came to doubt that electoral politics could transform Peru and end widespread poverty. In his opinion, career government bureaucrats and professional party machines always had and probably always would appease international corporations, foreign investors, and large landowners and export businesses while ignoring the sufferings of the rest of society. He therefore placed his faith in local direct democracy and vigilante justice rather than an elected parliament and career civil servants (Tarazona-Sevillano 1990: 18–19, 24–7).

Guzmán joined the Peruvian Communist Party around 1960. His persistence helped secure his admission, for many older party members argued that only sons and daughters of workers should join. At that time, the party was splintering between supporters of Stalin and supporters of Khrushchev. Guzmán, impressed by Stalin's book, *Problems of Leninism*, vigorously defended him. He later recalled that 'taking him [Stalin] away from us would have been like taking away our soul' (Guzmán 1988: 100).

In 1962 Guzmán took a teaching job in the newly opened University of San Cristóbal de Huamanga in the southern mountains. There, among Andean peasants in the department of Ayacucho, Guzmán began to think seriously about the countryside as a theatre for revolutionary politics and about the possibility of a peasant–proletarian revolutionary alliance. As he stated in a 1988 interview, 'Ayacucho allowed me to discover the peasantry. . . . I started to understand Chairman Mao Tse-tung' (Guzmán 1988: 101).

The Peruvian government had reopened the University of Huamanga to stimulate local economic development (see Chapter 8). The university was to combine instruction in traditional academic subjects with extension programmes in commercial agriculture for people in its environs. Guzmán looked askance at the extension programmes, for he was not convinced that the machinery, chemicals, and financial strategies they promoted actually helped the struggling farmers. He thought, instead, that the new agricultural and financial ways condemned the farmers to perpetual indebtedness – indeed, to greater poverty.

The involvement of both the US Peace Corps and international development agencies in the development of the university's extension programmes and academic curricula also troubled Guzmán. He reacted by helping organize student protests. The university administration, partly because of the pressure, soon terminated Peace Corps instructional contracts.

In 1969 university students, highschool students, and townspeople protested the government's proposed tuition increases. The local peasants and the urban middle class saw formal education as one means to change their personal circumstances in an otherwise highly stratified society. Guzmán performed liaison services among student, family, and community groups. The protests turned violent: police and youths began to exchange bullets and various projectiles. Police shot randomly into crowds, and gangs of students tore down telephone lines and destroyed bridges. Some officers believed that Guzmán had incited the students and in consequence jailed him. He was later released because of lack of evidence.

Throughout the 1960s and 1970s Guzmán relentlessly criticized most of the communist groups who, by and large, supported Khrushchev and hoped to persuade the military government to implement radical economic change. Guzmán, a steadfast admirer of Stalin and the radical policies of the early Russian Revolution, was outraged both by the rise of Khrushchev within the worldwide communist movement and by his de-Stalinization campaign. Most Peruvian communists, however, accepted and supported Khrushchev's efforts. Meanwhile, the Peruvian military government, though hardly procommunist, wanted the communists to function as a counterweight to APRA's labour organizations and therefore allowed them to organize workers. Many Peruvian communists, in turn, hoped to convince the military government of the wisdom of redistributing land, seizing foreign-owned assets, and collectivizing production. They therefore tried to dissuade peasants and workers from land invasions and other forms of protest lest they feed the officers' fears of social disorder. Guzmán – ever a gadfly in communist circles – argued that by trying to contain poor people's protests, Peruvian communists were needlessly perpetuating a system of exploitation and suffering. Furthermore, history had shown that the military was not a reliable agent of social change. It was only natural, then, that whenever a Peruvian communist organization split into more politically conciliatory 'Soviet' factions (such as the so-called Communist Party of Peru – Unity, or PCP-U) and more politically confrontational 'Chinese' factions (such as the so-called Communist Party of Peru – Red Flag, or PCP-BR), Guzmán would usually support the latter and denounce the former for being concerned more with placating the powers that be than with solving society's ills.

Specialists in Peruvian radical politics believe that during the middle 1960s Guzmán travelled with a delegation of Peruvian communists to the People's Republic of China and attended a cadre school. There, he became increasingly fascinated both with the idea of a peasant-based revolution and with the ongoing struggle between government bureaucrats and party radicals who were calling for a permanent Cultural Revolution. These radicals, Guzmán believed, correctly saw that political privilege was inherently corrupting and counterrevolutionary. Reportedly, Guzmán, while in cadre school, also was taken with the instructors' skilful use of light explosives (such as fireworks) in classroom demonstrations. He began seriously to entertain the notion of physical violence as a tool that could be applied with scientific precision and whose outcomes could be reliably foreseen (Poole and Rénique 1992: 33).

During his stay Guzmán systematically studied the writings of José Mariátegui, whom he would later identify as one of his mentors. Mariátegui's arguments about

Peru's peculiarly dependent and geographically uneven pattern of capitalist development were particularly convincing. Guzmán also concluded that Mariátegui's theories about the cultural and political weakness of the national bourgeoisie were valid, and concurred in Mariátegui's insistence on the primacy of popular education in a successful socialist revolution. Like his mentor, Guzmán believed that the proper role of a serious revolutionary party was to educate oppressed people as to the structural origins of their condition and as to their political opportunities and alternatives.

Back in Peru, Guzmán thought at length about how to educate peasants concerning the derivation of their condition and about social revolution. He also had returned more cynical than ever about the Peruvian Communist Party-Unity's attempts to build bridges to purportedly 'progressive groups' within the military government. He reasoned that any such alliance was doomed because the progressive wings in the military were half-heartedly committed to the equalization of property and because half-hidden conservative units within the military would repeal reforms at the first opportunity. But Guzmán was equally cynical about the recent guerrilla politics of ELN and MIR because they relied exclusively on guns and military tactics to inspire a revolution and foolishly failed to educate peasants beforehand. Guzmán held firmly that armed struggle, although sometimes necessary, must always complement, never overshadow, the painstaking educational preparation of the oppressed and exploited (Gorriti 1992: 156–7; Poole and Rénique 1992: 37–8).

Other faculty members and students at the University of Huamanga who shared elements of Guzmán's thinking soon gathered around him. Antonio Díaz Martínez, among others, became an ally and helped develop the early ideals and strategies of Shining Path. Díaz, a well-published and internationally travelled agricultural economist, had earlier worked as a government official, administering an agricultural development plan that, in theory, would increase productivity through publicly financed irrigation systems for private haciendas. Díaz soon became disillusioned with such technological solutions for ending poverty in Peru. He concluded that they only helped the rich get richer while condemning the nonrich to perpetual poverty.

Díaz then became an advocate of radical land redistribution and collective forms of production. After joining the university faculty in Ayacucho, he criticized the university for pressuring peasants into borrowing money for the purchase of machinery and chemicals with which to produce cash crops for sale in coastal cities. He argued that the university's reasoning was ridiculous, especially given local soil conditions and local farmers' comparative disadvantage in transporting harvests to distant markets. Local peasants' traditional habits of cooperative production and local consumption served them to greater advantage and had the impressive plus of solvency.

Díaz was hardly a romantic traditionalist or a blind opponent of social change. He abhorred the extreme poverty and inequality in the Andes and hoped to render them obsolete by helping establish a political and economic alternative to modern capitalism. Rural impoverishment could be overcome only if there were radical banking reform; if utilities were nationalized in order to direct more resources into the hinterland; if private transportation monopolies were legally compelled to develop badly needed infrastructure in the mountains; and if public universities provided rural communities with agriculturists to be consulted by peasants, informed by their Andean traditions of collective production, as they saw fit (Harding 1988; Starn 1991: 72–5, 80–4).

Over the years Guzmán, Díaz, and others on the faculty at the University of Huamanga established numerous political study groups on the plight of Andeans and better ways to develop the country's economy. The Ayacucho radicals also helped organize like-minded study groups at other major universities, such as the National University of Engineering and the National University of San Marcos in Lima. The groups gradually coalesced into a semisecret party that although Marxist in its theoretical orientation was also very critical of the politics of most other communist parties. Gradually, the Ayacucho-based coalition, which officially split from the PCP-BR in 1970, became informally known among radicals as Sendero Luminoso (Shining Path). (Some activists do not like the shorthand 'Shining Path' or 'SL' and prefer to have their organization called by its full name, 'Communist Party of Peru – Shining Path'.)

During the early 1970s Sendero Luminoso became highly influential within the University of Huamanga. Its representatives sat on the university's Executive Council and on bodies that selected faculty and designed and implemented curricula. Shining Path activists also opened the José Carlos Mariátegui Centre for Intellectual Study, where faculty members delivered public lectures on topics in philosophy, social science, and the natural sciences. Guzmán, always energetic and active, held several key administrative offices on campus; at one point, he was provost.

During the mid-1970s rival political groups won elections to the student union and the faculty union and began to displace key members of Shining Path. Losing its campus stronghold, Sendero Luminoso began to expend more energy on organizing off-campus constituencies and working in nearby villages, for example, in the university's community-education programmes for peasants and secondary-school youths. Shining Path activists also contacted teachers who during the military's rule belonged to Maoist labour groups and who had been recently trained at the university, encouraging them to set up 'people's schools' where students would be exposed to social criticism as well as to noncapitalist agricultural practices that might improve their standard of living. In addition, they began to organize small cells in cities throughout central and southern Peru and participated in squatter-settlement politics. Urban groups also for the first time addressed womens' issues.

Soon experienced peasant-union and mine-workers organizers in the Andes and members of urban squatter organizations – such as Julio César Mezzich, Félix Calderon, and the Red Star group in Lima – joined the Ayacucho-based radicals. By the early 1980s members of the Shining Path coalition could be found throughout southern and central Peru and in numerous major cities, including Lima. In membership and geographic reach it had become a serious rival to other reform and revolutionary organizations (Poole and Rénique 1992: 38–43; Smith 1992: 131–3).

Members of Shining Path, coming from different social backgrounds and working in different local political contexts, often disagreed over day-to-day tactics (to be discussed later). They agreed, however, that Peru's current economic problems originated in the Spanish conquest of South America and in the country's reliance for more than a century on international markets and foreign investors. Said one Shining Path document, 'the modern Peruvian economy was born retarded and ill at its roots' (Communist Party of Peru 1985: 26).

According to Shining Path theorists, the early owners of haciendas and plantations, relying on the cheap, forced labour of Indians, had never rationalized production or invested profits in expensive labour-saving machinery. Rather, large landowners adopted an easy lifestyle, often in Lima, and spent their wealth importing manufactured luxury items and imitating European fashions.

Since the mid-nineteenth century, argued spokespersons for Shining Path, US and European investors have removed irreplaceable natural resources. Peru's large landowners have used rents to foreigners and profits from exported raw materials to remain semi-European and nonproductive. The Peruvian government has propped up the socioeconomic order by forcing indigenous people to work for less-than-subsistence wages on haciendas, plantations, and foreign-owned mines and by repressing union drives among Peru's few industrial workers. Neither the largely corrupt state bureaucrats, nor the foreign investors, nor the self-indulgent hacienda and plantation owners have wanted to develop a light-manufacturing sector. Such investments have been discouraged by the country's weak domestic market. Peru's economy therefore cannot be viewed as an 'emerging' capitalist order with a multitude of small entrepreneurs risking hard-earned profits on expensive machinery. The economy is better depicted as a mixture of 'imperialism, semifeudalism, and bureaucratic capitalism' (Communist Party of Peru 1982; 1985).

To rescue Peru from its chronic poverty and profound inequalities in income and wealth, Shining Path strategists proposed a mixture of armed struggle and political education of wage earners, peasants, and small-business owners. Armed struggle was deemed necessary because Peru's current elite would not quietly give up its wealth and political privileges. After all, Peru's history of repeated oligarchic coups, launched whenever populist presidents had attempted to introduce modest social reforms, had proven that a peaceful road to social justice was illusory. In the words of Mao Tse-tung, whom the Shining Path often quoted with approval, 'Everything grows out of the barrel of a gun' (Communist Party of Peru 1986: 58).

Violence alone, however, would never generate economic development. In addition, the country's three major popular classes – the peasantry, the proletariat, and the petit bourgeoisie – needed to form a political coalition, plan a new constitutional order, expel the large landowners and foreign capitalists, and then pursue autarky and a humane form of small-scale capitalism. For this scenario to be realized, Shining Path must patiently teach the popular classes about politics and economics, because they currently see neither that their class interests converge nor that social revolution is necessary.

Shining Path writers proposed teaching peasants, workers, and small-business owners about their potential political power and socioeconomic options in hypothetical 'revolutionary base areas' where the Peruvian government had been forcefully expelled by guerrilla units and where local communities ruled themselves through a mixture of direct democracy and representative institutions. There, with advice from Shining Path activists, members of the popular classes would be able to make their own social and economic policies and learn by political practice about one another's interests. Shining Path theorists counselled movement activists to establish revolutionary base areas in remote parts of the Andes and then steadily expand the areas' borders until the entire nation, except for large cities, had become part of a 'New Democratic People's Republic'. If revolutionary base areas were properly nurtured, Peru's elite would prudently abdicate power rather than face the wrath of an organized popular polity. Ideally, a federated polity and autarkic economic system would follow the collapse of the imperialist, semifeudalist, and bureaucratic capitalist regime and would protect small-scale private property and encourage local entrepreneurship. In addition, the new political order would seize large estates and foreigners' holdings, would distribute them to the poor, and would promote wage earners' rights to bargain collectively.

Shining Path theorists, being communists, believed that complete elimination of exploitation and oppression required the abolishment of private property and introduction of collectivized property. They warned, however, that a communist revolution should not yet be attempted. Peru's productivity level was too low, and the country's proletariat was too small and politically inexperienced. Moreover, international superpowers, such as the US and Japan, would use their military might to destroy such 'a really free, sovereign country' (Communist Party of Peru 1982: 1). In the distant future, once Peru's manufacturing base had been adequately developed and a sufficiently large proletariat had emerged, a communist revolution might succeed. Until then, Shining Path should focus on establishing revolutionary base areas, meeting the government's repression with guerrilla violence, and educating the popular classes as to why the current social order is unredeemable and why a socioeconomic revolution through a broad interclass coalition is Peru's only hope (Communist Party of Peru 1982; 1985; 1986).

Despite government efforts to represent Shining Path simplistically as 'terrorist', the movement never relied solely on physical violence to achieve its ends, especially during its first decade. The national leadership only decided during the late 1970s (about seven years after the group's formation) that the movement should immediately use armed action to *supplement*, not follow upon, the time-consuming political education of the poor. The decision was preceded by and later generated much controversy within Shining Path and was never unanimously and unequivocally supported, even within the party's Central Committee (Guzmán 1988: 26, 42). Some of Shining Path's earliest leaders, such as Luis Kawata Makabe, argued that if the movement engaged in armed struggle, it was doomed to repression and self-destruction. But he and other opponents of armed action could never defeat its advocates, partly because the latter held key organizational positions in Ayacucho and from time to time successfully purged the most vocal naysayers. Still, even the momentarily victorious proguerrilla factions conceded that guns alone could not produce a social revolution and that priority must be given to the education objective (Gianotten et al. 1985: 193, 202; Gorriti 1992: 164–5; McClintock 1989: 78; Poole and Rénique 1992: 40, 48; Smith 1992: 135).

During its many minipurges, Shining Path developed two organizational and ideological dimensions. One was a sophisticated guerrilla wing, many of whose members graduated from Shining Path's military school, established in 1979. There, teachers taught – in addition to military skills and weapon making – Marxist, Leninist, and Maoist theories of historical change; the irreplaceable role of the proletariat in revolutionizing capitalist society (and therefore the futility of a premature communist revolution); and the need for a vanguard party to unite the peasantry, urban and rural proletariat, and small-business classes into a single, anti-imperialist coalition. In the words of Guzmán (1988: 48), 'Modern weapons are necessary, but their performance depends on the ideology of the man who wields them. Lenin taught us that.' The second dimension of the movement, which had existed at least since the early 1970s, was a diffuse set of nonviolent educational projects, typified by the so-called *organismos generados* (party-generated organisms) that burrowed within union chapters, neighbourhood schools, squatter settlements, and other local-level social institutions. These activists (who composed most of the movement) generally eschewed arms, laboured alongside Peru's nonwealthy in established social institutions, and encouraged residents to experiment with local forms of collective production.

In theory, the Shining Path movement *as a whole* acted in a coherent, unified manner because of the authority formally vested in its national executive committee, known as the *'Cupola'*. The committee, in principle, coordinated subordinate units in the peaceful, political education of the poor and in armed struggle against representatives of the state and, to a lesser extent, of the wealthy. The Cupola, with limited knowledge about different areas of Peru, was expected not to direct the day-to-day activities of local cells but to provide general guidelines. Only on occasion did the Cupola dispatch a group of activists on a specific mission. Usually cells of approximately four to five members were autonomously to choose appropriate tactics from their knowledge of local opportunities and from their familiarity with the movement's long-term goals. A common movement slogan – 'Centralized strategy and decentralized tactics!' (Communist Party of Peru 1986: 27; Guzmán 1988: 46) – suggested the tension between the movement's somewhat centralized authority structure and its often decentralized day-to-day decision making.

In practice it proved very difficult for the Cupola to supervise Shining Path's approximately ten thousand members[1] and to coordinate armed struggle with non-violent forms of political education. Most Shining Path cells, after all, were self-directed most of the time because of the need for security from government infiltration and because local social, economic, and political conditions vary so greatly that each cell tended to believe it could best decide on appropriate revolutionary activities for its locale. Neighbouring guerrilla and educative cells, normally unaware of one another's plans and activities, periodically worked at cross-purposes; for example, an unexpected bombing might undermine the efforts of a local cell to gain influence within a labour-union chapter. Different factions – guerrilla and educative – temporarily triumphed from region to region and from year to year. Those who lost in the local factional squabbles over the priority to be given to violent and nonviolent tactics sometimes left Shining Path rather than work with unpredictable colleagues (Gianotten et al. 1985: 193; McClintock 1989: 78–9; Poole and Rénique 1992: 43; Smith 1992; Tarazona-Sevillano 1990: 55–70). Because of the variety of local political activities, scholars have had difficulty generalizing about Shining Path's tactics. In the words of one US political scientist, 'Especially since 1982, it has seemed possible that there is more than one Sendero' (McClintock 1989: 83).

Armed struggle in the southern Andes

In 1981 hooded Shining Path guerrillas began to appear regularly in the more remote villages of the southern Andean department of Ayacucho. They occasionally bombed banks and government offices – architectural symbols of the socio-economic order – but channelled most of their energies into enforcement of village laws and norms. They punished cattle rustlers from neighbouring villages, local officials who were reputed to have abused their authority, unfaithful husbands, and any owners of small stores who in public opinion swindled costumers. Verbal humiliations, public whippings, and occasional executions were carried out, many of which earned Shining Path the villagers' gratitude (Isbell 1992: 65–6, 68, 71).

Shining Path guerrillas, however, saw themselves as revolutionary vanguards, not as institutional supports for local norms and notions of justice. Accordingly, after having enforced the moral economy of a village over several months, they often attempted to transform the village ethos and institutions. Frequently, for example, they imposed systems of communal planting and barter in lieu of commercial exchange. Some activists also insisted that villages terminate market relations with the rest of the country and become economically self-reliant, and tried to close roads on market days. In some places guerrillas tried to ordain sobriety and sexual abstinence at previously rowdy adolescent rituals (Isbell 1992: 66–7, 71–2; 'Nicario' 1995).

The guerrillas' zealotry usually backfired. Many peasants owned and treasured their individual private plots (even if the plots were very small) and were habituated to selling portions of their produce for cash to outsiders. These mini and part-time entrepreneurs found Shining Path's economic proposals impractical. In the words of one, 'We could not let them close the markets. Where would we get our salt and matches?' (Isbell 1992: 66). The guerrillas' puritanism also seemed foreign and culturally arrogant to many adolescent villagers who engaged in 'hedonistic' and 'indulgent' celebrations that violated the guerrillas' sense of propriety.

Not infrequently, residents in Ayacucho's villages rebelled against the more radical proposals of the revolutionaries. Many peasants who had earlier tolerated and even welcomed Shining Path guerrillas into their villages began to report them to the police and even asked the government to build police stations as protection. Rural support for the radicals thus constantly waxed and waned, depending in part on the specific goals and initiatives of particular Shining Path activists and on the congruence of their initiatives with local traditions (Crabtree 1992: 102–3; Harding 1987: 190–2; Isbell 1992: 66–9, 72–77; Poole and Rénique 1992: 60–4; Salcedo 1986: 38–9).

In 1981 and 1982 Shining Path guerrillas appeared for the first time in departments abutting Ayacucho. Once again, they physically and verbally attacked objects of popular resentment, such as recently upwardly mobile merchants and commercial farmers, and also offered to help villagers in their ongoing invasions of large farms and agrarian cooperatives. Once again, numerous rural communities initially supported Shining Path actions because they served local norms. According to some anthropologists conducting field work in the area, villagers, who initially had referred to the guerrillas as 'terrorists', by the mid-1980s were calling them 'buddy' and 'comrade' (Berg 1992: 98).

Only a small minority of rural residents supported the movement's periodic proposals for a new system of property ownership, however. Peasants feared that whenever Shining Path activists spoke glowingly of collectivization, they meant the seizure of the peasants' own plots. Further, proposals for village self-sufficiency troubled many peasants, who relied on cash crops to buy medicines, clothing, and other 'luxuries'. Thus, popular support for the radicals vacillated, as it did in the department of Ayacucho, according to the guerrillas' declared aims and immediate actions (Berg 1992: 90–103; Gianotten et al. 1985: 193–6, 198).

The government initially dismissed the geographic range and social bases of support for the Shining Path movement and described the Andean guerrillas as 'isolated criminal delinquents'. When local officials in the southern Andes began to resign in large numbers because of death threats (some were carried out), the Belaúnde government abandoned its indifference and dispatched an experienced counterinsurgency force known as the Sinchis, which two decades earlier had defeated the MIR guerrillas. The government also declared states of emergency in several provinces of Ayacucho (a Peruvian province approximates in size and administrative duties to a county in the United States or Britain) in which counterinsurgency units were constitutionally permitted to detain suspected terrorists and their supporters without formal charges, and could legally enter homes without warrants. Public demonstrations against purported military misbehaviour were outlawed. Freedom of speech and press were circumscribed; for example, anyone who spoke in favour of the guerrillas could be incarcerated for up to 25 years.

According to many observers, the Sinchis and other police and military units took political advantage of the new curbs on civilians' constitutional rights. Because many officers believed that Shining Path was part of an international communist conspiracy to overthrow the government, they did not limit themselves to members of Shining Path but investigated all local radicals, reformers, and known Marxists, including so-called red priests (clergy who worked among the Andean poor). Military units invaded villages said to have been friendly to Shining Path, indiscriminately arrested and tortured young males, and destroyed homes and property. By the mid-1980s more than 6,000 civilians had been killed in the military's campaign against Shining Path, and in some months, upwards of 1,000 would 'disappear', presumably either to be held in secret prisons or to be killed and deposited in unmarked mass graves (McClintock 1989: 89; Reid 1986: 44). Most of the repression occurred in Ayacucho, where military actions between 1983 and 1984 resulted in more than 5,000 deaths out of a local population of roughly a half million (Degregori 1994: 82). During the mid-1980s human rights organizations around the world reported widespread torture and extrajudicial executions by Peruvian security forces.

Amnesty International, for one, warned that human rights violations were taking place 'on a scale unprecedented in modern Peru' (Reid 1986: 44). A Peruvian Senate commission on human rights reported that security forces had killed 6,935 civilians in 1983 and 1984 (Poole and Rénique 1992: 7). Belaúnde ineptly responded to the reports by blithely ridiculing others' concerns. He joked at one press conference that he had recently tossed into dustbins Amnesty International's reports (Crabtree 1992: 96).

The military's presence in Ayacucho and neighbouring departments and the suspension of civil liberties did not noticeably diminish Shining Path violence. On the contrary, Shining Path guerrillas began to kill with greater frequency and to bomb bridges and the pylons that helped bring electrical energy to Lima.

In addition, the guerrillas began to set up scores of alternative local political institutions called 'People's Committees' in remote villages that security forces could not police. According to Shining Path leaders, several hundred People's Committees had been established by the mid-1980s, and several thousand Peruvians were participating in them. The movement hoped to establish several hundred more People's Committees before the decade's end (Communist Party of Peru 1985: 34; 1986: 34–5; Guzmán 1988: 20–3, 34–7, 43–6, 51, 73, 78–9).

According to Sendero spokespersons, the committees functioned as unrestricted town meetings, where wage earners, peasants, and small entrepreneurs could freely discuss public policy. In addition, members of each of the three major classes – the proletariat, the peasantry, and the petit bourgeoisie – were allowed to choose a third of the members to the Delegate Assembly, which met when the People's Committees were not in session. In principle, each class, if uncomfortable with its delegates' decisions, had the right of immediate recall.

In theory, the People's Committees and Delegate Assemblies were to provide political structure to the hypothesized revolutionary base areas and were, in the long run, to evolve into a highly decentralized, federated rival to the Peruvian state. When Peru's nonrich finally toppled the current elites (a process that was expected to take at least a few decades), members of popular classes would continue to rule themselves directly by means of People's Committees and Delegate Assemblies. In the meantime, the new political institutions would teach participants alternatives to the government's current economic policies, how to make public policy, and how to balance competing class interests. Referring to Peru's impoverished masses, Guzmán (1988: 51) stated and predicted that

> for the first time they are taking Power and they have begun to taste the honey on their lips. They will not stop there. They will want it all, and they will get it.

The Belaúnde government, embarrassed by its apparent impotence in stopping the revolutionaries' insurrectionary politics and outraged by the continuing murders of public officials, suspended civil liberties in additional provinces and departments. The increased suspensions, however, failed to contain the expanding movement or to deter the growing numbers of assassinations, which Shining Path now defended as a proper response to the government's indiscriminate 'genocide'. By 1985 both the Shining Path and the military had each begun to kill off entire populations of mountain villages suspected of aiding the opposition. Peasant hostility toward both mounted.

The guerrillas resorted to selectively executing rural residents whom they suspected of aiding the police. Often villagers, forewarned, would disagree with the guerrillas' judgment and plead for a suspect's life, which occasionally caused a guerrilla reversal but more often did not (Poole and Rénique 1992: 66–8; Rosenberg 1991: 207–8; Rudolph 1992: 89).

The guerrillas often avoided capture by fleeing from a village before government forces arrived. At most, a few unarmed educators would remain ('Nicario' 1995: 334). From one perspective, retreat was sensibly cautious; from another, it was cowardly and irresponsible. Locals, after all, were left to suffer the brunt of the repression provoked by the revolutionaries. In the words of one peasant:

> Why don't they take care of us? They got us into this problem, but they don't protect us; they ought to protect us, defend us. Why did they say they would be at the front of the battle and leave us behind? Where are they? Here you don't see them. They've gotten us into this mess and now they've gone.
>
> (McClintock 1989: 90)

Andean peasants responded variously to their increasingly violent and volatile environment. Many felt anger toward their seemingly fair-weather friends whose presence had brought down on them the wrath of the government. At least one village's residents sought to prove their loyalty to the regime by seizing more than a half dozen Shining Path activists who returned to the village once the Sinchis left, by stoning three to death, and by taking the others to government authorities (Salcedo 1986: 41).

The indiscriminate brutality of the Sinchis, however, exacerbated many peasants' dislike of the state and increased the attraction for some of Shining Path activists and their programme for radical change. According to social scientist Ronald Berg (1992: 98), Andean peasants generally believed that the police acted

> more cruelly and arbitrarily than the guerrillas. When the guerrillas struck, it was against people whose 'crimes' were well known or against specific targets such as the cooperatives. On the other hand, the police arrested and interrogated blindly, the numbers of 'disappeared' increased rapidly, and those whose relatives were taken away were left with great bitterness.

The escalating struggle between the military and Shining Path was complicated in 1984 by the appearance of another political organization – the Túpac Amaru Revolutionary Movement (MRTA) – that was also willing to use force to try to transform society. Composed primarily of former Apristas and of some members of a few radical communist parties, MRTA guerrillas primarily attacked symbols of foreign capitalism (such as property owned by multinational corporations) in cities. They viewed themselves as natural allies of the IU and as political realists because although they advocated revolutionary changes in the structure of society, they also believed that Peru's democratic government would immediately collapse if significant social reform did occur. According to MRTA theorists, the rich would protect their privileges and wealth with bayonets rather than tolerate redistribution of wealth or political privileges. MRTA activists therefore viewed their primary tasks as the cultivation of a martial spirit among the urban poor and the ever more numerous unemployed university graduates, and the preparation of these groups for an inescapable and imminent civil war. MRTA, interestingly, never developed a clear, detailed economic programme; it simply denounced the presence of international corporations on Peruvian soil and the world economy as the primary enemy of Peru's poor. To the extent that MRTA had an economic programme, it was to be the nation's Robin Hood: steal from foreign-owned factories and distribute the booty among the urban poor.

Leaders of Sendero Luminoso disdained MRTA as politically infantile; it failed to appreciate the need to educate the rural poor about the class bases of poverty and about the need for a comprehensive social, political, and economic revolution. Many leaders also accused MRTA of adhering to a nationalist-bourgeois ideology that was opposed primarily to the economic influence of US and western European corporations but not to capitalism per se.

The relationship between the two groups was strained throughout the mid and late 1980s, although the government generally viewed them as collaborators, not rivals. MRTA leaders initially expressed admiration for the courage of Shining Path activists and proposed unification, but Shining Path did not perceive a common interest and instead began to attack MRTA units (Bourque and Warren 1989: 17–18, 30; Crabtree 1992: 107–8, 189, 198–9; Poole and Rénique 1992: 12–13, 182–5; Rudolph 1992: 91–2; Woy-Hazleton and Hazleton 1992: 217–18).

Geographic expansion

Between 1982 and 1987 Shining Path activists extended their operations from Ayacucho and its neighbouring departments to the central Andean highlands and to the southernmost region of Peru. In some respects, little changed other than landscape. The guerrillas continued to assassinate and issue death threats to unpopular local officials and business owners, while other activists organized communal work sessions and popular schools (Crabtree 1992: 192–3). Nonetheless, the ratio of violent to nonviolent activity seemed to change, with nonviolent educational activity apparently receiving higher priority within the new rural territories. Members of Shining Path also began to collaborate with the more mainstream union and church leaders, whereas previously they had been more likely to denounce and even attack rival left-wing groups that advocated primarily a peaceful, legalistic road to social change.

The change in tactics was especially noticeable around Lake Titicaca, where many local peasants were already well organized into unions, church groups, and auxiliaries of the United Left. Since the mid-1960s groups such as the Vanguardia Revolucionaria had organized general strikes and encouraged producer and savings cooperatives. These religious and Marxist groups provided many of the local services, such as the provision of food for the hungry and protection of villagers against outlaws, that had earned Shining Path a small portion of trust and temporary support in Ayacucho. Shining Path activists, entering an organizationally dense environment, decided to seek out and win over established local leaders and their organizational resources rather than compete with them. On occasion guerrilla units attacked government officials (the mayor of Salina was murdered), but overall, Shining Path engaged in far less violence in the southern tip of Peru than it had in Ayacucho. Interestingly, the national Shining Path leadership instructed local activists to be far less cooperative with other left groups and to use threats of violence more regularly, but was ignored in favour of patient persuasion and cooperation (Crabtree 1992: 113–14; Taylor 1987).

In the mines of the central Andes, Shining Path also tried to collaborate with existing unions but enjoyed less success. Relations remained strained because the miners, having won hard-fought victories in the past, saw collective bargaining as a valuable route to wage increases and improved working conditions. Shining Path activists, many of whom repeatedly called for a tough, no-concessions style of contract negotiations, soon found themselves politically isolated from a majority of miners and union organizations. To compel more radical goals and a more combative negotiating style, some Shining Path radicals threatened and occasionally murdered recalcitrant labour leaders, actions that only intensified the hostility of established union partisans (Crabtree 1992: 114–15, 193; Poole and Rénique 1992: 78–83).

After the early 1980s Shining Path also expanded its activities in the eastern jungles, especially the subregion known as the Upper Huallaga Valley. Drug consumption in the United States since the mid-1970s had made coca a profitable crop on the eastern slopes of the Andes. The promise of decent wages and quick profits attracted hundreds of thousands of migrants to the valley from Peru's most impoverished rural communities. Even local farmers who previously had grown rice and fruit for coastal consumers turned to coca largely because of its low labour requirements and relatively high returns. By the late 1980s more than a quarter of a million Peruvian small farmers and entrepreneurs were in the coca business. The industry generated millions of dollars in foreign exchange and accounted for almost 40 per cent of the value of all Peruvian exports (Crabtree 1992: 115–18, 195–201; Gonzales 1992: 105–25; Poole and Rénique 1992: 167–202).

Middlemen in the coca trade came from Colombia, where leaves were turned into paste for sale in the United States. The traffickers attempted to underpay the Peruvian producers and threatened harm to any who tried to band together for bargaining strength. The police, poorly paid by the state and better paid by the Columbians, looked the other way as hired gangsters hassled the farmers. According to numerous observers, the eastern jungles resembled an anarchistic 'Wild West', lawless and without public services (Crabtree 1992: 117; Rosenberg 1991: 153).

Shining Path stepped into the valley's political vacuum during the mid-1980s. Its activists offered to protect small farmers from the traffickers, to secure good profits for the farmers, and to finance infrastructural improvements, such as roads, that the government in Lima had failed to provide. Its activists also organized local vigilante committees to control drinking and prostitution, created local-level representative government institutions, and even supervised wedding ceremonies. The movement also coordinated townwide litter-removal campaigns, in which all members of a community (even bankers) participated. The political services and organization became so extensive and sophisticated that local legends grew about a new 'republic' run by Shining Path (Crabtree 1992: 117–18; Gonzales 1992: 108–11; Poole and Rénique 1992: 185–6).

Shining Path did not provide its administrative services without cost. It directly and indirectly taxed local residents (for example, road tolls), and insisted on a share of coca revenues. Some experts estimate that during the middle and late 1980s, Shining Path took in somewhere between 20 million and a billion dollars annually from its 'governmental' operations (Gonzales 1992: 121; Rudolph 1992: 123). The movement used a portion of its revenues to finance guerrilla and educative operations in other parts of the country.

Members of Shining Path, perhaps having learned a lesson in the southern Andes, avoided trying to force collectivization in the eastern jungles. British scholar John Crabtree (1992: 118) notes that

> despite its dogmatic-sounding ideology, Sendero showed in the Alto Huallaga a notable pragmatism in responding to the needs and concerns of those it chose to work with. Though it would tend to enter a village, assemble the people and give its usual ideological harangue, it took care to tailor the message to those to whom it was intended. . . . [G]enerally it offered to organise the sort of services such as justice and even infrastructural improvements which governments in Lima had conspicuously failed to provide.

Repression under García

At the same time that Shining Path was extending its sphere of influence in the central mountains and eastern jungles, the government was trying to check the movement through less repressive and more conciliatory tactics. The Belaúnde government's heavy-handedness had resulted in a public relations black eye. At home and abroad the government was being criticized for its serious violations of human rights and for failing to stop the steady increase in Shining Path assaults on local authorities and business leaders. International companies and financial institutions were being pressured to stop investing in and lending money to Peru. Belaúnde's policy of pure repression, in short, had international political costs that the economically battered government could no longer afford.

After being elected president in 1975, Alan García Pérez immediately reined in the military commanders whose underlings seemed unusually prone to act against innocent civilians. He promised that the armed forces henceforth would scrupulously observe international norms concerning human rights and civil liberties, and organized a peace commission in hopes of convincing leaders of Shining Path that a legal road to social change was available. As well, he tried to use new programmes – including housing and educational programmes – to weaken Shining Path's growing popularity within impoverished rural and urban communities.

García's reconciliatory moves, although perhaps inspired by long-term political calculation and dreams of social harmony, created numerous political enemies in the short run. After journalists revealed that army troops had recently massacred scores of civilians and had left them in unmarked graves, García sacked three high-ranking generals. The dismissals troubled many officers, who were unused to such high-handed treatment from a civilian politician (a member of APRA no less). Military commanders also felt threatened by García's attempts to balance the budget by slashing weapons purchases. Rumours of an imminent military conspiracy soon circulated throughout Lima. García, a lifelong member of APRA, well aware of the military's long-standing hostility to the party, quickly reached an implicit compromise: if the military would regulate itself in regard to tortures, massacres, and disappearances, the government would protect it from external investigations of alleged human rights violations. Needless to say, human rights advocates in Peru and abroad erupted in denunciation of García's sudden solicitude for the military (Crabtree 1992: 108–10, 201–6; Poole and Rénique 1992: 8; Rudolph 1992: 18–20).

García also earned enemies because of his failure to implement the programme of economic development promised to poorer departments in the Andes. Many of the projects, which he had announced to great fanfare, existed on paper only; funding never arrived. The government also failed to repair many of the bridges, communication lines, and electrical systems that were being destroyed daily by Shining Path guerrillas. Many observers soon concluded that García was ineffectively fiddling while the rapidly declining highland economies burned (Crabtree 1992: 110; Mauceri 1995: 199).

In fairness to García, his promises were probably impossible to keep, given the catastrophic economic conditions. New schools, housing projects, and hospitals were luxuries that Peru simply could not afford. But García's problems were also to some extent by-products of his patronage-based style, of his fear of losing electoral advantage, and of the party's culture of corruption. To increase APRA's reputation and support, García often refused to give money to local governments and social groups in the Andes, for they were often affiliated with non-APRA left-leaning entities. In the department of Puno, for example, community leaders petitioned the government for release of legislated flood-relief funds and also of funds for food and medical care. Local APRA leaders, however, repeatedly talked García into postponing or drastically reducing government aid. García and his APRA chieftains believed that the monies would be locally dispensed by left-dominated community organizations and municipalities for their own partisan advantage. Many of the local APRA leaders, in addition, managed to pocket large shares of the money that the government sent to APRA-dominated municipalities, reasoning that their take was repayment for their services to the party. The government's repeated failure to fund programmes stoked the fires of resentment. Soon anti-García protests, including hunger strikes and general strikes, were being mounted in Puno and other Andean departments (Poole and Rénique 1992: 8–9; Rudolph 1992: 120; Taylor 1987: 147–9).

In 1986 García attempted to increase his international influence by hosting a meeting of the Socialist International. Representatives came from moderate socialist parties and social-democratic governments around the world. Numerous European leaders attended, happy to help their Third World cousin gain publicity and stature. The public relations spectacle turned sour when Shining Path inmates in three prisons organized a strike to protest their impending removal to a new prison where, they believed, their already frequently violated rights would be subject to more abuses. Embarrassed, García ordered military attacks on the prisons. Highly destructive weaponry, including aircraft and artillery, demolished the structures, and (perhaps with García's foreknowledge) more than 100 who had already surrendered were massacred. The bloody events outraged many of the country's foreign guests and saddled García with an unsavoury international reputation.

García subsequently unleashed the military and extended the suspension of civil liberties to additional departments. By the end of the 1980s more than half of the population of Peru lived in the so-called emergency zones, where due process of law had been suspended and where local military governments closely regulated citizens' exercise of the freedoms of speech, press, and assembly. Police by the thousands began to raid universities and arrest students suspected of ties with Shining Path; in February 1987 more than 750 students were arrested in Lima's universities alone. Secret detentions and mysterious disappearances, which had declined immediately after García's inauguration, skyrocketed. Numerous human rights groups, including Amnesty International, concluded in the late 1980s that Peru had the highest number of forced disappearances in the world, even exceeding the total set by the Pinochet regime in Chile (Degenhardt 1988: 292; Degregori 1994: 92, 97; Palmer 1990: 8; Rosenberg 1991: 186, 201–2; Woy-Hazleton and Hazleton 1992: 216–17).

Developing an urban presence

The last three years of García's presidency were a time of bloodshed and fear. Criminal violence, such as armed robbery and assault, became commonplace as seemingly endless economic insecurity pressed people to desperate acts. Paramilitary right-wing death squads appeared for the first time and killed scores of suspected Sendero members and sympathizers, including lawyers and teachers. Villages organized self-defence patrols, or '*rondas campesinas*', that protected their territories from, or at least gave warning of, encroachment by the military and the guerrillas. Sometimes, however, the rondas attacked neighbouring villages to gain land or avenge past injustices. In 1986 there were 1,327 reported guerrilla attacks; in 1990, 2,154. In 1987 alone, political violence by groups other than security forces accounted for approximately 850 deaths; in 1989, almost 2,000 (Crabtree 1992: 184–7; Poole and Rénique 1992: 9, 70; Rudolph 1992: 116; Woy-Hazleton and Hazleton 1992: 215–16).

Because the increased presence of security forces in the highlands had made mobilization very difficult, the national leaders of Shining Path at a plenary session in summer 1987 reflected on the effectiveness of their past educative and guerrilla strategies, the extent of government repression, and their assumptions about current social trends and economic conditions. They agreed that the movement should channel more energy and resources into mobilizing the poor in the coastal cities, where social discontent seemed to be rapidly rising. They also urged a change in policies regarding the urban middle classes, which had been viewed ambivalently as both potentially revolutionary and counterrevolutionary. Henceforth, the movement would see them more consistently as potential allies in a broad popular struggle against international capitalism. And third, the leaders advocated greater movement presence in established trade unions and squatter institutions controlled by IU and APRA (Dietz 1990: 142; Woy-Hazleton and Hazleton 1992: 213).

The decisions at the plenary session reflected a subtle shift in the ongoing struggle within the movement between the strong advocates of armed struggle and their critics. In addition, the outcome reflected the steady rise in the political stature of Lima-based factions within the nationwide movement.

As we noted earlier, Shining Path had been active in coastal cities since at least the late 1970s, particularly so in Lima's eastern industrial corridor, which had grown from 45,000 inhabitants in 1961 to 181,000 in 1986 (Smith 1992: 128). Shining Path's urban work during the late 1970s and early and mid-1980s was primarily small-scale propaganda, such as drawing revolutionary graffiti on the walls of buildings, and aid to newly arrived migrants from the countryside. Not everything remained pacifistic; by 1985 bombings and assassinations were becoming more commonplace. Indeed, in 1985 the number of Shining Path attacks in Lima exceeded the number in the department of Ayacucho, the original site of Shining Path's armed struggle (Poole and Rénique 1992: 84–95; Smith 1992: 129–34). Still, compared to activities undertaken by Shining Path units in other parts of Peru, Lima's cells were remarkably nonviolent. According to a 1986 Shining Path document, which statistically analysed the movement's tactics (or 'forms of struggle') between June 1984 and 1986, 80 per cent of Shining Path's actions throughout Peru involved either guerrilla warfare with the military units or selected executions of purported enemies of the people. Lima, however, was atypical. There, only 15.8 per cent of Shining Path's activities involved either guerrilla warfare or executions. Most of the radicals' energy was directed at educating and organizing industrial workers and shantytown residents (Communist Party of Peru 1986: 22–7).

From the beginning the Lima-based Metropolitan Committee of Shining Path acted largely independently of the Cupola. Its activists tended to be both less wedded to armed action and more open to collaboration with other left groups than were Shining Path activists in the southern Andes. The national leadership therefore periodically purged the Lima branch of nonrevolutionary 'debris', the first purge apparently occurring in 1975. Despite the executive committee's efforts at control, Lima remained a centre of more peaceable and collaborative activity than tended to exist in the Peruvian highlands (Crabtree 1992: 188–90; Degregori 1994: 95, 98–99; Poole and Rénique 1992: 84–5; Rudolph 1992: 112–14; Smith 1992: 131, 135).

According to students of Shining Path politics, after the 1987 plenary session, Shining Path became a much more urban-based phenomenon. The movement attempted to recruit radicals and reformers in Lima who were rapidly becoming disillusioned with the García government's failure to turn the economy around and improve the condition of the urban poor. Shining Path made inroads in the newest shantytowns, where other left organizations had not yet established themselves, and helped new arrivals secure land and diverse public services, including light, water, sewerage, and education. In some squatter communities, Shining Path activists ran in elections for community office. They also acquired positions of influence in three of the four major labour unions in Lima's eastern corridor (Mauceri 1995: 27; Poole and Rénique 1992: 84–96; Smith 1992: 136–41; Stokes 1995: 48–51; Tarazona-Sevillano 1990: 52–4; Woy-Hazleton and Hazleton 1992: 213).

Many of Lima's sorely deprived sympathized with the Shining Path's radical spirit. Occasionally, the new migrants even endorsed some acts of violence by Sendero guerrillas (such as the slaying of a highly unpopular company manager or the public beating of a drug trafficker). Many appreciated the guerrillas' functioning as a moral police force vis-à-vis thieves, prostitutes, and unprincipled moneylenders. Active participation in movement organizations was always modest, however.

By 1986 Shining Path activists in Lima were contacting the staff of *El Diario* (a newspaper that had traditionally supported the IU coalition and that was almost the only Lima daily that regularly covered labour disputes). About that time it sold more than 25,000 copies a day and was easily available at newsstands. Around 1987 it began publishing pro-Shining Path articles regularly and even occasional communiques from the group's spokespersons.

Lima's Shining Path activists also recruited young instructors from local universities to teach in various shantytown public schools and college preparatory academies. New pro-Shining Path associations of lawyers (troubled by the government's blatant violations of civil liberties) and of university students (angry because of the lack of job opportunities and shocked by García's brutal response to the 1986 prison strike) formed during the mid and late 1980s. The movement's activists also began participating in a broad range of new local institutions: soup kitchens, school milk programmes, and even 'rival' political parties (Poole and Rénique 1992: 86–90; Strong 1992: 79).

Shining Path assassination teams, often directed by the national executive committee, periodically appeared in Lima and dispatched scores of trade-union activists and community leaders who refused to work with Shining Path. After October 1987 the assassinations almost totally ceased for three years, and Lima activists instead engaged in organized 'armed general strikes', in which entire communities desisted from working as protest against government and companies' actions. Individuals who refused to participate were threatened with harm to either their property or themselves.

The struggle over the proper role of violence continued between Shining Path's original 'old guard' from Ayacucho and the newer urban-based members. The urbanists seemed to be gaining influence at the older activists' expense, although in public statements Guzmán played down the rifts within Shining Path. For example, in a 12-hour interview published in *El Diario*, he said that there were no profound intraorganizational disagreements over tactics or strategy. He insisted that the movement's members were simply engaging in pragmatic, nondogmatic experimentation:

we will advance, even if we begin by feeling our way in the dark, finding temporary solutions for certain situations or for brief periods of time, until we find the definitive one. As Lenin taught us, no revolution can be planned out completely ahead of time.

(Guzmán 1988: 91)

But the numerous local deviations from a common course of action belied the movement's purported ideological unity, as did the appearance in 1990 of Shining Path street leaflets calling for the abandonment of armed struggle (Crabtree 1992: 208–9).

Inevitably, as Shining Path became more active in urban politics, it faced the difficult practical question of how to relate to existing union, shantytown, and party organizations. It never developed a consistent position, at least at the national level, but vacillated during the late 1980s between peaceful infiltration within popular associations and violent destruction of rival organizations. Each alternative had costs. Working patiently within an organization meant that verbal and physical scuffles inevitably broke out between Shining Path activists (who called for militant rhetoric and open attacks on property) and supporters of collective bargaining and clientelism. Yet when activists intentionally tried to shout down speakers at neighbourhood meetings or hit squads harmed a rival organization (for example, by murdering a community activist), popular resentment and rage inevitably followed, sometimes leading to locals' cooperation with police and military units (Crabtree 1992: 189–91; Poole and Rénique 1992: 1–2, 89–95).

Shantytown and union leaders, in turn, were torn about how best to relate to the movement. On one hand, its radical programme of People's Committees often seemed impractical and its use of violence often seemed immoral and sometimes prompted police repression. On the other hand, Shining Path activists provided badly needed energy and enthusiasm to grassroots organizations, while peaceful petitioning of the government increasingly seemed ineffective. In the words of one Lima community organizer (who would be assassinated in 1992 by Shining Path guerrillas),

If there is a Shining Path member who believes in equality, in a better world, I ask him or her to think more. I don't believe they all are murderers. . . . Political parties are not monolithic and impenetrable. . . . Within the Shining Path, there are currents, and this is something we can take advantage of.

(Moyano 1995: 375)

Ironically, perhaps Shining Path's greatest ally in developing an urban presence was the government. The military tended to overlook the ideological and strategic differences within Shining Path and between the Shining Path and other left-wing organizations, and tended to treat union organizers, community activists, and radical priests as fellow travellers of Shining Path. More than one reformer became a sympathizer of Shining Path's after being arbitrarily arrested and detained in prison or tortured. Popular knowledge both of extralegal killings by the military and of poorly explained 'disappearances' of suspected Shining Path activists further nourished sympathy (if not always active support) for the movement. When trying to understand the popular sympathy for Shining Path, some of whose members did hurt civilians and the poor, one should never forget the magnitude of government brutality. Between 1982 and 1988 more than 10,000 Peruvians had either been killed or 'disappeared' because of security forces' actions, and between 1989 and 1990, one-third of Lima's metropolitan population had been subjected to police and military searches (Poole and Rénique 1992: 13; Bourque and Warren 1989: 24).

Conclusion

In 1990 Shining Path completed a decade of armed struggle. Many of its activists were aware that violence had not sparked the popular insurrection that advocates of guerrilla tactics had projected. The increasing arrests of activists and sympathizers (including labour lawyers) during the late 1980s led to new calls within the movement for the abandonment of armed struggle. However, before the growing division between the proguerrilla national leadership of Shining Path and its grassroots organizers could harden into another purge or a permanent organizational schism, Peru's constitutional order abruptly changed.

In 1992 President Alberto Fujimori, facing growing restlessness over his economic policies, dissolved Congress and declared himself a temporary dictator. Fujimori promised to destroy Shining Path and thus help the society regain a spirit of civility and safety, and to these ends immediately granted security forces expanded powers, ensured that military officers could not be tried in civilian courts for possible violations of human rights, tapped opposition parties' telephones, restricted journalists' rights to report on the government's struggle with guerrillas, and created special military courts to try terrorist suspects. He believed that to preserve democracy in the long run, civil liberties and judicial due process had to be suspended in the short run. In his words, 'Demagoguery allowed terrorists to take advantage of these, quote, democratic principles, unquote, to destroy democracy and the democrats' (Fujimori 1995: 444).

The government published a list of suspected Shining Path sympathizers that included several highly respected human rights activists whom few outside of government viewed as guilty. Accounts proliferated of arbitrary arrests, of torture, and of right-wing paramilitary groups posing as Sendero activists and attacking church groups and research centres. Fujimori dismissed the concerns of civil and human rights organizations, accusing Amnesty International of being part of an international campaign against Peru. The government's attitude toward complaints with respect to its repression of Shining Path was not new, for as we have seen, previous presidents were equally dismissive. Indeed, even before Fujimori suspended Congress, his minister of defence had declared that a human rights team sponsored by the World Council of Churches was functioning as the 'international missiles of Sendero Luminoso' (Poole and Rénique 1992: 17; see also Mauceri 1995: 23–5; McClintock 1993: 117).

Shining Path responded to the dictatorship in part by intensifying its educative work among the poor and in part by escalating its bombing campaigns in Lima, which for the first time included random explosions in residential neighbourhoods.

Such explosions certainly did not endear the guerrillas to civilians, but then the state's own violence alienated many citizens.

The armed forces captured Guzmán in September 1992. Fujimori was minimally involved in the operation, but he took credit for it and immediately declared that the Shining Path movement had been destroyed. The movement, however, did not immediately disappear. A wave of car bombings in Lima's wealthiest neighbourhoods reminded the government that several guerrilla units remained active. Pro-Sendero banners in marches also indicated that the movement's nonguerrilla cells were alive and well.

Some specialists in Peruvian politics have speculated that after Guzmán's arrest, the more political educative wing gained ascendancy within the movement's organizational apparatus. Most of the leaders who had been arrested with Guzmán were advocates of armed struggle, especially in the countryside. Their absence, it seems, allowed a shift in ideological weight toward the Lima faction, which has been more pacifistic, alliance-prone, and urban-oriented than Guzmán's so-called 'Chanka faction' (Degregori 1994: 94–9). The growing power of the more pacifistic wing may explain why in 1993 Guzmán called on all Shining Path activists to abandon armed struggle. Interestingly, several local cells ignored Guzmán's command and continued to bomb and kill (Burt and Ricci 1994). One group declared that Guzmán lacked authority to reorient the movement towards more pacific politics, for 'It is a norm of the Communist movement that Party leadership cannot be exercised from prison' (Izaguirre 1996: 38).

In 1995, Fujimori, under intense international economic and political pressure, permitted presidential elections to be held. He won handily. There were some local irregularities in the counting of votes, and many election procedures (including the design of the ballots) were obviously arranged to divide opposition parties and to insure Fujimori's re-election. Still, most observers agreed that the elections were on the whole free and fair and that there was evidence that a genuine transition to a democratic constitutional order had begun (Palmer 1996: 74).

Sounds of political instability nonetheless crackled. Antigovernment demonstrations and clashes between police and protesters representing diverse social groups, including construction workers, municipal workers, university students, and retirees, escalated during 1994 and 1995. Levels of unemployment remained very high, and standards of living remained disturbingly low. According to one study, approximately two-thirds of all Peruvians lived in absolute poverty (Rochabrún 1996: 24).

Shining Path, meanwhile, reduced the frequency and scale of its armed attacks. Military actions did not completely cease. At one point, local Shining Path units attacked and briefly occupied a score of district and provincial capitals. The movement, however, seemed to be entering a new phase. Even leaders of those cells opposed to Guzmán's request to put down arms conceded that guerrilla attacks needed to be curbed and that the movement needed to direct more energy into clandestine involvement in local community and labour organizations and into nonviolent forms of popular education (Izaguirre 1996: 38).

Why did the government have so many difficulties containing Shining Path between 1980 and 1995, especially given the movement's oddly Maoist rhetoric (certainly not part of the Andean peasants' experience and self-understanding); given the movement's violence against villagers, other left-wing rivals, and accused informers; and given the government's own violence against the insurrectionists?

Indiscriminate government violence (which affected almost every family in the mountains and in metropolitan Lima) and the rapid deterioration of the economy certainly predisposed many citizens to take an antigovernment stance. Martial law was exceedingly onerous and had steadily expanded from the emergency zones of Belaúnde to the dictatorship of Fujimori. Moreover, the economy was in the worst tailspin in recent Latin American history, and a crash seemed imminent. The total annual productivity of Peru declined by a third between 1988 and 1991. The standard of living had deteriorated to such an extent that the hemisphere's first cholera epidemic in current history broke out, laying more than 250,000 Peruvians low by 1991, and killing a tenth of that number (Andreas and Sharpe 1992: 77). All of these circumstances created acute dissatisfaction and a greater openmindedness toward radical politics.

In addition, Shining Path attracted recruits and sympathy from many rural Peruvians and new shantytowners because of its demonstrated interest in the problems of the poor. In Andean departments (such as Ayacucho) and in the Upper Huallaga Valley, it provided services – such as schools, the enforcement of local norms, and protection from coca-leaf buyers – that were desired but not supplied by the government. Similarly, in Lima's newest squatter communities, the popularity of Shining Path rested mostly on its ability and willingness to help new migrants find their way through an unfamiliar and often hostile environment. Conversely, the movement's popularity quickly dissipated whenever Shining Path activists departed from local norms and attempted to impose their own visions of proper economic arrangements and moral values on others. Overt radicalism almost always alienated the very people the movement wanted to help and represent.

Violence per se did not appear to generate much favour for the movement. In fact, it periodically drove potential supporters away; the cold-blooded murder of popular Lima community leader María Elena Moyano in 1992 is an instance (Poole and Rénique 1992: 92). But unlike earlier guerrilla organizations in Peru, such as MIR and ELN, Shining Path participated in grassroots and local-community politics, and used social services as a tool to arouse peasant and urban-worker backing. Ironically, popular opinion in regard to this often stern, self-consciously violent social movement rested on very pragmatic grounds: its social and economic services met a crucial need (Berg 1986–87; McClintock 1989: 95–96; Smith 1992).

These observations about the sources of popular support for Shining Path seem to corroborate Joel Migdal's more general conclusions about the social bases of support for revolutionary parties. In his classic study of peasant politics, Migdal (1974: 212) asked why revolutionary social movements in Third World countries sometimes attract peasants and sometimes do not, and then replied,

Peasants join when there is something tangible to be had. . . . Their initial aims in joining are not to implement a particular ideology. . . . Instead they seek immediately useful concessions that will aid them in navigating their social and economic environment.

Like the popular Third World revolutionary groups of the 1960s that Migdal studied, Shining Path survived and prospered in parts of rural and urban Peru during the 1980s and early 1990s largely because it offered immediate, tangible benefits in times of sudden economic change and dislocation. Perhaps in its public-service projects – and not in its acts of violence or its semi-Maoist revolutionary doctrines – Shining Path is representative of successful agrarian social movements around the world.

Note

1. Estimates of the number of activists in Shining Path during the 1980s vary between 2,000 and 15,000. The Peruvian government contended in the late 1980s that Shining Path had 5,000 members. The movement in the mid-1980s said it had 15,000 members. Observers agree that a small number of Shining Path members are combatants (McClintock 1989: 63).

Part V

Conclusions

Chapter 11

From history to theory

We began our study by surveying three major theoretical approaches to the study of social movements. We used themes and selected hypotheses from the approaches to collect information about three movements that flourished during the 1980s and early 1990s. We explored each movement's social and political backdrop, nonelite political antecedents, and evolving goals and strategies. Let us compare some findings and then evaluate the theoretical traditions' strengths and weaknesses on the basis of our new knowledge.

Three social movements in comparative perspective

West Germany's Greens, Poland's Solidarity, and Peru's Shining Path were attempts by thousands of nonelites to re-create their society. Activists in each movement dreamt of establishing a radically new social order. They straddled the line between legal and illegal activity, openly defied government orders and expectations, and at times employed socially disruptive tactics.

Although the three movements were abstractly similar (and hence meet the minimum definition of a social movement found in Chapter 1) there were noticeable differences among them. One can categorize these differences under four headings: (1) general strategies; (2) social and political contexts; (3) political antecedents, and (4) intramovement politics.

The Green party-movement from the outset relied on elections to transform the West German society. Elections would afford an opportunity not only to enter government and affect policy but to disseminate new values and proposals among nonelites: the extension of political rights to foreign guest workers; withdrawal from NATO; support of national liberation movements in the Third World; the dismantling of the current system of consultation between business and government; and creation of an extremely decentralized and participatory political and economic order. Over time, the Greens toned down their harsh criticisms of other parties, countercultural clothing, and antibourgeois language. They called less frequently for a thoroughgoing reconstruction of the country's political economy. These attempts to become more palatable to socially moderate voters and to enter governing coalitions caused some observers to question whether the Greens in the 1990s should still be viewed as a social movement. Had they now become a conventional party, seeking voters and leaning toward reform rather than reconstruction?

Solidarity, in contrast, tried to check the arbitrariness of the Polish party-state by means of large-scale work stoppages. Organizations of industrial workers, private farmers, and intellectuals challenged government policies on prices, civil liberties, and cultural freedom. After martial law was imposed in 1981, the movement became primarily a set of underground publications. In the late 1980s a few factions broke with the movement's national leadership, which cautioned against strikes and other disruptive actions, and formed independent unions in hopes of improving workers' wages and working conditions through industrial action. In 1989 Solidarity's national leadership, in exchange for restraining striking workers, negotiated constitutional reforms and then pursued an electoral strategy of social transformation. Disagreement over the desirability of free-market reforms splintered the movement after 1990. Solidarity's organizational legacy was a constellation of rival parties, unions, and interest groups with very different social goals.

Shining Path attempted to transform Peru through a protracted armed struggle, combined with services to the urban and rural poor and the establishment of alternative political and economic orders in the rural areas where the state's armed forces were absent. The movement's long-term goal was to repel international capital; to redistribute property from the big bourgeoisie to smaller capitalists, wage earners, peasants, and the chronically poor; and, afterwards, to prepare Peru for communism. The movement contended that to transform oligarchic Peru, violence would be needed because the privileged classes and their international supporters would otherwise not give up their wealth and political power. The killing of politicians, civilians, and soldiers distinguished Shining Path from almost all other radical and reformist groups in Peru. Within Shining Path, different cells and factions disagreed over the timing of violent acts and over the proper ratio of violent to nonviolent activities, but they concurred that radical change could not be accomplished without the use of guns.

Besides strategy, the three movements differed in economic aims, partly reflecting each country's unique economic character. For example, West Germany's standard of living in the 1980s, as measured by per capita gross national product, was much higher than Poland's or Peru's. Official unemployment was much lower. True, West Germany's postwar economic boom had slowed by 1980, and the jobless rate, which during the 1960s had been almost zero, was temporarily rising (which partly explains the Greens' appeal among the young and unemployed). Relative poverty was restricted primarily to foreign workers and younger adults. The Greens' proposed federal programmes, not surprisingly, never called for further enrichment of the haves. The Greens instead focused on distributional justice and advocated greater entitlements to squatters, foreign workers, and other groups who were not beneficiaries of the country's postwar boom. They pressed for decentralization of the economy, with local residents and the employees in each enterprise participating in the making of business decisions. In theory, this would lead to greater attention to the human and environmental costs of production processes, and less to short-term profit maximization. The Greens, in addition, advocated greater state regulation of environmentally harmful products and production methods, and greater state education of consumers about the ecological consequences of their spending habits. Distributional justice and ecologically sensitive production and consumption, not further prosperity and wealth, were the primary aims.

Solidarity's activists, in contrast, desired prosperity. Poland's standard of living, as measured by per capita gross national product, was a tenth of West Germany's. Moreover, the gap between Poland and the economies of western Europe seemed to be increasing. Between 1980 and 1991, the average annual growth of Poland's economy was 1.2 per cent, West Germany's 2.3 per cent, and all the OECD nations 3.0 per cent (Haq 1995: 207–8). Solidarity, not surprisingly, decried conditions and called for growth to enable a higher standard of living. Though movement activists disagreed about how to promote growth (some called for workplace democracy, others for a free-market system, and still others for more efficient state planning and an end to corruption), they agreed that hard times must end as soon as possible.

Shining Path also pursued materialist aims. After all, Peru's per capita income during the 1980s was half of Poland's and a twentieth of West Germany's. According to United Nation statistics and definitions, more than 30 per cent of Peruvians lived in 'absolute poverty' during the 1980s. To make matters worse, the future looked bleak: during the 1980s, Peru's gross national product 'increased' at an average annual rate of –0.4 per cent (Haq 1995: 207–12, 222). Moreover, the distribution of wealth and income was remarkably skewed. During the 1970s and 1980s, the richest 10 per cent of Peruvian households received 40 per cent of the nation's total income; the poorest 40 per cent received 7–12 per cent. To place these figures in a comparative perspective: the richest 10 per cent of West German and Polish households during the 1970s and 1980s received 30 and 20 per cent of their respective countries' total incomes; the poorest 40 per cent received between 15 and 20 per cent and between 20 and 25 per cent (Taylor and Jodice 1983: 134–5; World Bank 1991: 115, 245, 249).

It is not surprising, then, that Shining Path stressed the need for a new strategy of national economic development and for a radical redistribution of wealth. Its leaders were far less interested than were some leaders of Solidarity in promoting rapid economic growth through market reform, increased foreign investment, and continued free trade. Past Peruvian governments had tried these strategies to no avail. Shining Path activists also were far less interested than the leaders of the West German Greens in preventing further industrial degradation of the environment (approximately half of Peru's factories were shut down, in any event) and curbing consumers' environmentally insensitive purchasing habits. The Peruvian radicals instead advocated immediate transfer of wealth and income from international corporations and large businesses to the poor, wage earners, peasants, and small entrepreneurs, protection of small businesses from foreign competition, development of indigenous forms of industry and commerce, and local experiments in collective production.

Each of the three movements drew upon a distinct set of social classes for support. The Greens attracted urban white-collar professionals and unemployed young adults, including recent college graduates who had once hoped to secure public-sector jobs. Solidarity was largely a movement of industrial workers suffering declining standards of living, independent family farmers frustrated by government controls, and dissident intellectuals with patriotic and civil libertarian goals. Shining Path received support from university students and recent graduates who either could not find work or were employed at extremely low wages and salaries (for example, the schoolteachers who joined Maoist unions). Peasants in the remote southern Andes, shantytown dwellers in Lima, and coca farmers in the eastern jungles were also numbered among the adherents.

Each movement's proposals for economic change partly reflected the actual economic problems its supporters faced. The white-collar professionals in the Greens found environmental protection and workplace rights important. The proletarian activists in Solidarity were initially concerned with union rights and protecting real wages, and its agrarian members wanted the government to help finance private farmers, halt food imports, and deregulate food prices. The supporters of Shining Path sought greater public services for the poor and protection from international market forces, including Colombian drug lords, who were driving down coca-leaf prices.

The three social movements evolved in different political environments, which influenced the activists' strategies and tactics. The West German constitutional order – with its multiple layers of government, elected legislatures, and modified proportional representation – predisposed Green activists to pursue electoral politics. An electoral strategy made no sense in pre-1989 Poland, given the PZPR's domination of the Sejm, the precarious status of freedoms of speech and assembly, and the threat of a Soviet invasion should Poland depart from the Stalinist mode of one-party rule. Large-scale work stoppages, however, had proven effective in changing government policies in the past and therefore seemed a more viable tactic, so long as the Soviet Union was not provoked to intervene. Shining Path worked within an impoverished, constitutionally unstable, and often corrupt political system that was rife with racism. Government officials at all levels treated Indians (approximately 40 per cent of the population) as second-class citizens. Since the Second World War, elite factions repeatedly ignored liberal democratic constitutions and established dictatorships rather than share power. Confronting an unloved and inefficient political system, Shining Path adopted a strategy of armed struggle and dual power. In West Germany or Poland, such a strategy might seem utopian, but Peru's constitutional order was not as secure as West Germany's liberal democratic order nor as efficiently policed as Poland's communist order. A gradual replacement of the state with Peoples' Committees and a prolonged armed struggle seemed a plausible way to effect change.

Activists in the three movements chose strategies that appeared reasonable in the national political context: electoral and parliamentary politics in West Germany, general strikes and factory occupations in pre-1989 Poland, and armed struggle and People's Committees in Peru. It would be an exaggeration to say that the choices were inevitable. Rather, the nations' distinctive political contexts 'softly' determined certain courses of action as more self-evidently useful than others.

Nonelite political activities predated each movement and provided prototypical goals and strategies. But neither the Greens, nor Solidarity, nor Shining Path simply repeated previous nonelite politics. Family resemblances, however, were evident. West Germany's new social movements, squatters' and spontis' subcultures, and JUSO experiments with local-level and participatory democracy provided the Greens with activists, critiques of the environmental status quo, and tested political tactics and strategies. Solidarity inherited Poland's postwar tradition of repeated working-class protest against PZPR policies and Polish intellectuals' experiences with legally scrupulous methods of resistance. Shining Path echoed earlier twentieth-century efforts at guerrilla warfare, land invasions, and, at least since the early days of APRA, armed attacks on state officials.

At the same time, each movement's selection of goals and strategies reflected only part of its country's entire tradition of nonelite politics. Armed struggle, after all, had been part of West German radical politics at least since the formation of terrorist groups in the late 1960s, but it was forgone by Green activists. Solidarity in general lacked the ultranationalist, anti-Soviet, and anti-Semitic agendas of such groups as the Young Poland Movement and Confederation for an Independent Poland. Shining Path shunned the parliamentary strategies of most of Peru's Marxist and Aprista parties. In short, the leaders of the Greens, Solidarity, and Shining Path adopted only some elements of their respective countries' intricate traditions of nonelite politics. The movements' politics were not simply recapitulations of each country's nonelite politics. Movement activists selected only some of the various ways that nonelites previously had defied authorities, defined their problems and goals, and fought for their interests.

The movements inevitably contained factions that battled over goals, strategies, and tactics. The predominant factional cleavages within the Greens and Solidarity changed over time, whereas the sources of ideological disagreement within Shining Path seemed relatively constant. The first major Green factional struggle involved socially and culturally conservative environmentalists, such as Gruhl, who fiercely opposed socialism, feminism, and libertine countercultural values, and ardent pro-feminist and anticapitalist radicals, such as Dutschke, who wanted to dismantle West Germany's capitalist order. During the late 1980s the major factional division within the Greens involved the so-called realos, who favoured parliamentary coalition-building and moderate rhetoric during election campaigns, and the so-called fundamentalists, who distrusted the corruptive potential of government and who favoured more revolutionary rhetoric and extraparliamentary mobilizations. Solidarity contained a plethora of ideologies and suborganizations before the declaration of martial law in December 1981. They included advocates of factory councils associated with 'Network', industrial trade-unionists, commercial farmers, civil libertarians, and advocates of greater independence from the Soviet Union. Following the 1989 parliamentary elections, the movement quickly fragmented into political and social organizations with wildly different economic visions. Wałęsa's heavy-handed leadership style also created rifts. The factions within Shining Path disagreed over the usefulness of specific forms of armed struggle – for example, arson, industrial sabotage, the assassination of civilian politicians – and how best to combine violent acts with nonviolent organizing efforts in villages, unions, and shantytowns. In various regions, different mixes of opinion prevailed. By and large, the use of armed tactics was least frequently questioned among activists in the Southern Andes and most frequently questioned in Lima.

In each movement, national leaders pledged loyalty to democratic values and promoted some democratic procedures and institutions. They also adopted from time to time nondemocratic methods of rule toward either rival movement factions or nonmovement political organizations. The leaders of the West German Greens, for example, advocated the rank and file's right to control movement leaders through recall procedures and limited, nonrenewable terms for any activist elected to a national governmental post. Over time, the Greens' national leaders jettisoned these procedural checks on their powers and, in the opinion of some of their intramovement opponents, flaunted their autonomy from the movement's base. Struggles over internal democracy were also visible in Solidarity. Wałęsa frequently ignored the views of dissenting groups and acted unilaterally, without consulting other movement activists and governing bodies. Nonetheless, participatory democracy was evident in many of Solidarity's local and national meetings, where members freely spoke their mind, publicly criticized the national leaders' decisions, and frequently rejected their advice. In Shining Path, Guzmán permitted some differences of opinion. He also endorsed the Peoples' Committees and Delegates' Assemblies, which in principle were radically democratic institutions where all popular interests could be heard and nonresponsive representatives could be immediately recalled. There were, however, obvious nondemocratic features in Shining Path politics. Guzmán periodically tried to purge activists whose commitment to armed struggle seemed either lukewarm or undisciplined, and the movement periodically assassinated opposing politicians, soldiers and police, and wealthy citizens.

Thus, democratic and nondemocratic elements were evident in all three movements. These contrary tendencies may explain why scholars frequently disagree about the implications of social-movement politics for democracy. Depending on the specific events and actions that one has in mind, the same movement can appear to embody, promote, destroy, or threaten democratic values.

Theoretical insights and oversights

We have reviewed some parallels and differences between the West German Greens, Solidarity, and Shining Path. Let us now consider how the logic of each postwar theoretical tradition illuminates some features of modern social movements and obscures others.

Social movements and modernization

As noted in Chapter 1, immediately after the Second World War and before the late 1960s, many scholars who studied social movements interpreted them primarily as by-products of a set of worldwide, interconnected, and irreversible social changes called 'modernization'. According to modernization theorists, these changes – such as the diffusion of literacy, the secularization of culture, industrialization, urbanization, and the expansion of capitalist modes of production – were in many ways beneficial. Even so, they generated feelings of social disorientation, anomie, and loneliness. These feelings were especially acute among newcomers to bustling, large-scale, and industrialized cities and among owners of small businesses, small farmers, and self-employed urban artisans. Reputedly, members of these classes enthusiastically followed movement leaders, who coined ideologies that berated modernity, celebrated older lifestyles, and identified convenient scapegoats for citizens' problems and discomfort. The ideologies prescribed not piecemeal correction of remedial social problems but a radical destruction of the status quo and the reconstruction of past society. In addition, the ideologies provoked movement activists into violating the civil liberties of the scapegoats and physically harming them.

The three cases we have examined partly corroborate the first postwar wave of social-movement theorizing. In West Germany, Poland, and Peru, rapid social change either immediately preceded or coincided with the formation of the Greens, Solidarity, and Shining Path. The official programmes of each movement criticized the types of worldwide, fundamental change that scholars commonly associate with the term *modernization*, such as rapid industrialization (the Greens), bureaucratic organization of the workplace (Solidarity), and commercialization of the countryside (Shining Path). Leaders of these movements, moreover, advocated not merely the replacement of political leaders but a root-and-branch transformation of the entire social system.

Still, the histories of the Green party-movement, Solidarity, and Shining Path do not completely fit the modernization view of social movements. What are some of the mismatches?

First, the modernization scenario about social movements does not cover all the kinds of social and political conditions that contributed to the rise of the Greens, Solidarity, and Shining Path. Government threats to civil liberties and high unemployment among recent college graduates motivated some people to vote for and to join the Greens. Increasing hunger and joblessness pushed many people to join Solidarity and Shining Path, as did patriotic opposition to perceived Soviet imperialism (Solidarity) and US imperialism (Shining Path). Modernization, in other words, accounts for only part of the social context of these movements; other discernible problems and circumstances played a role as well.

Second, the postwar modernization theories exaggerate the amount of social nostalgia in movement programmes. Take the West German Greens. Their federal programmes advocated an alternative, radically decentralized economy and numerous soft restrictions on modern consumer habits (for example, by way of regulations on advertising) to sustain the environment. The programmes, however, neither rejected industrialization in toto nor called for a return to a preindustrial, preliterate, preurban, and precommercial past. Solidarity's leaders, likewise, were hardly advocates of a back-to-the-countryside movement. Even the programmes of Rural Solidarity embraced the commercialization and mechanization of farming. Although Shining Path activists wished to protect peasants and farmworkers from commercialization and sometimes coerced rural folk into not exchanging goods in markets and into establishing self-sufficient communal economies, these projects never entailed a return to the 'good old days' of paternalistic haciendas encircled by impoverished villages. Instead, the activists urged Peru's rural poor to experiment with non-traditional collective forms of production and distribution. All three movements, in short, strongly condemned the status quo, but their positive programmes were much more than a resurrection of premodern social orders. Granted, there were some conservative wings to each movement (for example, the Gruhl conservatives, who were especially numerous in the formative days of the Greens), but the movements on the whole advocated not total resurrection of a romanticized past but social innovation.

Finally, close examination of the official programmes of the Greens, Solidarity, and Shining Path suggests that the modernization theorists overstated the tendency of movements to use scapegoats in explanations for current social problems. The ideologists and national leaders of the three movements tended to interpret current conditions not simply in terms of conspiracies but also as the result of impersonal social forces and historical trends, such as the spread of industrial capitalism and Enlightenment thinking (the German Greens), the influence of Soviet-style communism (Solidarity), and changing international market conditions (Shining Path). True, each movement vilified selected members of the political elite, such as SPD leader Schmidt and newspaper mogul Springer in West Germany, PZPR leaders Gierek and Jaruzelski in Poland, and prime ministers Belaúnde, García, and Fujimori in Peru. The three movements' theoreticians, however, saw social problems as solvable only through systematic social change; elimination of disliked individuals would not by itself set the world aright.

In summary, the modernization approach to social movements seems partly accurate but not an entirely valid interpretation of social movements (at least of the three we have examined). The German, Polish, and Peruvian case studies suggest that movements may indeed be prompted by large-scale social changes occurring around the globe, such as industrialization, urbanization, and commercialization. But other social conditions also generate movements; their official programmes entail much more than nostalgic recollections of the past; and their plans of action are much more comprehensive than vicious attacks on convenient scapegoats.

Organizational resources and political opportunities

As we have seen, the next wave of postwar theorizing focused on how current political and local social circumstances affect nonelites' decisions on whether to participate in social movements. According to this wave of theorizing, participation is a result of cost-benefit reasoning, not of particular types of socially induced suffering. Nonelites join movements not because they are unusually disoriented and lonely – on the contrary, movement participants tend to be unusually sociable and level-headed about social situations. Nor do nonelites join because they are victims of unwanted social changes and suddenly feel exploited and disenfranchised. After all, the second-wave theorists argued, nonelites are always exploited and disenfranchised – even in societies characterized by liberal-democratic constitutions and free-market systems. Nonelites join social movements when the perceived benefits of participation outweigh the perceived costs, such as the threat of arrest or of being fired from work. Consequently, to understand the emergence and lifespans of social movements, one must study local history and see how the calculus of participation may have changed.

In their explanations for nonelites' decisions to join movements, the second generation of movement theorists has tended to separate into three groups: resource-mobilization theorists, indigenous-community theorists, and political-process theorists. Resource-mobilization theorists argue that nonelites join only if leaders first secure enough resources – such as legal expertise, money, and meeting places – to increase substantially the movement's chances for success. Indigenous-community theorists contend that nonelites join only if local social institutions, such as churches and recreation clubs, have first supplied the organizational resources necessary for a movement's success. Such resources range from meeting places to experienced community leaders. Movements, moreover, tend to appear in urban settings because compact living fosters associations. Political-process theorists look at international, national, and local political events for conditions that might reduce the costs of movement participation and might induce nonelites to join a movement. Generally speaking, the more repressive and tyrannical the local politics, the less likely that nonelites will join. Contrariwise, the more tolerant, peaceable, and constitutional the political order, the more divided the elites, and the more available the powerful political allies, the greater the chance that nonelites will join. Chances are even higher if elites cannot agree on how to respond to rebellious nonelites and if a significant fraction of the elite helps the protesters.

The three cases we examined partly jibe with all three subtypes of second-wave theorizing. Movement activists, such as Kelly, Wałęsa, and Guzmán, astutely mobilized the resources, including national publicity and foreign supporters, needed for their respective movements to succeed. Local social institutions, such as colleges, neighbourhood churches, and squatters' associations, provided each movement with valuable resources. Finally, auspicious political circumstances – such as the desertion of many Jusos from the SPD, international pressures on the PZPR not to put down regime opponents, and the Peruvian government's weak presence in the mountains and jungles – reduced the costs to nonelites for joining these particular movements.

However, the second tradition of theorizing is also deficient in accounting for the rise of the three movements. True, one can identify in hindsight numerous circumstances that, when combined, conceivably reduced the costs to nonelites of joining the Greens, Solidarity, and Shining Path. But one also could cite circumstances that probably raised the costs. Recall, for example, the controversial laws regulating movement activism among civil servants in West Germany, the PZPR's harassment of KOR and Solidarity activists even before the declaration of martial law, and the suspensions of civil rights and the brutality of the government's security forces throughout Peru. Once one considers all conceivable circumstances, it becomes much more difficult to assume that movement participation was obviously less costly than nonparticipation in the eyes of nonelites. Moreover, it becomes more plausible that other, less prudential motivations – such as moral outrage over economic inequality or a thirst for revenge after experiencing state repression – played important roles in people's decisions to join these movements.

In addition, the second-generation theorizing is somewhat disappointing because of its narrow thematic focus. Its hypotheses address few of the many facts that we uncovered about each movement and ignore many potentially interesting topics. Factions, for example, were quite visible in all three movements, and leaders endlessly struggled, with varying success, to unify the movement's colliding groups. The hypotheses, however, say surprisingly little about politics within movements. Resource-mobilization theorists, for example, focus on how movement leaders scrounge resources *outside* a movement. Indigenous-community and political-process theorists likewise emphasize how the social and political *environment* of a movement generates support and do not analyse movements' internal decision-making processes, structures of authority, or patterns of rebellion and contestation.

Another blind spot in the second wave of movement theorizing has to do with leaders' periodically autocratic decision-making styles. Such behaviour deserves detailed interpretation and systematic explanation but receives neither in the second-generation literature.

Finally, the second-generation theories, perhaps because they focus almost exclusively on the costs and benefits of joining social movements, say relatively little about the origins of social movements' ideologies. Why are particular goals, values, and strategies embraced by a movement and others rejected? Where do dominant ideologies come from, and why do they command such fervent loyalty? Why, for example, did Guzmán, Díaz, and other founders of Shining Path embrace the notion of prolonged armed struggle when so many other Peruvian radicals had not?

Identity-formation theory

The problem of ideology leads us to the third generation of social-movement theorizing: the identity-formation approach. This approach rests on a simple assumption: people's actions are structured by deeply held beliefs. Nonelites construct their beliefs in at least two ways. Either they develop ideas autonomously in local social institutions, such as churches, quilting bees, and coffeehouses, and then bring these ideas with them to a movement (the autonomous popular-culture thesis), or they create new belief systems while participating in movements and partaking of their countercultural milieus (the autonomous movement-culture thesis).

Some observations about the Greens, Solidarity, and Shining Path correlate with the basic logic of identity-formation theory. As autonomous popular-culture theorists might expect, many Green, Solidarity, and Shining Path members had previously been active in social groups and institutions, such as peace marches, religious organizations, and college study groups. There, they developed many of the goals and strategies that they would later pursue as movement activists. In addition, as autonomous movement-culture theorists might expect, some activists adopted new beliefs after joining their social movement. The post-1981 conversion of much of Solidarity's national leadership to free-market beliefs perhaps best exemplifies this phenomenon.

Although these findings seem compatible with scenarios commonly found in identity-formation writings, the historical record once again does not fully match the theory. Although there are numerous cases of nonelites forming deeply held political beliefs before joining a movement and then consistently acting on those beliefs later (Guzmán may be a good example of this process), there are also numerous counterexamples. Recall, for example, the former spontis and Jusos who joined the Greens *after* shedding previous, presumably deeply held political beliefs. Here, ideological discontinuity seems as striking as continuity. So, are activists' actions shaped primarily by long-standing and deeply held beliefs, or are additional factors involved?

The image of movements as sites of unfettered 'free thought' also seems unsatisfactory once we have closely examined the historical record. True, heated ideological debates occurred in the three movements and, from national elites' perspectives, the movements were hothouses of heresy, but there also were limits as to what notions members could explore without fearing consequences. Movement leaders, such as the Greens' Federal Executive Board, Wałęsa, and Guzmán, repeatedly tried to pressure ideological mavericks into conformity either through purges or through exclusion from the movement's decision-making process. Although all three movements were partly havens from conventional ways of looking at society, leaders' efforts to discipline thinking should not be forgotten. Paradoxically, the three movements were ideologically open and closed.

Identity-formation theories, in addition, overlook several questions about movements' popular appeal that we might want to ask. For example, why do some movement programmes and ideologies resonate among the population at large, while others do not? And why do levels of electoral support fluctuate so greatly in the course of a few years? (Why, for instance, did the Greens' electoral fortunes steadily rise during the mid-1980s, suddenly drop during the late 1980s and early 1990s, and then rise again during the mid-1990s? And why did Solidarity's electoral fortunes plummet between 1989 and 1993?) To explain a movement's changing electoral and ideological popularity, one must go beyond microlevel analysis of the origins of activists' goals and strategies and look at nonelites' shifting attitudes, which may be products of emotion, temperament, and short-term prudence (not only thought and conviction) and which also may be responses to political events and developments.

Finally, identity-formation theorists have thus far failed to explain how leaders in a large movement manage to unite members with diverse deeply held beliefs. How, for example, did leaders in the Greens temporarily reconcile the realos' and fundis' very different beliefs about electoral politics? How did Guzmán manage to unite the ideologically distinctive Ayacucho and Lima factions? And how did Wałęsa manage to keep the highly diversified Solidarity movement unified for more than a decade? To explain how leaders unite activists who have logically discordant belief systems, it is necessary to think explicitly about power struggles, expedient compromises, and the art of rhetoric.

Towards a fourth generation of social-movement theorizing

We have found that each postwar tradition of movement theorizing matches and explains some of the historical record, distorts other aspects, and fails altogether to account for still other key developments. This is not surprising. One purpose of theory is to make our innumerable experiences understandable and manageable through a few convenient and valid generalizations. This condensing of experience necessarily entails omission and distortion. Stated differently, there is always a tension between the useful simplicity of a theory and the complexity of experience that the theory tries to sum up.

Sometimes we are tempted to relinquish a theory solely because it fails to represent all aspects of reality. To do so is hasty and unwise. We need simplifying theories – to paraphrase Tocqueville, only God has no need of generalizations. Without theories, we would have no way of organizing our myriad observations, venturing predictions, or giving meaning to our actions. Instead of relinquishing theories because they simplify, which is one of their primary virtues, we should keep them but also be aware of their insights and limitations. In addition, we should supplement our store of generalizations by constructing new theories that address known oversights.

One recurrent blind spot in postwar traditions of social-movement theory involves the study of internal politics. Early modernization theorists seldom, if ever, portrayed movements as containing rival wings, currents, and factions that continually jostle with one another and that leaders must somehow reconcile. The second generation of theorists also seldom looked closely at ongoing factional struggles within movements or at how leaders find common ground among a movement's ideologically disparate parts. Identity-formation theories similarly do not ponder patterns of intramovement conflict and reconciliation.

How, then, to begin theorizing about such matters? One modest proposal is to re-examine our intellectual inheritance. Perhaps older political theories can provide some suggestive starting points. They might, after all, complement the sociologically and ideologically oriented theories about social movements that have characterized scholarly thinking since the Second World War. For example, Machiavelli's maxims about the prince's dilemmas and alternatives, and Lenin's analyses of the demands and dilemmas of revolutionary vanguards might help us ponder more systematically the nature of movement leadership. Aristotle's and Marx's analyses of divergent class interests, class struggle, and the fragility of interclass alliances might help us formulate generalizations about the centrifugal forces haunting modern movements. The political tales of Moses' ruthless leadership and the rebellious 'murmuring' in *Exodus*, which some political theorists have creatively used to make sense of twentieth-century revolutionary regimes (Walzer 1985), may similarly provide insights as to the sequence of factional struggles that movements undergo.

The reflections in *The Federalist Papers* and *The English Constitution* about the advantages and dangers of different decision-making processes could be used as a springboard for a systematic investigation of alternative patterns of intramovement policy making.

In short, one might find in classic political theory concepts and themes that can help us make sense of politics within social movements. This may be a desirable theoretical move if we decide to make sense not only of the economic, social, and political contexts and ideological components of social movements but also of their internal fights and adjustments.

The development of a fourth theoretical approach – one that focuses on (1) the plural viewpoints, interests, and ambitions that exist within any movement; (2) the conflicts over goals, priorities, and activities that naturally arise from members' different interests and aims, and (3) the methods that leaders use to reduce friction among activists and to promote agreement and unity – would enhance our understanding of social movements in at least two ways. First, close examination of disputes would induce us to note the contingent, ambiguous, and tentative nature of many movement decisions and would dissuade us from presuming that movements must be fixed in their programmes and activities – a mistake often made in journalistic accounts of contemporary movements. We would become more aware of the dynamic nature of movements' aims and plans of action, of the sorts of twists and turns in goals and strategies that we observed in the cases of the Greens, Solidarity, and Shining Path.

Second, greater sensitivity to intramovement political processes would aid us in thinking about the ways that movement participation educates nonelites about political conflict and thereby indirectly shapes a society's political culture. We know that people acquire many politically relevant beliefs, skills, and values through small-scale interactions in formal and informal social settings, such as schools, workplaces, and churches (Almond and Verba 1963; Pateman 1971; Verba 1961). Movements provide yet another classroom where nonelites can acquire a perspective on conflict that can later be used in other political contexts. The content of an activist's education can vary greatly; through processes of struggle and reconciliation, movement activists might learn democratic norms, but they might also be trained in authoritarian practices. What a participant learns depends in part on the specific methods that leaders of the movement use to forge agreement among members, and in part on the methods that factions and cliques in the movement use to advance their distinctive aims.

The time may have arrived for us to develop a fourth theoretical approach (for convenience, let us call it a 'discord' approach) that explicates intramovement struggles and borrows themes from classic political theory. A new approach, by emphasizing disagreement and divisions within movements and the efforts by leaders to forge unity, would complement the insights of already established theoretical approaches, but would ask questions about phenomena that are now often overlooked. Previous waves of theorizing invited us to think systematically about (1) the relationships between movements and worldwide social changes; (2) the political resources, political opportunities, and strategic choices facing social movements; and

(3) the multiple beliefs and cultural creativity of movement activists. The discord approach would draw our attention to the clashing rhetoric, priorities, interests, and decisions of different factions and circles. We would notice both leaders' initiatives and dissenters' resistance. Each social movement would appear polymorphous, with multiple, competing personalities and possible lines of development.

Since the writings of Robert Park in the early twentieth century, scholars have offered many responses to the question 'are social movements historically important?'. A discord approach would not enable a person to discover a simple answer to this question. One instead would see social movements as constantly evolving yet transforming – as they are internally dialectical – and therefore bearing multiple legacies for future generations.

References

Ackelsberg, M. A. (1991) *Free Women of Spain: anarchism and the struggle for the emancipation of women*, Bloomington: Indiana University Press.

Adam, B. D. (1987) *The Rise of a Gay and Lesbian Movement*, Boston, Massachusetts: Twayne.

Alber, J. (1989) 'Modernization, cleavage structures, and the rise of green parties and lists in Europe' in F. Müller-Rommel (ed.) *New Politics in Western Europe: the rise and success of green parties and alternative lists*, Boulder, Colorado: Westview Press, pp. 195–219.

Allen, C. S. (1992) 'Germany' in M. Kesselman and J. Krieger (eds) *European Politics in Transition* 2nd edn., Lexington, Massachusetts: D. C. Heath, pp. 233–326.

Almond, G. A. and Verba, S. (1963) *The Civic Culture: political attitudes and democracy in five nations*, Princeton, New Jersey: Princeton University Press.

Anderson, Jr. R. D. (1982) 'Soviet decision-making and Poland', *Problems of Communism* 31(2): 22–36.

Andreas, P. R. and Sharpe, K. E. (1992) 'Cocaine politics in the Andes', *Current History* 91(562): 74–8.

Angell, A. (1981) 'Classroom Maoists: The politics of Peruvian schoolteachers under military government', *Bulletin of Latin American Research* 1(1): 1–20.

Anonymous (1982) 'Yes, there is a women's movement in Poland' in S. Persky and H. Flam (eds) *The Solidarity Sourcebook*, Vancouver, British Columbia, pp. 149–51.

Anonymous (1988) 'Gnomes, revolution, and toilet paper: The Orange Alternative in Wroclaw', *Across Frontiers* 4(2–3): 1–5.

Apter, D. E. (1987) *Rethinking Development: modernization, dependency, and postmodern politics*, Newbury Park, California: Sage Publications.

Apter, D. E. and Sawa, N. (1984) *Against the State: politics and social protest in Japan*, Cambridge, Massachusetts: Harvard University Press.

Arendt, H. (1951) *The Origins of Totalitarianism*, New York: Harcourt, Brace.

Arendt, H. (1965) *On Revolution*, New York: Viking Press.

Ascherson, N. (1987) *The struggles for Poland*, New York: Random House.

Ash, T. G. (1991) *The Polish Revolution: Solidarity* revised and updated edn., London: Granta Books.

Ash, T. G. (1993) *The Magic Lantern: the revolution of '89 witnessed in Warsaw, Budapest, Berlin and Prague*, New York: Vintage Books.

Ash, T. G. (1995) '"Neo-Pagan" Poland', *New York Review of Books* 43(1): 10–14.

Berg, R. H. (1986–87) 'Sendero Luminoso and the peasantry of Andahuaylas', *Journal of Interamerican Studies and World Affairs* 28(4): 165–96.

Berg, R. H. (1992) 'Peasant responses to Shining Path in Andahuaylas' in D. S. Palmer (ed.) *Shining Path of Peru*, New York: St. Martin's Press, pp. 83–104.

Bernhard, M. (1990) 'Barriers to further political and economic change in Poland', *Studies in Comparative Communism* 23(3–4): 319–39.

Bernhard, M. (1991) 'Reinterpreting Solidarity', *Studies in Comparative Communism* 24(3): 313–30.

Bernhard, M. H. (1993) *The Origins of Democratization in Poland: workers, intellectuals, and oppositional politics, 1976–1980*, New York: Columbia University Press.

Betz, H-G. (1995) 'Alliance 90/Greens: from fundamental opposition to black-green' in D. P. Conradt, G. R. Kleinfeld, G. K. Romoser and C. Søe (eds) *Germany's New Politics: parties and issues in the 1990s*, Providence, Rhode Island: Berghahn Books, pp. 203–20.

Biezenski, R. (1994) 'Workers' self-management and the technical intelligentsia in people's Poland', *Politics and Society* 22(1): 59–88.

Black, C. E., Helmreich, J. E., Helmreich, P. C., Issawi, C. P. and McAdams, A. J. (1992) *Rebirth: a history of Europe since World War II*, Boulder, Colorado: Westview Press.

Błaszkiewicz, A., Rydowski, Z. W., Szwajcer, P. and Wertenstein-Żuławski, J. (1994) 'The Solidarność spring?', *Communist and Post-Communist Studies* 27(2): 125–34.

Blondet, C. (1995) 'Villa El Salvador' in O. Starn, C. I. Degregori and R. Kirk (eds) *The Peru Reader: history, culture, politics*, Durham, North Carolina: Duke University Press, pp. 272–7.

Boggs, C. (1986) 'The green alternative and the struggle for a post-Marxist discourse', *Theory and Society* 15(6): 869–99.

Bourque, S. C. and Warren, K. B. (1989) 'Democracy without peace: the cultural politics of terror in Peru', *Latin American Research Review* 24(1): 7–34.

Bracher, K. D. (1969) 'The problems of parliamentary democracy in Europe' in A. J. Milnor (ed.) *Comparative Political Parties*, New York: Thomas Y. Crowell, pp. 340–64.

Braunthal, G. (1995) 'The perspective from the left', *German Politics and Society* 13(1): 36–49.

Breines, W. (1982) *Community and Organization in the New Left, 1962–1968: the great refusal*, New York: J. F. Bergin.

Brinton, C. (1938) *The Anatomy of Revolution*, New York: Prentice-Hall.

Bromke, A. (1978) 'The opposition in Poland', *Problems of Communism* 27(4): 37–51.

Brown, J. F. (1988) *Eastern Europe and Communist Rule*, Durham, North Carolina: Duke University Press.

Brown, J. F. (1991) *Surge to Freedom: the end of communist rule in eastern Europe*. Durham, North Carolina: Duke University Press.

Brown, M. F. and Fernández, E. (1991) *War of Shadows: the struggle for utopia in the Peruvian Amazon*, Berkeley: University of California Press.

Bürklin, W. P. (1985) 'The German greens: the post-industrial non-established and the party system', *International Political Science Review* 6(4): 463–81.

Bürklin, W. P. (1987) 'Governing left parties frustrating the radical non-established left: the rise and inevitable decline of the greens', *European Sociological Review* 3(2): 109–26.

Bürklin, W. P. (1988) 'A politico-economic model instead of a sour grapes logic: a reply to Herbert Kitschelt's critique', *European Sociological Review* 4(2): 161–6.

Burns, R. and van der Will, W. (1988) *Protest and Democracy in West Germany: extra-parliamentary opposition and the democratic agenda*, New York: St. Martin's Press.

Burt, J. and Ricci, J. L. (1994) 'Shining Path after Guzmán', *NACLA Report to the Americas* 28(3): 6–9.

Caen, P. (1982) 'Interview with Zbigniew Iwanow' in S. Persky and H. Flam (eds) *The Solidarity Sourcebook*, Vancouver, British Columbia: New Star Books, pp. 151–5.

Cameron, M. A. (1991) 'Political parties and the worker–employer cleavage: the impact of the informal sector on voting in Lima, Peru', *Bulletin of Latin American Research* 10(3): 293–313.

Campbell, L. G. (1973) 'The historiography of the Peruvian guerrilla movement, 1960–65', *Latin American Research Review* 8(1): 45–70.

Capra, F. and Spretnak, C. (1984) *Green Politics: the global promise*, New York: E. P. Dutton.

Carlessi, C. (1989) 'The reconquest', *NACLA Report on the Americas* 23(4): 14–21.

Castells, M. (1983) *The City and the Grassroots*, Berkeley: University of California Press.

Chong, D. (1991) *Collective Action and the Civil Rights Movement*, Chicago, Illinois: University of Chicago Press.

Clark, R. P. (1984) *The Basque Insurgents: ETA, 1952–1980*, Madison: University of Wisconsin Press.

Cohen, J. L. (1985) 'Strategy or identity: new theoretical paradigms and contemporary social movements', *Social Research* 52(4): 663–716.

Cohn, N. (1961) *The Pursuit of the Millennium*, New York: Harper.

Communist Party of Peru (1982) *Develop Guerrilla Warfare*, Berkeley, California: Committee to Support the Revolution in Peru.

Communist Party of Peru (1985) *Don't Vote! Instead, expand the guerrilla war to seize power for the people*, Berkeley, California: Committee to Support the Revolution in Peru.

Communist Party of Peru (1986) *Develop the People's War to Serve the World Revolution*, Berkeley, California: Committee to Support the Revolution in Peru.

Conradt, D. P. (1986) *The German Polity* 3rd edn., New York: Longman.

Cooper, A. H. (1988) 'The West German peace movement and the Christian churches: an institutional approach', *Review of Politics* 50(1): 71–98.

Cooper, A. and Eichner, K. (1991) 'The West German peace movement', *International Social Movement Research* 3: 149–171.

Cornelius, Jr. W. A. (1971) 'The political sociology of city-ward migration in Latin America: toward empirical theory', *Latin American Urban Research* 1: 95–147.

Costain, A. N. (1992) *Inviting Women's Rebellion: a political process interpretation of the women's movement*, Baltimore, Maryland: Johns Hopkins University Press.

Crabtree, J. (1992) *Peru under García: an opportunity lost*, Pittsburgh, Pennsylvania: University of Pittsburgh Press.

Curry, J. L. (1992) 'The puzzle of Poland', *Current History* 91(568): 385–9.

Dalton, R. J. (1993) *Politics in Germany* 2nd edn., New York: HarperCollins.

Degenhardt, H. W. (1988) *Revolutionary and Dissident Movements* 2nd edn., London: Longman.

Degregori, C. I. (1994) 'Shining Path and counterinsurgency strategy since the arrest of Abimael Guzmán' in J. S. Tulchin and G. Bland (eds) *Peru in Crisis: dictatorship or democracy?*, Boulder, Colorado: Lynne Rienner, pp. 81–100.

Die Grünen (1983) *Programme of the German Green Party*, London: Heretic Books.

Dietz, H. (1986–87) 'Electoral politics in Peru, 1978–1986', *Journal of Interamerican Studies and World Affairs* 28(4): 139–63.

Dietz, H. (1990) Peru's Sendero Luminoso as a revolutionary movement', *Journal of Political and Military Sociology* 18(1): 123–50.

Dobson, A. (1990) *Green Political Thought: an introduction*, London: HarperCollins.

Drzycimski, A. (1982) 'Growing' in S. Persky and H. Flam (eds) *The Solidarity Sourcebook*, Vancouver, British Columbia: New Star Books, pp. 110–12.

Dyson, K. (1989) 'Economic policy' in G. Smith, W. E. Patterson and P. E. Merkle (eds) *Developments in West German Politics*, Durham, North Carolina: Duke University Press, pp. 148–67.

Eckersley, R. (1989) 'Green politics and the new class: selfishness or virtue?', *Political Studies* 37(2): 205–22.

Eckert, R. and Willems, H. (1986) 'Youth protest in western Europe: four case studies', *Research in Social Movements, Conflicts and Change* 9: 127–53.

Edelman, M. (1988) *Constructing the Political Spectacle*, Chicago, Illinois: University of Chicago Press.

Escobar, A. and Alvarez, S. (1992) *The Making of Social Movements in Latin America*, Boulder, Colorado: Westview Press.

Esser, J., Fach, W. and Dyson, K. (1983) ' "Social market" and modernization policy: West Germany' in K. Dyson and S. Wilks (eds) *Industrial Crisis: a comparative study of the state and industry*, New York: St. Martin's Press, pp. 102–27.

Evans, S. (1979) *Personal Politics: the roots of women's liberation in the civil rights movement and the new left*, New York: Knopf.

Evans, S. M. and Boyte, H. C. (1986) *Free Spaces: the sources of democratic change in America*, New York: Harper & Row.

Eyerman, R. and Jamison, A. (1991) *Social Movements: a cognitive approach*, University Park: Pennsylvania State University Press.

Fallenbuchl, Z. M. (1982) 'Poland's economic crisis', *Problems of Communism* 31(2): 1–21.

Fantasia, R. (1988) *Cultures of Solidarity: consciousness, action, and contemporary American workers*, Berkeley: University of California Press.

Ferree, M. M. (1987) 'Equality and autonomy: feminist politics in the United States and West Germany' in M. F. Katzenstein and C. M. Mueller (eds) *The Women's Movements of the United States and Western Europe: consciousness, political opportunity, and public policy*, Philadelphia, Pennsylvania: Temple University Press, pp. 172–95.

Fogt, H. (1989) 'The greens and the new left: influences of left-extremism on green party organisation and policies' in E. Kolinsky (ed.) *The Greens in West Germany: organization and policy making*, Oxford: Berg, pp. 89–121.

Frankland, E. G. (1989) 'Federal Republic of Germany: "Die Grünen"' in F. Müller-Rommel (ed.) *New Politics in Western Europe: the rise and success of green parties and alternative lists*, Boulder, Colorado: Westview Press, pp. 61–79.

Frankland, E. G. and Schoonmaker, D. (1992) *Between Protest and Power: the green party in Germany*, Boulder, Colorado: Westview Press.

Fromm, E. (1941) *Escape From Freedom*, New York: Holt, Rinehart & Winston.

Fujimori, A. (1995) 'A momentous decision' in O. Starn, C. I. Degregori and R. Kirk (eds) *The Peru Reader: history, culture, politics*, Durham, North Carolina: Duke University Press, pp. 438–45.

Gamson, W. A. (1968) 'Stable unrepresentation in American society', *American Behavioral Scientist* 12(2): 15–21.

Gamson, W. A. (1975) *The Strategy of Social Protest*, Homewood, Illinois: Dorsey Press.

Garner, R. and Zald, M. N. (1985) 'The political economy of social movement sectors' in G. D. Suttles and M. N. Zald (eds) *The Challenge of Social Control: citizenship and institution building in modern society – essays in honor of Morris Janowitz*, Norwood, New Jersey: Ablex, pp. 119–45.

Gaventa, J. (1980) *Power and Powerlessness: quiescence and rebellion in an Appalachian valley*, Urbana: University of Illinois Press.

Gianotten, V., de Wit, T. and de Wit, H. (1985) 'The impact of Sendero Luminoso on regional and national politics in Peru' in D. Slater (ed.) *New Social Movements and the State in Latin America*, Amsterdam: CEDLA, pp. 171–202.

Gitlin, T. (1980) *The Whole World is Watching: mass media in the making & unmaking of the new left*, Berkeley: University of California Press.

Goldberg, R. A. (1991) *Grassroots Resistance: social movements in twentieth century America*, Belmont, California: Wadsworth.

Goldman, M. F. (1986) 'Soviet policy toward the political turmoil in Poland during the fall of 1980', *East European Quarterly* 20(3): 335–57.

Gonzales, J. E. (1992) 'Guerrillas and coca in the Upper Huallaga Valley' in D. S. Palmer (ed.) *Shining Path of Peru*, New York: St. Martin's Press, pp. 105–25.

Gonzales de Olarte, E. (1993) 'Economic stabilization and structural adjustment under Fujimori', *Journal of Interamerican Studies and World Affairs* 35(2): 51–80.

Gonzales de Olarte, E. (1994) 'Peru's difficult road to economic development' in J. S. Tulchin and G. Bland (eds) *Peru in Crisis: dictatorship or democracy?*, Boulder, Colorado: Lynne Rienner, pp. 155–85.

Goodwyn, L. (1978) *The Populist Moment: a short history of the agrarian revolt in America*, New York: Oxford University Press.

Goodwyn, L. (1991) *Breaking the Barrier: the rise of solidarity in Poland*, New York: Oxford University Press.

Gorriti, G. (1992) 'Shining Path's Stalin and Trotsky' in D. S. Palmer (ed.) *Shining Path of Peru*, New York: St. Martin's Press, pp. 149–70.

Graham, C. (1994a) 'Commentary' in J. S. Tulchin and G. Bland (eds) *Peru in Crisis: dictatorship or democracy?*, Boulder, Colorado: Lynne Rienner, pp. 73–8.

Graham, C. (1994b) 'Introduction: democracy in crisis and the international response' in J. S. Tulchin and G. Bland (eds) *Peru in Crisis: dictatorship or democracy?*, Boulder, Colorado: Lynne Rienner, pp. 1–20.

Green, S. (1995) 'Postscript: the Land elections in Hessen, Nordrhein-Westfalen and Bremen', *German Politics* 4(2): 152–8.

Guzmán, A. (1988) *Interview with Chairman Gonzalo*, Berkeley, California: Committee to Support the Revolution in Peru.

Halebsky, S. (1976) *Mass Society and Political Conflict: towards a reconstruction of theory*, Cambridge: Cambridge University Press.

Hancock, M. D. (1989) *West Germany: the politics of democratic corporatism*, Chatham, New Jersey: Chatham House.

Hancock, M. D. (1993) 'The SPD seeks a new identity: party modernization and prospects in the 1990s', in R. J. Dalton (ed.) *The New Germany Votes: unification and the creation of a new German party system*, Providence, Rhode Island: Berg, pp. 77–98.

Handelman, H. (1975) *Struggle in the Andes*, Austin: University of Texas Press.

Haq, M. (1995) *Reflections on Human Development*, New York: Oxford University Press.

Harding, C. (1987) 'The rise of Sendero Luminoso' in R. Miller (ed.) *Region and Class in Modern Peruvian History*, Liverpool: University of Liverpool Institute of Latin American Studies, pp. 179–207.

Harding, C. (1988) 'Antonio Díaz Martínez and the ideology of Sendero Luminoso', *Bulletin of Latin American Research* 7(1): 65–73.

Harvey, N. (1994) *Rebellion in Chiapas: rural reforms, campesino radicalism, and the limits to Salinismo*, La Jolla, California: University of California at San Diego Center for US–Mexican Studies.

Haya de la Torre, V. R. (1995) 'The APRA' in O. Starn, C. I. Degregori and R. Kirk (eds) *The Peru Reader: history, culture, politics*, Durham, North Carolina: Duke University Press, pp. 240–4.

Hermens, F. A. (1951) *Europe Between Democracy and Anarchy*, Notre Dame, Indiana: University of Notre Dame Press.

Hermens, F. A. (1984) 'Representation and proportional representation' in A. Lijphart and B. Grofman (eds) *Choosing an Electoral System: issues and alternatives*, New York: Praeger Publishers, pp. 15–30.

Hill, C. (1972) *The World Turned Upside Down: radical ideas during the English revolution*, New York: Viking Press.

Hill, P. (1985) 'Crisis of the greens: "Fundis", "realos", and the future', *Radical America* 19(5): 35–43.

Hoffer, E. (1951) *The True Believer: thoughts on the nature of mass movements*, New York: Harper & Row.

Holc, J. P. (1995) 'Competing visions of Polish parliament, 1989–1993', *East European Quarterly* 29(1): 69–87.

Holmes, K. R. (1983) 'The origins, development, and composition of the green movement' in R. L. Pfaltzgraff Jr., K. R. Holmes, C. Clemens and W. Kaltefleiter (eds) *The Greens of West Germany: origins, strategies, and transatlantic implications*, Cambridge, Massachusetts: Institute for Foreign Policy Analysis, pp. 15–46.

Hosking, G. (1991) *The Awakening of the Soviet Union* enlarged edn., Cambridge, Massachusetts: Harvard University Press.

Hülsberg, W. (1985) 'The greens at the crossroads', *New Left Review* 152: 5–29.

Hülsberg, W. (1988) *The German Greens: a social and political profile*, London: Verso.

Inglehart, R. (1990) *Culture Shift in Advanced Industrial Society*, Princeton, New Jersey: Princeton University Press.

Inter-University Coordinating Commission (1982) 'The Lodz agreement' in S. Persky and H. Flam (eds) *The Solidarity Sourcebook*, Vancouver, British Columbia: New Star Books, pp. 143–9.

Isbell, B. J. (1992) 'Shining Path and peasant responses in rural Ayacucho' in D. S. Palmer (ed.) *Shining Path of Peru*, New York: St. Martin's Press, pp. 59–81.

Izaguirre, C. R. (1996) 'Shining Path in the 21st century: actors in search of a new script', *NCALA Report on the Americas* 30(1): 37–8.

Janiszewski, J. (1982) 'Solidarnosc: design for a logo' in S. Persky and H. Flam (eds) *The Solidarity Sourcebook*, Vancouver, British Columbia: New Star Books, pp. 79–80.

Jenkins, J. C. (1981) 'Sociopolitical movements' in S. L. Long (ed.) *The Handbook of Political Behavior*, New York: Plenum Press, vol. 4, pp. 81–153.

Jenkins, J. C. (1983) 'The transformation of a constituency into a movement: farmworker organizing in California' in J. Freeman (ed.) *Social Movements of the Sixties and Seventies*, New York: Longman, pp. 52–70.

Joppke, C. and Markovits, A. S. (1994) 'Green politics in the new Germany', *Dissent* Spring: 235–40.

Judkins, B. M. (1983) 'Mobilization of membership: the black and brown lung movements' in J. Freeman (ed.) *Social Movements of the Sixties and Seventies*, New York: Longman, pp. 35–51.

Kamiński, B. (1991) *The Collapse of State Socialism: the case of Poland*, Princeton, New Jersey: Princeton University Press.

Karabel, J. (1993) 'Polish intellectuals and the origins of solidarity: the making of an oppositional alliance', *Communist and Post-Communist Studies* 26(1): 25–46.

Karpiński, J. (1987) 'Polish intellectuals in opposition', *Problems of Communism* 36(4): 44–57.

Katzenstein, P. J. (1987) *Policy and Politics in West Germany: the growth of a semisovereign state*, Philadelphia, Pennsylvania: Temple University Press, pp. 104–5.

Katzenstein, P. J. (1989) 'Stability and change in the emerging third republic' in P. J. Katzenstein (ed.) *Industry and Politics in West Germany: toward the third republic*, Ithaca, New York: Cornell University Press, pp. 307–53.

Kelley, R. D. (1994) *Race Rebels: culture, politics, and the Black working class*, New York: Free Press.

Killian, L. (1964) 'Social movements' in R. E. L. Faris (ed.) *Handbook of Modern Sociology*, Chicago, Illinois: Rand McNally, pp. 426–55.

Kitschelt, H. (1988) 'The life expectancy of left-libertarian parties. Does structural transformation or economic decline explain party innovation? A response to Wilhelm P. Bürklin', *European Sociological Review* 4(2): 155–60.

Kolinsky, E. (1984) *Parties, Opposition and Society in West Germany*, New York: St. Martin's Press.

Kolinsky, E. (1989) 'Women in the green party' in E. Kolinsky (ed.) *The Greens in West Germany: organization and policy making*, Oxford: Berg, pp. 189–221.

Kornhauser, W. (1959) *The Politics of Mass Society*, New York: Free Press.

Kowalewski, Z. (1982) 'Solidarity on the eve' in S. Persky and H. Flam (eds) *The Solidarity Sourcebook*, Vancouver, British Columbia: New Star Books, pp. 230–40.

Kowalik, T. (1994) 'A reply to Maurice Glasman', *New Left Review* 206: 133–44.

Kramer, D. (1994) 'The graying of the German greens', *Dissent* Spring: 231–4.

Kramer, M. (1995) 'Polish workers and the post-communist transition, 1989–1993', *Communist and Post-Communist Studies* 28(1): 71–114.

Kubik, J. (1994) *The Power of Symbols Against the Symbols of Power: the rise of Solidarity and the fall of state socialism in Poland*, University Park: Pennsylvania State University Press.

Kuroń, J. and Modzelewski, K. (1982) 'Open letter to party members' in S. Persky and H. Flam (eds) *The Solidarity Sourcebook*, Vancouver, British Columbia: New Star Books, pp. 35–56.

Laba, R. (1991) *The Roots of Solidarity: a political sociology of Poland's working-class democratization*, Princeton, New Jersey: Princeton University Press.

Laclau, E. (1985) 'New social movements and the plurality of the social' in D. Slater (ed.) *New Social Movements and the State in Latin America*, Amsterdam: CEDLA.

Lakeman, E. (1984) 'The case for proportional representation' in A. Lijphart and B. Grofman (eds) *Choosing an Electoral System: issues and alternatives*, New York: Praeger Publishers, pp. 41–51.

Lipset, S. M. (1950) *Agrarian Socialism: the cooperative commonwealth federation in Saskatchewan – a study in political sociology*, Berkeley: University of California Press.

Lipset, S. M. (1955) 'The radical right: a problem for American democracy', *British Journal of Sociology* 6(2): 176–209.

Lipset, S. M. (1960) *Political Man: the social bases of politics*, New York: Doubleday.

Lopiński, J., Moskit, M. and Wilk, M. (1990) *Konspira: Solidarity underground*, Berkeley: University of California Press.

Mariátegui, J. C. (1970) *Seven Interpretive Essays on Peruvian Reality*, Austin: University of Texas Press.

Mariátegui, J. C. (1995) 'Reflections' in O. Starn, C. I. Degregori and R. Kirk (eds) *The Peru Reader: history, culture, politics*, Durham, North Carolina: Duke University Press, pp. 228–33.

Markovits, A. S. (1982) 'The legacy of liberalism and collectivism in the labor movement: a tense but fruitful compromise for model Germany' in A. S. Markovits (ed.) *The Political Economy of West Germany: Modell Deutschland*, New York: Praeger Publishers, pp. 141–87.

Markovits, A. S. and Allen, C. S. (1989) 'The trade unions' in G. Smith, W. E. Patterson and P. H. Merkle (eds) *Developments in West German Politics*, Durham, North Carolina: Duke University Press, pp. 289–307.

Markovits, A. S. and Dalton, R. J. (1995) 'Spin doctors and soothsayers: the *Bundestag* elections of October 16, 1994', *German Politics and Society* 13(1): 1–11.

Markovits, A. S. and Gorski, P. S. (1993) *The German Left: red, green and beyond*, New York: Oxford University Press.

Marody, M. (1995) 'Three stages of party system emergence in Poland', *Communist and Post-Communist Studies* 28(2): 263–70.

Mason, D. S. (1983) 'Solidarity, the regime and the public', *Soviet Studies* 35(4): 533–44.

Mason, D. S. (1989) 'Solidarity as a new social movement', *Political Science Quarterly* 104(1): 41–58.

Mason, D. S. (1992) *Revolution in East-central Europe: the rise and fall of communism and the cold war*, Boulder, Colorado: Westview Press.

Mauceri, P. (1995) 'State reform, coalitions, and the neoliberal *autogolpe* in Peru', *Latin American Research Review* 30(1): 7–37.

McAdam, D. (1982) *Political Process and the Development of Black Insurgency, 1930– 1970*, Chicago, Illinois: University of Chicago Press.

McAdam, D. (1988) *Freedom Summer*, New York: Oxford University Press.

McCarthy, J. D. and Wolfson, M. (1988) 'Exploring sources of rapid social movement growth: the role of organizational form, consensus support, and elements of the American state' presented at the American Sociological Association workshop, Frontiers in Social Movement Theorizing, in Ann Arbor, Michigan on 9 June.

McCarthy, J. D. and Zald, M. N. (1977) 'Resource mobilization and social movements: a partial theory', *American Journal of Sociology* 82(6): 1212–41.

McClintock, C. (1981) *Peasant Cooperatives and Political Change in Peru*, Princeton, New Jersey: Princeton University Press.

McClintock, C. (1984) 'Why peasants rebel: the case of Peru's Sendero Luminoso', *World Politics* 37(1): 48–84.

McClintock, C. (1987) 'Capitalist expansion and the Andean peasantry', *Latin American Research Review* 22(2): 235–44.

McClintock, C. (1989) 'Peru's Sendero Luminoso rebellion: origins and trajectory' in S. Eckstein (ed.) *Power and Popular Protest: Latin American social movements*, Berkeley: University of California Press, pp. 61–101.

McClintock, C. (1993) 'Peru's Fujimori: a caudillo derails democracy', *Current History* 92(572): 112–19.

Melucci, A. (1985) The symbolic challenge of contemporary movements, *Social Research* 52(4): 789–816.

Melucci, A. (1988) 'Social movements and the democratization of everyday life' in J. Keane (ed.) *Civil Society and the State: new European perspectives*, London: Verso.

Mewes, H. (1983) 'The West German green party', *New German Critique* 28: 51–85.

Michnik, A. (1987) *Letters from Prison and Other Essays*, Berkeley: University of California Press.

Michnik, A. and Lipski, J. J. (1987) 'Some remarks on the opposition and the general situation in Poland 1979' in A. Michnik (ed.) *Letters from Prison and Other Essays*, Berkeley: University of California Press, pp. 149–54.

Migdal, J. S. (1974) *Peasants, Politics, and Revolution: pressures toward political and social change in the Third World*, Princeton, New Jersey: Princeton University Press.

Millard, F. (1994) *The Anatomy of the New Poland: Post-communist politics in its first phase*, Brookfield, Vermont: Edward Elgar.

Morris, A. D. (1984) *The Origins of the Civil Rights Movement: Black communities organizing for change*, New York: Free Press.

Morris, A. D. and Herring, C. (1981) 'Theory and research in social movements: a critical review' in S. L. Long (ed.) *Annual Review of Political Science* 2(1981): 137–98.

Moyano, M. E. (1995) 'There have been threats' in O. Starn, C. I. Degregori, and R. Kirk (eds) *The Peru Reader: history, culture, politics*, Durham, North Carolina, Duke University Press, pp. 371–6.

Mushaben, J. M. (1984) 'Anti-politics and successor generations: the role of youth in the West and East German peace movements,' *Journal of Political and Military Sociology* 12(1): 171–90.

Mushaben, J. M. (1985) 'Cycles of peace protest in West Germany: experiences from three decades', *West European Politics* 8(1): 24–40.

'Nicario' (1995) 'Memories of a cadre' in O. Starn, C. I. Degregori and R. Kirk (eds) *The Peru Reader: history, culture, politics*, Durham, North Carolina: Duke University Press, pp. 328–35.

Nowak, J. (1982) 'The church in Poland', *Problems of Communism* 31(1): 1–16.

Offe, C. (1987) 'Challenging the boundaries of institutional politics: social movements since the 1960s' in C. Maier (ed.) *Changing Boundaries of the Political: essays on the evolving balance between the state and society, public and private in Europe*, Cambridge: Cambridge University Press, pp. 63–105.

Ost, D. (1988) 'Indispensable ambiguity: Solidarity's internal authority structure', *Studies in Comparative Communism* 21(2): 189–201.

Ost, D. (1989) 'The transformation of Solidarity and the future of central Europe', *Telos* 79: 69–94.

Ost, D. (1990) *Solidarity and the Politics of Anti-politics: opposition and reform in Poland since 1968*, Philadelphia, Pennsylvania: Temple University Press.

Padgett, S. (1987) 'The West German social democrats in opposition, 1982–86', *West European Politics* 10(3): 333–56.

Padgett, S. and Burkett, T. (1986) *Political Parties and Elections in West Germany: the search for a new stability*, London: C. Hurst & Company.

Palmer, D. S. (1986) 'Rebellion in rural Peru: the origins and evolution of Sendero Luminoso', *Comparative Politics* 18(2): 127–46.

Palmer, D. S. (1990) 'Peru's persistent problems', *Current History* 89(543): 5–8, 31–4.

Palmer, D. S. (1996) '"Fjuipopulism" and Peru's progress', *Current History* 95(598): 70–5.

Papadakis, E. (1984) *The Green Movement in West Germany*, New York: St. Martin's Press.

Park, R. E. (1972) *'The Crowd and the Public' and Other Essays*, Chicago, Illinois: University of Chicago Press.

Pastor, M. and Wise, C. (1992) 'Peruvian economic policy in the 1980s: from orthodoxy to heterodoxy and back', *Latin American Research Review* 27(2): 83–117.

Pateman, C. (1971) *Participation and Democratic Theory*, Cambridge: Cambridge University Press.

Perlman, J. E. (1975) 'Rio's favelas and the myth of marginality', *Politics and Society* 5(2): 131–60.

Persky, S. (1981) *At the Lenin Shipyard*, Vancouver, British Columbia: New Star Books.

Petras, J. (1968) 'Revolution and guerrilla movements in Latin America: Venezuela, Colombia, Guatemala, and Peru' in J. Petras and M. Zeitlin (eds) *Latin America: reform or revolution? A reader*, Greenwich, Connecticut: Fawcett, pp. 329–69.

Petras, J. F. and Havens, A. E. (1981a) 'Peasant movements and social change: Cooperatives in Peru' in J. F. Petras, A. E. Havens, M. H. Morley and P. DeWitt (eds) *Class, State and Power in the Third World with Case Studies on Class Conflict in Latin America*, London: Zed Press, pp. 222–37.

Petras, J. F. and Havens, A. E. (1981b) 'Urban radicalism in Peru' in J. F. Petras, A. E. Havens, M. H. Morley, and P. DeWitt (eds) *Class, State and Power in the Third World with Case Studies on Class Conflict in Latin America*, London: Zed Press, pp. 238–54.

Piven, F. F. (1976) 'The social structuring of political protest', *Politics and Society* 6(3): 297–326.

Poguntke, T. (1992a) 'Between ideology and empirical research: the literature on the German green party', *European Journal of Political Research* 21(4): 337–56.

Poguntke, T. (1992b) 'Unconventional participation in party politics: the experiences of the German greens', *Political Studies* 40(2): 239–54.

Poguntke, T. and Schmitt-Beck, R. (1994) 'Still the same with a new name? Bündis 90/Die Grünen after the fusion', *German Politics* 3(1): 91–113.

Poole, D. and Rénique, G. (1992) *Peru: time of fear*, London: Latin America Bureau.

Powell, J. D. (1971) *Political Mobilization of the Venezuelan Peasant*, Cambridge, Massachusetts: Harvard University Press.

Powell, Jr. G. B. (1982) *Contemporary Democracies: participation, stability, and violence*, Cambridge, Massachusetts: Harvard University Press.

Pravda, A. (1982) 'Poland 1980: from "premature consumerism" to labour solidarity', *Soviet Studies* 34(2): 167–99.

Pulzer, P. (1995) *German Politics, 1945–1995*, Oxford: Oxford University Press.

Quijano Obregón, A. (1968) 'Tendencies in Peruvian development and in the class structure' in J. Petras and M. Zeitlin (eds) *Latin America: reform or revolution? A reader*, Greenwich, Connecticut: Fawcett, pp. 289–327.

Reid, M. (1986) 'Building bridges? García confronts Sendero', *NACLA: Report on the Americas* 20(3): 43–6.

Roberts, G. K. (1995) '*Superwahljahr* 1994 and its effects on the German party system', *German Politics* 4(2): 4–25.

Rochabrún, G. (1996) 'Deciphering the enigmas of Alberto Fujimori', *NACLA Report on the Americas* 30(1): 16–24.

Rogers, D. E. (1995) *Politics after Hitler: the western allies and the German party system*, New York: New York University Press.

Rogin, M. P. (1967) *The Intellectuals and McCarthy: the radical specter*, Cambridge, Massachusetts: M.I.T. Press.

Rosenberg, T. (1991) *Children of Cain: violence and the violent in Latin America*, New York: William Morrow and Company.

Roth, R. (1991) 'Local green politics in West German cities', *International Journal of Urban and Regional Research* 15(1): 75–89.

Rothacher, A. (1984) 'The green party in German politics', *West European Politics* 7(3): 109–16.

Rudé, G. (1959) *The Crowd in the French Revolution*, Oxford: Oxford University Press.

Rudolf, J. D. (1992) *Peru: the evolution of a crisis*, Westport, Connecticut: Praeger.

Rule, J. B. (1988) *Theories of Civil Violence*, Berkeley: University of California Press.

Sachs, J. (1993) *Poland's Jump to the Market Economy*, Cambridge, Massachusetts: MIT Press.

Salcedo, J. M. (1986) 'The price of peace: a report from the emergency zone', *NACLA: Report on the Americas* 20(3): 37–42.

Sanford, G. (1990) *The Solidarity Congress, 1981: the great debate*, New York: St. Martin's Press.

Scharf, T. (1989) 'Red–green coalitions at local level in Hesse' in E. Kolinsky (ed.) *The Greens in West Germany: organization and policy making*, Oxford: Berg.

Scharf, T. (1994) *The German Greens: challenging the consensus*, Oxford: Berg.

Scharf, T. (1995) 'Waving not drowning: the consolidation of the German greens', *German Politics* 4(2): 172–81.

Schattschneider, E. E. (1960) *The Semisovereign People: a realist's view of democracy in America*, New York: Holt, Rinehart and Winston.

Schoonmaker, D. (1988) 'The challenge of the greens to the West German party system' in K. Lawson and P. H. Merkl (eds) *When Parties Fail: emerging alternative organizations*, Princeton, New Jersey: Princeton University Press, pp. 41–75.

Schoonmaker, D. (1995) 'Unifying the greens' in P. H. Merkl (ed.) *The Federal Republic of Germany at Forty-five: union without unity*, New York, New York University Press, pp. 296–311.

Schoonmaker, D. and Frankland, E. G. (1993) 'Disunited greens in a united Germany: the all-German election of December 1990 and its aftermath' in R. J. Dalton (ed.) *The New Germany Votes: unification and the creation of a new German party system*, Providence, Rhode Island: Berg, pp. 135–62.

Schorske, C. E. (1972) *German Social Democracy, 1905–1917: the development of the great schism*, New York: Harper & Row.

Schwartz, M. and Shuva, P. (1992) 'Resource mobilization versus the mobilization of people: why consensus movements cannot be instruments of social change' in A. Morris and C. M. Mueller (eds) *Frontiers in Social Movement Theory*, New Haven, Connecticut: Yale University Press, pp. 205–23.

Scott, A. (1990) *Ideology and the New Social Movements*, London: Unwin Hyman.

Scott, J. C. (1976) *The Moral Economy of the Peasant*, New Haven, Connecticut: Yale University Press.

Scott, J. C. (1985) *Weapons of the Weak: everyday forms of peasant resistance*, New Haven, Connecticut: Yale University Press.

Semmler, W. (1982) 'Economic aspects of Model Germany: a comparison with the United States' in A. S. Markovits (ed.) *The Political Economy of West Germany: Modell Deutschland*, New York: Praeger Publishers, pp. 22–52.

Sheahan, J. (1994) 'Commentary' in J. S. Tulchin and G. Bland (eds) *Peru in Crisis: dictatorship or democracy?*, Boulder, Colorado: Lynne Rienner, pp. 187–93.

Singer, D. (1982) *The Road to Gdansk: Poland and the USSR*, New York: Monthly Review Press.

Skidmore, T. E. and Smith, P. H. (1992) *Modern Latin America* 3rd edn., New York: Oxford University Press.

Smith, C. (1991) *The Emergence of Liberation Theology: radical religion and social movement theory*, Chicago, Illinois: University of Chicago Press.

Smith, E. O. (1983) *The West German Economy*, New York: St. Martin's Press.

Smith, E. O. (1989) 'A survey of economic policy' in K. Koch (ed.) *West Germany Today*, London: Routledge, pp. 52–81.

Smith, G. (1984) *Politics in Western Europe: a comparative analysis* 4th edn., New York: Holmes & Meier Publishers.

Smith, G. (1989) *Livelihood and Resistance: peasants and the politics of land in Peru*, Berkeley: University of California Press.

Smith, M. L. (1992) 'Shining Path's urban strategy: ate vitarte' in D. S. Palmer (ed.) *Shining Path of Peru*, New York: St. Martin's Press, pp. 127–47.

Solidarity National Congress (1982) 'The Solidarity program' in S. Persky and H. Flam (eds) *The Solidarity Sourcebook*, Vancouver, British Columbia: New Star Books, pp. 205–25.

Staniszkis, J. (1984) *Poland's Self-limiting Revolution*, Princeton, New Jersey: Princeton University Press.

Staniszkis, J. (1989) 'The obsolescence of Solidarity', *Telos* 79: 37–50.

Starn, O. (1991) 'Missing the revolution: Anthropologists and the war in Peru', *Cultural Anthropology* 6(1): 63–91.

Starn, O., Degregori, C. I. and Kirk, R. (1995) *The Peru Reader: history, culture, politics*, Durham, North Carolina: Duke University Press.

Starski, S. (1982) *Class Struggle in Classless Poland*, Boston, Massachusetts: South End Press.

Stefancic, D. R. (1992) *Robotnik: a short history of the struggle for worker self-management and free trade unions in Poland, 1944–1981*, New York: Columbia University Press.

Stein, S. (1980) *Populism in Peru: the emergence of the masses and the politics of social control*, Madison, Wisconsin: University of Wisconsin Press.

Stepan, A. (1978) *The State and Society: Peru in comparative perspective*, Princeton, New Jersey: Princeton University Press.

Stephens, E. H. (1983) 'The Peruvian military government, labor mobilization, and the political strength of the left', *Latin American Research Review* 18(2): 57–93.

Stokes, S. C. (1991a) 'Hegemony, consciousness, and political change in Peru', *Politics and Society* 19(3): 265–90.

Stokes, S. C. (1991b) 'Politics and Latin America's urban poor: reflections from a Lima shantytown', *Latin American Research Review* 26(2): 75–101.

Stokes, S. C. (1995) *Cultures in Conflict: social movements and the state in Peru*, Berkeley: University of California Press.

Strong, S. (1992) *Shining Path: terror and revolution in Peru*, New York: Times Books.

Taras, R. (1996) 'The end of the Walesa era in Poland', *Current History* 95(599): 124–8.

Tarazona-Sevillano, G. (1990) *Sendero Luminoso and the Threat of Narcoterrorism*, New York: Praeger.

Tarrow, S. (1989a) *Democracy and Disorder: protest and politics in Italy, 1965–1975*, Oxford: Oxford University Press.

Tarrow, S. (1989b) *Struggle, Politics, and Reform: collective action, social movements, and cycles of protest*, Ithaca, New York: Cornell Studies in International Affairs Western Societies Paper.

Tarrow, S. (1994) *Power in Movement: social movements, collective action and politics*, New York: Cambridge University Press.

Taylor, C. L. and Jodice, D. A. (1983) *World Handbook of Political and Social Indicators* 3rd edn., New Haven, Connecticut: Yale University Press.

Taylor, L. (1987) 'Agrarian unrest and political conflict in Puno, 1985–1987', *Bulletin of Latin American Research* 6(2): 135–62.

Taylor, L. (1990) 'One step forward, two steps back: the Peruvian *Izquierda Unida* 1980–90', *Journal of Communist Studies* 6(3): 108–19.

Taylor, L. (1993) 'Peru's "time of cholera": economic decline and civil war, 1985–1990', *Third World Quarterly* 14(1): 173–9.

Thompson, E. P. (1963) *The Making of the English Working Class*, London: Gollancz.

Thompson, E. P. (1971) 'The moral economy of the English crowd in the eighteenth century,' *Past and Present* 50: 76–135.

Tilly, C. (1978) *From Mobilization to Revolution*, Reading, Massachusetts: Addison-Wesley.

Tilly, C. (1986) *The Contentious French*, Cambridge, Massachusetts: Harvard University Press.

Tilly, C., Tilly, L. and Tilly, R. (1975) *The rebellious century, 1830–1930*, Cambridge, Massachusetts: Harvard University Press.

Touraine, A. (1981) *The voice and the Eye: an analysis of social movements*, Cambridge: Cambridge University Press.

Touraine, A. (1985) 'An introduction to the study of social movements', *Social Research* 52(4): 749–87.

Touraine, A., Dubet, F., Wieviorka, M. and Strzelecki, J. (1983) *Solidarity: Poland 1980–81*, Cambridge: Cambridge University Press.

Velarde, J. (1994) 'Macroeconomic stability and the prospects for growth, 1990–1993' in J. S. Tulchin and G. Bland (eds) *Peru in Crisis: dictatorship or democracy?*, Boulder, Colorado: Lynne Rienner, pp. 139–54.

Velasco, J. (1995) 'The master will no longer feed off your poverty' in O. Starn, C. I. Degregori and R. Kirk (eds) *The Peru Reader: history, culture, politics*, Durham, North Carolina: Duke University Press, pp. 264–9.

Verba, S. (1961) *Small Groups and Political Behavior: a study of leadership*, Princeton, New Jersey: Princeton University Press.

Wade, L. L., Lavelle P. and Groth, A. J. (1995) 'Searching for voting patterns in post-communist Poland's Sejm elections', *Communist and Post-Communist Studies* 28(4): 411–25.

Walzer, M. (1985) *Exodus and Revolution*, New York: Basic Books.

Wejnert, B. (1988) 'The student movement in Poland, 1980–1981', *Research in Social Movements, Conflicts and Change* 10: 173–81.

Werlich, D. P. (1984) 'Peru: the shadow of the Shining Path', *Current History* 83(490): 78–82, 90.

Werlich, D. P. (1988) 'Peru: García loses his charm', *Current History* 87(525): 13–16, 36–7.

Werlich, D. P. (1991) 'Fujimori and the "disaster" in Peru', *Current History* 90(553): 61–4, 81–3.

Weschler, L. (1984) *The Passion of Poland: from Solidarity through the state of war*, New York: Pantheon Books.

Weschler, L. (1988) 'Skirmish', *New Yorker* 64(28): 48–67.

Weschler, L. (1989) 'A grand experiment', *New Yorker* 65(17): 59–104.

Weschler, L. (1990) 'Shock', *New Yorker* 66(43): 86–136.

Weschler, L. (1992) 'Deficit', *New Yorker* 68(12): 41–77.

West, C. (1993) *Keeping Faith: philosophy and race in America*, New York: Routledge.

Wilson, J. (1973) *Introduction to Social Movements*, New York: Basic Books.

Wise, C. (1986) 'The perils of orthodoxy: Peru's political economy', *NACLA: Report on the Americas* 20(3): 14–26.

World Bank (1991) *Social Indicators of Development, 1990*, Baltimore, Maryland: Johns Hopkins University Press.

Woy-Hazleton, S. and Hazleton, W. A. (1992) 'Shining Path and the Marxist left' in D. S. Palmer (ed.) *Shining Path of Peru*, New York: St. Martin's Press, pp. 207–24.

Wozniuk, V. (1986) 'Determinants in the development of the Polish crisis of 1980: the interplay of domestic and external factors', *East European Quarterly* 20(3): 317–34.

Zirakzadeh, C. E. (1989) 'Traditions of protest and the high-school student movements in Spain and France in 1986–87', *West European Politics* 12(3): 220–37.

Zubek, V. (1991a) 'The threshold of Poland's transition: 1989 electoral campaign as the last act of a united Solidarity', *Studies in Comparative Communism* 24(4): 355–76.

Zubek, V. (1991b) 'Wałęsa's leadership and Poland's transition', *Problems of Communism* 40(1–2): 69–83.

Zubek, V. (1992) 'The rise and fall of rule by Poland's best and brightest', *Soviet Studies* 44(4): 579–608.

Zubek, V. (1993) 'The fragmentation of Poland's political party system', *Communist and Post-Communist Studies* 26(1): 47–71.

Zubek, V. (1995) 'The phoenix out of the ashes: the rise to power of Poland's post-communist SdRP', *Communist and Post-Communist Studies* 28(3): 275–306.

Zuzowski, R. (1991) 'The origins of open organized dissent in today's Poland: KOR and other dissident groups', *East European Quarterly* 25(1): 59–90.

Author index

Adam, Barry D. 167
Alber, Jens 81, 83
Allen, Christopher S. 42n
Anderson, Richard D. Jr 110n
Andreas, Peter R. 184n
Apter, David E. 22n
Arendt, Hannah 6, 8, 22n
Ascherson, Neal 98, 106, 109n, 110n, 128n
Ash, Timothy Garton 126, 128n, 160, 163, 165n, 166n

Berg, Ronald H. 209, 211
Bernhard, Michael H. 110n, 128n
Betz, Hans-George 91, 93n
Biezenski, Robert P. 143
Black, Cyril E. 42n
Braunthal, Gerard 91, 93n
Brinton, Crane 6
Bromke, Adam 110n, 128n
Brown, James F. 165n
Brown, Michael F. 184n
Burkett, Tony 42n
Bürklin, Wilhelm H. 38, 83, 85
Burns, Rob 62n

Castells, Manuel 195
Chong, Dennis 4
Cohen, Jean L. 22n
Cohn, Norman 22n
Cooper, Alice Holmes 61
Cornelius, Wayne A. Jr 13
Costain, Anne W. 14
Crabtree, John 214

Dalton, Russell J. 54, 93n
Dyson, Kenneth 42n

Eckersley, Robyn 83, 84, 85
Eichner, Klaus 61
Esser, Josef 42n
Eyerman, Ron 22n

Fach, Wolfgang 42n
Fernández, Eduardo 184n
Fogt, Helmut 93n
Frankland, E. Gene 41, 52, 74, 89, 90, 93, 93n
Fromm, Erich 6

Gamson, William 5
Garner, Roberta Ash 11
Goldberg, Robert A. 21n
Goldman, Minton F. 110n
Gonzales de Olarte, Efraín 184n
Goodwyn, Lawrence 18, 98, 115, 128n, 165n
Gorski, Philip S. 43, 53, 62n, 65, 67, 83, 93n
Green, Simon 93n

Halebsky, Sandor 22n
Hancock, M. Donald 42n
Havens, A. Eugene 198n
Herring, Cedric 22n
Hill, Phil 93n
Hoffer, Eric 3, 6, 8–9
Holmes, Kim R. 43
Hülsberg, Werner 43, 62n, 93n

Inglehart, Robert 82

Jamison, Andrew 22n
Jenkins, J. Craig 4, 12, 22n
Joppke, Christian 90, 92

Karpinski, Jakub 110n
Katzenstein, Peter J. 42n

Killian, Lewis M. 21n
Kitschelt, Herbert 82, 85
Kolinsky, Eva 81, 85
Kornhauser, William 6
Kowalik, Tadeusz 166n
Kramer, David 91
Kubik, Jan 121, 128n

Laba, Roman 114, 115, 128n
Lipset, Seymour Martin 6, 22n, 169n
Lopinski, Maciej 165n

Markovits, Andrei S. 42n, 43, 53, 62n, 65, 67, 83, 90, 92, 93n
Marody, Mira 166n
Mason, David S. 165n
McAdam, Doug 4, 14, 22n
McCarthy, John D. 12
McClintock, Cynthia 170, 182, 184n, 194, 208, 223n
Melucci, Alberto 17
Mewes, Horst 55
Michnik, Adam 110n
Migdal, Joel S. 14, 222–3
Millard, Frances 165n, 166n
Morris, Aldon D. 13, 21n, 22n
Mushaben, Joyce Marie 83

Nowak, Jan 128n

Obregón, Aníbal Quijano 170
Offe, Claus 83, 84, 85
Ost, David J. 110n, 128n, 153, 164, 165n

Padgett, Stephen 42n
Papadakis, Elim 43, 62n
Park, Robert E. 6, 240
Pastor, Manuel, Jr 184n
Perlman, Janice E. 13
Persky, Stan 165n
Petras, James F. 198n
Piven, Frances Fox 5, 11, 22n
Poguntke, Thomas 81
Powell, John Duncan 14, 22n
Pravda, Alex 126
Pulzer, Peter 42n, 91

Roberts, Geoffrey K. 93n
Rogers, Daniel E. 42n

Rogin, Michael Paul 22n
Rudé, George 22n
Rudolf, James D. 184n
Rule, James B. 10, 22n

Sawa, Nagayo 22n
Scharf, Thomas 92
Schattschneider, E. E. 11
Schoonmaker, Donald 41, 52, 74, 89, 90, 93, 93n
Scott, James C. 22n, 169–70
Semmler, W. 42n
Sharpe, Kenneth E. 184n
Sheahan, John 170, 184n
Singer, Daniel 110n, 128n, 165n
Skidmore, Thomas E. 170, 179
Smith, Christian 14, 22n
Smith, Eric Owen 37, 42n
Smith, Peter H. 170, 179
Staniszkis, Jadwiga 110n
Starn, Orin 191
Stefancic, David R. 128n
Stepan, Alfred C. 184n
Stokes, Susan C. 198n
Strarski, Stanisław 128n, 165n

Taras, Ray 166n
Tarrow, Sidney 167
Thompson, E. P. 11
Tilly, Charles 13, 167
Tilly, Louise 13
Tilly, Richard 13
Touraine, Alain 165n

van der Will, Wilfried 62n
Velarde, Julio 184n

Wade, Larry L. 166n
Walzer, Michael 238
Werlich, David 176, 184n
Weschler, Lawrence 152, 154, 155, 162, 165n, 166n
West, Cornel 4
Wilson, John 4
Wise, Carol 184n
Wozniuk, Vladimir 110n

Zald, Mayer N. 11, 12
Zubek, Voytek 163, 166n
Zuzowski, Robert 128n

Subject index

Action for a Third Way (A3W) 68–9
Action Group for an Independent Germany
  (AUD) 68–9, 70, 71
active strikes 142–3, 144
Afghanistan 109
AL *see* Berlin, Alternative Slate
Albania 147
Alliance for Progress 173
Alliance '90
  electoral showing of 92–3
  Greens merge with 90–2, 93n
Alpinists 119, 122
Alternative Political Alliance–Greens
  (SPV–Greens) *see* German Greens
Amazon basin
  economy of 172, 174, 177, 183
  Shining Path in 213–14, 222, 230
American Revolutionary Popular Alliance
  (APRA)
  MIR and 192
  MRTA and 211
  programme of 185–9, 231
  repression of 187, 189
  Shining Path and 200, 215, 217, 218
  see also Haya de la Torre, Víctor Raúl;
    García Pérez, Alan
Amnesty International, Peruvian government and
  210, 216, 220
Andes
  class conflict in 173–4, 191–4
  relative poverty of 168, 171, 173–4, 181–3
  Shining Path and 168, 199, 201, 202, 204,
    208–9, 210–11, 212–13, 222, 230
Andrzejewski, Jerzy 122
antinuclear politics (Germany)
  beginnings of 38
  and formation of alternative parties 56, 64–5

Greens and 74, 82, 86, 88
  and occupation of construction sites 55–6,
    58, 64, 88
anti-Semitism
  Nazis and 27
  among Polish patriots 125–6, 145, 231
  within PZPR 118–19, 120–1, 144
  within Solidarity 145, 160, 231
APO *see* extraparliamentary protests
APRA *see* American Revolutionary Popular
  Alliance
Arequipa 201
Argentina, Peruvian economy compared to 170,
  184
Aristotle 238
armed struggle, *see* guerrilla organizations; Red
  Brigades; Shining Path; terrorism
A3W *see* Action for a Third Way
AUD *see* Action Group for an Independent
  Germany
autonomous movement-culture approach *see*
  third wave of social-movement theorizing
autonomous popular-culture approach *see* third
  wave of social-movement theorizing
Ayacucho (city)
  economy of 182–3
  Shining Path's origins in 201–3
Ayacucho (department)
  economy of 181, 182–3
  repression in 209–10
  Shining Path in 199, 204, 208, 222

Baden-Württemberg
  antinuclear politics in 58
  conservatism of Green politics in 69, 74
  Green voting in 80
Bahro, Rudolf 85

Bałuka, Edmund 116
Battle Against Nuclear Threat 45
Bavaria
    interwar revolutionary experiment in 34
    conservatism of Green politics in 69
    Green voting in 82
BBU *see* Federal Association of Citizens'
    Initiatives for Environmental Protection
Beddermann, Carl 65
Belaúnde Terry, Fernando
    economic policies of 177
    Shining Path and 209–10, 214, 234
Believers' Self-Defence Committee 123
Berlin
    Alternative Slate (AL) 66, 70
    counterculture of 65–6, 68
    economy of 69
    ecosocialists in 74
    Green voting 80
    Jusos in 50
    protests in 46, 47
    squatters' settlements 48–9, 55
Blanco, Hugo 192, 197
Bolivia
    free market reform in 158
    Peruvian economy compared to 184
Bolshevik Revolution 34, 201, 202
Brandenburg, Green voting in 92
Brandt, Willy
    decree against radicals and 53
    early JUSO support for 50, 51–2
    KOR supported by 123
Brazil, Peruvian economy compared to 170,
    184
Bremen
    counterculture of 65–6
    educational experiments in 52
    Greens and 65, 67, 70, 80, 92
Brezhnev, Leonid 109, 152
BUF *see* Federal Conference of Independent
    Peace Groups
Bujak, Zbigniew 116
Bulgaria 147
Bydgoszcz crisis 139–42, 146–7, 165n

Calderon, Félix 204
Campaign for Democracy and Disarmament
    45–6
Campaign for Disarmament 45
Canada *see* Saskatchewan Cooperative
    Commonwealth Federation
Carter, Jimmy 126
Castro, Fidel 189, 192–3
Catholic Church

German politics and 44
Peruvian politics and 195–6, 200, 209, 212,
    220
Polish politics and 101–2, 104, 106, 120–1,
    122, 123, 128n, 132, 140, 141, 152, 156,
    157, 161
United States politics and 12
CDU/CSU *see* Christian Democrats
CGTP *see* General Confederation of Peruvian
    Workers
Chavez, Cesar 12–13
Chernobyl nuclear disaster 86
Chiapas, rebellions in 4
Chile
    human-rights violations in Peru compared to 216
    Peru's war with 171
    Peruvian economy compared to 184
Chinese Communist Party *see* People's Republic
    of China
Christian Community of Working People 123
Christian Democrats (CDU/CSU)
    citizen-action groups and 54, 55
    civil liberties and 46–7, 52–3
    foreign policy and 41, 44
    in government 39–41, 46–7, 90
    Greens and 63, 65, 73, 74, 86–7, 88, 89
    voters for 81, 82
Christian National Union 159
churches
    movements' origins in 8, 12, 13, 235, 236
    popular culture and 13, 16, 17, 236
    see also Catholic Church; Protestant churches
Churchill, Winston 98–9
Chuschi 199, 200
civil rights movement (United States), as model
    in social-movement theorizing 3, 10, 14, 22n
citizen-action groups
    ecological thinking within 58–60
    Greens and 62, 63, 66, 67
    political evolution of 54–6
Citizens' Committees (KO) *see* Solidarity
classical political theory 238–9
Club of the Crooked Circle 117, 122
Club of Rome 38
Cold War
    German economic recovery and 29–30
    Greens opposition to 78–9
    militarization of West Germany and 32
    nuclear weapons in Germany and 33, 60–1,
        78, 109
    partition of Germany and 25–6
    Soviet foreign policy and 108–9
    see also Korean War; United States, foreign
        policies of; Vietnam War

Cologne 68
Colombia, drug trafficking and 213, 230
Commandos 118
Committee for the Defence of Life and Family 123
Committee for Social Self-Defence (KSS-KOR)
  dissolution of 145
  Lenin Shipyard strike and 130, 132, 134
  origins of 124–6
  repression and 140
Communist League (KB) 65, 66
  see also K-groups
Communist parties
  China and 108, 202
  Germany and 25, 27, 33, 34, 35, 44–5, 48, 51, 52, 55, 59–60, 65–7, 68, 70
  France and 29
  Italy and 108, 123
  Peru and 189, 199, 200, 201–23
  United States and 17
  Yugoslavia and 108
Communist Party of Germany (KPD) 25, 35, 44, 51, 66
  see also German Communist Party
Communist Party of Peru (PCP) 193, 201
Communist Party of Peru–Red Flag (PCP-BR) 202, 204
Communist Party of Peru–Shining Path (PCP-SL)
  armed struggle and 199, 205–8, 208–9, 210–11, 212–13, 216–19, 220–1, 228, 230, 231
  democratic and nondemocratic features of 205–6, 208–9, 210–11, 213–14, 217, 219, 220, 230, 231, 232, 237
  drug trade and 213–14, 230
  factionalism within 204, 206–8, 213, 217–20, 221, 228, 231–2, 237–8
  formation of 200–4
  government responses to 209–11, 214–16, 219–21, 222, 235
  organization of 206–7
  oscillating popularity of 197, 208–9, 211, 214, 217–20, 221, 222–3, 223n
  programme of 199–200, 204–8, 212–13, 216–19, 220–1, 228, 229, 230, 233–4
  shantytowns and 196, 197, 217–19, 221, 222, 230
  theory of revolutionary base areas and 205–6, 210, 219, 230, 232
  traditions of protest and 185, 189, 197–8, 231
Communist Party of Peru–Unity (PCP-U) 202, 203

Confederation for an Independent Poland (KPN)
  anti-Semitism and 231
  militancy of 125, 126
  shipyard workers aided by 127, 131, 231
Confederation of Peruvian Workers (CTP) 186, 189
constitutions, social-movement development and 23–4, 26–8, 42, 95–6, 165, 230
countercultures
  in Germany 48, 57, 65–6, 68
  in Poland 103, 114, 117–20, 126, 155
crisis-of-modernity interpretation of the Greens 83–5
CTP see Confederation of Peruvian Workers
Cuban revolution 175, 192–3
Czechoslovakia
  repression in 101, 137
  social unrest in 95, 108
  Solidarity letter to 147
Czuma, Andrzej 125

Debray, Regis 193
democracy
  movements as contributors to 3, 6, 10–11, 15, 16, 22n, 232, 239–40
  movements as threats to 3, 6–10, 15, 22n, 232, 236, 237, 239–40
democratic norms, processes, visions and practices
  of Jusos 50–1, 53
  of KOR 117–18, 122–4, 127
  of new women's movement (Germany) 56–7, 88
  of Peruvian shantytowns 195–7, 198n, 219
  of spontis 48
  see also German Greens, democratic and nondemocratic features of; Communist Party of Peru–Shining Path, democratic and nondemocratic features of; Solidarity, democratic agenda of; Solidarity, nondemocratic features of
Democratic Party 156, 157
Democratic Union (UD) 160, 161
Díaz Martínez, Antonio 203–4, 236
dictatorships, social movements in 95, 164–5, 189–90, 193–4, 195–6, 230
  see also Solidarity
discord theory see fourth wave of social-movement theorizing
Ditfurth, Jutta 85, 90
Dmowski, Roman 125
drug trade 183, 213, 230
Dutschke, Rudi 46, 47, 67, 68, 70, 231

East Asia
  Cold War and 33
  world economy and 32
  see also Korean War; Vietnam War
East Germany *see* German Democratic Republic
Easter March of the Opponents of Atomic
    Weapons 45
ecology movement *see* new social movements;
    see also antinuclear politics
ecological theorizing
  conservative ecological theory of Herbert
    Gruhl 67–8
  eco-Christians 60
  ecofeminism 59–60
  ecolibertarianism 71–2, 74
  ecological humanism 58
  eco-pax alliance 60–1
  ecosocialists 59–60, 66, 72–3, 74, 75
  Greens and 69, 71–3, 74–7, 79
EEC *see* European Economic Community
El Diario
ELN *see* National Liberation Army
English Constitution 239
Enlightenment, Green critique of 75, 79, 234
Environmental Protection List 64–5
Environmental Protection Party (USP) 65
European Economic Community (EEC) 30, 56,
    64, 70, 92
Exodus 238
extraparliamentary protests (APO)
  opposition to emergency-power laws and
    46–7
  veterans of 48–50, 52, 55, 67

factionalism, social movements and 20, 231–2,
    236, 237–8
  see also fourth tradition of social-movement
    theorizing
Fascism 7, 9
Fanon, Franz 45–6
FDP *see* Free Democratic Party
FDR *see* Federal Republic of Germany
Federal Association of Citizens' Initiatives for
    Environmental Protection (BBU) 58–9, 60,
    61, 70
Federal Conference of Independent Peace
    Groups (BUF) 61
Federal Republic of Germany (FRG)
  civil-rights controversies in 46–7, 49, 53, 63,
    64, 67, 88, 233, 235–6
  constitutional court of 28, 33, 35, 44
  federalism and 28
  foreign policy of 32–3, 39–42, 44, 46, 51–3,
    59, 60, 61

formation of 25–8
parties and party system of 36–7, 39–41, 42,
    42n, 45, 64, 67, 86–7, 89, 92
proportional representation in 28, 26–8, 42
see also German economy; German Greens;
    Germany
Federalist Papers 239
Fighting Poland 119
Fighting Solidarity 154
first wave of social-movement theorizing
  basic argument of 6–10, 15, 19, 22n,
    232–3
  critique of 233–4
  frustration with modernity and 7–11, 19, 24,
    41–2, 111, 169–70
  scapegoats and ideological reasoning 7–10,
    233
Fischer, Joschka 85
Flick scandal 86
Flying University 126
fourth wave of social-movement theorizing
    238–40
France
  environmental politics in 64
  foreign policies of 25–30, 32, 33, 99
  Lenin Shipyard strike and 133
Frankfurt
  counterculture in 68, 69
  Greens in 68, 69, 74
  guest workers in 31
  Jusos in 50
  police brutality in 88
Free Democratic Party (FDP)
  civil liberties and 39, 47, 49
  free-market orientation of 39–40
  in government 39–40, 41
  Greens and 73–4, 80, 86–7, 89, 92
  voters for 81, 82
French Revolution 6, 10, 22n
Fujimori, Alberto
  as dictator 220–1, 222
  economic policies of 180, 184, 220
  Shining Path and 220–1, 234

García Pérez, Alan
  economic policies of 178–9, 184
  protests against 215–16, 217–18
  Shining Path and 214–16, 234
  Socialist International and 215–16
gays and lesbians
  Nazism and 27
  election campaigns by 63, 66
  German Greens and 71, 73, 79
GAZ *see* Green Action Future

Gdańsk
  industrial struggles in 114, 116, 127, 130, 131
  Lenin Shipyard strike 116, 127, 130–4, 165n
  opinion surveys in 111
  Solidarity and 135–6, 145, 149
  student politics in 114, 125–6, 132
Gdańsk agreement (twenty-one demands) 132,
    133, 134–5, 137, 138, 141, 144
Gdańsk Polytechnic University 132
GDR see German Democratic Republic
Gdynia 114
General Confederation of Peruvian Workers
    (CGTP)
  formation of 188
  revolutionary military government and 189–90
  Shining Path and 189
Geremek, Bronislaw 157
German Communist Party 25, 35, 44, 51, 52,
    55, 66
German Democratic Republic (GDR) 25, 44,
    91, 92, 101, 108, 147
German economy
  big business and 29, 30, 35–6, 40, 41
  education of workforce and 31, 41
  environmental damage and 38–9, 41–2, 71–2,
    228–9
  evolution of 23–6, 29–32, 34–9
  government's role in 35–6, 37, 38, 39
  guest workers 30–1, 36, 37, 42, 46, 63, 66,
    68, 73, 78, 227, 228
  inequality within 37, 69, 93, 229
  international trade and 29–30, 32, 37, 38,
    39–40
  labour relations and 32, 34–6, 37–8, 42n
  and 1960s and 1970s recessions 32, 37, 38,
    41, 83
  postwar boom and 29–31, 36–7, 38–40,
    82–3
  unemployment and 29, 30, 32, 37, 38, 41, 42,
    68–9
German Greens
  democratic and nondemocratic features of 68,
    72, 77–8, 87–8, 91, 232, 237
  factionalism within 63, 64, 65, 66–9, 70–5,
    79–80, 85–6, 87–91, 92–3, 93n, 231, 234,
    237–8
  Federal Executive Board of 87–8, 237
  formation of 53, 56, 64–71
  fundamentalist/realist struggle within 72–5,
    85–91, 93, 93n, 231
  interpretations of 82–5
  in government 86, 87, 88, 90, 92
  programmes and goals of 68–9, 71–3, 74–80,
    89, 91–3, 227–9, 230, 233–4

traditions of protest and 43–4, 53, 56, 62,
    62n, 63, 68, 75, 82, 231
  voters for 41, 64–7, 80–5, 86, 89–90, 92,
    93n, 230, 233
  see also Alliance '90
Germany
  occupation of 25–9, 33, 35, 42n
  unification of 25–6, 27–8, 44, 89, 91
  Weimar Republic 26–8, 47
  see also German Democratic Republic;
    Federal Republic of Germany
Gierek, Edward 137, 149, 234
  economic programme of 105–7, 115, 126
  opposition groups and 119, 122–3, 126
Global 2000 38
GLU see Green List for Environmental
    Protection
Gomułka, Władysław
  anti-Semitism and 119
  early popularity 101–3, 117
  economic programme of 104–5, 113–14
  revisionists and 102–4, 116–19
  Soviet Union and 101, 102, 105
Gorbachev, Mikhail, Poland's transition to
    democracy and 152–3
Grace Contract 172
Great Britain 209
  economic history of 34, 160
  foreign policies of 25–9, 32–3, 98–9
  political system of 209
  Peruvian economy and 172, 183
  Solidarity's programme and 160
Great Depression 82, 170, 177
Green Action Future (GAZ) 67, 70–1
Green Forum 71
Green List for Environmental Protection (GLU)
    65, 68–9, 70
Green Slate (Hamburg) 66–7
Group for Defending the Interests of Working
    People 159
Group Z 71
Gruhl, Herbert 67–8, 70, 71, 231, 234
guerrilla organizations 45, 192–3, 197, 203,
    211–12, 222, 231
  see also Shining Path
Guevara, Ernesto 'Che' 45, 193
Guzmán Reynoso, Abimael 200–3, 207, 210,
    218–19, 221, 232, 235, 236, 237
Gypsies, 27

Haiti, Peruvian economy compared to 184
Hamburg
  counterculture in 65–6
  Greens of 65, 66–7, 70, 80, 90, 92, 74

guestworkers in 31
peace movement in 45
Rainbow Slate of 66–7, 70
Havel, Václav 160
Haya de la Torre, Víctor Raúl 186–8
Helsinki accords 126
Hesse
educational experiments in 52
Greens in 69, 74, 80, 92
see also Frankfurt
Hitler, Adolf 26, 27
horizontal movement 139, 144
Hungary
repression in 101, 137
social unrest in 95
Soviet invasions and occupations of 25,
137
Solidarity letter to 147
Hyde park 114

identity formation see third wave of social-
movement theorizing
Independent Germans' Action 66
interest groups, social movement contrasted with
4–5
International Monetary Fund, Peruvian economic
crisis and 178, 180
Iran, Shah of 46, 47
issue entrepreneurs 12
Italy
European Economic Community and 30
social movements in 7, 9
see also Communist parties
IU see United Left

Janiszewski, Jezy 134
Jaruzelski, Wojciech 149, 152–3, 234
Japan 22n, 206
John Paul II, Pope 121, 141
Jurczyk, Marian 116
Juso see Working Group of Young Socialists

Kania, Stanisław 137–8
Kawata, Makabe, Luis 206
Kelly, Petra 61, 64, 79, 235
Keynes, John 40
K-Groups 51, 59–60
see also Communist League; Communist
Party of Germany
Khrushchev, Nikita 101, 102, 201, 202
KKW see National Executive Commission
KO see Solidarity
KOR see Workers' Defence Committee
Korean War 30, 33

KPN see Confederation for an Independent
Poland
Kraków
heavy industry and 99
as religious centre 121
repression in 123
KSS-KOR see Committee for Social Self-
Defence – KOR
Kuhn, Thomas 10
Kuroń, Jacek
and defence of militancy during martial law
151–2
in KOR 123
in KSS-KOR 125
letter against PZPR by 117–18, 119
Wałęsa challenged by 163
Kwaśniewski, Aleksander 163

labour conflict 6, 13
in Germany 32, 34, 37–8, 41, 42n, 44, 46,
47
in Peru 174, 176, 179, 186, 188, 189, 190,
191–2, 194, 204, 212–13, 217–19, 221
in Poland 102, 104–5, 106, 108, 111,
112–16, 121, 127, 128n, 130–4, 135, 138,
140–1, 142–3, 144, 149, 151, 155–6,
159–60, 162, 165n, 228, 230, 231
labour-market interpretation of the Greens 83,
84–5
Lake Titicaca 212
land invasions 191–2, 194, 231
leadership in movements, theories of
charismatic leader 9–10
community leaders 13–14, 235
issue entrepreneur 12–13, 235
political opportunities and leadership 14–15,
235
Leinen, Jo 61
Lenin Shipyard Strike see Gdańsk
Leninist thought
development of discord theory and 238
in Guzmán's statements 201, 207, 209
and autonomous reasoning of movement
activists 17, 197
Polish politics and 103–4, 124–5, 132, 134,
201, 207, 219, 238
levelers 114
Lima
economy of 171, 172, 181, 182, 187, 189,
205
labour conflict in 189, 218–19
shantytowns in 194–5, 196, 217–18, 219
Shining Path in 204, 205, 210, 217–21
Lipiński, Edward 122, 124

Łódź
  active strikes and 142
  free-market reforms and 159
  labour struggles in 112, 115
Lower Silesia, active strikes in 143
Lower Saxony
  electoral experiments in 64–5
  Green radicals and centrists in 69, 74
  Green voting in 80, 92

Machiavelli, Niccolo 238
Mann, Thomas 201
Maoism and Maoist parties
  in Germany 45, 55
  in Peru 189, 201, 202, 204, 205, 207, 221–3,
    230
  in Poland 118
Marcuse, Herbert 45, 51, 73, 117
Mariátegui, José Carlos
  anti-imperialist thinking of 184n, 188
  Shining Path and 200, 202–3, 204
Marshall Plan 29–30
mass media
  criticisms of 18, 20, 21, 46, 60, 77
  in Germany 30, 44, 57, 64
  in Peru 179, 218–19
  in Poland 113, 132, 133, 134, 138, 140,
    156–7
  see also countercultures; popular culture;
    Springer newspaper chain
Mazowieck, Tadeusz 157, 160
McCarthyism 7, 10
Mexico
  Chiapas rebellion in 4
  Peruvian economy compared to 170, 173
Mezzich, Julio César 204
Michnik, Adam 124, 125
Middle Ages, social movements during 10, 22n
Middle East politics, oil and 38, 106
MIR see Movement of the Revolutionary Left
Modernity
  community and 13, 18
  loneliness and 7–10
  hierarchical culture and 18
  see also first wave of social-movement
    theorizing
Modzelewski, Karol 117–18, 119, 141–2
  letter against PZPR by 117–18, 119
  Wałęsa criticized by 141–2
Montgomery Bus Boycott 10
  see also civil rights movement
Morgenthau, Henry 29
Moses 238
Mothers Against Drunk Driving 3

Movement 119, 124
Movement for Silesian Autonomy 161
Movement for the Defence of Human and Civil
  Rights (ROPCiO)
  KSS-KOR contrasted with 124–5
  militant nationalism of 124–6
  shipyard workers supported by 127, 131, 132
Movement of the Revolutionary Left (MIR)
  failure of 192–3, 203, 209, 222
  Guzmán's critique of 203
  Shining Path compared to 222
Moyano, María Elena 219, 222
MRTA see Túpac Amaru Revolutionary
  Movement

National Council of Churches 12
National Democratic Party (NPD) 40
National Executive Commission (KKW) 153
National Federation of Trade Unions (OPZZ)
  Polish government and 152
  Solidarity's rivalry with 150, 155, 157
National Liberation Army (ELN)
  failure of 193, 203, 222
  Guzmán's critique of 203
  Shining Path compared to 222
National Socialism (Nazism)
  Allies' response to 25–8
  labour movements repressed by 34–5, 40
  as model of social-movement politics 3, 7,
    10
  Polish politics and 98, 99, 122
National System of Support for Social
  Mobilization (SINAMOS) 189
National University of San Cristóbal de
  Huamanga
  economic mission of 182–3, 201
  Shining Path's origins in 201, 203–4
  student protests at 201–2
NATO see North Atlantic Treaty Organization
  (NATO)
Nazism see National Socialism
Netherlands 30
Network see Solidarity
New Beginning '88 71
New Culture Movement/Orange Alternative
  155
new Left
  Germany and 45–6, 51, 73
  Poland and 118, 133
new social movements (Germany)
  emergence of 56–62
  Greens' cooperation with 56, 64–7, 68–9, 74,
    75, 82, 87–8, 231
Nordrhein-Westfalen, Green ideologies and 69

North Atlantic Treaty Organization (NATO)
formation of 33
German foreign policy and 32, 44, 50, 51,
52, 53, 59, 60, 61, 89
Greens' opposition to 68, 71, 78, 86, 91,
93n
North Sea 65
Norway 133
NPD *see* National Democratic Party
Nuclear Power, 'No Thanks' 65

oil crisis 32, 38, 106, 115
'Open Letter to the Party' (PZPR) 117–18, 119
OPEC *see* Organization of Petroleum Exporting
Countries
OPZZ *see* National Federation of Trade Unions
Organization of Petroleum Exporting Countries
(OPEC) 106
Orwell, George 126

Panama Canal 172, 186
Park, Robert 6, 240
party-movements, concept of 23–4, 227–8, 230
Pax 120, 156, 157
PCP *see* Communist Party of Peru
PCP–BR *see* Communist Party of Peru–Red
Flag
PCP–SL *see* Communist Party of Peru–Shining
Path
PCP–U *see* Communist Party of Peru–Unity
peace movement, Germany
before Greens 32–3, 44–5, 46–7, 49, 60–1,
63, 66
Greens and 68–9, 71, 74, 78–9, 82, 86, 91,
92
peasant pragmatism 191–2, 193, 194, 197,
208–9, 211, 213–14, 217, 222–3
People's Republic of China 105, 108, 202–3
Peruvian economy
evolution of 170–80, 184n
Fujishock and 180, 184n, 220
inequality and 171, 173–5, 181–4, 184n, 191,
193–4, 201, 203, 229
post-1970 crisis 169–70, 176–80, 182–4,
184n, 197, 217–18, 221, 222, 223n, 229
world economy and 170–4, 175, 176–8, 179,
180, 184n, 187, 234
Peruvian politics
human rights controversies 209–11, 214–16,
218–20, 221, 235
1980 constitution 190, 199
populism and 173–4, 178–9, 185–8, 192–3,
199, 203, 205, 211–12, 214–16, 217–18,
231

Revolutionary Government of the Armed
Forces 175–6, 184n, 189–90, 193–4,
195–6, 202, 203
A Planet is Plundered 67–8
Po Prostu 117
Poland Peasant Party 100
Polish Academy for Sciences 123
Polish economy,
agricultural sector 99, 100–1, 102, 103,
104–5, 106, 107, 153, 162
factory councils and 100, 102, 103, 104,
112–14, 156, 158
inequality and 107, 112, 113, 114, 162, 229
market reforms and 154, 158–9, 162
post-1970 crisis 107–8, 115, 126, 128, 138,
142, 148, 150, 154, 158–60, 162, 229
post-war boom 98–9, 100–1, 102, 103, 112
price increases and 104–5, 114, 115, 130,
153, 159
world economy and 101, 104, 105–6, 107,
110n, 115, 126, 154, 158, 159, 162
Polish League for Independence (PPN) 119
Polish politics
democratic transition and 152–3, 155–8,
165n, 166n
martial law and 149–50, 152, 165, 165n
one-party rule and 99–101, 106, 120, 152
parliamentary parties and 152, 156–8,
159–63, 166n
Sejm and 100, 103, 117, 122, 144, 156, 157,
163, 230
Soviet Union and 98–103, 105, 106, 108–9,
110n, 118, 119, 120, 124, 125, 127, 133,
137, 139, 140–1, 142–3, 147–8, 151,
152–3, 165n
see also Gierek; Gomułka
Polish Scouts 122
Polish Socialist Party 159
Polish United Workers' Party (PZPR)
anti-Semitism in 118–19, 144
horizontal movement and 139, 144
origins and dissolution of 100, 157–8
revisionism 101–2, 103–4, 116–19, 110n, 122
Solidarity and 132–4, 137–9, 140–1, 143–4,
148–9, 151, 152–3, 155–7, 165, 231, 235
Polish Workers' Party (PPR) 99–100, 101
political parties
social movements contrasted with 4, 5
social movements working with 12, 14
see also party-movements
Polish Peasant Party 163
popular culture
concept of 15–17, 199
sources of 16–18, 22n, 129–30, 199, 236

urban settings for 18, 167
  see also countercultures; third wave of social-
    movement theorizing
Populist movement 10, 22n, 24
postmaterialist interpretation of the Greens
  82–3, 84–5
Poznań 102, 112, 113, 118, 133
PPN see Polish League for Independence
PPR see Polish Workers' Party
proportional representation
  in Germany 28, 39, 42
  Greens and 64–7, 70, 80, 89, 92, 230
  in Poland 160, 162
  theories about 26–7
Protestant churches, political protest and 12, 13,
  44–5, 60, 62
Provisional Peasant Self-Defence Committees
  123
Puno 215
PZPR see Polish United Workers' Party

Racism, Peru and 171, 182, 183, 184, 188, 230
Radom 115, 121
Radio Free Europe 157
Rainbow Slate see Hamburg
Reagan, Ronald 61
Red Brigades 150
Red Star 204
revisionism see Polish politics
revolutionary base areas see Communist Party
  of Peru–Shining Path
Revolutionary Government of the Armed Forces
  see Peruvian politics
Rhineland-Palatinate
  conservative and centrist Greens in 69
  Green voting in 80
RMP see Young Poland Movement
Robotnik 127, 132
Romania
  social movements of 25
  Solidarity letter to 147
'rondas campesinas' 216
ROPCiO see Movement for the Defence of
  Human and Civil Rights
rural-based movements 5, 12–13, 167–8, 222–3
Rural Solidarity 138, 139–41, 157, 233

Saint Stanisław 121
Sachs, Jeffrey, shock therapy and 158
Saarland, weakness of Greens in 69, 80
Saskatchewan Cooperative Commonwealth
  Federation 22n, 24
Saxony, Green voting in 92
Schily, Otto 66, 85, 89

Schleswig-Holstein 65, 69, 80
  Green voting in 65, 80
  weakness of Greens in 69, 80
Schmidt, Helmut
  Greens and 234
  Jusos and 52, 53
  NATO missiles and 52, 59, 60–1
SdRP see Social Democracy of the Polish
  Republic
SDS see Socialist German Students' League
second wave of social-movement theorizing
  basic argument of 10–15, 19, 234–5
  critique of 235–6
  indigenous-community approach 11, 13–14,
    22n, 43, 63, 111, 112, 235
  political-process approach 11, 14–15, 22n,
    23, 63, 95, 96, 235
  resource-mobilization approach 11–13, 22n,
    43, 63, 111, 112, 235
  traditions of protest and 14, 20, 43–4, 62,
    62n, 111–12, 115–16, 128, 185, 197–8,
    231
Second World War
  German politics and economics following 25,
    29, 32–3, 34–5
  Guzmán's thinking and 200
  Polish politics and economics following 98–9
  postmaterialist theory and 82
Self-Defence 162
Shakespeare, William 201
shantytown politics (Peru)
  military government and 195–6
  nonpartisanship within 195, 196–7, 198n, 219
  Shining Path and 196, 197, 204, 217–20, 222,
    230, 231
Shining Path see Communist Party of
  Peru–Shining Path
Silesia
  nationalist sentiments in 145, 161
  labour struggles in 112
  Solidarity and 138, 143, 145
  see also Lower Silesia
SINAMOS see National System of Support for
  Social Mobilization
SKS see Students' Solidarity Committee
Sobieszek, Lech 116
Social Democratic Party of Germany (SPD)
  and civil liberties controversies 47, 49, 53,
    64, 67
  early years of 23, 34–5
  in government 40–1, 47, 49–54, 55, 59,
    60–1, 64, 67, 86, 90
  Greens and 64–7, 68, 69, 71, 72–4, 86–7,
    89, 90

Jusos and 41, 49–53, 63, 64, 235
programmes and goals of 39–42, 42n, 43,
44–5, 46–7, 51, 55, 57, 69, 86–7, 89
voters for 80, 81–2, 89
Social Democracy of the Polish Republic
(SdRP)
as successor to PZPR 157
electoral strength of 161, 163
social movement, concept of 3–5, 21n–22n, 23,
97, 227
Socialist German Students' League (SDS)
extraparliamentary protests by 46–7
impact on Green thinking 62, 75
new left orientation of 45–6
sexism within 56–7
and terrorist and sponti movements 49
Solidarity
Citizens' Committees (KO) 157, 158, 160
democratic agenda of 135–6, 137, 145, 147,
152, 155–7, 232
factionalism 128, 135, 137, 140–1, 142–5,
151–2, 153, 154, 155–6, 158, 159–60,
162, 163, 164, 165n, 228, 231, 237–8
formation of 130–6
free-market debate 145, 146, 153–4, 155,
157–8, 159, 160, 163, 164
fundamentalist/pragmatist struggle within
144–5, 146, 148, 149, 151, 154, 155–6,
164, 237
in government 157–60, 161–2, 164
martial law and 149–52, 164–5, 165n
Network and 143, 145, 150, 164, 231
nondemocratic features of 141–2, 143, 153,
157, 160, 161, 232, 237
organization of 135–6, 142, 151, 153, 157,
158, 160
programmes and goals of 128, 130, 137, 140,
142–8, 150–2, 153–4, 159, 160, 163–5,
165n, 228, 229, 230, 233–4
parliamentary elections and 156–7, 160–1,
162–3, 166n
size of 95, 139, 148, 150
as symbol 134, 135, 138, 139
as trade union 134–6, 138–9, 140–3, 148–9,
150, 153–6, 158, 159, 162, 165n
traditions of protest and 121, 127–8, 231
Solidarity '80
break with Solidarity 154
as parliamentary party 161
wildcat strikes and 155
Solidarity Peasant Party 159
Soviet Union (USSR)
foreign policies of 25, 29, 98–100, 105,
108–9, 110n, 118, 126, 148, 149, 152–3,
165n, 233

German Greens and 78–9
Peruvian left and 187, 202
Polish economy and 99, 101, 108, 153
Polish dissidents and 102–3, 118–19, 120,
124–6, 145, 233
PZPR and 100–1, 105, 106, 108–9, 110n,
120, 133, 138–9, 149, 152–3, 165n
social movements in 95
Solidarity and 135, 137, 140–1, 144, 145–6,
147–8, 149, 151, 233, 234
West Germans' fears of attack from 60
see also Bolshevik Revolution; Stalin and
Stalinism
SPD *see* Social Democratic Party
spontis
citizen-action groups and 54
democratic spirit of 48
Greens and 62, 63, 65, 66, 68, 75, 92, 164,
231, 237
new peace movement and 61
SDS roots of 48–9
Springer newspaper chain
countercultures contrasted with 48
Left represented by 30, 44, 47, 52–3, 67
protests against 47, 234
SPV-Greens *see* German Greens
squatter movement (Germany)
citizen-action groups and 55
emergence of 48–9
Greens and 62, 63, 66, 228, 231, 235
new peace movement and 61
and Springer chain 52–3
Stalin and Stalinism
Green criticism of 67, 88
Guzmán and 200–2
Polish Stalinism 97, 100–1, 120, 125
Soviet Union and 10, 100–1
Steffen, Jochen 64
Students' Solidarity Committee (SKS) 123, 125,
126
Sweden 160
Szczecin, labor struggles in 114–15, 116, 133

Taz 71
Temporary Coordinating Commission (TKK)
151–2, 153, 154
terrorist groups, German 41, 49, 53, 64, 88,
231
see also armed struggle
Thatcher, Margaret, Wałęsa admiration of 160
third wave of social-movement theorizing
autonomous movement-culture approach 17,
22n, 129–30, 236
autonomous popular-culture approach 16–17,
22n, 43, 111–12, 129, 163, 236

basic argument of 15–16, 18, 19, 22n, 63, 199, 236
critique of 237–8
identity-formation theory 15–16, 18, 22n, 236–7
see also popular culture
Three Mile Island nuclear disaster 38
Tito, Josip Broz 101
TKK *see* Temporary Coordinating Commission
Tocqueville, Alexis de 238
Trotskyism and Trotskyist parties
in Germany 45, 51
In Poland 118
in Peru 189, 192, 197
Trybuna Ludu 117
Tshombe, Moise 46
Túpac Amaru Revolutionary Movement (MRTA) 211–12
Turkey
Cold War and 29
guest workers from 31
twenty-one demands *see* Gdańsk agreement
Tygodnik Powszechy 120

UD *see* Democratic Union
UFW *see* United Farm Workers
Union of Polish Writers 123
Union of the Democratic Left 163
United Farm Workers (UFW) 12–13
United Left (IU)
factionalism within 190–1, 196–7
grassroots organizing 212–13
MRTA and 211
Shining Path's rivalry with 212–13, 217, 218
United Nations 158, 178, 180, 195, 229
United Peasant Party 156, 157, 163
United States (US)
economy of 34, 36, 172, 173
foreign policies of 25–30, 32–3, 35, 39, 41, 42, 43, 44, 46, 60, 61, 98–9, 109, 110n, 126, 145, 175, 179, 201, 205, 206, 233
Greens and 71, 74, 78–9
Peruvian left and 172–3, 185–6, 188, 201, 206, 233
political system of 28, 50, 56, 182, 209
social movements in 3, 7, 10, 12–13, 14, 17, 22n, 24, 56
university students, politics of 10, 12, 235, 236
in Germany 31, 38, 40, 42, 45–7, 48, 65–6, 81, 83–5, 230, 233
in Peru 182–3, 190, 201–4, 216, 218, 221, 230
in Poland 103–4, 114, 117–20, 122, 123, 125–6, 128n, 131, 132, 138, 149, 152, 155
Upper Huallaga Valley, Shining Path in 213–14, 222, 230

urbanization
in Europe 13, 30–1, 41, 99, 103
in Latin America 13, 179, 181, 194–5, 197
social-movement theorizing and 7–8, 13, 18, 167, 235
Ursus 115, 121
US *see* United States
USP *see* Environmental Protection Party
USSR *see* Soviet Union

Velasco Alvarado, Juan 193–4
Vanguardia Revolucionaria 212
Vargas Llosa, Mario 180
Vietnam War 41, 43, 46–7, 48, 56, 60, 67
Vogt, Roland 61
Vollmer, Antje 88, 90
von Hindenburg 26
Voters League, Nuclear Power, No Thanks! (WGA) 68

Wałęsa, Lech
as labour activist 116, 131–2
as leader of Solidarity 136, 140, 141–2, 143, 144, 147, 148, 149, 152, 154, 155, 156, 160
as politician 157, 160–1, 163
Warsaw 71, 98, 113, 115, 117, 118, 123, 127, 135
Weimar Republic *see* Germany
WGA *see* Voters League, Nuclear Power, No Thanks!
women's movements
in Germany 56–61, 63, 66, 74, 75, 79, 88
in Poland 138, 161
West Germany *see* Federal Republic of Germany
Workers' Defence Committee (KOR)
factionalism within 123–4
legalist strategy of 122, 123–4, 127, 231
martial law and 149, 150
opposition to Wałęsa and veterans of 160, 163
Workers Group 154
Working Group of Young Socialists (JUSO)
democracy and 50–1, 54–5, 231
Greens and 59, 63, 64, 68, 75, 231
Stamokap faction 51, 62
see also Social Democratic Party

Young Poland Movement (RMP)
anti-Semitism within 125–6, 231
shipyard workers aided by 127, 131, 132
Yugoslavia 101, 108, 160

Zakrzewski, Tadeusz 158
Znak 121